ID0435732

VAN NOSTRAND POLITICAL SCIENCE SERIES

Editor

FRANKLIN L. BURDETTE
University of Maryland

GODSHALL, W. L. (Editor)—*Principles and Functions of Government in the United States*

LONDON, K.—*How Foreign Policy Is Made*

PLISCHKE, E.—*Conduct of American Diplomacy*

DIXON, R. G., JR. and PLISCHKE, ELMER—*American Government: Basic Documents and Materials*

SPROUT, HAROLD and MARGARET—*Foundations of National Power, 2nd Ed.*

LANCASTER, LANE W.—*Government in Rural America, 2nd Ed.*

JORRÍN, M.—*Governments of Latin America*

GOVERNMENTS OF LATIN AMERICA

BY

MIGUEL JORRÍN

Professor of Government and Citizenship
University of New Mexico

D. VAN NOSTRAND COMPANY, INC.

TORONTO   NEW YORK   LONDON

VICTORIA COLLEGE
LIBRARY
VICTORIA, B.C.

NEW YORK

D. Van Nostrand Company, Inc., 250 Fourth Avenue, New York 3

TORONTO

D. Van Nostrand Company (Canada), Ltd., 25 Hollinger Rd., Toronto

LONDON

Macmillan & Company, Ltd., St. Martin's Street, London, W.C. 2

COPYRIGHT, 1953, BY
D. VAN NOSTRAND COMPANY, INC.

Published simultaneously in Canada by
D. VAN NOSTRAND COMPANY (Canada), LTD.

All Rights Reserved

*This book, or any parts thereof, may not be
reproduced in any form without written permission from the author and the publisher.*

Library of Congress Catalogue Card No. 53-6194

PRINTED IN THE UNITED STATES OF AMERICA
By GEORGE S. FERGUSON COMPANY, Philadelphia, Pa.

To

TESSIE

who was most helpful

Preface

This book is the outcome of courses on Latin American Government that I have taught in American universities during the past ten years. When the book was begun, there was no text in English in the field, and only the excellent compilation of Professor Fitzgibbon on the Latin American constitutions was found to be of valuable help to instructors and students. Later, MacDonald's book was published, filling a needed gap. More recently, Christensen's book on Readings has enriched the source material. Of course, there are good studies on specific countries, but they do not cover the whole field. These recent contributions indicate an interest of the political scientists in the Latin American area.

My book is designed primarily as a text for upper-classmen in a Liberal Arts college who are interested in Latin America or in comparative government. In these cases, the student will be familiar with the history of the area and will undoubtedly have some knowledge of political science. For those not so well informed, it is hoped that the first part on Colonial Governments will serve as a general introduction. The purposes of Parts II, III and IV are fully explained in the brief introductory notes preceding each section. The constitutional summaries, printed in small type, that follow the chapters in Parts II and III, are only to illustrate the points with which I deal previously and to serve as a quick source of reference for comparative analysis and class discussion.

The subject matter in *Governments of Latin America* presents, in a relatively short volume, material that is introductory in nature. There is adequate opportunity, indeed there are rich possibilities, for future research in this subject. Specialists in the field, as well as students, should find this book and its bibliography stimulating for further investigation.

I have tried to be objective, within the limitations that I am a product of my native cultural environment. I have tried to offer the North American reader an understanding of the complexities of the phenomena of government in a foreign area. To me, conclusions and opinions in a textbook are valid only to indicate the author's point of view. I trust that instructors and students will challenge them and reach, in all probability, a more enlightened viewpoint. After all, a textbook is merely an educational tool, and the success of any course rests always on the capacity of the instructor and the interest of the students.

My sincere thanks are due to the Committee on Research of the University of New Mexico for a small grant that made possible the final typing of the manuscript, and to my colleagues and students, first at Williams College and then at the University of New Mexico who, during the past ten years, have borne patiently with me on their campuses.

Albuquerque, New Mexico,
September, 1952.

M. J.

Contents

PART I

Colonial Government

CHAPTER 1

The Spanish State in America

INTRODUCTION

Spain was in the midst of a political transition when America was discovered. Like other countries of Europe, she was in the process of passing from the feudal state to the nation state, destined to be the predominant political structure of the majority of countries up to the present day.

In 1492, there existed in Spain a dynastic unity but not a national unity. In spite of the marriage of Isabella of Castile and Ferdinand of Aragon, the two kingdoms retained their own legal and administrative institutions. Because it was Queen Isabella of Castile who backed Columbus' voyage, the territory he discovered was incorporated politically to Castile, and thus it was the Castilian institutions which especially influenced the political structures that appeared in the new world.

For a study of the present governments of Latin America, it is not necessary to note in detail the governmental institutions of Castile. The only institutions of a political nature which disappeared completely with the independence of the Spanish colonies were those of a purely national character, that is to say, those organs of the national government dealing administratively with the colonies and keeping them under strict control of the mother country. Upon achieving independence, the Latin-American countries broke their political connections with Spain. But this was the only important change introduced by independence. On gaining sovereignty, the countries had to adjust their new political structures to the administrative, economic, fiscal and juristic institutions which had been functioning in the area. It is, therefore, more important to investigate carefully the Spanish provincial and municipal governments as well as the judicial machinery, and to offer only an over-all view of the central government of Castile.

3

Castile was a monarchy, but not an absolute monarchy. The theory and practice of the absolute monarchies did not appear in Europe until later. Castile was in the process, as we have noted, of becoming an absolute monarchy. There were limitations to the power of the monarch that should be mentioned in order to understand the political institutions established by Spain in America. Some of these limitations were the result of the prevalent political conceptions in Europe in the later Middle Ages. Others were a consequence of the existing social and economic conditions of Spain at the end of the War of Reconquest against the Moors. In the first group, we shall place the Law and the *Cortes;* in the second, the strong position occupied by the members of the nobility and the clergy.

It was recognized in fifteenth-century Spain that the law was common and applicable to all, regardless of status, and included the King. The law was either customary or codified. This principle may sound democratic but it was far from being so in practice. Spain, like the majority of the European countries, lacked the administrative machinery and representative institutions to enforce the law against the King and the higher members of the nobility, the Church, or the army.

The *Cortes*—to which we shall refer later in more detail—by the end of the thirteenth century had become a normal and important organ of government and remained as such until the early part of the sixteenth century. They constituted the most important limitation to the power of the King. The lawmaking power of the *Cortes* dates from 1387, when King Juan I agreed that laws could not be annulled or changed except with the authorization of the *Cortes.* Another important power of the *Cortes* was the power of the purse. In 1329, the *Cortes* of Madrid requested that no taxes be levied without their consent.

The nobility had great political power in the time of the Catholic Kings. It is estimated that the rents the nobility received amounted to one third of those of the entire Kingdom. Their large feudal holdings were bulwarks of the forces of decentralization that unquestionably weakened the monarchy. The lords also occupied, by hereditary title, important posts in the government and in the army.

The power of the clergy, too, was great, because of the large revenues from the metropolitan churches. The church of Toledo, for example, had the reputation of being the wealthiest in Christendom, and its revenues equaled those of the entire city. Higher members of the clergy exercised great political power that undermined the authority of the monarch.

Legal, administrative and social conditions limited the power of the monarchy; and we must remember also that the Catholic Kings did not have an important standing army—usually a great force of the absolute monarchs. The army raised by Ferdinand and Isabella for the conquest of Granada was still feudal. In 1484, the nobles forced the King to retire from action earlier than he wished, because they were tired of fighting.

The monarchy of Castile, in the fifteenth century, was therefore limited by law, by the *Cortes,* and by the rights and privileges of the nobility and the clergy. This realization is necessary in order to understand why, when America was discovered and government was established in the new territory, the natural reaction of a weak monarchy was to set up strict political control over the dependencies. Consequently the centralization of the Spanish colonial government cannot be explained in terms of institutions created by an absolute monarchy, because an absolute monarchy did not exist at that time in Spain. It can be explained only in terms of a monarchy that was itself struggling for power, that had just achieved territorial unity, and that was greatly concerned over the conservation of that power. A more mature and powerful kingdom, like that of Portugal, which was not fearing the possibly loss of its political position, established a less rigid governmental system in Brazil.

To make the picture of the Spanish colonial government more complex, two institutions which were gradually dying out in Europe—slavery and feudalism—were transplanted to America. It is true that slavery existed in Spain, but not on a large scale. Nevertheless, slavery of Indians, at the beginning, and especially slavery of Negroes, were established in America. Feudalism in Europe was changing from the landed type of nobility to the nobility of the court, because of the increasing power of the kings. In Latin America, feudalism took root under the type of court nobility that enjoyed the privileges of large landholdings, and a social structure based upon a hierarchy of titles granted by the

Crown of Spain dominated the colonies. These two obsolete political forms were not the only ones flourishing in the new world, because transplanted also were many ingredients of the modern state, such as administrative centralization and the great power of the kings. Elements of the new commercial state, based upon large-scale trade, influenced the colonies as well. Thus, one finds in the new world a mixture of the political ingredients of many centuries, and these ingredients have undoubtedly conditioned the present governmental structure of the Latin American republics.

THE CENTRAL GOVERNMENT

The Monarch. The central power of Castile was vested in the monarch, whose power embraced diverse geographical units linked together through their relations with the person of the King. The link was predominantly personal and did not represent a concrete and determined administrative organization. After the discovery of America, the new territories were considered united to Spain by the same link that united the various geographical units of Spain to the monarch. It is important to remember that the idea of a colonial empire with territories geographically and administratively separated from the mother country, and as dependencies of it, did not appear clearly defined by Spanish statesmen until much later. Madariaga reminds us that the Spanish King referred to America as "esos reinos"—(those kingdoms)—an expression analogous to that which he used when speaking of the other kingdoms then existing in the Iberian peninsula. The King, however, possessed not only political but economic power. The new territories were considered to be his property, so that all concessions, privileges, or rights in America emanated directly from the King. It must be remembered that, at the beginning of the sixteenth century, the idea of the state, with its own patrimony and a budget independent of that of the person of the sovereign, had not made its appearance in political science.

The power of the monarch was based upon the tradition of Visigothic and Roman laws, and upon a social organization which was the reflection of the philosophical and religious ideas then predominant in Spain. The Spanish social structure of that period was founded upon the medieval conceptions of a social hierarchy; the social group was rigid and stratified. Each person, by birth, occupied a particular place in society. Each human being came to the world to fulfill a certain role in his community, and this justified the existence of inequalities, there being no convention or human norm that might alter these dispositions. One must realize this in order to understand the complex political phenomenon that occurred in America when the power of the Spanish monarchy was extended to the New World. At this time, the King enjoyed considerable political authority; and, as we will see later, the two so-called democratic organs of any importance, the *Cortes* and *Municipios,* had lost the greater part of their power. The Spanish kingdoms, before the dynastic unification of the end of the fifteenth century, had enjoyed certain liberties, but those liberties had begun to wane by the time the Spanish dominion in America had been established.

The Cortes. The Spanish *Cortes* were not, strictly speaking, a permanent organ of the government. For centuries, the monarchs had maintained the custom of holding meetings with the important people of the kingdom. To these assemblies came representatives of the three social classes, sometimes called "states"—the nobility, the clergy, and the delegates from the chartered towns and cities. At first, they functioned as consultive organs; but later, compelled by political necessities (in the struggle against the feudal nobility), they were frequently used as a means of securing the support of the bourgeoisie and more particularly of raising the funds necessary to support royal projects. The King convoked the *Cortes* at his convenience, many times promising to hold meetings at stated intervals, but rarely keeping these promises. During the sessions of the *Cortes,* each "state" was entitled, separately, to make requests of the King. The latter would usually ask the advice of the *Cortes* on legislative measures, and the meeting would close by fixing the amount of tribute that each individual city was to contribute toward defraying royal expenses. Such organs of government had some legislative power, and on some historical occasions the influence of the *Cortes* was great.

By the beginning of the sixteenth century, the *Cortes* were in open decay, because little by little they had been losing ground to the absolutism of the Catholic Kings. With such an important event as the discovery of America, the *Cortes* were not even convoked in

Castile. The *Consejo Real*,[1] during this period, had acquired the power of revising the acts of the *Cortes*, and the president of the *Consejo* functioned as president of the *Cortes*.

In 1528, an assembly was convoked of representatives of the cities and towns of New Spain which fixed the amount that each town would have to contribute to the central government. At the same time, a delegate was named to negotiate with the Spanish King concerning the right of the City of Mexico to vote in the *Cortes*. Politically, however, the influence of the *Cortes* in the government of Latin America was relatively unimportant.

The Consejo Real was an organ of the central government, composed of members of the nobility and of the clergy, which functioned as the King's advisory board. Its duties were purely consultative, and it had no authority over the Indies. By the time of the discovery, the *Consejo*, too, had undergone important changes. At the same time that the feudal nobility was losing its political power in the face of the rising administrative centralization of the Catholic Kings, it was also losing its ascendancy in the *Consejo Real*. The rulers preferred to avail themselves of a new bureaucracy attached and faithful to them personally. In the *Consejo Real* of Castile, there came to be more *letrados* [2] than nobles, and the *Consejo* represented more and more the absolute will of the monarch. The increasing complexity of administrative problems led to the creation of other *Consejos* which functioned as consultative bodies directly subordinate to the King. They were the Councils of the Inquisition, the Military Orders, and the Indies. The latter is of special interest for us as it was the highest organ of the central power in its relation with the New World.

The Consejo de Indias.[3] *El Real y Supremo Consejo de las Indias* was created by Emperor Charles V, in August, 1524. In 1493, when Columbus had returned from his first voyage, Queen Isabella placed Juan Rodríguez de Fonseca in charge of all affairs relating to the new territories. Fonseca, at first aided by a secretary and later by a more extensive staff, occupied this post until his death in 1524. Thus

---

[1] For translation, see the Glossary.
[2] Educated persons—as a rule, lawyers.
[3] Indian council.

it can be said that the *Consejo de Indias* started functioning, rudimentarily, a few months after the discovery of America.

The *Consejo de Indias* was the highest legislative and administrative authority of the Spanish empire, with the exception of the King. It exercised jurisdiction over all Spanish possessions in America and the Philippines.

The powers of the *Consejo de Indias* came to embrace all functions of government: legislative, financial, military, ecclesiastical, commercial, and legal. The body approved all laws relative to America, naturally with the sanction of the King and in his name. It functioned as the highest court in the judicial hierarchy as regards cases arising in the overseas possessions and tried important cases brought up from the *Audiencias*, which will be discussed later. It also had jurisdiction over civil and criminal cases proceeding from the *Casa de Contratación*. Furthermore, it exercised censorship over all publications having to do with the *Indias;* no book appeared without its approval. The *Consejo* met every day except Sundays and holidays to transact business. When the colonial administration became more complex, especially during the reign of Philip II, other commissions were created, composed of members of the *Consejo* and other representatives of the central government, with jurisdictional power in special fields such as naval defense and Indian policy. The authority of the *Consejo* in religious affairs stemmed from the Royal Patronage which the Spanish monarch enjoyed with regard to the Roman Catholic Church.

One if the most serious defects in the *Consejo de Indias,* which in other aspects functioned laudably, was the absence of personal responsibility on the part of its members. There was no unity of action. An affair could come and go from the *Consejo* to the King, with recommendations, suggestions, and corrections for an unlimited time. The *Consejo de Indias* has, however, bequeathed to us in the well-known *Recopilación de las Leyes de los Reinos de las Indias,* published in 1681, one of the best administrative codes of its time. These laws of the *Indias* overemphasized minutiae and were unscientifically arranged, but they were, as C. H. Haring has said,[4] "altogether one of the most humane and one of the most comprehensive codes published for any colonial empire."

---

4 Haring, C. H., *The Spanish Empire in America*, New York, Oxford University Press, 1947, p. 111.

Casa de Contratación. Another institution of great importance was the *Casa de Contratación* of Seville. The lack of a clear separation of powers in the administration of the colonies is proved in the role played by this organ of government. In 1493, shortly after the discovery of America, the mercantile interest that had begun to appear in Europe as a characteristic form of the commercial state was evidenced by the creation, in Cadiz, of a customs-house for the Indies.

Ten years later, the *Casa de Contratación de las Indias* was established in Seville. This was the first Spanish institution created especially to arbitrate American affairs. The *Casa* was an economic, political, judicial, and scientific institution. All commerce with the Indies was placed under its control, making possible the monopoly which was the economic policy of the Spanish state. It was an institution of government with political attributes, in that it had the power to regulate the administrative relations of the colonial empire. It functioned as a court of law and, finally, as an important factor in the study of geography and navigation in America. To carry out these functions, the staff of the *Casa* consisted of a bookkeeper, business manager, chief pilot, postmaster, and even a professor of cosmography. The judicial power of the *Casa* extended to all civil suits relating to the commerce of the Indies and to crimes committed between Spain and the colonies. Politically, the *Casa de Contratación* was subordinate to the King and the *Consejo Real de Indias*.

Adelantados. Although in Spain there existed no separation of powers, as we understand it today, the monarchy, by itself, was unable to take complete charge of the complex executive problems stemming from the discovery and colonization of the new territories, so that some of its executive functions had to be delegated to subordinate organs. Among these organs of the central government, the most important were the *Adelantados, Virreyes,* and *Capitanes Generales*.

The post of *Adelantado* was a venerable Castillian institution that had been functioning since the twelfth century. Such functionaries were "put forward" in the place of the King. They were especially active during the Reconquest and were of two classes: *Adelantados Mayores,* who above all exercised judicial power, and *Adelantados Menores,* also called *fronterizos,* who were stationed along the borders of the state and performed chiefly military functions. In America, the rank of *Adelantado* was conferred upon all the *conquistadores,* whose function in this respect closely resembled that of the *Adelantado Menor* or *fronterizo.* When a new territory was occupied, the *Adelantado* was the most important officer of the government, and remained thus until the appearance of the *Virreyes,* when it fell into disuse. Ots Capdequi calls these functionaries *Adelantados Gobernadores,* and states:

> In the Indies, it is difficult to give a complete account of the attributes peculiar to the *Adelantados,* because usually the *Adelantado* was at the same time the governor. As one or the other, they were in charge of the political and administrative organs of government, but in addition possessed powers of a military and jurisdictional nature.[5]

The increase in administrative complexities, the ever-expanding amount of territory to be governed, and the international rivalries resulting from the ambition of other countries who wished a part in the rich commerce of America, led the Spanish monarchs to a realization of the necessity to affirm their sovereignty more forcefully. To do this, another organ, the Viceroyalty, was established possessing considerable local political power. The *Virrey* acted in place of the King, with supreme power over a specified territorial unit. The Viceroyalty in America embraced essentially the proportions of a state. The first two to be founded were those of Nueva España and Peru, created in the sixteenth century; later, in the eighteenth century, there appeared the viceroyalties of Nueva Granada and Río de la Plata.

In his territory, the *Virrey* was the supreme military and civil authority and exercised supervisory powers over the judiciary and financial institutions and the Roman Catholic Church. He was charged likewise with safeguarding the welfare of the Indians. Attempts were made to transplant to America the administrative centralization then existent in Spain, but in practice the system did not function as it had been conceived. In theory, the *Virrey* enjoyed almost absolute powers, naturally within the complicated

---

[5] Ots, Capdequi, J. M., *El Estado Español en Las Indias,* México, D. F., p. 4. (Author's translation.)

political machinery indicated above. Actually this power was limited by jurisdictional conflicts with the *Audiencias*. The *Virreyes* came and went, while the *Audiencias* were more permanent organs of government. The formalistic and highly detailed Spanish system of administration of the period further restricted the vice-regal power. The entire system was hedged about with complicated administrative rules which constituted an impediment to the rapid and effective exercise of the powers of office. Moreover, in the political realm, the *Virreyes* were never able to formulate long-range policies, for this was a function of the *Consejo de Indias* which, in turn, recommended such measures to the monarch. Furthermore, political power cannot truly exist without the accompanying authority to appoint subordinates. Since appointments to important administrative posts in America were made in Spain, the *Virrey* was far from the scene, and it was the political group at the time in favor with the King that exerted the greatest influence on him in such matters. Administrative subordinates enjoyed a privilege which today appears insignificant, but which in the sixteenth and seventeenth centuries represented an important arm of the government. This privilege consisted of the right to communicate directly with the monarch. Today the right of petition is consecrated in all modern constitutions but, in the times to which we are referring, it was not a general rule. The exercise of this right by the administrative subordinates of the *Virreyes* disrupted the administrative hierarchy and diminished the power of the latter.

In spite of these limitations, however, in America the *Virrey* was always the center of the highest political power. His influence in Spain and the universality of his functions made this post the nucleus of the public life of the colonies. The length of appointment of the *Virreyes* was, at first, for an unlimited period; later the term was restricted to three years, and finally was extended to five. Through "instructions," they prescribed the powers and functions of the subordinates in the governmental hierarchy, and designated— a function of great importance in many cases—their temporary successors until such time as a new *Virrey*, named in Spain, might arrive in the colonies.

The *Capitán General*, as a functionary of the Spanish state, is looked upon by many students of America's colonial past as an institution of primarily provincial or local character. It is included among those of the central government, because this seems more appropriate in view of the fact that the *Capitán General* was often-times independent of the central jurisdiction of the *Virrey*. The *Capitán General* was primarily a military official, and the *Virreyes,* as we have seen, also enjoyed military powers. In practice, the *Virrey* was the *Capitán General* of his district. Nevertheless, the *Capitanes Generales* enjoyed autonomous powers within their respective jurisdictions, being dependent upon and giving account of their administration directly to the King. Furthermore, in the sixteenth century the term *"Capitán General"* designated the governors of certain regions of America, which were completely independent of the *Virreyes* and tied politically to the *Consejo de Indias* and the monarch.

The Audiencias. Let us repeat that in the nation-state which was developed in Spain, the separation of powers did not exist; nevertheless, faced with the necessity of delegating authority and creating additional organs in order to govern the colonies more efficiently, certain institutions appeared in America which were of a purely judicial character in Spain. These, the *Audiencias,* had been functioning in Spain for several centuries when America was discovered. When brought to America they underwent a radical transformation, like other Spanish institutions. Perhaps due to the mistrust of the monarchs, it seemed necessary to authorize this organ to perform certain functions that were not purely judicial, in order to avoid the possibility of abuse of powers by the *Virreyes* and *Capitanes Generales.*

The *Audiencias* in America served as the highest appellate courts within their respective districts and, moreover, possessed a corporate character, exercising functions of a consultative body for the *Virrey* or *Capitán General,* as the case might be. They were granted some legislative powers allowing them to enact statutes of a local nature, subject to the approval of the monarch. The *Virreyes* and *Capitanes Generales* were the presidents ex officio of the *Audiencias,* and in those places where there were no such officials in residence, the *Audiencia* designated its own president, although in these cases it would be under the jurisdiction of the nearest *Virrey.*

These tribunals were composed of *oidores,*[6] whose number

---

6 Judges who must necessarily be attorneys.

varied in relation to the importance of the locality. As courts of justice, they tried cases (usually civil) appealed to them from the lower courts of the interior. Cases of an important nature could afterward be appealed from the *Audiencias* to the *Consejo de Indias.* The *Audiencias* possessed jurisdiction over criminal cases; that is, they served as original trial courts for such crimes. In addition, they were charged with protecting the rights of the Indians and usually reserved certain days of the week for hearing suits involving them and their complaints against Spaniards. Likewise, they tried complaints against the Church, as the decisions of the ecclesiastical courts could be appealed to the respective *Audiencias.*

Thus, in addition to being simple courts of justice, the *Audiencias* were administrative and political organs of the central power of Spain. The laws of the Indies specified clearly that the *Audiencias* were subject to the authority of the *Virreyes;* but, on the other hand, these tribunals could hear complaints formulated by the local inhabitants against the *Virreyes* and *Capitanes Generales,* and on many occasions halted their abuses. For their part, the *oidores* usually made a career of their positions; they resided permanently in the one locality and identified themselves closely with the varying local problems. Today in Latin America the *Audiencia* still functions as a judicial body. Stripped of its consultive and administrative powers, it resembles the old Spanish institution from which it emanated.

Functioning of the Central Government. In practice, the Spanish central governmental system was controlled by two institutions which the monarchs held like a threat over the heads of the functionaries to whom they delegated authority. These institutions were the *visitas* and the *juicios de residencia.* The former was an investigation, ordered by the central power, into the conduct of a colonial functionary. It could be undertaken at any time, when a subordinate's actions were under suspicion or subject of accusation. The *visitador* possessed wide powers and could prohibit the agent in question from exercising his duties, rendering an immediate account to the *Consejo de Indias* and other authorities.

When colonial officials terminated their appointments, their activities were reviewed by the *juicios de residencia.* This review consisted chiefly of a submittal of accounts during the process of which interested parties might file charges. In short, we could say that the Spanish monarchs wished to retain in their power all functions of government in the new territories. Distrust and suspicion of colonial authorities led them to exaggerate instructions to the point of extreme detail and produced serious complications and great confusion.

Professor C. H. Haring has rightly said that Spain did not establish any division of powers in America, but rather created a division of authority which increased the difficulty of administration. No words can be found better suited to sum up these observations than those of Professor Haring:

> It was apparent, therefore, that two principles were characteristic of Spanish imperial government in America: a division of authority and responsibility, and a deep distrust by the crown of initiative on the part of its colonial officials. These circumstances often prevented adequate and effective administration in the colonies. Through the necessity of constant reference to the home government, procrastination, delay, and red tape were the rule. The only real centralization was in the king and his council in Spain. Spanish imperial government was one of checks and balances; not secured as in many modern constitutional states by a division of powers, legislative, judicial, executive, but by a division of authority among different individuals or tribunals exercising the same powers. There was never a clear-cut line of demarcation between the functions of various governmental agencies dealing with colonial problems. On the contrary, a great deal of overlapping was deliberately fostered to prevent officials from unduly building up personal prestige or engaging in corrupt or fraudulent practices.[7]

THE LOCAL GOVERNMENT

The Provinces. For administrative reasons, the extensive territories that constituted the Spanish colonial empire were subdivided into units of small size and governed by officials called *gobernadores,* *corregidores,* or *alcaldes mayores.* Generally the *presidencia* or *gobernación* was the largest of them, at the head of which was the *gobernador,* considered as an official of highest rank, due to his power

---

7 Haring, C. H., *The Spanish Empire in America*, New York, Oxford University Press, 1947, p. 121.

and his remuneration. In cities of importance, the functionary who possessed political power was either a *corregidor* or an *alcalde mayor,* according to the region. The system which Spain set up in America, based upon division of authority without definite delimitations of function, was carried through to the provincial administration.

The picture is even more complicated if we remember that the governors were on many occasions *Capitanes Generales* and used the titles of *presidentes* at will. Political control was frequently exercised by an official designated as *presidente, gobernador,* or *Capitán General.* When the latter title was used it signified that the user also held military power. The *gobernadores, corregidores,* and *alcaldes mayores* possessed political and judicial authority within their respective territorial jurisdictions. They were, of course, subject to the control of the organs of central power to which we referred previously and faced problems of jurisdiction—as it was logical to expect—not only with the central government, but with municipal authorities. Although differing in name, rank, and the extension of territory under their rule, these provincial functionaries had the same powers and responsibilities, so that they can be studied together, to avoid unnecessary repetitions.

These provincial authorities (*gobernadores, corregidores,* and *alcaldes mayores*) were named by the King, those from Spain serving for five years, those already in America at the time of their appointment for three. Certain rules and limitations existed regarding their designation. No one could serve in the district in which he resided nor could he own land or mines in the district. Furthermore, such offices were prohibited to those whose relatives, to the fourth generation, occupied superior ranks in the administrative hierarchy (*Virreyes* or *Capitanes Generales*). Those selected for provincial posts had to declare all their goods and deposit an inventory with the *Audiencia* before assuming the position. This last requirement is especially interesting today, because it has been re-established in some of the new constitutions of Latin America for the majority of important public posts, including that of President of the Republic. The provincial official enjoyed political authority within his territory and moreover possessed some judicial powers. He exercised appellate jurisdiction over important cases, civil as well as criminal, originating in municipal courts. His decision could, in turn, be appealed to the *Audiencia.* Relations between these officials and municipal authorities were complex and not clearly defined. Conflicts were frequent, and in some cities the *corregidor* often intervened in the municipal government and acted jointly with the *alcaldes* and *regidores*. This was a direct consequence of the centralizing tendency and decadence of municipal authority existing in Spain at the time the new world government was being organized. The post of *corregidor* arose in Castile as a consequence of the desire of the King to restrict the local political power enjoyed by the municipalities.

The government of the Indian communities which paid tribute to the crown of Spain was also in charge of functionaries called *Corregidores de Pueblos de Indios*. These had political and judicial authority, and in theory were charged with protecting the well-being of the Indians. In practice, however, due to their relatively low salary, their rule was converted into frequent exploitation and abuses which caused many protests and even revolts. The provincial system thus briefly sketched came to an end with the reforms introduced by Charles III, when the *Intendencias* were created (Chapter 3).

THE MUNICIPAL SYSTEM

The Spanish municipal system was important in Latin America. Many authors maintain the erroneous idea that the municipality in Latin America was the democratic cell which Spain transplanted to the new territories, to flourish there and stimulate the movement for independence. This is an exaggeration. The municipality is important, not because in it the Creoles became familiar with the exercise of democracy, but because it was the only institutional nucleus around which the coherent forces of new nations were able to gather in the days of the struggle for independence. In this sense, the municipalities play a more important role than the other territorial units of the Spanish empire.

The Spanish Municipality. The democracy enjoyed by the Castillian municipality was a political phenomenon and a military necessity which was a direct consequence of the wars of Reconquest against the Moors. There are, of course, other causes of a different nature, such as the geographical conditions favoring the concentration of population in cities, the pastoral economy requiring urban protection in a country at war, and many others. These causes explain the creation of cities and municipalities, but they, alone, are not sufficient to justify the liberties which the Castillian munici-, pality enjoyed. The Spanish monarch, in the midst of the struggle for Reconquest, was faced with the problem of repopulating lands taken from the enemy. There was a "no man's land" to be put into production, but this could not be done through simple agricultural units or villages scattered over the territory. Thus there arose the necessity for the walled city, to function also as a military outpost, and it was essential to make the venture attractive in order to draw settlers to these dangerous spots. As is often the case, when rulers have nothing else to offer, they offer liberty. There was, con-sequently, a political and military reason which led the monarchs to consent to those special privileges which we know as *fueros municipales.*

The problem of the origin of the Spanish municipality has been the object of considerable historical controversy. In the nineteenth century, the predominant thesis among investigators was to the effect that the local institutions of Castile and León were of Roman origin. This opinion was advanced by the Portuguese historian Herculano and was repeated as an article of faith by almost all those who followed him. But toward the end of the nineteenth century, Hinojosa, the Spanish historian, took issue with Herculano's thesis. Hinojosa's disciple, Claudio Sánchez Albornoz, concludes a book which amplifies his stand by saying:

> No tie, no link, no matter how tenuous or loose it may be, can be established between the old municipal regime, definitely extinguished and forgotten in the Spain of the Reconquest, and the new medieval municipality.

He later adds:

> The medieval municipality of Castilla-León rose as the ripe fruit of the social, economic and political organization of the north, and with no foreign influences or ingredients. How could this be? This is a question involving a complex and diffi-cult problem: that of the origin of the municipal regime which, at the time of the Reconquest, crossed rivers and mountains toward the Mediterranean; which afterward *moved across the Atlantic* with the Conquistadores and finally extended through-

out the New World from Florida to the pampa, traversing all
Ibero America.[8]

The importance attached to the thesis of Albornoz is that it
clarifies the characteristic of a political phenomenon of the Reconquest and post-Reconquest of the modern Spanish municipalities;
a political phenomenon whose environment is reproduced in America
due to the necessity of overcoming territorial problems stemming
from the discovery.

The central government of Castile found itself constrained to
cede many of the powers it originally possessed in order to stimulate
the establishment of cities. The rights and liberties consigned in
the *fueros* varied with the situation of the new center of population,
and often their liberality was directly proportionate to the amount
of danger existing in the locality. Evident proof of this is that the
degree of risk involved was taken into consideration. Nevertheless,
there were certain essential characteristics which were uniform, and
they will be pointed out now.

The municipal *fueros* granted to residents, called *vecinos*, who
were heads of families and property owners, the right to meet in
an assembly called the *Consejo*. In this assembly the municipal
authorities were elected. Methods of election varied, officeholders
frequently being drawn by lot, but the important fact was that the
Consejo had the right to approve the appointments. The authorities
thus elected were called *regidores;* their number varied according to
the importance of the center of population, and they exercised
supreme authority in the municipal administration. In addition to
the *regidores*, the *Consejo* designated two *alcaldes*, or magistrates,
charged with the administration of municipal justice. There were,
of course, other categories of administrative officials who carried
out diverse public functions. This municipal corporation integrated
by the functionaries designated by the *Consejo* received the name
of *Ayuntamiento* and possessed its own legal personality. The
Consejos had one other important prerogative: that of naming the
procuradores to represent the city in the *Cortes*, as members of a
third state.

---

8 Sánchez Albornoz, Claudio, *Ruina y Extinción del Municipio Romano en España*,
Buenos Aires, Facultad de Filosofía y Letras, 1943, pp. 126, 129. (Author's translation
and italics.)

There is no doubt that, at a certain period in history, the Castillian municipality was one of the most democratic institutions existing in Europe, although its political power was purely local and not of a national character. Before the discovery of America, this power had already begun to decline; and when the kings became stronger and no longer needed to induce pioneers to found cities, the political reason for granting these liberties ceased, diminishing the power of the municipalities. One of the methods used by the central power was the creation of the post of *corregidor* who, as the name implies, was to govern with the *regidores,* the post to be held for life. Little by little, the practice of selling these posts was established by the central government. The kings, who conserved the legislative power, created other municipal offices, and the power of the *Consejo* was substituted by that of the *Ayuntamiento,* formed by these new functionaries subject to the national government.

The Municipality in America. The Castillian *Ayuntamiento* was transplanted to the new world, with the repetition in America of the phenomenon occurring in Spain during the Reconquent. Although the territory was a frontier and it was necessary to fight and conquer the indigenous population, the more democratic municipality was in operation. Some historians are surprised, for example, that Emperor Charles V would concede the right to some groups to elect their own *regidores* when this right had already disappeared in Spain. This is understandable, however, in view of the fact that the same necessity of establishing urban centers and attracting population, which existed in Spain during the Reconquest, was now being repeated in America. This political function of the municipality which Spain established in America must be taken into account, since it explains similar practices. The municipal corporation in America was called the *cabildo* (from the Latin, *capitulum,* chapter). The term originally designated the body of ecclesiastics of a church or the community of ecclesiastics of a village, and was sometimes used to distinguish the groups of brothers of certain religious orders of laymen or clerics. In Cuba, the meaning was extended to include the groups of *ñáñigos,* composed of Negroes, and at times of underworld Europeans. Often the word was used to indicate a building occupied by the municipal corporation.

The composition of the municipality in America was at first similar to that of Europe. The *regidores* were chosen by the inhabitants, and the former elected the *alcaldes ordinarios*. There were two *alcaldes* in important settlements and one in the smaller ones. The number of *regidores* was variable also, there generally being four or six in the towns and villages and more than a dozen in the cities. In America, there appeared with the foundation of the municipalities a series of administrative posts whose holders were considered ex-officio members of the *cabildo* as, for example, the *alguacil mayor* (constable), the *depositario general* (public trustee), and many others.

The *cabildos* exercised municipal authority within certain demarcations, carrying out functions relating to the entire sphere of local government. They levied and collected taxes, distributed land to the inhabitants, issued construction permits, and were in charge of public order and the militia for the defense of the city. The *regidores, alcaldes,* and other members of the *cabildo* met behind closed doors in the so-called *cabildos cerrados,* this being the usual way of handling administrative affairs. The decisions thus reached had legal validity and were not revealed until it was necessary, the members of the *cabildo* taking an oath to maintain secrecy.

Regarding affairs of great importance, such as epidemics, public calamities, or when the city was in danger of attack, the officers of the *Ayuntamiento* usually convoked an assembly of important citizens and distinguished members of the clergy to deliberate with the *cabildo.* Such meetings were called *cabildos abiertos,* their sole purpose being to hear the opinion of persons not connected with the government of the city. The decisions taken were not obligatory for the *cabildo,* which might freely accept or reject them. Seemingly, these *cabildos abiertos* took place more frequently in the more remote or less important cities. It would be inaccurate to consider the *cabildos abiertos* as the exercise of direct democracy or a referendum, or even as consultation with the total opinion of the populace, as only those invited could attend such deliberations. In spite of this, they played an important role in the emancipation movement of the Latin American republics, as we shall see later.

The *alcaldes ordinarios* were, as in Spain, judicial officers and possessed original jurisdiction over civil and criminal matters of the locality. They were elected annually by *regidores,* the law prohibiting the *regidores* from being *alcaldes,* although this provision was not always fulfilled.

The democratic structure of the municipality in America suffered the same fate as the Spanish *Ayuntamiento.* Little by little the centralizing power of the monarch and his functionaries infringed upon its liberties, especially when American cities and towns were no longer outposts of the empire. The *regidores* were named by the governors or by the King himself, and often retiring *regidores* appointed their own successors. Later perpetual *regidores* were designated, and it was not unusual for a newcomer from Spain to carry among his effects his appointment as *regidor,* without the population of the locality knowing anything of the affair. Philip II, compelled by economic necessity, introduced the practice of selling the posts of *regidores* in America, and thus municipal administration was converted into the private property of the King. It was common practice to find not only perpetual but hereditary *regidores,* since those who had purchased their posts demanded the right to bequeath them to their sons. Thus, families of *regidores,* with all the characteristics of dynasties, were established in America.

The social conditions of the Indians will be discussed later when studying the other institutions created by the Spanish state in America, and in this section will be pointed out only the existence of other governmental officers who were a part of the colonial administrative system. These, the *alcaldes* and *regidores* of the Indian settlements were closely connected with the municipalities. In each pueblo there were usually four *regidores* and one *alcalde.* Appointed annually by the inhabitants of the village, they constituted the government. The *alcaldes* shared their authority with the *cacique* or hereditary chief of the tribe and exercised judicial functions over minor cases and misdemeanors. In such localities, the Church also intervened to a certain extent in local administration, the parish priests (*curas doctrineros*) being in charge of ecclesiastical functions, conversion of the indigenous population, and enjoying considerable influence in the community.

The political autonomy of the *regidores* and *alcaldes* of the Indians was quite limited, which is understandable if one takes into account the small amount of autonomy enjoyed by municipalities in general. Intervention in the local administration by the *Corregidor de Indios* was frequent, and there were many cases of abuse of authority. Often the appointment of a *Corregidor de Indios* was only a formality, so that he functioned in practice as an *encomendero* (see Chapter 2), with the accompanying exploitation and ill-treatment.

The Church and the Government. The Roman Catholic Church functioned in Spanish America in many cases as an instrument of the political machinery of local administration. As such an institution let us consider it, since it is impossible to explain the reasons for the strict regulation of the Church in some of the modern constitutions of Latin America without taking into account the political position of the Church in the administrative structure which preceded independence.

As indicated earlier, the nation-state made its appearance in Europe in the sixteenth century. This state form, still existent today, had to overcome two political forces before being established. The first of these was feudalism—the traditional enemy of centralized governments—which in spite of having declined in Europe, was brought to America, although with peculiar characteristics. The other force was the temporal power of the Papacy, and in this struggle the nation-state triumphed; so that when America was discovered, the Papacy was already aware that it had to make concessions to the new nationalistic spirit and political power which the European monarchies enjoyed. One of these concessions was the institution of the Royal Patronage of the Indies, by virtue of which Popes Alexander VI and Julian II granted to the Spanish monarchs political and administrative control of all the ecclesiastical affairs of America, with the exception of those having to do with dogma and religious discipline.

In the economic aspect, the Spanish government had the right of collecting the *diezmo* or ecclesiastical tax, and the obligation of defraying the cost of maintenance and construction of new churches and other centers devoted to religious practices. Politically, the King was empowered to intervene in the appointment of ecclesiastical authorities, whatever their rank might be. Archbishops, bishops, and abbots were named by the King directly, who sent the proposed name to the Pope, the latter acting upon his recommendation rather than independently. The King also named those composing the lower ecclesiastical ranks, their names being sent to the Council of

Prelates of America for approval. Parish priests were appointed by the *Virreyes* in their capacity as vice-patrons of the Church, as the personal representatives in America of the Spanish monarchs.

The political absolutism which reached its height in Spain as the sixteenth century advanced caused the Royal Patronage of the Indies to be considered as one of the prerogatives which the Kings exercised with greatest pride. Because of this system, the Church functioned in practice as an integral part of the public administration of the period. The central government intervened in everything. It divided ecclesiastical territories, was in charge of the erection of new churches, monasteries, and convents, and in many cases named bishops and other high officials, authorizing them to take possession of their offices and carry out their duties without waiting for the sanction of the Holy See. There were cases in which the bishops performed their functions and were transferred to other dioceses without having received the apostolic sanction.

The great power of the Kings was felt not only in the administrative and economic realms of the Church, but at times in its spiritual and religious spheres. Papal bulls and other dispositions of Rome could not be promulgated in America without the approval of the *Consejo de Indias*. The latter organ of the central government carried on a type of censorship of pontifical authority. Later, during the Bourbon dynasty, this intervention of the state in Church affairs was extended to include even questions of dogma, and the monarchs considered the Royal Patronage a direct consequence of the exercise of sovereignty.

It is important to point out that, in Spanish America, relations between the Church and state were so intimately connected that it is difficult to separate them. What existed in America was not only a political state, but a Church-state. The Church succeeded in maintaining the unity of faith, and the state offered it its protection at the same time incorporating it into its administrative machinery. Today it is an accepted principle that the state is responsible for the establishment and maintenance of certain public services. In the sitxeenth century, the idea was not yet clearly defined. We have heard on many occasions that the Spanish state did not concern itself with public services in America, and that the Church had to take charge of these. One should keep in mind that the public services, which the Church maintained, were done as an organ of the state.

The same could be said with regard to the problem of education. The Church organized and directed it, as part of the state. Among public services in charge of the Church-state, outside of education which was the most important, were the establishment and administration of hospitals and asylums, which, in spite of the natural limitations of the period, performed a great service in the new territories. In the sixteenth century, the hospitals served also as poor houses, and the monasteries as inns for travelers. The history of Mexico and Peru is full of the admirable achievements which today we would call "social work" of the religious orders and famous clergymen. The work of the missionaries and the father-protectors of the Indians, as we will see in the next chapter, was a social work of outstanding importance.

The identification, in its administrative aspects, of the state with the Church was not complete. The latter retained the right of holding its own property and received large grants of land which it later exploited for its own benefit. This laid the groundwork for the ecclesiastical *latifundia* which has caused so many past and present problems in Latin America. In this and other ways, the Church acquired an economic power which even today it retains in the majority of the countries, and thus it was converted from an organ of the state to a state within a state, which is still the seat of discord.

As a political machine, the Church carried out, first during the Conquest and later during the consolidation of the empire, another function of great importance through its system of missions. The mission was an outpost of a religious-military nature, functioning like a bridgehead at first, spiritually as well as materially. When the empire was integrated, the mission, with its crude buildings adapted as much to defense and production as to religion, was the sentinel guarding the frontiers of the great colonial empire. It was not unusual for a garrison of soldiers, or *presidio,* to reside permanently in a mission. The governmental function carried on by the missions was so evident that they generally received an annual sum directly from the central government to defray their expenses.

When the threat of the Reformation appeared in Europe, another function was entrusted to the Church in America. This was the preservation of the faith, and to this end the Inquisition was established. It had existed in Spain since before the discovery of the new world. At the beginning of the sixteenth century, the bishops of the Indies already possessed inquisitorial powers, but it was not until the end of the century that the tribunals of the Inquisition were established. The first of these, set up in Lima, was followed by that of Mexico in 1571. Before their establishment, *autos de fe* were held in America by the bishops in charge of the Inquisition, but it was not until the latter part of the sixteenth century that the system functioned with the most clearly defined political characteristics. Because this aspect of the Inquisition is extremely well known, we need only point out that it was a direct result of the policy of the counter-Reformation which Philip II maintained. It was a defensive measure, both religiously and politically.

The tribunals of the Inquisition still further complicated the governmental machinery functioning in America. Their powers were not clearly defined, and the institutions of government were supposed to aid them as the secular arm, in which capacity the Inquisition could invade the jurisdictions of the organs of government, both in the civil and ecclesiastical realms. Abuses of power were frequent, and history is full of the protests of administrative authorities against the ecclesiastics of the Inquisition, but the influence of the latter was so great that not even the *Virreyes* dared oppose them openly. The administration of property confiscated from accused persons brought about corruption. There were scandals which caused public alarm, and concrete cases of inquisitors and fiscal agents who became wealthy so rapidly that they were the object of investigations, or *visitas* by the government.

The tribunal was created to combat heresies against the faith, but few important cases regarding dogma occurred in the colonies. An examination of the trials of the Inquisition in America shows that the tribunals had to content themselves with cases of Jews and Dutch and English Lutherans. There were others in which the crime punished was that of superstition and blasphemy, especially among Negro slaves. Cases of witchcraft and superstition were the most frequent, also among the Negro slaves, and a few among the Indians, although the latter were outside the jurisdiction of the Inquisitors. The methods of the Inquisition and its torments do not fit into this study, dedicated to an understanding of the political influence of the Church.

In the writer's opinion, the tribunal of the Inquisition left a more definite mark on the political development of America in its ideological aspect. The tribunal maintained a rigorous censorship of all books distributed in the continent. The scientific ideas of the Renaissance and the political ideas which were propagated in the countries of the Reformation did not penetrate into America due to the fervor displayed by the tribunals of the Inquisition. The Spanish colonies were maintained isolated from western culture for more than two centuries, as it was not until the end of the seventeenth century that Encyclopedism succeeded in breaking the blockade.

SUGGESTED READINGS

English:

Altamira, Rafael, *A History of Spain,* New York, D. Van Nostrand Co., Inc., 1949.

Bourne, Edward G., *Spain in America,* 1450-1580 (American Nation Series, Vol. III), New York, Harper & Brothers, 1904.

Diffie, Bailey W., *Latin American Civilization; Colonial Period,* Harrisburg, Stackpole & Heck, Inc., 1945.

Fisher, Lillian E., *Viceregal Administration in the Spanish American Colonies,* Berkeley, University of California Press, 1926.

Hanke, Lewis, *The First Social Experiments in America,* Cambridge, Harvard University Press, 1935.

Haring, Clarence H., *The Spanish Empire in America,* New York, Oxford University Press, 1947.

Madariaga, Salvador de, *The Rise of the Spanish Empire,* New York, The Macmillan Co., 1947.

Madden, Marie R., *Political Theory and Law in Medieval Spain,* New York, 1930.

Means, Philip A., *The Spanish Main, Focus of Envy, 1492-1700,* New York, Charles Scribner's Sons, 1935.

Merriman, Rogers B., *The Rise of the Spanish Empire in the Old World and the New,* 4 vols., New York, The Macmillan Co., 1938.

Moses, Bernard, *The Establishment of Spanish Rule in America,* New York, G. P. Putnam's Sons, 1898.

Prescott, William H., *Ferdinand and Isabella,* 3 vols., New York, 1872.

Scholes, France V., *Church and State in New Mexico, 1610-1650,* Albuquerque, University of New Mexico Press, 1937.

Smith, Donald E., *The Viceroy of New Spain,* Berkeley, University of California Press, 1913.

Wilgus, A. Curtis (Ed.) *Colonial Hispanic America,* Washington, The George Washington University Press, 1936.

Spanish:

García, Antonio, *Bases de la Economía Contemporánea,* Bogotá, 1948.

Hanke, Lewis, *Bartolomé de las Casas,* La Habana, 1949.

Levene, Ricardo, *Introducción a la Historia del Derecho Indiano,* Buenos Aires, 1924.

Mayer, E., *Historia de las Instituciones Sociales y Políticas de España y Portugal durante los Siglos,* V a XV., Madrid, 1925.

Ortiz, Fernando, *Contrapunteo Cubano del Tabaco y el Azúcar,* La Habana, 1940.

Ots Capdequi, J. M., *El Estado Español en las Indias,* Mexico, D.F., 1941,

Pereyra, Carlos, *Historia de la América Española,* Madrid, 1920-1926, 8 vols.

Sánchez Albornoz, Claudio, *Ruina y Extinción del Municipio Romano en España,* Buenos Aires, 1943.

Serrano y Sanz, Manuel, *Origenes de la Dominación Española en América,* Madrid, 1918.

Zavala, Silvio A., *Las Encomienda Indiana,* Madrid, 1935.

————, *Las Instituciones Jurídicas en la Conquista de América,* Madrid, 1935.

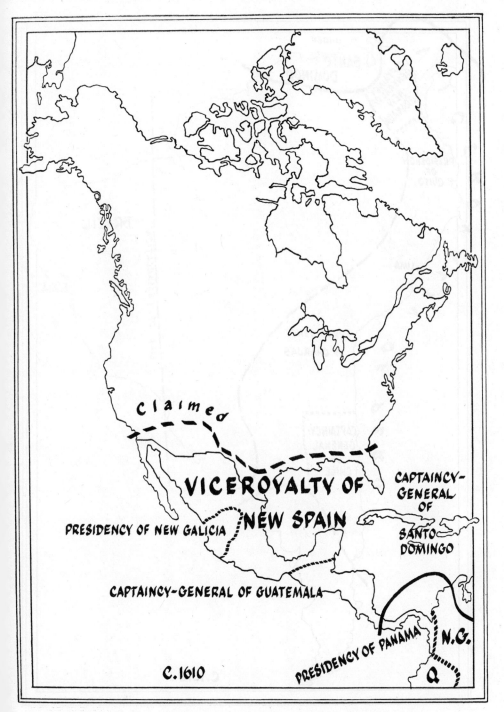

Southern North America and Central America about 1610.

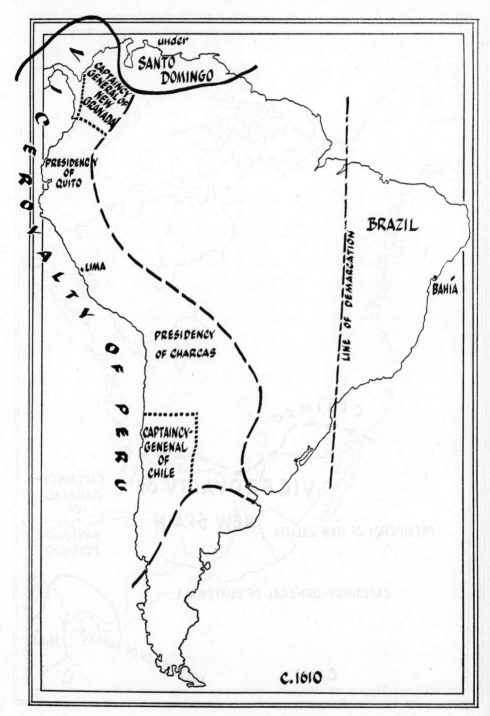

under
SANTO
DOMINGO

CAPTAINCY
GENERAL OF
NEW
GRANADA

PRESIDENCY
OF
QUITO

LIMA

VICEROYALTY OF PERU

PRESIDENCY
OF CHARCAS

CAPTAINCY-
GENENAL
OF
CHILE

BRAZIL

BAHÍA

LINE OF DEMARCATION

C. 1610

South America about 1610.

CHAPTER 2

Spanish Colonial Institutions

The preceding chapter has dealt with the political structure established in America by the Spanish state. This structure should be studied together with other characteristics of the social group to which it applies; therefore, the economic, legal and social institutions of colonial America will now be considered. Only the purely essential and institutional aspects will be covered, as a background for the realities which the Latin American republics had to face. A complete analysis of an economic, legal, or sociological character is not the purpose of this work, and only the Spanish institutions will be dealt with in this chapter. In a later chapter on Brazil, the colonial institutions of Portugal will be examined.

Economic Structure. Spanish economic policy rested upon the mercantilist principle, which was predominant during this period. According to this policy, the colonies existed solely for the benefit of the mother country and functioned as a market for the merchants of that nation. As a consequence of this principle, America played the role of an economic complement of Spanish production, in which it was to contribute only those things which would not compete with the products of the mother country.

Another consequence of mercantilism was the establishment of a commercial monopoly between Spain and America, principally through the port of Seville where the *Casa de Contratación* was located. Still another result of this policy was the importance attributed to the acquisition of precious metals, especially gold, which explains the national protectionism enjoyed by mining interests to the detriment of agriculture and industry. This policy logically produced, as is known, commercial backwardness not only in America but in Spain itself, and contributed to the development of manufacturing in other European countries where the gold of the Indies was spent.

31

Spain exercised a rigid control over the sources of wealth in its colonial empire. The institution created for this purpose was the system of *regalías* of the Crown. In theory, America was part of the private patrimony of the kings, who granted privileges, reserving for themselves a part of the sources of wealth. It is important to remember some of these *regalías,* for they were the forerunners of many of the limitations upon private property today found in the modern constitutions of Latin America. For example, the mines, gold found in the rivers, salt pits, precious stones, treasures found in the tombs of the Indians, and the lands, waters, pastures, and mountains not granted to others remained the property of the Crown. It was customary to grant the rights of exploitation to individuals with the obligation on their part to pay to the King one fifth (*el quinto*) of all the wealth obtained from such grants. Regarding mines, the principle was always maintained that the surface and the subsoil were two different things, and that exploitation of the latter was through government concession. The owner of the surface had to denounce the mine, like any other individual, in order to put it into production. The concessionaire, if he did not own the surface, had to pay the owner for its use. This principle is today the object of strict regulation in many constitutions of Latin America and produced serious international controversies at the time of the Mexican expropriation of foreign-owned oil holdings.

With regard to land ownership, granting of the title was in the hands of the royal authority or of its political delegates, *Adelantados, Virreyes, Presidentes,* and even *cabildos* enjoying this power. Such grants as these did not bestow full title, and, in order to do so, the concessionaire had to cultivate the land, maintain it, and reside thereon for a period of time. This characteristic is important because it is included in some of the contemporary constitutions. The ownership of property gave some jurisdictional powers over the inhabitants of the estate. That is, the landowner acted as a sort of feudal lord.

After the Conquest, and even while it was being consummated, the original system of land distribution suffered important alterations. The royal grants were abandoned, and the practice of auctioning state lands was introduced. Also authorized was the system of the so-called *composiciones,* by which the possession of land without a title could be legalized through the payment of a sum of money to the government. This resulted from the need of money experienced by Spain during the dynastic and religious wars.

Agriculture and stock raising developed in America, conditioned by geographical environment, regional necessities, and the spirit of initiative of the colonizers. There was no uniform Spanish policy, as Ots Capdequi indicates: "It cannot be said that, with respect to the territories of the Indies, there was a true policy on the part of the representatives of the Spanish government regarding agriculture and stock-raising." [1] It is true that in the laws there were certain regulations on agriculture and livestock industries for the purpose of encouraging them, but, as the same author adds, the end in view throughout these regulations was the Spanish economy and its necessities.

Legal Structure. The first documents from which emanated the legal relations between the central government of Spain and the *conquistadores* were those called *capitulaciones*. These were contracts between the above-mentioned parties in which certain concessions were granted to the settlers and obligations to the monarchs were specified. Generally the organizers of discovery expeditions paid all their own expenses, the *capitulación* giving to the discoverer almost absolute powers in the lands under his command. This institution, which was of medieval character and very similar to the municipal charters used in Spain in the founding of cities (Chapter 1), suffered the same consequences as the municipal system in America. Thus, as the Conquest advanced, the Spanish state accentuated its centralizing tendency and the *capitulación* declined in importance. Let us keep in mind that, in spite of the private character of the relations between the monarch and the discoverer, they were not of a purely commercial nature, since the discoverer always acted in the name of the Spanish crown. Private initiative was rewarded and stimulated, but without impairing the sovereignty of the state.

National sovereignty was manifested also in the sphere of individual relations by the transplanting of Castillian legal norms to America; and, even more important, by the creation of special laws which contributed to the formation of the American social body and that conditioned, and still affects, its political conduct.

---

1 Ots Capdequi, J. M., *op. cit.*, p. 40.

The Spanish law which came to America, or that which was created especially for America, was a written law. Custom and judicial autonomy did not play an important role. Laws were formulated in Spain and many of the institutions and dispositions thereby created were wise and just, but as a rule they were completely divorced from the existing realities of the colonies. Judges and magistrates were able to do little, faced with the rigor of the written law. This was the result of the same centralizing political principle which absorbed and regulated all else. As a typical case of the influence of Castillian law in the sphere of private relations, the institution of marriage should be noted. Marriage was a sacrament of the Church and was subject to the provisions of canon law, which became more rigid after the Council of Trent. Union between Spanish men and Indian women was recognized by the law and was encouraged from the first years of colonization. An attempt was made to induce Spaniards living in concubinage with Indians to contract marriage, as well as for Indians to marry among themselves.

In the first years of colonization, very few Spanish women came to America, and many married men who resided in the new territories were separated from their wives. The government tried to correct this situation by arranging for wives to be brought to America, and later prohibited married men from coming to the colonies without being accompanied by their wives. The government also sought to maintain the conjugal home with regard to the unions which existed among the Indians, and prohibited taking Indian women from their places of habitual residence if they were not accompanied by their mates. In general, the tendency was to protect and stimulate marriage as a social and religious institution.

Regarding the position of the woman in colonial life, it is important to point out that, in accordance with the laws of the period, she lacked legal capacity. When single, she was under the authority of her father, eldest brother, or closest male relative, regardless of her age. The married woman was subordinate to her husband, and only widows enjoyed legal capacity. Women were not incorporated into society in their own right until many years after Independence, and today there are still Latin American countries where they lack political rights, and others where they need their husbands' permission to take part in commercial relations.

The foregoing was the general rule, although there were important exceptions especially as regards political activities. There were
women who temporarily occupied the post of *Virreina,* and many
others who held governmental positions. These, nevertheless, were
exceptions sanctioned by the Spanish monarchs due to extraordinary
circumstances and, as such, confirmed the rule.

In the economic realm, women were often authorized to receive
encomiendas, especially as a result of inheritance, but this was always
contrary to the prevailing legal order. In the Royal Order of
August 9, 1546, *encomiendas* received by women were ordered annulled because "they are not qualified for or capable of having
Indians under their custody." It was also ordered that in case a
woman holding an *encomienda* should marry, the *encomienda* be
registered in her husband's name. As may be seen from these and
many other cases that can be cited, the purpose was always to maintain the principle of feminine legal incapacity.

Regarding the right of property, some of the frequent interventions of the political power of the Spanish government in the sphere
of individual activities should be noted. What was pointed out
earlier with regard to the royal grants should be kept in mind, as
well as the fact that capitalism, with its essential characteristic of
individual and private initiative, never did become established in
colonial America. To illustrate this, only a few cases need be mentioned where private and public interests co-existed or, in other
words, where the individual undertaking was limited by the power
of the state. When treasure was found, the state kept half for itself,
leaving the other half for the discoverer. Ownership of public services, as stated earlier, was sold to the highest bidder; the owners
acquired only the use of them, the crown conserving the *dominium
directum.* The system of collective ownership of land, and even of
slaves, was established. In cities and towns, the well-known *ejidos*
or lands for the joint use of the inhabitants, and commons for the
grazing of livestock were created. The laws of the Indies specified
that "the pastures, hills and waters are held in common in the Indies."
We shall see the legal and political consequences of this forerunner
of collective property included in many modern Latin American
constitutions.

The legal status of the Indians was the object of scrupulous
regulation in Spanish law. From the date of the discovery until

1500, Indians could legally be converted into slaves. In this period of legalized slavery, extraordinary abuses took place. Oftentimes the *conquistadores* captured the Indians and made slaves of them. Through the Royal Order of June 20, 1500, the system was changed and it was decreed that Indians should be treated as subjects of Castile, slavery being authorized only for prisoners of war. But from this measure other abuses arose, especially that of simulating a state of war; and, in 1530, slavery of the Indians even in this case was prohibited. Later the laws were modified and, in the *Recopilación de las Leyes de Indias* (Chapter 1), slavery was authorized of those tribes which rebelled against the crown, such as the Caribs, Araucanians, and Apaches.

The right of not being submitted to slavery enjoyed by the Indians was limited by other legal institutions which in practice produced almost the same results as slavery. Such institutions were the *repartimiento* and the *encomienda*.

The *repartimiento* was the practice of distributing Indians among the colonizers so that the latter would benefit from their work. Abuses were frequent, and the indigenous population diminished as a result of these forms of forced labor. An institution which played a more important role was the *encomienda*. Through it, a group of Indian families was placed under the legal power of an *encomendero,* who was in charge of their religious instruction, in return for which they were to afford him personal service. At first this privilege was granted only for the lifetime of the *encomendero,* but later it was extended to the fourth generation through the payment of a sum of money to the crown. In practice this institution converted the Indian into a serf. Many protests arose from the abuses; in fact, such a point was reached that in 1542 personal service was replaced by the obligation, on the part of the Indians, to pay a tribute to the *encomendero. Encomiendas* were maintained until early in the eighteenth century, when they were officially abolished. It should be noted there that the grant did not implicitly include the land, as many writers have indicated. It was always an obligation of a personal character upon the Indian, and had no legal relation to the system of landholding.

Indians not submitted to the *encomienda* lived on *reducciones* under the authority of their own *alcaldes* and *alguaciles,* an authority which was later placed in the hands of the *corregidores* of Indian villages.[2] The condition of the Indians who lived on *reducciones* will be dealt with later when studying the organization of labor. In order to gain an idea of the legal situation of the Indians, the characteristics of the tribute that they had to pay to the Spanish government should be described, as well as other forms of servitude to which they were subjected. This tribute was a consequence of equalization of the Indian with other subjects of the crown. Indians of both sexes between the ages of 18 and 50 were obliged to pay tribute to the Spanish crown. In the pueblos or *reducciones* this tax was collected by the local governmental officials. The amount was set by officials designated by the *Audiencia,* and payment was sometimes made in money, sometimes in kind, depending upon the circumstances. To facilitate collection of the tax, the Indians were *empadronados* [3] and considered as contributors. This census was, of course, unpopular among those obliged to pay tribute and is one of the reasons why even today the indigenous masses in Latin America look upon governmental officials with dislike.

Another institution of considerable importance was the *mita.* Through it, the Indians were selected by drawing lots to work temporarily for a Spanish master and were paid by the day.[4] The length of work varied with the type of occupation, and those Indians who tilled their own lands or made their living as artisans were exempt. The agricultural and mining *mitas* were very important. The amount of tribute to be paid by the Indian was discounted from his daily wage, and thus the institution functioned as a new form of servitude which was one of the severest of the personal services which oppressed the Indian laborer.

In addition it is necessary to recall other forms of servitude because they constituted the historical antecedent of the agrarian problems which exist in Latin America. They bound the Indian, and later the *mestizo,* to a rural landholding (generally to a latifundia). The names of such institutions vary from country to country, but they are essentially the same; therefore, only the best known term will be used: *peonage.* Chaves Orozco, the Mexican sociologist, describes it in the following manner:

---

2 See Chapter 1.
3 Registered in a local census.
4 The institution was Indian in origin.

Theoretically and legally, the peon was a lessee or copartner (*mediero*) of the hacienda, who at times worked for a salary, or who might work for a salary exclusively. The "lessee" or "wage-earner" was such only in name, as in fact they were serfs. The lessee did not own the instruments of production. Oxen, implements and plows (the rudimentary Egyptian plow) belonged to the land-owner, who rented them to the *arrendatario* or lessee. In addition, the land-owner advanced the necessary seeds which the lessee paid back after the completion of the harvest. As the latter did not have sufficient resources to subsist until the harvest, he received cereals from the "master's" granary and the indispensable groceries from the plantation store to keep himself and his family from starvation. Operating on this basis, the harvest, its outcome generally problematical, was not enough to pay the land-holder the following: (1) 50% of the total harvest; (2) rent for the implements of production; (3) cost of the seeds advanced by the land-holder; (4) cost of the goods and food-stuffs obtained from the *tienda de raya* or plantation store.[5]

Another juridical institution which must be taken into account was slavery. The importation of Negro slaves to America was authorized by the Royal Order of the Catholic Kings, dated September 16, 1501. Before this, slavery of the Indians had already been established. A well-known authority in this field, Dr. Fernando Ortiz, says in this regard:

It is undeniable that there was Spanish slavery of Indians here before that of Negroes; that in Castilla there always was slavery of Negroes and whites, both before and after the discovery. . . . It is not amiss to remember that many slaves were brought to the Indies, even white Christian women, by the Catholic King, through his Royal Order of Burgos, February 26, 1512.[6]

Thus slavery took root in Spanish America as a legal and social institution when it was already disappearing in some countries of the old world and being replaced by other forms of labor. In ancient times, the institution of slavery—in spite of its odious aspects—

---

[5] García, Antonio, *Bases de la Economía Contemporánea*, Ediciones R.F.I.O.C., Bogotá, 1948, p. 79. (Author's translation.)

[6] Ortiz, Fernando, *Contrapunteo Cubano del Tabaco y el Azúcar*, La Habana, 1940, p. 354. (Author's translation.)

made its economic contribution and aided in the development of great cultures. But in the sixteenth century, when it was transplanted to America, it had exhausted its historical function. A similar phenomenon occurred with regard to Feudalism.[7] In America,

> . . . a negative feudalism was united with a negative slavery,
> with no objectives of economic construction; thus was produced
> a true mixture of cultural dregs without the capacity to create
> what slavery and feudalism had created in Asia and Europe.[8]

José Carlos Mariátegui,[9] the Peruvian writer, has pointed out that with the introduction of slavery the Spanish *conquistador* abandoned the task of assimilating the Indian and sought help in the Negro. With this, the policy of assimilation came to an end and was substituted by the policy of exploitation in which the Indian was considered the same as the Negro, in spite of the legal differences existing in the *Leyes de Indias*.

Moreover, in colonial social life slavery produced that aversion toward manual labor which is characteristic of the Creole aristocracy that inherited the political power of Spain with the coming of independence. Antonio García, cited above, has singled out as the most important consequence of slavery

> . . . the disqualification of work, upon being converted into a
> specifically slave-servile activity, stimulating leisure and para-
> sitism as the characteristic of the free population and as an ob-
> jective demonstration of the purity of blood.[10]

System of Work. One interesting characteristic of the political structures of the Latin American countries is the incorporation in the modern constitutions of rules and precepts designed to protect the working classes and harmonize their relations with their employers. The salient features of the system of work in the colonial period should be noted, as a background for the present situation.

---

[7] American feudalism was not the same as its European counterpart, since the latter carried out the important function of offering protection to the serf in the wars between the various feudal lords, in the chaotic state then found in Europe as a result of the fall of the Roman Empire.

[8] García, Antonio, *op. cit.*, p. 83.

[9] Mariátegui, José Carlos, *Siete ensayos de Interpretacion de la Realidad Peruana*, Editorial "Libreria Peruana," Lima, 1934.

[10] García, Antonio, *op. cit.*, p. 83.

In Spain, as in the other countries of Europe, the free workers were associated in the guilds. The Spanish guild was inspired by a religious spirit and mixed spiritual ends with economic and technical purposes. Under the Spanish law, the municipality intervened and regimented the production and commerce of certain necessities, such as bread, wine, and meat, in order to safeguard the poorer classes. The *Leyes de Partidas* prohibited associations of workers with the purpose of artificial setting of the price of labor, and established a maximum salary which was in relation to the articles of primary consumption. The *Cortes* of Valladolid, for example, established as the maximum working day the period from sunrise to sunset, and protected all types of persons so that they might freely teach their trades.

The Spanish guild was no different from the medieval European one. It was a corporation with its own legal capacity, made up of the masters of the trade. The apprentices and companions did not form a part of the guild. The rank of master was not acquired by simply having been an apprentice or companion for a required length of time; rather, it was necessary to pass an examination to prove ability and to open one's own shop. This signified not only technical knowledge of the trade but also economic capacity to establish oneself.

In colonial America, there were two legal sources of importance in the field of labor. The *Leyes de Indias* dealt with the system of work of the aborigines, while the municipal ordinances regulated free work in the population centers.

The purpose of the municipal ordinances regarding guilds was to distribute among the workers of the locality the acquisitive capacity of the population in an equitable and economically useful form. It was a planned economy, as we would say today, and an intervention of the government in the sphere of private initiative. J. Jesús Castorena [11] has pointed out the important fact that the object of the ordinances of guilds in America was not the regulation of labor but the creation of a system of economic production. The apprentices and companions did not form a part of the guild, but were under its authority because the ordinances were applicable to them. On the other hand, the ordinances did not fix the conditions of

---

[11] Castorena, J. Jesús, *Tratado de Derecho Obrero*, México, Editorial Jaris, 1942.

work of the apprentices and companions. In this respect they were subject to the will of the masters.

The ordinances of guilds regulated the process of production in Hispanic America in painstaking and minute form. There were those of a sanitary character (use of certain raw materials in food products) ; others of purely economic content (price-fixing) ; some designed to avoid dangerous competition (fixing of locations and number of shops) ; and those regulating relations between various guilds (prohibition of masters from contracting work outside their specialty). This system placed free labor and individual initiative under the political control of the municipal administration. The *cabildos* approved the ordinances of guilds, and officials called *veedores* were in charge of passing on the promotions of apprentices and companions. There is no doubt but that this rigid system slowed down the economic development of colonial America and, moreover, created a deep division of classes which Antonio García says was

> . . . not only anti-capitalistic, in the sense of impeding competition, free determination of prices, and accumulation of reserves, but it was racial and negative in the establishment of artisan hierarchies: differing from the medieval establishment in that not only was there an examination of manual skill or virtuosity necessary in the Indies (conducted by the respective *veedores* of the guild, under the control of the *Cabildos*) but also a 'blood test.' [12]

That is, with the object of impeding the economic autonomy of certain ethnic groups considered inferior, achievement of the title of master implied the proof of purity of blood; thus, the direction of the guilds remained in a minority group of Spanish and Creoles.

In the European guild, all workers had the legal capacity to become masters. In America, through its subordination to the *cabildo,* the political and centralizing power of the crown reached even to the guild. The apprentices and companions of non-white races functioned as salaried workers of the guild corporation, not through lack of technical capacity, but for reasons of politics and caste.

[12] "Pureza de Sangre" meaning investigation of their "race." García, Antonio, *op. cit.,* p. 88.

The closed nature of the guild system impeded the development of private commerce in America, since the artisan masters had the exclusive privilege of the sale of their products. The economic monopoly which Spain established in international commerce permeated the lesser spheres of economic life, with the state exercising its control over the local production of the artisans in the guilds. Such guilds had "community chests" (*cajas de comunidad*) and pawnshops (*montes píos*) to help their members economically through the creation of funds held in common upon which the members could draw in case of necessity. In practice, it appears that these institutions functioned only as a means of permanent savings with principally religious ends, using their money to defray the costs of the fiestas of patron saints, religious services, burials, etc.

Not all of the work of colonial America was dedicated to artisan or agricultural pursuits. There was a beginning of industry which absorbed a great part of the population and led to the origin of *obrajes*. These were woolen or cotton textile factories, the products of which were important locally because only the upper classes could afford the rich materials imported from Spain, the rest of the population depending on the goods manufactured in America. Such *obrajes* were productive undertakings for the owners, and severe exploitation of workers occurred in them.

Labor was on a piecework basis, the usual working day being fourteen or fifteen hours, with Sunday work the custom, since the violation of religious holidays was justified by the pretext that the work was voluntary on the part of the worker. Tribute (when the worker was obliged to pay any) was subtracted from the worker's wages, as was the priest's salary on many occasions. Women and children worked alongside men, and the system of borrowing on one's future salary, which made the employee a virtual prisoner of the owner, existed in many *obrajes*. Many of these maintained their own systems of repression (prison, chains, and corporal punishment). This system of manufacturing was extremely advantageous to owners of *obrajes*, and their numbers multiplied throughout the colonial territory. *Obrajes* were owned by religious communities, individuals, churchmen, indigenous communities, and *caciques* in their capacity of individuals, as well as by Spanish *encomenderos* and *hacendados*.

Together with the work of the guilds and *obrajes* should be mentioned the condition of the Indians who were not a part of *encomiendas,* but lived on the *reducciones* or pueblos. Some of them, of course, worked in the *obrajes* of their own *caciques,* but there were others who served under contract as salaried employees and laborers and were under the protection of the *Leyes de Indias.* The latter had as their object the protection of all Indians, although in practice this protection was side-stepped in view of the forms of servitude we have noted. It is well to keep in mind that such laws constitute an interesting historical antecedent to present measures regarding workers' rights. Some of them include the following: (1) the contract for work could not cover a period longer than one year; (2) payment must be by the week in accepted currency (not wine, chicha, honey or Paraguayan *yerba*); (3) minimum wages (the amount to be fixed by the city or zone of production); (4) no work on Sundays; (5) payment directly to the wage earner. It is true that many of these rights were not practiced in America, but most of these provisions have been included in the modern constitutions of Latin America.

The Indian *reducciones* were objects of special attention and measures for the defense of their inhabitants. For example, it was ordered that "no Spanish, Negroes, mestizos or mulattoes are to live in the Indian pueblos." This was later explained with that traditional frankness which characterized the legislators of the Indies, by saying: "because it has been found that some Spaniards who deal with, live and travel among the Indians are troublesome, of bad habits, robbers, vicious and lost souls." [13]

The *Leyes de Indias* also sought to impede alcoholism among the Indians. The Spaniards made use of alcohol in order to subjugate the Indians, but the laws prohibited the sale of wine and its introduction into the *reducciones,* although the sale of *pulque* was admitted in New Spain.

Social Structure. It cannot be said that a society with homogenous characteristics existed in America until the latter half of the sixteenth century. The period of conquest was marked by the policy of assimilation of the Indians. There was, as we have seen, slavery of Indians and Negroes, but as yet the organization of slave labor

---

[13] Castorena, J. Jesús., *op. cit.,* pp. 101-102. (Author's translation.)

had not produced its economic consequences, and the zeal of missionaries and other religious leaders to incorporate the Indian into the Hispanic culture remained.

The social characteristics of that period were later changed completely by two factors. The first of these was of economic content caused by the effects of slave labor which created a wealthy and privileged class of Spaniards, settling in population centers. The other was of a social character and consisted in the appearance of a growing *mestizo* population. The superior *peninsular* and Creole class adopted a defensive and discriminatory attitude toward this group which was rising from below. Such an attitude remained until the last years of Spanish domination and persists today in many countries where there is a large *mestizo* population.

The social group which came into being after the first half of the sixteenth century conserved—in general lines—the same structure until the end of the eighteenth century, when the first thoughts of independence appeared. At this time the Spaniards, whites, and those who passed as such, constituted the superior class and were subdivided into two subgroups: the so-called *peninsulares* who were those born in Spain, and the Creoles or Spanish born in the New World. This sector of society usually occupied the high administrative, ecclesiastical, or military posts, had land or mine holdings, and engaged in large-scale import or export activities. But, after the first years of social integration, a pronounced schism developed between the *peninsular* and the Creole. In Cuba, there is an old proverb which says, "The Spaniard was able to have everything here except Spanish sons." [14] This proverb expresses a great social reality. From the beginning of colonization the more important posts were always occupied by *peninsulares*. This held true equally for the religious hierarchy. The law, it is true, made no distinction between the *peninsulares* and the Creoles, but the separation was maintained in administrative and ecclesiastical policy. That old policy of distrust which we have pointed out extended even to the social and economic realm. It would appear that Spain had no faith in her overseas sons. The separation into subgroups reached even to the business world where the rich peninsular merchants who en-

---

[14] "El español puede tener de todo en Cuba menos hijos españoles."

joyed a monopoly of business in the Indies did not employ any Creole in an important position.

This division among the components of the class comprising the social elite has been explained away in various manners. It has been said, for example, that the Creole element was indolent, due to having been born in America and thus influenced by the climate. This affirmation cannot withstand even the most elemental criticism, since it is known that the most important centers of population in colonial America were established in the temperate zone. The so-called indolence of the Creoles was undoubtedly an effect and not a cause. The Creole sought to avoid hard work not through indolence, but, because with the system of slavery, work was considered a social stigma. He was caught between two social groups. He could not rise, because the doors were closed to him, and of course he did not desire to descend and mix with the lower groups. Therefore, he adopted a negative attitude, one of escape, and had to be content with living almost at the margin of his own group. There was no other possible solution.

The Spaniard, who came to America to reinforce the peninsular group after the period of Conquest, did so to profit more than to fight. The men of action of the Conquest were replaced by officials who, according to the expression of Bishop Zumárraga, came "to inflate themselves." [15] Decadence began in Spain and was reflected in America in the social, political, economic, and religious spheres. Picón Salas reminds us that:

> The destruction of the Invincible Armada in the stormy northern seas had the value of a symbol; in contrast to the old warlike and religious ideals of the Spaniards rose England's economic achievement, the bourgeois culture of the Protestant countries, the very concrete absolutism of the French state, the appearance of the natural and mechanical sciences; all historical trends which were opposed to those defended by Spain with such stubborn faith.[16]

However, a radical change in social values took place. Life, which during the period of the Conquest had an exchange value for which

---

[15] Picón Salas, Mariano, *De la Conquista a la Independencia*, México, D. F., 1944. p. 88.

[16] *Ibid.*, p. 89. (Author's translation.)

it offered itself gladly in the quest for glory and the Christian mission, came to be valued only for luxurious living in the centers of population, while economic production was entrusted to the servile arms of Indians and Negroes. The *criollo* group also desired this type of life, and the descendants of the *conquistadores* who inherited the titles of nobility, the great *encomiendas*, and the rich haciendas made up a colonial aristocracy which, although excluded from political and administrative functions, enjoyed a privileged position. Other less fortunate *criollos* sought power and social prestige in the liberal professions, especially law, and went in search of titles of nobility. Spain, impoverished by the European wars, sold titles of nobility and the Creoles founded entailed estates (*Mayorazgos*) with their lands, creating latifundism which has influenced the political and economic life of the Latin American republics to such a great degree.

The peninsular and Creole group considered itself superior to the great anonymous mass that constituted the remainder of the population. It is true that "purity of blood" was sometimes a ridiculous myth. Influence and especially money corrupted the so-called informations of blood purity, and many mestizos and even mulattoes acquired titles of nobility.

The Indians, as was pointed out earlier, formed a separate social group. A few lived outside the *encomiendas* and *reducciones*, managing to share the life of the Creole group, but in the colonial period they were never numerous. Some *caciques* came to occupy positions of prestige, but in general they owned their social rise to an understanding with the local Spanish officials, with whom they cooperated in the exploitation of other Indians.

The *mestizo* group occupied a position in the social scale immediately below that of the *peninsular* and the *criollo*. The law made no distinction between *mestizos* and whites, but a social and economic inequality existed. The *mestizo* found himself at a crossroad. He could not bring himself to descend and be assimilated into the Indian group, nor did the latter group favor such a process; and he could not ascend because of the rigid caste system which existed. A religious career was as a rule closed to him, so that he could occupy only very inferior positions, and the Church refused him admittance to the sacred orders as it did the Indians and Negroes. Some *mestizos* formed a sort of inferior middle class and became small farmers, domestic and administrative employees, and small-scale businessmen. The rest comprised the great mass of workers and artisans who served in the guilds and *obrajes* with only the slightest possibility of improving their condition. Negroes, mulattoes, and *zambos* (mixture of Indians and Negroes) occupied the lowest positions in the colonial social scale. Many of them, of course, were slaves. Freedmen were considered inferior beings and also lived at the margin of their social group, making their living as best they could, many as laborers on the haciendas, some in domestic service, others in the trades and as street venders.

The inferior position of this group was not only from an economic and social standpoint, but from a legal one as well. Municipal and police ordinances made their condition extremely difficult. For example, they were not allowed to carry arms, appear on the streets after curfew, and the women were forbidden to wear costly dresses or use ornaments. Some freedmen adopted an attitude of escapism and sought refuge in the underworld, placing themselves at the margin of the law, in secret societies such as the *ñáñigos* in Cuba, or in groups of habitual delinquents.

To complete this brief picture of colonial society, some of the characteristics of the educational system should be mentioned. Education in the colonies was a direct consequence of the social structure already pointed out and the caste system established in America. In this regard, Spain was no further advanced nor more backward than the rest of Europe. She brought to America what she had and what she believed in. Education was limited to the superior class of *peninsulares* and Creoles, and, to a certain degree, reached the *mestizos*. The Indians were the object of special attention, in theory at least.

Primary education was concentrated in religious schools or through a system of private tutors in the homes. In theory, the municipalities were entrusted with maintaining public schools, but due to lack of funds, this measure was not put into practice, especially in poorer localities. Secondary education was organized through the creation of colleges (*colegios*) which remained in the hands of religious orders, and important private colleges of a lay or semi-lay nature appeared only at the end of the colonial period. Religious instruction, preparing one for a church career, was in charge of the seminaries.

The law stipulated that there be a public school in each Indian pueblo. This requirement was fulfilled in the important *reducciones,* but in others it was limited to religious instruction in charge of a priest *(cura doctrinero)*. While the zeal and enthusiasm of the first years of the colony lasted, worthy efforts were made to educate the Indians and *mestizos.* The names of great educators such as Pedro de Gante, Zumárraga, Motolinía, and others, as well as the institutions they founded should be remembered in this respect. But, when the epic and utopian period of colonization had passed, those institutions decayed and disappeared.

Universities came early to America. The first center of higher learning which received the authorization of the Pope was the University of Santo Domingo (1538), but there is no evidence that the bull in question received the approval of the Spanish government, which was necessary as a consequence of the existence of the Royal Patronage. In 1551 authorization by the Pope and by the government of Spain was granted to the universities in Mexico and Lima, and the former was inaugurated with pomp. Later, other centers of higher education were created elsewhere.

Colonial universities were organized along the line of the Spanish ones, principally the famous University of Salamanca. Their government was in the hands of a general faculty of professors to which graduates residing in the vicinity belonged. The general faculty elected the Rector. Colonial universities enjoyed considerable autonomy, although there were frequent interventions by the political power of the *Virrey* and the religious power of the bishops and archbishops. This should be kept in mind in studying the important role which universities, as well as the professors and students themselves, have played in the political life of Latin America.

SUGGESTED READINGS

English:

Barber, R. K., *Indian Labor in the Spanish Colonies,* Albuquerque, Historical Society of New Mexico, 1932.

Christensen, Asher N., "The Spanish American Colonial System," in *The Evolution of Latin American Government,* New York, Henry Holt & Co., 1951.

Diffie, Bailey W., *Latin American Civilization; Colonial Period,* Harrisburg, Stackpole & Heck, Inc., 1945.

García Calderón, Francisco, *Latin America, Its Rise and Progress,* New York, Charles Scribner's Sons, 1913.

Hanke, Lewis, *The First Social Experiments in America,* Cambridge, Harvard University Press, 1935.

————, *The Spanish Struggle for Justice in the Conquest of America,* Philadelphia, University of Pennsylvania Press, 1949.

Haring, Clarence H., *The Spanish Empire in America,* New York, Oxford University Press, 1947.

————, *Trade and Navigation between Spain and the Indies in the Time of the Hapsburgs,* Cambridge, Harvard University Press, 1918.

Kirkpatrick, F. A., *Latin America: A Brief History,* New York, The Macmillan Co., 1939.

Lanning, J. T., *Academic Culture in the Spanish Colonies,* New York, Oxford University Press, 1940.

Lea, H. C., *The Inquisition in the Spanish Dependencies,* New York, The Macmillan Co., 1908.

Simpson, Lesley B., *The Encomienda in New Spain,* Berkeley, University of California Press, 1913.

Zavala, Silvio A., *New Viewpoints on the Spanish Colonization of America,* Philadelphia, University of Pennsylvania Press, 1943.

Spanish:

Arciniegas, Germán, *Este Pueblo de América,* México, D. F., 1945.

Henríquez, Ureña, Pedro, *Historia de la Cultura en la América Hispánica,* México, D. F., 1947.

Navarro Lamarca, C., *Compendio de Historia de América,* Buenos Aires, 1910.

Orozco y Berra, Manuel, *Historia de la Dominación Española en México,* México, D. F., 1938.

Parra Pérez, C., *El Régimen Español en Venezuela,* Madrid, 1932.

Pereyra, Carlos, *La Obra de España en América,* Madrid, 1920.

Picón Salas, Mariano, *De la Conquista a la Independencia,* México, D. F., 1944.

Quesada, Vicente G., *La Vida Intelectual de la America Española,* Buenos Aires, 1917.

Reyes, Alfonso, *Ultima Tule,* México, D. F., 1943.

Terán, J. B., *El Nacimiento de la América Española,* Buenos Aires, 1931.

Zavala, Silvio A., *La Encomienda Indiana,* Madrid, 1935.

————, *Las Instituciones Jurídicas en la Conquista de América,* Madrid, 1935.

CHAPTER 3

Colonial Evolution

CHANGES IN THE SPANISH STATE

During the period of colonial domination, Hispanic America did not remain stationary. Important changes took place once the various social groups had become organized with definite characteristics, until finally the political ties with Spain were broken by all countries early in the nineteenth century, with the exceptions of Cuba and Puerto Rico. In this chapter, some of these important changes will be examined, to analyze later the consequences they produced and the various factors conditioning the new republics.

Economic Evolution. During the eighteenth century, Spain's policy of a closed commercial monopoly with America underwent several modifications. In some cases, the strict supervision which the Spanish government had exercised over the maritime traffic was relaxed. Foreign ships, chiefly French, received authorization to enter and trade with certain ports of the Spanish Empire. Years later, this commerce stopped, and once again the system of *flotas*, which facilitated monopoly, was established. The system functioned more like a public service carried on by the Spanish state, since the departures were at regular intervals, and each trip followed a fixed route and schedule. The government made every effort to keep merchants well informed of market conditions, and *"navíos de aviso"* crossed the Atlantic every three months, carrying essential news with reference to prices, demand, and production.

The monopoly enjoyed by the powerful merchants of Sevilla and Cádiz was also greatly diminished by the royal authorizations granted to private companies located in other Spanish cities to trade with certain American ports. The most important of these companies was the *Compañía Guipuzcoana*, and there were others in Barcelona and Galicia. This shift was due to economic innovations in Spain, by means of which the government sought to balance the budget, reform the tax system, overcome regionalism, and stimulate foreign trade.

In spite of the aforementioned changes which took place both in Spain and in her colonies, it is obvious that free trade was non-existent. Monopoly continued along with its corollary, contraband. The commercial monopoly was economically disastrous for Spain and her colonies, and in addition caused serious moral, social, and political consequences. It is true that during the reign of Carlos III, all limitations on commerce among the colonies were removed, and all Spaniards were permitted to trade directly with America from any port of the peninsula. This made the *Casa de Contratación* superfluous, and it was abolished in 1790. Nevertheless, free trade, as we understand it today, was never established, since freedom was limited to relations between peninsular Spain and Spanish America, and between the various political units of America. In spite of the narrowness of these measures, commerce developed rapidly, so that by the end of the eighteenth century, the colonies were enjoying a prosperity such as they had never before experienced. But, as always happened when Spain granted concessions to her colonies, they came too late to stop the consequences of long years of colonial exploitation.

Governmental Evolution. Early in the eighteenth century, when the Bourbons occupied the Spanish throne, important changes were introduced in those organs of the central government responsible for colonial administration. These political reforms followed the pattern of the administrative centralism of the French government. The King created a council of ministers, or cabinet, composed of officials named by him from among his close associates. A Ministry of Navy and Indies was created in 1714. The Minister had executive power in all affairs pertaining to the American colonies and, subject only to the King's approval, could name the members of the *Consejo de Indias* and the *Casa de Contratación*. It is easy to see why these two institutions were then relegated to secondary roles. Years later, almost at the close of the eighteenth century, a Ministry of the Indies was created which lasted only three years; and, afterward, affairs concerning the colonies were distributed among the Ministries of Finance, Justice, War, Navy, and Foreign Affairs, according to the nature of the matter. With these reforms, the venerable *Consejo de Indias* was converted into nothing more than a consultative organ of the crown, and was later abolished by the Liberal Cortes of Cádiz in 1812. When Ferdinand VII was re-established on the Spanish throne, the *Consejo de Indias* was revived (1814) and continued in operation until 1834, although, in the latter years of its existence, Spain's only remaining "Indias" were the islands of Cuba and Puerto Rico.

Another modification of considerable importance introduced during the last century of Spanish colonial government was the system of *Intendencias*. The *Intendente* was a provincial official who replaced the *corregidores, gobernadores,* and *alcaldes mayores* (see Chapter 1). The system had worked well in France and was used in America for the first time in Cuba, with the new official's jurisdiction limited to some specific matters. Later, the *Intendentes* were installed with greater powers in other provinces, and in 1790 the system was in use throughout the entire colonial empire. The *Intendente* was named directly by the central government and enjoyed military, political, and judicial powers within his jurisdiction, which was usually larger than that of the functionaries he had supplanted. He was especially entrusted with the collection of taxes and was in charge of developing agriculture, commerce, and industry as well as security measures, public order, and urban improvement. He also had the power to supervise ecclesiastical functions, being the Vice-Patron of the Church within his territory.

The *Intendentes* were partly under the authority of the *Virreyes.* In financial matters they were not dependent upon them but were directly responsible to an official called the *Superintendente General,* who was entirely independent of the *Virrey.* The division of authority gave rise to many conflicts, and later the post of *Superintendente* was combined with that of *Virrey,* so that the latter continued with the same powers he had formerly enjoyed. The *Intendentes* had better salaries than the officials they replaced and were better administrators, largely because they were freer from economic temptation. However, they were opposed by businessmen and farmers long accustomed to tax evasion, by the *Virreyes* whose authority they had decreased, and by the Bishops, because of their intervention in the affairs of the Church. The *criollos,* too, objected to the system, as provincial posts were among the few to which they could aspire and these new officials were *peninsulares* appointed directly from Spain.

The *Intendencias,* then, were established as a general system in Spanish America at the end of the eighteenth century and only a few years before the first independence movements. There was not enough time for them to take root, but they were taken into account when organizing the provincial structure of some of the new republics. The boundaries of the *Intendencias* in many cases influenced the geographical outline of the nations when they came into existence.

Social Evolution. The sixteenth century, the century of the discovery of part of America and of the Conquest, constitutes the most important period of colonial society. The historical development of Spanish America has been very different from that of British America. In the former, as Arciniegas aptly points out,

> . . . conquest came first, and was followed by the colony, by colonization. The Latins were, at this time, dispersed over an area several times greater than all of fifteenth century Europe. In British America, colonization came first; the conquest followed. The English came as families, established themselves on small islands like Jamaica or along the Atlantic coast of North America. They did not advance into the interior until the centers of colonization had become large enough to support such an advance with force.[1]

In the century of the Spanish Conquest, military and defense institutions were predominant over those of administrative organization. There was an underlying thought of a social utopia, represented by the attempts to adapt the indigenous masses to the new civilization. The social phenomenon of that century was the necessity of adjusting to the new environment, which called for a radical change on the part of the European *conquistador.* For the Indian, it meant a complete alteration of every aspect of his life, while the African slave was uprooted from his cultural environment. The political consequences of this were not felt at the time, but they were obvious in

---

[1] Arciniegas, Germán, *Este Pueblo de América,* México, D. F., 1945, p. 38. (Author's translation.)

the roles played by these different social groups when independence appeared upon the scene.

The following century was in direct contrast. The Conquest had been completed, and Spain felt sure of herself. The utopian attempts of the missions at social incorporation were followed by urbanization of the new centers of population. The clergy preferred to live iñ convents or monasteries, and the secular population in the comfortable baroque mansions of the cities. Cheap labor provided by the Indians, *mestizos,* and Negroes made life easy and agreeable, and economic differences accentuated caste distinctions. The *peninsular* kept his political power, but the *criollo* opposed him with his economic strength based on the income from the great latifundias. Both groups held similar political and religious views, and a like outlook toward society insofar as this meant the exclusion of the *mestizos,* Indians, and Negroes.

In the realm of ideas, there was an important event which brought about a radical change in Spanish policy: the Reformation. Toward it, Spain adopted a defensive attitude which deeply affected her colonies. To defend something implies satisfaction with what this "something" represents. In this struggle, Spain was not concerned with acquiring new lands or conquering new peoples. What did concern her was the conservation of her political power; and, to achieve this, she considered it necessary to defend, at all costs, the ideas which made possible the triumphs of the preceding century. The Spanish Empire was the result of the approval granted to the *conquistadores* by Roman Catholic authority. To keep this empire, it was indispensable to uphold the religious faith and, for this purpose, the principles of the counter-Reformation were established in America as well as in Spain.

The policy of counter-Reformation was not a negation of progress, but the conviction that the height of progress had already been achieved and must now be conserved. The conduct of the sixteenth century Spanish Americans was far different from its seventeenth century counterpart. Social values had changed, and leadership was in the hands of a semi-cultured bureaucracy that enjoyed economic power or political influence. Life became static and sedentary, and, although some European countries experienced the cultural Renaissance that rose from the Reformation, nothing of the sort occurred in Latin America, whose doors were closed to ideas. The defensive attitude delayed the arrival of the European cultural contributions which constituted the indispensable preparation for the great transitions of the eighteenth century. In France, for example, there was the new logic and methodology of Descartes' school of thought. Bacon's scientific method and the political thought of the rationalists contributed to England's progress. In Spanish America, the counter-Reformist theology imposed by the Inquisition was reaffirmed. As a modern Latin American investigator says, "while Europe sought to establish the kingdom of man upon earth, the sole concern of Spain and Portugal was to maintain the kingdom of God." [2]

At the beginning of the eighteenth century, social changes took place which forecast what was to happen in the nineteenth. It is important to note that before the ideological influence of European liberalism, and before the philosophy of the Enlightenment was felt, there were serious attempts in Latin America to gain individual freedom. The influence of European thought is not denied, nor is the contribution of the American Revolution, but the Latin American independence was not such a simple thing and had roots which could be found in the eighteenth century. This entire period was filled with protest movements of groups of Indians and *mestizos,* attempting to modify the administrative abuses of colonial policy. It is true that there was no definite purpose in these movements toward a complete political emancipation, but they were an indication of popular unrest. Many of these only demanded a change in the administration, which is not a surprising fact considering that the French Revolution of 1789 was originally not a republican movement, but merely a movement to establish a constitutional monarchy.

Some of these objections by the Latin American masses, who resorted to force to obtain betterment and liberties under colonial dominion, should be recalled. There were the rebellions of Paraguay (Cabildo de Asunción) ; of the Cuban tobacco planters; of the Venezuelans against economic monopoly; of the Argentines against obligatory military service; of the Yucatecans against the Viceroy; and very especially, the uprising of Túpac-Amaru and the rebellion of the *Comuneros* of Colombia. In the history of ideas, there were two noteworthy phenomena. The first one was the attitude of

---

2 Picón Salas, Mariano, *op. cit.,* p. 90. (Author's translation.)

so-called political protest by the exiled Jesuits who, driven out of America, settled in Italy and Germany; and the second one was the influence of the Spanish Enlightenment. As a natural reaction, the Jesuits became enemies of the Spanish crown and published a number of books in which they no longer supported the counter-Reformist thought of the preceding century, fearlessly expressing their opinions regarding political problems which before had been forbidden them. Among other things, they preached the equality of men, with no distinctions, and defended the doctrine of sovereignty of the people. The Enlightenment, which some authors have called enlightened despotism, had a profound effect upon the inhabitants of the colonies. The faith in science produced an eagerness to see for themselves and prove everything, which led to a desire for travel and an inter-American cosmopolitanism.

Toward the end of the eighteenth century, the American and French revolutions made their impression in Latin America. The North American independence, at that time, influenced only a small group of educated men in the Spanish colonies. Its ideas were felt more deeply after the independence, when the new republics modeled their own political institutions upon the North American structure. The ideas of the French Enlightenment reached only the cultured minorities. Those of the Revolution of 1789, as a political event, had a much greater influence on the masses. Thus the Latin American picture under colonial domination was a complex phenomenon of the transculturation of economic, political, and social forms. "Transculturation," the term coined by Fernando Ortiz,[3] is used here because it does not imply merely a change of culture, a diffusion, or migration of social forms, but it includes the results of these changes or transmissions of cultures. What Ortiz says with regard to Cuba may be applied to all Latin America:

> The true history of Cuba is a history of an intricate transculturation. First, the transculturation of the paleolithic to the neolithic Indians, and the disappearance of the latter because they could not adjust themselves to the new Castillian culture. Later, the transculturation of an incessant stream of white immigrants, Spaniards, but of different backgrounds and cultures,

---

[3] Ortiz, Fernando, *El Fenómeno Social de la Transculturación*, Revista Bimestre Cubana, vol. XLVI, No. 2, pp. 273-274. (Author's translation.)

and "torn," as they themselves expressed it, from their Iberian peninsular society, to be transplanted in a new world, new to them in nature and humanity, where they in turn must adjust themselves to a new fusion of cultures. Simultaneously, the transculturation of a steady human flow of African Negroes of varied races and cultures, hailing from all the coastal territories of Africa, from Senegal . . . to Mozambique. They, too, were torn from their social nuclei, and their cultures destroyed, oppressed beneath the weight of the dominating cultures, as the sugar canes are crushed beneath the weight of the mills. There were still other migratory cultures; continental Indians, Jews, Portuguese, Anglo-Saxons, Frenchmen, North Americans and yellow men, Mongolians from Macao, Canton and other regions of the once Celestial Empire, and each immigrant rooted out of his native soil in the turmoil of disadjustment and readjustment, of deculturation and acculturation that is, briefly, transculturation.[4]

The European ingredient transcultured in Latin America was not purely Spanish or Portuguese, but Mediterranean, formed by Arabian, Celts, Jewish, Gothic, Italian, French, with even a contribution from Irish and English civilizations. The white Mediterraneans were followed by the Negroes from different regions of Africa, many of them in different stages of cultural evolution. Later, the appetite of other parts of Europe was awakened, and their peoples came, seeking their part in the distribution of the virgin lands of Latin America.

America was the new world for Europe, but Europe was more than a new world to America. As Ortiz has also indicated, Europe descended upon America in the form of iron, the wheel, gunpowder, the compass, the horse, currency, wages, capital, writing, printing, books, Kings, and churches, and even a new God that was Almighty and who, nevertheless, was so humble that He allowed Himself to be killed by men. The Spanish *conquistador* was followed by agriculturalists, shepherds, priests, and miners. He brought domestic animals and the plants he had cultivated in Europe. Nevertheless, the socio-political pattern did not harmonize with this cultural contribution which showed the ideas of progress. The regime of authority and the arrangement of the human groups was a direct result

---

4 *Ibid.*

of the desire to centralize political power and to maintain a rigid social structure. The *conquistador* was not alone. He brought the Negro, and he had to co-exist with the Indian. In view of the Negroes' different cultural levels, their forced migration and acculturation affected them in different ways. Those who had been slaves in their own lands merely changed masters, and their shock was not so violent. Those who had been farmers, or otherwise accustomed to hard labor, suffered from the loss of liberty, but many became adjusted to their new surroundings. Those who came of warlike tribes resorted to flight and force to free themselves from the yoke of slavery. Many of them became *"cimarrones,"* or runaways, in some countries for centuries. The first Negro rebellion took place in Hispaniola in 1522, and the Negro Quilombo of Palmares, in Brazil, was perhaps the first free Latin American nation.

The Negroes left their material cultures in Africa, but they brought their gods with them. Their religious flexibility allowed them to use the symbols and images of the Roman Catholic faith, but they kept their own religious beliefs. They also brought with them their primitive medicines, as well as their traditions and superstitions, witchcraft, voodooism, and other practices that have endured to this day, as a survival of this complex phenomenon of transculturation. But all Negro contributions were not negative. The slaves' strong arms made the Conquest possible, and, while the *conquistador* devoted his time to warfare, the slaves cultivated the land and produced the food necessary for the armies and the inhabitants of the cities. Many of them adjusted well to the Iberian culture and became part of the European families, imitating their customs and accepting their way of life. The cultural survival of the African contribution to America is well expressed today by Negro music and poetry.

The Spaniard's cultural impact on the aborigines was of a different nature. The Indians of Spanish America "discovered" Europe and Africa. Their first explanation was supernatural. They thought the *conquistadores* were gods, but as soon as the newcomers began to behave like men, the hearts of the natives filled with doubt. The indigenous cultures suffered a violent upheaval. The conquering class destroyed all the symbols that could possibly undermine their political, religious or social institutions. The subdued race, with some exceptions, received the cultural and spiritual contributions of the invaders, but it was not the weapons of the *conquistador* or the new spiritual culture forced upon them that transformed the aborigines, but the destruction of their economy that brought to them the misery and poverty they still endure today. The Indians accepted the changes, adjusted themselves to their new masters, and, with exquisite tolerance, adored their God. But they could never understand why they were not allowed to work their land to feed their families, or why they were forced to search for metals which, for them, had only an ornamental value. They may have understood why even their musical instruments were destroyed, but they could not grasp why their system of irrigation and their agricultural implements were also ruined.

One of the first results of the impact following the discovery was that the socio-political structure of the new dominions was the product of only one of the ingredients of the process of transculturation— the European one. The institutions that we have in Latin America are the product of the evolution of the Mediterranean cultures. The other two cultures, the Indian and the Negro, have played an insignificant role. For this reason, their components react unfavorably toward something they cannot consider theirs, and that is why, in many countries, they constitute a serious social problem. The social attitude of the nonincorporated group was of defense. Today, the large mass of Indians, mestizos, Negroes, and mulattoes still condition the political development of many Latin American countries in a negative manner. The early nineteenth century witnessed the political phenomenon of independence. All Ibero-America, with the exception of Cuba and Puerto Rico, broke the ties that bound it to the mother country and endeavored to become organized as independent states. This chain of events marked the opening of a period when the new nations, although possessed of the external symbols of political power, behaved in their economic and social lives like mere colonies. Furthermore, they retained certain ingredients which we shall now examine.

COLONIAL REPUBLICS

The political ideas of liberalism were established in completely constituted nations, such as France, England, and the United States. The situation was altogether different in Latin America. Spain left in America a colonial sub-state, upon which it was impossible, throughout the nineteenth century, to establish liberal republics. This is true even today in many of the Spanish American countries.

Administrative centralization, economic monopoly, social hierarchies, and the political absolutism of Spain brought about a profound anti-State feeling in Latin America. In the Latin American mind, the institution of the State was represented by Spain's abuse of power, and the natural result was political apprehension or distrust of everything that might be intervention by the authorities. Furthermore, the exponents of the liberal doctrine made no effort to build states in Latin America, because the idea of interference was contrary to the philosophy of *laissez faire* which inspired the movement for independence. The paradox was especially harmful, because the ideology that made independence possible was in direct opposition to the economic and social necessities of the new nations. A number of contemporary Latin American authors, such as Moisés Poblete Troncoso,[5] and Antonio García point out this characteristic. García says:

> Upon this stage should be placed Latin America, defined as an aggregation of countries whose populations have the lowest standards of living, and the lowest levels of technical and political culture. These populations exist gregariously, as though mechanically stacked together within the framework of a nation, but without a living or organic relationship with it. The adherents of liberalism abstained, through liberal orthodoxy (the same one to inspire the policies of the great capitalistic powers) not only from organizing the state, but even from bringing up the problem of the necessity for organization. We find, then, the paradoxical phenomenon—though an easily explainable one—that it is precisely in countries like the Latin American ones, which correspond to colonial areas, that the activity of the state is more vitally essential, and that here it does not exist as a dynamic and national construction, authorized to rebuild society, to modify systems of work and of living, and to revive ideologically a population in a regressive state.[6]

---

[5] Poblete Troncoso, Moisés, *El Standard de Vida de las Poblaciones de América*, Universidad de Chile, 1942.

[6] García, Antonio, *op. cit.*, pp. 215-216. (Author's translation.)

Another phenomenon resulting from colonial domination was that long-term submission to a foreign power made the Latin American republics depend upon some factor outside of themselves to solve the problems of their own existence. This situation touches not only the international matters, but the individual affairs of many of the Latin Americans during the nineteenth century. The custom of waiting for something "from outside" to attend to the domestic and personal necessities becomes a habit. From the highest social circles to those who live most modestly, we find many waiting for a solution or for help to come. Defeated politicians seek foreign assistance. Ruined businessmen hope for government help. Governments with financial troubles resort to international loans. The harsh agrarian economy and the rigid system of social hierarchies, the result of years of colonial despotism, have caused the complex to spread to the social customs and to life itself. The poor peon in the country and the laborer in the city count on luck for their liberation and save their pennies to buy lottery tickets, hoping to improve their lot.

The financial condition of the nations and international politics have made this complex still more intense. Independence had hardly been achieved when there appeared the menace of the Spanish Reconquest and the peril of the Holy Alliance. Spain made war on Peru and Chile and reconquered Santo Domingo. France subjugated Mexico, and years later even Germany blockaded and cannonaded Venezuela. The new states had no peace in their international life, and they were not considered a part of the community of nations. The United States effected most of its territorial expansion at the expense of Latin America, and the latter was not thought of in equal terms by its powerful northern neighbor throughout the nineteenth century. Any student of history of the United States can easily verify this fact by merely recalling the names given to different foreign policies in this country. The countries south of the Rio Grande were "territories" which should not change hands following the principles of the Monroe Doctrine, and later were simply geographic units placed in the path of the "manifest destiny." If the new republics misbehaved in their domestic affairs, they should be punished with the "big stick" in order to develop into places where money could wisely be invested, following the dictates of "dollar diplomacy." It was not until well into the twentieth century that the nations of Spanish America were given equal consideration by the United States, under the "Good Neighbor policy." Therefore, one must add to the psychological complex, a result of the colonial administration, the international realities, and the national economic situations as conditioning ingredients of Latin American political life.

The complex extended even to the cultural sphere. The movement for independence, as we have seen, was inspired by a foreign philosophy. Liberalism stimulated the patriciate in the struggle against Spain, and romanticism was the directing principle of the first generation following independence. This romantic period (1830-1860) was characterized by political anarchy, *caudillismo,* and the exile of the best thinkers of the various countries. Each nation semed to be influenced by two groups: a group of officials gathered around the established government and lending its culture to dictatorship, and the émigrés group living in foreign countries. Each country waited for something "from outside," either an invasion of a military or revolutionary nature, or of a cultural or literary character. When the *caudillos* were subdued and the dictatorships started on the decline around 1860, there appeared a *"criollista"* culture. Native characteristics were glorified. The Gaucho, the Indian, and the Negro made their appearance in literature. Foreign investments came to the scene and gradually took over the natural resources of some countries. The Latin Americans discovered, to their amazement, that the "nature" of which they sang in their *"criollista"* culture was no longer theirs. The impact of hard, economic reality caused the revival of the complex. It was not until the twentieth century, starting with the Mexican Revolution, that the Latin American nations made a new effort to overcome this complex.

The influence of the colonial complex was not limited to the cultural generations of Spanish America but was manifested as well in a characteristic of Latin American thought that we may describe as normativistic. This type of thought consists in lending more attention to the ideal conduct than to the social realities. The study of crude facts and the consideration of the causes of political phenomena have been given but little time by the majority of Latin American statesmen. Instead, they have presented solutions, and outlined norms with a view to changing reality. The political leader in Latin America has thought more of what "ought to be" than what "is." This normativistic, and not realistic, attitude is typical of the nineteenth century. Many authors have pointed out the characteristic preference for literary and philosophical studies in the Latin American countries, in contrast with the cultivation of the physical and natural sciences in countries with more solid material surroundings. This is an exact observation, and it is due not only to the Spanish educational tradition, but to the normativist characteristic of Latin American thought.

José Gaos, among others, has remarked [7] on an opposition in intellectual history, between thought and philosophy, which is typical of all Spanish-speaking countries. There has been a dialectic contrast between a line of thought that aspired to innovate and renovate, which has been generally popular, unsystematic and normative, and a systematic philosophy, conservative and governmental. Ever since the utopian thought of the sixteenth century missionaries, which was opposed to the official and centralizing philosophy of the Spanish government, up to the struggle between the revolutionary ideas of the twentieth century and the conservative governments of many Latin American countries, the opposition has been constant.

The struggle and the normative character of thought have deeply influenced political life and the governmental structure of Spanish America. Again, the politician thinks of what should be, and ignores what actually is. There is a preoccupation for the ideal norm to be followed, and none for the reality which should be observed and explained. Professor Northrop has wisely remarked:

> The statesman, when he acts scientifically and wisely, must think and operate literally in two worlds. He must know things as they are; he must also know things as they ought to be. To demand more of the normative in fact than possible changes in the factual will permit may mean the defeat of one's ideals completely, whereas to ask less than perfection may be to achieve more. Scientifically grounded, wise statesmanship consists in possessing scientifically verified factual history concerning what is the case, and scientifically verified normative social theory of what ought to be the case and then achieving as much of the ideal as possible changes in the factual will permit.[8]

---

[7] Lectures at University of Havana, 1938.

[8] Northrop, F. S. C., *The Logic of the Sciences and the Humanities*, The Macmillan Co., New York, 1947, p. 264.

The Latin American statesman has not stopped to find out the "scientifically verified normative social theory" and has not taken the pains to observe the practical results of a law or a constitutional principle, when he is already working for the abolition or modification of these norms.

The exaggeration of the normative tendency is also due to the role played by the Roman Catholic Church during the wars of independence and later during the early years of the republics. Although many components of the Church were even initiators of the wars, as in Mexico, the Church as an official institution supported the colonial government in Latin America. Without being actually religious wars, the struggles for independence were clashes of a generation against the Church as a political institution, and they produced a society that was not atheistic, but was definitely anti-clerical. Christian ethics, which had been the cohesive force and normative principle, were undermined. Latin America lost her moral faith, if not her religious one, in the Roman Catholic Church. Religious norms had to be replaced by others, and this increased the normative tendency of the generation following independence.

In order to comprehend this phenomenon, one may merely compare it to the similar period in the United States. There was no religious conflict in this country during the War of Independence. The North American liberators were firm believers, and Protestant ethics not only accepted the liberal ideas of independence, but offered it the support of its best thinkers. The founders of the state in North America had no pressing normative problems; therefore, they were free to attend to reality. The cohesive social force, represented by religious ethics, was not broken when political independence from England was achieved.

Latin American normativism reaches not only ethical conduct, but the legal part of society. Together with ethics, law is the other normative discipline of importance. The outstanding political leaders of Latin America were jurists, and even today one finds an ever-present interest in philosophy of law. This is simple to understand. There is dissatisfaction with the existing norms of law, with positive law, hence the escape toward a philosophy in search of a better law and an ideal norm.

This, too, contrasts with the North American phenomenon, where, because it is basically a country of common law, there is not as great a need for this normative and philosophic thought in order to modify legal institutions.

It is not the intention to convey the impression that normativism is, in itself, a negative factor. The author merely indicates its peculiar characteristics. What is negative and harmful is the exaggeration of normativism on a purely subjective and personal basis, overlooking the necessity of verifying the results of the normative theories. This characteristic, so distinctive of Latin American culture, is what has weighed heavily against the republics in the scales of their political existence.

Nationalism. After more than three centuries of being conditioned by the factors and ingredients described before, the inhabitants of the different political units of the Spanish colonial empire broke off their ties with the metropolis. During those early centuries, the countries of Spanish America were colonies in the political sense of the word, and continued to be so for years after their independence. The new republics acquired all the exterior symbols of political power, but economically and socially they retained all their colonial characteristics. The wars of independence, with the exception of the Mexican war in its early stages, were not actually revolutions. There was no change in the system of control, since those that conquered political power belonged to the same social group that previously held it, with similar functions, status, and outlooks.

The struggle in Latin America was carried on against the abuses of power by Spain, and not necessarily against the use of this power as expressed in economic relations and social customs. The wars of independence were a struggle between two groups who occupied the same position in the social hierarchy, who disagreed politically as to who should control power, but who concurred, fundamentally, in social matters. This situation and the conflicts within the same group caused a series of paradoxes that affected the political life of the continent for more than half a century. The French Revolution, that produced the liberation of the middle class and swept away the power of the nobility simultaneously, created the political structure necessary to guarantee the use of power by the bourgeoisie. In Latin America, there was no bourgeoisie to liberate, and the Creole patriciate or semi-feudal nobility consolidated its power as a result of independence. For this reason, many Latin American authors have said that most Latin American countries have not yet had their French revolution. What they did was to imitate the political forms of a new class that appeared in history, when this class did not yet exist in Latin America. They did something even more singular: they left intact the economic structure that hindered the establishment of that new class.

As a result of this paradoxical situation, two political phenomena occurred in the American hemisphere, radically opposed to each other. North of the Rio Grande, the thirteen British colonies gradually enlarged their original territories, reached out toward the south and west, and integrated the states that formed the North American union. To the south, the Spanish colonies gained their independence and broke up into numerous nations. To the North, therefore, there was integration and unification; to the South, disintegration and division. And the political ingredients that caused that disintegration were nationalism combined with liberalism.

The idea of the nation-state as a unit of cultural homogeneity, joined by economic, geographic, and spiritual ties, was not a novelty when the Spanish American republics achieved their independence. The political phenomenon of the nation-state made its appearance in Europe in the first years of the modern era, with the victory of the kings over the feudal lords and the Pope. In the nineteenth century, nationalism fused with the liberal ideology and produced the movements for independence in Belgium, Greece, Poland, Hungary, and Italy. The liberal ideology made use of nationalism not only to fight for the emancipation of subjugated peoples under absolute monarchies, but to realize the unification of countries divided among themselves, as in the cases of Italy and Germany. This independentist ideology was caused by the liberal philosophy of the eighteenth century, which grew into a political reality in the nineteenth. The nationalism that inspired the founders of the new countries of Latin America is therefore not the nationalism represented by the idea of the nation-state, which had triumphed in Europe long before, but the liberal and romantic nationalism of nineteenth century European political thought. The modern nations made their political appearance long before the independence of Latin America. Therefore, one must differentiate between the two concepts and examine the reasons why Latin American democratic liberalism marched side by side with exaggerated nationalism.

As has been stated, the independence of the Latin American nations was nothing more than the displacement of one group of controllers by another. During the years of the armed struggle, the leaders of political movements had no difficulty in finding symbols with which to keep the members of their parties united. The symbols they used were the liberty to be gained, and the defense of the nationality still to be created. It is a simple thing to keep a political group closely united during the period of struggle for power, no matter what sort of campaign is to be carried out, an electoral one or a military. However, once in power, the victorious group must find a substitute for the symbol once used, in order to remain in power. The Latin American nations endeavored to become organized as democratic governments. The democratic government is based upon the consent of the majority, but this consent must be elicited by the manipulation of adequate symbols. While Latin American patriots fought against Spanish colonial power, they were closely knit as a direct consequence of the effort to reach their objective. But, as soon as they reached their goal, their ranks opened and divided. When Latin American liberalism achieved power, it substituted for the symbol of liberty, expressed in the necessity of gaining independence, the symbol of nationalism, expressed in the necessity of retaining its prize.[9]

The exaggerated nationalism of Latin America was doubtless the result of the political tendency of the times, but it was also the means used by the new governing class to continue in power. The historical atmosphere of the nineteenth century was an additional factor to this exaggeration. No sooner had military victory been attained than the threat of Spanish Reconquest arose. The absolute monarchies triumphed in Europe, with the defeat of Napoleon and the formation of the Holy Alliance. There was the very real danger of a European attack which might sweep away the conquests of independence. The Latin American republics were small and poor and felt insecure against the rest of the world. When a country is weak, it tends to exaggerate the symbols of a power it does not possess, and this was done in Latin America by means of nationalistic patriotism. This exaggerated nationalism was caused by the pre-

---

[9] In the next chapter, the special type of Latin American liberalism will be described.

vailing political ideas, the political insecurity of the new ruling class, and the international insecurity of the new republics.

In Latin America, sovereignty was attributed to the people or to the nation, but it was actually exercised by a minority, since economic and educational qualifications were established for the exercise of the right of suffrage. The principle of equality before the law was no more than a formal declaration in the constitutional texts, because economic and caste inequalities continued to divide the individuals. Economic neo-feudalism was maintained with the system of latifundia, and the same colonial practices of servitude were kept, such as peonage and the other means of exploitation of the rural masses.

Caudillismo. Political nationalism presupposes and implies unity of command and administrative centralization. However, together with nationalism, there appeared an ingredient that fostered disunion and decentralization and that contrasted with it. This phenomenon is what authors like to call *"caudillismo"* or the concentration of authority in the hands of one person, which to a certain extent deprives the institution of the state of this authority.

"Caudillo" is a Castillian word, meaning leader, and it did not always have the derogatory meaning that we tend to give it today. Nineteenth century writers called the great leaders of the indepence movements "caudillos," and Franco's adherents use the term in this sense. Our interest is in the political significance of *caudillismo* in Latin America, and when we use the word we mean the political action of a chief, which makes its influence felt in national politics. The *caudillo* should not be confused with the *cacique,* who is the political head of a minor territorial area. Politically, *caudillismo* is a phenomenon somewhat like nationalism. During the process of independence and the half century following the constitution of the republics, *caudillismo* reached alarming proportions in Latin America. The curious thing is that the political symbol used by the *caudillos* in their struggle against the central power was federalism, that is, the demand for political autonomy for the regions of the new states. Federalism was merely the means used by the local groups to rationalize their desire for political power. There were no great economic or cultural differences between the regions of the Spanish empire. Many Latin Americans, impressed

by the federalist principles of North America, believed they could
solve their local problems by the establishment of federal republics.
An interesting development occurred with this federalistic *caudillismo.* The achievement of the North American federalists was that
they succeeded in knitting together thirteen colonies, which were
unlike each other. The principles served to unite. Latin America
used the same means to disunite regions that had not already been
divided under Spain's administrative centralization. The difference
between federalistic *caudillismo* and nationalistic centralism was
not based on reality. The necessity for local autonomy was not what
caused the nineteenth century *caudillos* to struggle for federation.
They used the federalist ideology as a justification of their struggle
against the central government and in order to conserve political
power.

Caudillismo has economic, juristic, social, and even religious
roots. There are different sorts of *caudillos,* according to the means
used to exercise power. In inaccessible regions, the economic power
of the owner of the latifundia was the center of all the region's activities, and whether he willed it or not, he was forced to wield political
power and become a *caudillo.* The local *cacique,* and through him,
the feudal landowner, took the place of the parish priest in the sphere
of community influence. Civil wars increased *caudillismo,* and the
military or revolutionary chief found himself possessed of a power
he was later reluctant to give up. There are permanent factors that
have brought about *caudillismo,* such as the imitation of foreign
state forms without considering the political and economic conditions of the new nations; the absence of a middle class; the force that
created and gave impulse to the liberal democracies and established
these in more advanced countries; and the inertia and absolute lack
of political awareness in the great masses of Indians, Negroes, mulattoes, and *mestizos* who were not considered legally or economically
incorporated to the new state.

During the first years of republican life, the exercise of power
was controlled by the landowning oligarchy, with the cooperation
of the professional classes and a small minority of businessmen, generally composed of foreigners satisfied to carry on their commercial
activities without participating in the civic life of the state. One
should again recall that not only the spiritual but the economic and
political power of the potent Catholic Church did not cooperate

with the new republics, but either kept aloof or actively opposed them. Thus, it is simple to understand how these countries, with no economic or geographic basis, pieces of a territory arbitrarily sliced from what had been the Spanish Empire, became victims of political *caudillismo*.

The effects of *caudillismo* were the short duration of the first constitutions, anarchy, and a number of civil wars. Of the three branches of the State, the legislative had the least participation in national affairs. During the last years of Spanish rule, under the Bourbon dynasty, political centralization became stronger, and this tendency resulted in the establishment of the strong executive. This strong executive exercised political control not only over the legislative but over the judicial power, and it was not until the end of the nineteenth century, and early in the twentieth, that the tendency to strengthen these other two organs could be noted. As Professor Wise correctly states:

> Although dictatorship will doubtless be a frequent occurrence as long as human society lasts, caudillismo (sic) appears to be a temporary phenomenon. It will likely gradually disappear as the conditions that gave rise to it disappear. In different parts of Latin America and at different rates, social and economic modernization is taking place. Education, urbanization and industrialization, improved health and more international contact—these are all going ahead and showing signs of giving the sort of social milieu in which genuine democracy can provide an adequate government. In this new situation dictatorship may reappear from time to time, but the old-style caudillo (sic) seems on the wane.[9]

SUGGESTED READINGS

English:

Crow, John A., *The Epic of Latin America,* Garden City, Doubleday & Co., Inc., 1946.

Fisher, Lillian E., *The Intendant System in Spanish America,* Berkeley, University of California Press, 1929.

Haring, Clarence H., *The Spanish Empire in America,* New York, Oxford University Press, 1947.

---

10 Wise, George S., *Caudillo: a Portrait of Antonio Guzmán Blanco,* New York, Columbia University Press, 1951, p. 176.

Kirkpatrick, F. A., *Latin America: A Brief History*, New York, The Macmillan Co., 1939.

Moore, David R., *A History of Latin America*, New York, Prentice-Hall, Inc., 1938.

Moses, Bernard, *South America on the Eve of Emancipation*, New York, G. P. Putnam's Sons, 1908.

————, *Spain's Declining Power in South America*, 1730-1806, Berkeley, University of California Press, 1919.

————, *The Spanish Dependencies in South America*, New York, Harper & Brothers, 2 vols., 1914.

Simpson, Lesley B., *The Encomienda in New Spain*, Berkeley, University of California Press, 1929.

Wilgus, A. Curtis, Ed., *The Development of Hispanic America*, New York, Rinehart & Co., Inc., 1941.

Wise, George S., *Caudillo: A Portrait of Antonio Guzmán Blanco*, New York, Columbia University Press, 1951.

Zavala, Silvio A., *New Viewpoints on the Spanish Colonization of America*, Philadelphia, University of Pennsylvania Press, 1943.

Spanish:

Arciniegas, Germán, *Este Pueblo de América*, México, D. F., 1945.

Arguedas, Alcides, *Pueblo Enfermo*, Barcelona, 1910.

————, *Los Caudillos Bárbaros*, Barcelona, 1929.

Ayarragaray, Lucas, *La Anarquía Argentina y el Caudillismo,* Buenos Aires, 1904.

Carianca y Trujillo, Raúl, *La Evolución Política de Iberoamérica*, Madrid, 1925.

García, Antonio, *Bases de la Economía Contemporánea*, Bogotá, 1948.

Henríquez Ureña, Pedro, *Historia de la Cultura en la América Hispánica*, México, D. F., 1947.

Levene, Ricardo, *Introducción a la Historia del Derecho Indiano*, Buenos Aires, 1924.

Mijares, Augusto, *La Interpretación Pesimista de la Sociología Hispana Americana*, Caracas, 1938.

Ortiz, Fernando, *Contrapunteo Cubano del Tabaco y el Azúcar*, La Habana, 1940.

————, *Los Negros Esclavos*, La Habana, 1916.

Picón, Salas, Mariano, *De la Conquista a la Independencia*, México, D. F., 1944.

Ponce de León, Salvador, *Análisis Crítico de las Dictaduras*, México, D. F., 1935.

Terán, J. B., *El Nacimiento de la América Española*, Buenos Aires, 1931.

DISPUTED

PRESIDENCY
OF
GUADALAJARA

CAPTAINCY-
GENERAL
OF
SANTO DOMINGO

NEW SPAIN

ST. DOMINGUE

AUDIENCIA OF MEXICO

CAPTAINCY-GENERAL OF GUATEMALA

NEW GRANADA

C. 1784

Southern North America and Central America about 1784.

CAPTAINCY-
GENERAL OF CARACAS

NEW GRANADA

AUDIENCIA OF SANTA FE

GUIANA

PRESIDENCY OF QUITO

BRAZIL

AUDIENCIA
OF LIMA
PRESIDENCY
OF CUZCO

PRESIDENCY
OF
CHARCAS

P
E
R
U

LA PLATA

CAPTAINCY
GENERAL
OF CHILE

AUDIENCIA
OF
BUENOS AIRES

C.1784

South America about 1784.

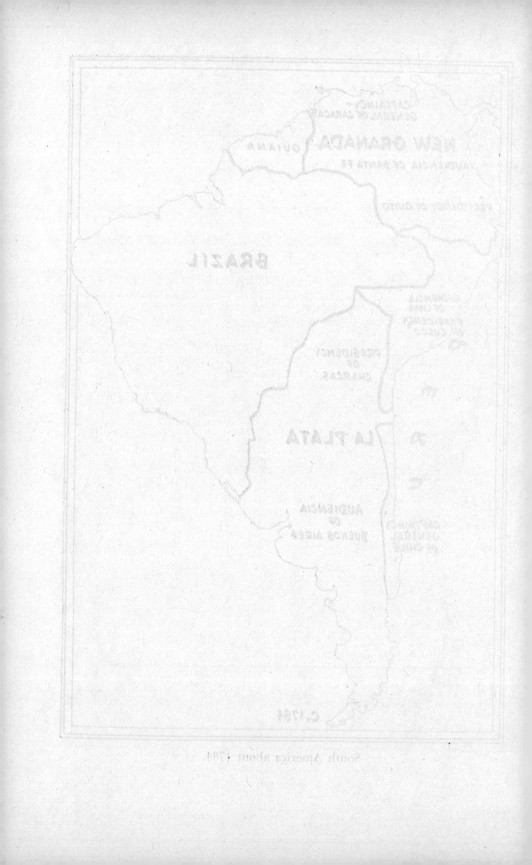

South America about 1784.

PART II

The Powers of the State

CHAPTER 4

The Executive Power

Throughout Latin America, the head of the state is designated with the title of President. The twenty nations are republics, because the executive power does not belong to a dynasty based on hereditary rights. This does not mean that all the republics have a presidential form of government like the United States. In this type of government, the executive is politically independent of Congress, and there are countries in Latin America in which the President is, in a limited way, responsible to Congress. In other countries he must act together with the Council of Ministers. In various nations the acts of the President, in order to have validity, require the approval of the Minister of the department to which the matter refers.

The general over-all characteristic of the Latin American presidency is, and always has been, its great political power. In the history of the United States, it is common to find strong presidents and leaders, but in Latin America we should speak not of the individual, the strong man, but of the institution, "the strong executive." It is the office of the president that, because of the administrative and constitutional setup, has more power than the other two branches of government. Many factors have contributed to this pattern. Some of them have already been indicated in the preceding chapters. But before considering the institutional aspects that make the executive strong, the theoretical background of the strong executive should be examined.

The Strong Executive. The conceptions of political liberalism, rooted in Latin America, created the strong executive. In European countries, including Spain and Portugal—in the brief democratic moments of their history—the same ideology gave more political power to the legislative branch of government. The United States, in spite of adopting the presidential form of government, also gave, in its Constitution, the larger power to Congress.

How the political liberalism allied itself with nationalism to keep the Creole group in power in Latin America has already been discussed. When the Spanish colonies became independent in the 1820's, the liberalism of the Enlightenment was no longer influential in Europe. It had been substituted by the romantic and nationalistic liberalism, which was not a middle-class movement but an aristocratic philosophy with an exaggerated cult of heroes and strong leaders. This is the type of liberalism that most influenced the new republics of South America, and its influence can explain the evils of *caudillismo* and the institutional aspect of the strong executive created in the constitutions of the new countries. There is a tendency to confuse the early political liberalism of the British and French Enlightenment with the romantic and nationalistic liberalism of the nineteenth century. This confusion is an oversimplification of a long period of Western intellectual history. There is a need for clarification, and it should be made when the intellectual history of Latin America is written. This discussion will be limited to point out the distinction. It has been well done, with regard to Europe, by Bertrand Russell, in the following words:

> Early liberalism was individualistic in intellectual matters, and also in economics, but was not emotionally or ethically self-assertive. This form of liberalism dominated the English eighteenth century, the founders of the American Constitution, and the French encyclopaedists. During the French Revolution, it was represented by the more moderate parties, including the Girondins, but with their extermination it disappeared for a generation from French politics. In England, after the Napoleonic wars, it again became influential with the rise of the Benthamites and the Manchester School. Its greatest success has been in America, where, unhampered by feudalism and a State Church, it has been dominant from 1776 to the present day, or at any rate to 1933.[1]

This liberalism did not influence Latin America after the independence. Of course, it inspired some of the forerunners of the

---

[1] Russell, Bertrand, *A History of Western Philosophy*, New York, Simon and Schuster, Inc., 1945, p. 599.

movement in the eighteenth and early nineteenth centuires. What really influenced the new republics was the other type of liberalism. It was, in Bertrand Russell's words:

> A new movement, which has gradually developed into the antithesis of liberalism, begins with Rousseau, and acquires strength from the romantic movement and the principle of nationality. In this movement, individualism is extended from the intellectual sphere to that of the passions, and the anarchic aspects of individualism are made explicit. The cult of the hero, as developed by Carlyle and Nietzsche, is typical of this philosophy. Various elements were combined in it. There was dislike of early industrialism, hatred of the ugliness that it produced, and revulsion against its cruelties. There was a nostalgia for the Middle Ages, which were idealized owing to hatred of the modern world. There was an attempt to combine championship of the fading privileges of Church and aristocracy with defence of wage-earners against the tyranny of the manufacturers. There was vehement assertion of the right of rebellion in the name of nationalism, and of the splendour of war in defence of "liberty." Byron was the poet of this movement; Fichte, Carlyle, and Nietzsche were its philosophers.[2]

This second type of liberalism ends by establishing a government of the successful hero. In many cases this government forgets the moral values of the old liberalism, and suppresses freedom. This was the case in many of the Latin American countries in the nineteenth century, and the situation still prevails in some of them. The cult of the hero, from a purely ideological conception finds its way into the structure of government and takes form in the constitution in normative precepts creating the strong executive.

Some attempts, to be described later, have been made to correct the situation and introduce institutional changes in order to give more participation to Congress in the administration. Some countries have established a semi-parliamentary form of government, but in spite of these institutional changes, the President is still the most powerful man in the government. This situation can be illustrated with a brief anecdote. In Cuba, a semi-parliamentary government was created in the constitution of 1940. The change was due to the

---

2 Russell, Bertrand, *op. cit.*, 600.

natural reaction against the abuses of power of the dictator, Machado. While the constitutional modifications were being considered, during the provisional presidency of Carlos Mendieta, a reporter asked him if he favored the parliamentary form of government. President Mendieta, an honest leader of the old *caudillo* type, answered in the affirmative, adding: "Of course, in that case, I shall be your Prime Minister." Parliamentarism in Cuba has never been sufficient to overcome the problem of the strong executive. Maybe the Uruguayans were right when they decided that the only way to solve the problem is to avoid the office of the President, as they did recently.

The ideas of romantic liberalism contributing to the creation of the strong executive also helps to explain the mental attitude of the Latin American masses with regard to what is called *"el hombre providencial"* (the providential man). Many strong presidents, that assume dictatorial powers, sincerely believe they are the only ones who can do something for their country. The phenomenon is not limited to Latin America, but it is found more frequently in that area. There are sincere Mexicans who today defend the regime of Díaz, and Dominicans and Peruvians who argue in favor of Trujillo and Odría. Their rationalizations are always the same, and they tell us that those leaders are doing something for the country. They tell us of the achievements in public works, finances, education, employment. Of course, their conception of democracies is that government is *for* the people, forgetting the other two aspects, *of* and *by* the people.

Classes of Executive. The majority of the Latin American republics have adopted the presidential form of government. Under it, the President freely appoints the members of his Cabinet, and the Secretaries or Ministers have no responsibility before Congress. In some countries there is an institution that makes the members of the Cabinet more independent than cabinet members of the United States. It is the duty of the Ministers or Secretaries to countersign the President's acts, and precise provisions in the constitutions state that the Presidential acts are invalid without their signatures. In these countries there is no political intervention of Congress in the executive sphere of action, but there is the tendency to limit the power of the President, obliging him to share his authority with the Secretaries or Ministers.

In the purely parliamentary governments, which prevail in Europe, executive power is exercised by a Prime Minister appointed by the President or Chief of State from among the majority party in Parliament, or from a majority group or coalition. The essential characteristic of pure parliamentarism is the political responsibility of the Prime Minister or of the members of his cabinet with regard to the legislative power. Some Latin American countries have tried this form of government, but today no purely parliamentary forms exist. However, there are semi-parliamentary forms. In these the object is to restrict the power of the executive, thus deviating from the doctrine of absolute separation of powers, and giving more political ascendancy to the legislative branch of the government. The Latin American republics in which this system is clearly established are Cuba, Peru, and Uruguay.

The Cuban system under the abolished constitution of 1940 was interesting, because it has combined the presidential form with European parliamentarism. Article 138 of the constitution reads: "The executive power is exercised by the President of the Republic *with the* [3] Council of Ministers . . .", and adds, "The President of the Republic acts with directive power and as moderator of national solidarity." Later, in Article 164, we read: "The Prime Minister and the Council of Ministers are responsible to the Chamber and the Senate for their acts of government . . ." In Cuba, therefore, the legislative power may grant or refuse its confidence to the entire Council of Ministers, to the Prime Minister alone, or to one of the members of the cabinet. This system attempts to avoid the frequent cabinet changes so common in the parliamentary governments of Europe, because the power of Congress to interpellate the ministers is limited to once every six months. The Cuban system has not been subjected to a real test, for the Presidents who have governed since 1940 have generally enjoyed a majority in Congress.

The designation of the President as political moderator is also an interesting innovation, because it shows the tendency to place the problems of government in the hands of political functionaries supported by the majority groups in Congress, and it puts the Presi-

---

[3] Italics added by the author.

dent in the same position as the head of the government of the purely parliamentary systems. In practice, this has not been the fact, inasmuch as the presidents since 1940 have been political leaders with a strong majority throughout the country.[4]

The Peruvian system is different from the Cuban.[5] The constitution contains no concrete precepts with regard to the political responsibility of the Council of Ministers, nor does it express that the President must act together with the Council. In spite of this, the Peruvian constitution authorizes Congress to intervene in the acts of the Ministers, who are obliged to appear to be interpellated, and who must resign when they are censured.[6]

In Peru, the Ministers of State form the Council of Ministers, which has its own president. There are, therefore, a President of the Council of Ministers and a President of the Republic. The President of the Republic appoints and removes the President of the Council. He also appoints and removes the Ministers, but upon the proposal and with the consent of the President of the Council.

In the Peruvian system, therefore, the legislative power can compel the executive to give account of its acts by means of interpellation, and oblige a member of the cabinet to resign through a vote of censure. It is a moderate parliamentarism, and the separation of powers is still fairly well delineated.

The semi-parliamentary system of Uruguay also had interesting features.[7] Article 145 of the constitution said: "The executive power shall be exercised by the President of the Republic who shall act with a Council of Ministers. . . ." The legislative power is authorized to judge politically the Ministers of State, under Article 136, which states: "The General Assembly, at the request of either of the Chambers, may judge politically the conduct of the Ministers of State, denouncing their administrative or governmental acts." The censure exercised in Uruguay by the legislative power was of two kinds:

---

[4] For an interesting study of the Cuban system, see "The Cuban Parliamentary System in Action, 1940-47," William S. Stokes, *The Journal of Politics*, Vol. II., pp. 335-364.

[5] For the recent changes in Cuba, see Chapter XIII.

[6] "The presence of the Council of Ministers, or of any of the Ministers, is obligatory, provided that the Congress or either of the Chambers may call them for interpellation." (Art. 169). "A motion of censure against the Council of Ministers, or against any of the Ministers, may be presented by only one Deputy or Senator, and shall be voted upon in the same session." (Art. 172). "The censured Minister must resign. The President of the Republic shall accept the resignation." (Art. 173).

[7] Uruguay has today a plural executive.

collective censure when it affected a majority of the members of the cabinet, and partial censure when it referred to only one minister or to a minority of the members.[8]

In December of 1951, a constitutional amendment was approved, abolishing the presidential office and replacing it with a nine-man Executive Council. This was, in substance, the old program of reforms advocated by Batlle (see Chapter 15). Six members of the Council are to come from the party which had the majority in the national elections, while the remaining three are to come from the party of the opposition. The Council elects its own president, but the whole body represents the nation. The president is not the president of the republic, but the president of the Council.

In spite of this reform, Uruguay continues with its parliamentary form of government. Congress reserves the right to disapprove, by majority vote, the actions of any member of the Council, who would then be obliged to resign. If the Council wishes to keep the minister, it refers the case to a combined session of the two houses of Congress, whose vote is final in the matter. Therefore, in the new Uruguayan executive, Congress continues exercising strong supervision and constitutes the closest approximation of European parliamentarism.

The tendency to limit the sphere of action of the executive is not so clear in some other countries, although the legislative branch may censure the conduct of the members of the Cabinet and force them to resign from their posts.

In Ecuador, the vote of censure not only obliges the censured minister to resign, but he may not hold this office again until two years have passed. Censure in that country is an individual matter, referring exclusively to the functionary who is being censured, giving this action the nature of judicial sanction. The individual is punished, not the government. The action of the legislature implies no vote of lack of confidence in the executive.

In Guatemala, on the other hand, legislative action against one or several ministers constitutes a vote of lack of confidence. The

---

8 The disapproval (of Congress) may be collective or not, but in one or the other case, it shall be pronounced by an absolute majority of the members of the General Assembly in special public session. It shall be understood that collective disapproval is that which affects a majority of the Cabinet." (Art. 138). "Disapproval by the General Assembly shall cause the resignation of the Ministers or of the Council, as the case may be." (Art. 139).

minister or ministers must resign. There, the power of censure may not be exercised until six months after the appointment of the censured minister or ministers, and never during the last six months of the presidential term.

In Panama, the National Assembly may censure the ministers in cases of "illegal acts or grave errors" that may injure the interests of the state. This censure is considered one of the administrative prerogatives of the National Assembly, indicating that the legislative branch exercises supervisory control over the executive.

In Venezuela, the Congress may censure a minister, as in these other countries. The interesting feature of the Venezuelan system is that the Congress, itself, decides when the censure should cause the removal of the minister, and in that case notifies the President of the Republic, who in turn removes the official in question. This indicates that the vote of censure implies no vote of lack of confidence in the head of the executive.

These last four systems are not, properly speaking, a parliamentary or even a semi-parliamentary form of government, but they do show the tendency to restrict the abuses of power of the executive.

Powers of the President. The powers of the President are in many cases like those of the heads of state in other countries with the republican form of government. A few of the most important should be mentioned, as they illustrate the relations between the head of the state and the other powers of the nation. With regard to his relations with the Congress, the President is empowered to present bills, by means of a message to the legislature, and he must sanction, veto, or promulgate the laws. He may call the Congress into extraordinary session when circumstances require it.

The executive enacts regulations, decrees, and resolutions. All constitutions sanction this right, it being understood that presidential resolutions must not violate or change the nature of the text of the laws. This power to enact regulations has caused difficult problems in practice and has resulted in serious political disturbances. It is not easy to delimit the field of the law from that of the regulation, and it is simple to give an interpretation to the law, by means of a regulation, which might either invalidate it or make it more radical. In the exercise of regulatory powers, many abuses have been committed in the Latin American countries. Cases in which presidential decrees should have been no more than administrative resolutions have been given such force that they have infringed upon the sphere of action of the legislative power. It has been the constant and continued practice of many presidents to govern by decree. The Paraguayan system is a typical case in point. In that nation, in order to prevent the Congress from disregarding presidential recommendations on new legislative measures, the President's message becomes law. It is a case of legislation by decree, by omission, or default of the legislative power. Furthermore, the Paraguayan President is invested with legislative power when the Congress is not in session.

The President's most important power, in his relations with the judiciary, is in connection with the execution of sentences. He may grant total or partial pardons, in some countries needing the approval of the Council of Ministers. This traditional power of chiefs of state, in practice, has produced complications. On the occasion of national holidays, or before going out of office, presidents have frequently abused their authority to pardon, favoring members of their party or personal friends. The Cuban constitution, in order to prevent this, prohibits the President from pardoning officials or public employees who have committed electoral frauds or crimes, unless they have served at least one third of their sentence.

The right to grant amnesties, according to constitutional theory, is a legislative and not an executive power. However, in Latin America there are several countries where this power is given to the President: Bolivia (Article 94, section 13); Costa Rica (Article 109, section 20), and Haiti (Article 84). This right to grant amnesties is limited to political offenses and may not be used for common crimes. No doubt, the use of this privilege gives rise to favoritism and places the executive above the other branches of the state precisely in the realm of political matters, where abuse of power is most frequent. On the other hand, in other countries only the Congress is authorized to grant amnesties.

In their relations with the armed forces, the Latin American Presidents have an important role. They are, of course, commanders-in-chief of the forces, as is the case in most countries. They may also grant promotions and appoint important officials. Some countries require the approval of the Congress to grant these promotions or make the appointments. Two countries establish interesting limitations with regard to the direct command of troops, which the

President may assume. In Chile (Article 72, section 14), the President must have the approval of the Senate to command personally the sea and land forces. In Peru, he needs not only the authorization of Congress to assume personal command of the army, but it is definitely established that in order to do so, he is subjected to military jurisdiction (Article 153). Furthermore, Article 145 clearly states that the exercise of the presidency of the republic is suspended when the President takes command of the armed forces in person. The object of this constitutional limitation of the presidential power is not only to require legislative approval to command troops, but particularly to avoid the abuse of power on the part of the President, who must temporarily cease in the exercise of his office and lose his position as a civil functionary.[9]

In their connection with the Roman Catholic Church, there are presidents who, as heads of the executive power, still exercise ecclesiastical Patronage, no longer called "royal," but "National Patronage." These are the Presidents of Argentina, Bolivia, Costa Rica, Paraguay, Peru and Venezuela. This right of ecclesiastical Patronage is exercised by the national executive approximately as it was by the Crown in colonial America. The civil branch of the government intervenes in ecclesiastical administration, proposes to the Vatican appointments of important ecclesiastics, and has the privilege held by the Council of the Indies to authorize the promulgation of the Papal bulls in the nation's territory. In Argentina, the President must have the approval of the Supreme Court in order to exercise this right, while in Bolivia, Peru, and Paraguay the authorization of the Congress is required. In Peru, bishops and archbishops appointed by the President must be natives of the country.

As Supreme Chief of the nation, the Latin American President represents his country in all official acts, personally or through delegates. He signs treaties with foreign nations, appoints high functionaries of public administration, grants pensions, retirements and naturalizations, and in general enjoys the traditional powers of the office.

Requirements to Be President. As a general rule, the requirements with regard to age, nationality and the enjoyment of civil and

---

9 This has not prevented today's army rule in Peru. (See Chapter 14.)

political rights essential in Latin America to occupy the position of President of a republic follow the lines accepted by the constitutions of most of the nations of the world. In Cuba, there is one exception. The requirement to be a citizen by birth is not exacted of those who have served at least ten years in the army of liberation during the wars of independence (Article 139).

A requirement in Argentina and Paraguay, however, is in open conflict with the democratic principle of freedom of worship. There, one must be a Roman Catholic in order to be eligible to the Presidency of the Republic. These limitations contradict the principle of freedom of religion expressed in Article 26 of the Argentinian constitution and Article 19 of the Paraguayan one.

Another interesting requirement is set forth in Article 45 of the constitution of the Dominican Republic. Under it, it is essential that the President shall have resided in Dominican territory during the five years immediately preceding the elections. The object, of course, is to prevent the possibility of political exiles attaining the presidency, as it is easy to understand that a political leader who is allowed to remain in the country for five years under a President like Trujillo must necessarily be politically favorable to the government. This precept definitely limits a free presidential election.

Presidential Substitution. The problem of the presidential vacancy has been thoroughly considered in the Latin American countries. The first constitutions followed the example of the United States of America, creating the office of Vice-President. Political struggles and the ambitions of Vice-Presidents brought about the gradual elimination of the office and the tendency to find another means to fill the vacancy in case of absence, death or incapacity of the President. The tendency to do away with the Vice-Presidency was followed by the modern Latin American constitutions; however, the Cuban constitution of 1940 re-established the office, and its example was followed by the Brazilian constitution of 1946. Several of the nations have Vice-Presidents under their present constitutions.

There are three different systems for presidential substitutions in the other nations. One of them, and the most common, consists in the election by the Congress of a designate to fill the vacancy, should it occur, for the remainder of the term. Under another, the constitution names the Ministers who, in order of importance, are called upon to fill the vacancy. The third system, followed in Paraguay, has the provisional President elected by a National Assembly composed of the members of the Council of State and the Chamber of Representatives.

The Mexican system is different. If a presidential vacancy occurs during the first two years following the election, Congress is constituted as an Electoral College and appoints a provisional President, but general elections are immediately called to choose a new President to occupy the office for the remainder of the term. If the vacancy occurs during the last four years of the presidential term, Congress appoints the substitute to conclude the term.

Presidential Re-election. The re-election of the President of the Republic has been one of the most disturbing issues in the political life of the Latin American continent. The attraction of power, the abuses of *"caudillismo"* and *"personalismo"* have made many Presidents resort to extreme means in order to continue in office. The long, traditional dictatorships of Latin America have always tried to cover their abuses of power with the cloak of legality, and the simulation of presidential elections. Faced with such practices, the people and the statesmen have attempted to create constitutional barriers against presidential continuance, and the problem of re-election has been carefully regulated.

The most common system prohibits immediate re-election; that is, the President may not be re-elected at the end of his term. His place must be taken by another, and he may not be nominated again until after a certain length of time. The object of this is clear: to prevent fraudulent elections influenced by the party in power. Mexico, whose revolutionary movement of 1910 was started with the political slogan of "effective suffrage—no re-election," has in its constitution the most definite prohibition of all:

> The President shall enter into the performance of his office on December first and shall continue in it six years. Any citizen who has discharged the office of President of the Republic, popularly elected or in the character of interim, provisional or substitute, may in no case and for no reason again hold this office (Art. 83).

That is to say, in Mexico the act of once having served as President incapacitates a citizen from occupying the office again.

In Argentina, the new constitution of March 11, 1949, modified Article 77 of the constitution of 1853 that prohibited presidential re-election. Today re-election is authorized for the period immediately following the term in office.[10]

The constitution of Paraguay also differs from the general trend, and its article 47 states that the President may be re-elected.

Other Organs of the Executive. The executive power is not exercised exclusively by the President of the Republic and his Secretaries or Ministers, since some countries provide for special organs charged with the supervision of public administration and sometimes with the duty of advising the head of the state. Among these organs are the Tribunals of Account and the Councils of State.

The Tribunals of Account supervise revenues and expenditures of the government. In some countries, they function as part of the judiciary; that is, they possess all the characteristics of tribunals of justice entrusted with the examination of the accounts of the municipal, provincial, and central governments. In other republics these duties are assigned to a Comptroller. There are countries where this organ is considered as a part of the executive power in all matters related to the administration of public funds. Because of these differences, a general description of the institution is very difficult, and it is best to offer a brief outline of its characteristics in two countries where it operates.

In Brazil, the Tribunal has the following powers:

> 1st. To follow and control directly, or through delegations created by law, the execution of the budget. 2nd. To judge the accounts of those responsible for funds and other public properties, and those of the administrators of autarchic entities. 3rd. To judge the legality of contracts and retirements, removals and pensions . . . (Art. 77) .

In the Cuban constitution, we find a clear and precise definition of this organ of government:

> The Tribunal of Accounts is the supervising body for reve-

---

10 See Chapter 15.

nues and expenditures of the State, Province and municipality,
and of the autonomous organizations created under the protection of the law, which receive their incomes directly or indirectly
through the State. The Tribunal of Accounts is dependent only
upon the law, and its differences with other bodies shall be
submitted to the decision of the Supreme Tribunal of Justice
(Art. 266).

The members of the Tribunal are elected by the Supreme Tribunal of Justice, the President of the Republic, the Senate, and the
University of Havana.

The Council of State. This organ of government functions with
powers somewhat like that of the executive, and sometimes with
quasi-legislative and judicial faculties. Its composition, powers, and
the form of election of its members vary according to the countries,
so it should be studied separately.

In the Republic of Colombia its principal function is of a purely
consultive nature in matters referring to administration, but it
also has judicial powers in questions concerning administrative
litigation.[11]

The members of the Council of State are elected by the Congress
from a panel submitted by the President of the Republic.[12]

In Ecuador, the Council of State must see to the strict enforcement of the constitution and of the laws of the republic, especially
the individual rights of the citizens. Its powers are not consultive, as
in Colombia, but rather are supervisory with regard to the legal and
constitutional structure of the nation. It also has semi-legislative
powers, when the Congress is not in session, and functions as a tribunal in cases of administrative litigation. The composition of this

---

11 See Chapter 6.

12 Powers of the Council of State are:

1st. To act as a supreme consultative body for the Government in matters of
administration, it being necessarily heard in all those that the Constitution and the
laws specify.

Opinions of the Council are not obligatory for the Government, except in the case
of Article 212 of this Constitution.

2nd. To prepare bills and codes that must be presented in the legislative Chambers,
and to propose suitable amendments in all branches of legislation.

3rd. To discharge the functions of a supreme tribunal of administrative litigation,
in conformity with the rules specified by law.

4th. To enact its own by-laws, and to exercise the other functions determined
by law. (Art. 141).

THE EXECUTIVE

Country	Term	Vice-President	Immediate Re-Election	Form of Election	Ministers Politically Responsible to Congress	Council of State	Tribunal of Account
Argentina	6 years	Yes	Yes	Direct vote	No	No	No
Bolivia	6 years	Yes	No	Direct vote	No	No	No
Brazil	5 years	Yes	No	Direct vote	No	No	Yes
Chile	6 years	No	No	Direct vote	No	No	No
Colombia	4 years	Designate	No	Direct vote	No	Yes	No
Costa Rica	4 years	2 Vice-Pres.	No	Direct vote	No	No	Yes
Cuba	5 years	Yes	Yes	Direct vote	Yes	No	Yes
Dominican Republic	4 years	No	No	Direct vote	No	Yes	Yes
Ecuador	4 years	Yes	No	Direct vote	No	No	Yes
El Salvador	6 years	Yes	No	Direct vote	No	No	Yes
Guatemala	6 years	No	No	Direct vote	No	No	No
Haiti	6 years	No	No	By assembly	No	No	Yes
Honduras	6 years	Yes	No	Direct vote	No	No	No
Mexico	6 years	No	Never	Direct vote	No	No	Yes
Nicaragua	6 years	Designate	No	Direct vote	No	No	Yes
Panama	4 years	2 Vice-Pres.	No	Direct vote	No	No	No
Paraguay	5 years	No	Yes	Direct vote	No	Yes	Yes
Peru	5 years	Yes	No	Direct vote	Yes	No	No
Uruguay	Council	No	......	Congress	Yes	No	Yes
Venezuela	5 years	No	No	Direct vote	Yes	No	No

organ is extremely interesting, since it is made up of functionaries of the executive, legislative, and judicial branches of the government, as well as representatives of the armed forces and two private citizens elected by the Congress. The Ministers of the executive participate in the sessions of the Council, but have no right to vote.

In Paraguay, the Council of State passes upon the legality of decrees issued by the executive power, which are to have the force of law. This means that if the executive attempts to legislate by decree, these decrees must first be approved by the Council of State. The Council functions as a consultive body to the President in economic and financial matters, and especially with regard to the international relations of the nation. The most interesting feature of this organ is its composition, since it is a sort of government corporation closely resembling the European fascist constitutions. The executive power, by means of its ministers, is represented in the Council, but they act together with the Rector of the University, the Archbishop of Paraguay and representatives of business, banking, various branches of industry and the armed forces.[13]

THE PRESIDENCY [14]

Argentina. The President and Vice-President hold their offices for the term of six years and may be re-elected. They are elected directly by the people, by majority vote. The despatch of matters corresponding to the executive is in the hands of the Ministers of State, who legalize the presidential acts without which they have no efficacy. Senators and deputies may not be appointed Ministers. The President and Ministers may attend the sessions of Congress, and participate, but may not vote.

Bolivia. The executive power is exercised by the President of the Republic, together with the Ministers of State. There is a Vice-President, and the constitutional term is six years. The President and Vice-Presi-

---

13 "There shall be a Council of State which shall be composed of the Ministers of the executive branch, the rector of the national university, the archbishop of Paraguay, a representative of business, two representatives of the farming and cattle industries, one representative of the manufacturing industries, the president of the Bank of the Republic, and two retired members of the military institutions, one from the army and the other from the navy, with rank not lower than colonel. The manner of designation of the Councilors not holding public office shall be determined by law. The members of the first Council of State shall be designated by the President of the Republic." (Art. 62).

14 The following notes are designed only to supplement the preceding chart. They may serve as reference material for discussions and analyses of current political events, and also to give a general view of the office of the presidency.

dent may not be re-elected until six years after the end of their term. The Ministers of State are appointed by the President, and they are required to appear before the Congress upon request. The President and Vice-President are elected by direct suffrage.

Brazil. Brazil has a President and a Vice-President, who hold office for five years and are elected by direct vote. The President is assisted by the Ministers whom he freely appoints, and who are required to countersign presidential acts. The Ministers are obliged to appear before the Chamber of Deputies and the Senate when called to report, but they are not politically responsible before the Congress.

Chile. The executive power belongs to the President; there is no Vice-President. In the case of the absence or illness of the President, his place is taken by a Minister designated by law, who then assumes the title of Vice-President of the Republic. The President holds office for six years and may not be re-elected for the term immediately following. He is elected directly by the people. Presidential orders must be signed by the Minister of the respective department. Ministers are obliged to give account of their acts, but there is no political responsibility of the Cabinet before the Congress.

Colombia. The President of the Republic is elected by direct vote of the people, for a four-year term. No citizen may be elected to the Presidency who has held the office during the year immediately prior to the elections. There is no Vice-President, but every two years Congress elects a Designate who takes the President's place in his absence. If the President's absence should be permanent, the Designate shall convoke general elections, and the new President shall hold office for the remainder of the term. The Ministers of State countersign the President's acts and are appointed by him.

Costa Rica. The executive power belongs to the President, who holds office for four years and may not be reelected for the following term. There is no Vice-President, but in its first regular session, the Congress appoints three Designates for each presidential term, who are called First, Second and Third, and who substitute for the President in that order. The resolutions of the President must be signed by each Secretary, or they are not considered valid. The President is elected by popular vote.

Cuba. The President exercises the executive power with the Council of Ministers. There is a Vice-President, and both are elected by universal suffrage, for a term of four years. No one who has held the office of President or Vice-President may occupy it again until eight years after the expiration of the term. The President is assisted by a Council of Ministers, one of whom holds the title of Prime Minister. These Ministers are politically responsible before the Congress, but the President is the administrative head of the nation, so the Prime Minister does not possess the political power held by Prime Ministers in the parliamentary systems.

Dominican Republic. The executive power is exercised by the President of the Republic, elected every five years by direct vote. In the case of the temporary absence of the President, his place is taken by the Secretary of War. Secretaries are freely appointed by the President, and they have no political responsibility before the Congress.

Ecuador. A President and a Vice-President are elected by direct and secret vote for a four-year term. The President may not be re-elected until four years after the expiration of the term for which he was elected. Decrees and resolutions of the President must be authorized by the respective **Ministers.**

El Salvador. The executive power is in the hands of a President, elected for four years, and he may not be re-elected for the term immediately following. The President is elected by the people, but when a candidate does not obtain a majority of votes Congress elects the President by public vote, from among the three candidates who have obtained the largest number of votes. A Vice-President is elected in the same manner. Decrees and orders of the President must be authorized by the Ministers, or they are not to be obeyed. The Ministers shall attend the sessions of the Assembly and answer interpellations, but must retire before voting takes place.

Guatemala. The President acts with his Ministers, individually or collectively. The presidential term is for six years, and re-election is prohibited until twelve years after the expiration of the term. The election is carried out by universal and direct suffrage. There is no Vice-President, and the temporary or permanent absence of the President is filled by the President and Vice-President of the Congress, in that order. Guatemalan ministers are politically responsible before the Congress. They must countersign the President's acts to make them valid.

Haiti. The executive power is exercised by the President of the Republic. In case of a vacancy, the Cabinet is temporarily invested with executive power, but it must immediately convoke the National Assembly for the election of a new President. The President is elected, by secret ballot and absolute majority, for a six-year term by the

National Assembly. All presidential measures must be deliberated in the Council of Secretaries (cabinet), but there is no political responsibility of its members before the Congress.

Honduras. The executive power is exercised by the President and, in his absence, by the Vice-President. The presidential term is for six years, and both the President and Vice-President are elected by popular vote and may not be re-elected for the term immediately following. The Secretaries of State must countersign presidential measures. The Secretaries may attend the deliberations of Congress, answer interpellations referring to matters of administration, but Congress may not exact political responsibility of them.

Mexico. The President is elected by direct suffrage for a six-year term, and in no case and for no reason may he be re-elected. If a presidential vacancy occurs during the first two years of the term, the Congress appoints a substitute, and if the Congress is not in session, the permanent committee makes the appointment, but in either case, a presidential election is called immediately. When the vacancy occurs during the last four years of the term, the provisional President is appointed by the Congress to conclude the term. The President is assisted by the Secretaries of the Cabinet, whose countersignatures are required on all presidential measures for validity. There is no political responsibility of the Secretaries before the Congress.

Nicaragua. The President is elected by direct and popular vote for a six-year term, and he may not be re-elected for the following term. In the case of a presidential vacancy, his place is taken by one of the three Designates appointed annually by the Congress from among its members. The Secretaries countersign the President's acts and are obliged to answer interpellations, but this implies no political responsibility.

Panama. The President is elected by direct and popular vote for a four-year term. In the same election, a first and second Vice-President are chosen, who take the President's place if necessary. The President may not be re-elected for the two terms immediately following. The ministers may attend the debates of the legislature, report on matters of administration and participate in the debates, but they may not vote. There is no political responsibility before Congress.

Paraguay. The President is elected by direct suffrage for a five-year term and may be re-elected for one more term. In case of a presidential vacancy during the last three years of the term, the National Assembly appoints a substitute to conclude the term. If the vacancy occurs during the first two years, the provisional President calls for elections to be held within two months. The Secretaries of State authenticate and legalize the acts of the President. They have no political responsibility to Congress.

Peru. The President is elected by direct suffrage for a six-year term and may not be re-elected for the term immediately following. In case of a presidential vacancy, the substitute is elected by Congress. The Ministers of State exercise the executive power together with the President and are politically responsible to Congress.

Uruguay. Executive power corresponds to a nine-man Executive Council. Six members of the Council are selected from the majority party in the National elections and the remaining three from the opposition parties. The Council elects its own president. The members of the Council are politically responsible to Congress.

Venezuela. The President is elected by universal, secret, and direct vote for a five-year term and may not be re-elected for the term immediately following. Temporary absences of the President are filled by one of the ministers, designated by him, and permanent absences by the president of Congress. However, the substitute must convoke Congress so that it may provide for the election of a new President. The Ministers of State are politically responsible to Congress.

Suggested Readings

English:

Clevan, N. A. N., *The Political Organization of Bolivia,* Washington, D. C., Carnegie Institution, 1940.

Crampton, Ethel M., "The Executive Office in Latin American Constitutions," *Southwestern Political Science Quarterly,* March, 1921.

Fitzgibbon, Russell H., "Executive Power in Central America," *Journal of Politics,* August, 1941.

————, Ed. *The Constitutions of the Americas,* Chicago University Press, 1943.

Gibson, William M., *The Constitutions of Colombia,* Durham, N. C., Duke University Press, 1948.

Hambloch, Ernest, *His Majesty the President,* New York, E. P. Dutton & Co., Inc., 1936.

Hanson, Simon, *Utopia in Uruguay,* New York, Oxford University Press, 1938.

MacDonald, Austin F., *The Government of the Argentine Republic,* New York, Thomas Y. Crowell Co., 1942.

————, *Latin American Politics and Government,* New York, Thomas Y. Crowell Co., 1949.

Stuart, Graham, *The Governmental System of Peru,* Washington, D. C., Carnegie Institution, 1925.

Stokes, William S., "The Cuban Parliamentary System in Action, 1940-1947," *The Journal of Politics,* Vol. IX, pp. 335-364.

Wise, George S., *Caudillo,* New York, Columbia University Press, 1951.

Other Languages:

Álvarez Tabío, Fernando, *Teoría General de la Constitución Cubana,* La Habana, 1946.

Cavalcanti de Carvalho, Manuel, *Evoluçao do Estado Brasileiro,* Rio de Janeiro, 1941.

Echeverría S. Buenaventura, *Derecho Constitucional Guatemalteco,* Guatemala, 1944.

Herrera Guerrero, Héctor V., *La División de Poderes en la Constitución de 1917,* México, D. F., 1946.

Lazcano y Mazón, Andrés María, *Constituciones Políticas de América,* La Habana, 1942.

Morales, Elizondo, Oscar, *El Principio de la División de Poderes,* México, D. F., 1945.

Partido Peronista, *Rèforma de la Constitución Nacional,* Anexo III, Buenos Aires, 1949.

Pereda, Setembrino Ezekial, *El Poder Ejecutivo,* 4 vols., Montevideo, 1918-1923.

Pérez, Francisco de Paula, *Derecho Constitucional Colombiano,* Bogotá, 1942.

Raveau, Rafael, *Tratado Elemental de Derecho Constitucional Chileno y Comparado,* Santiago de Chile, 1939.

Ruggeri Parra, Pablo, *Derecho Constitucional Venezolano,* Caracas, 1944.

Tagle, Carlos A., *Estado de Derecho y Equilibrio de Poderas en la Constitución Argentina,* Santa Fe, 1944.

CHAPTER 5

The Legislature

One of the conquests of liberalism was to give the people the right to make their own laws, as a consequence taking away that power from the executive branch of the government. In some countries, such as England, France, and the United States, this philosophy resulted in the creation of strong legislative bodies. In Latin America, this was not the case. The philosophy of the strong executive prevailed, and one of the characteristics of the contemporary governments—with the exception of Uruguay—is still the weakness of congress.

Apart from the theoretical reasons indicated in the previous chapter, historical circumstances contributed to the weakness of the Latin American legislative assemblies. The most important one is the absence, in colonial days, of important deliberative bodies on the national level, or similar institutions of government. The Latin American congress had to be improvised without any antecedent. In the United States and in England, there had been centuries of parliamentary experience. France had its States General, and Spain its *Cortes*. The other two branches of colonial government, the executive and the judiciary, could be adapted, and in many cases they were, to the organs created by the new republics. This was not the case with the legislature. The only semi-representative institution, the *Cabildo*, functioned solely on a local level, and nevertheless played an important role as a deliberative body in the struggle for independence. Today, the Latin American legislature functions with the general characteristics of this organ of government, but it is in essence a weak organ. It possesses, however, some typical institutions and practices that are worth considering.

Bicameral Legislature. With the exception of Costa Rica, El Salvador, Guatemala, Honduras, Panama, and Paraguay, which have maintained the unicameral system, the Latin American countries, some as small as Ecuador, Nicaragua, and Haiti, have preferred the bicameral one. The two-chamber system in the United States and the European countries is the result of the historical origin or federal structure; yet in many of the Latin American countries where the system has been adopted, these conditions have not existed. The necessity of a higher chamber is obvious in a large federation such as in the United States, or in countries where the purpose has been to maintain a specialized body integrated by the aristocracy of politics or of birth, as in Europe. But in Latin America, we can find no such justification, and the explanation lies in the political or bureaucratic necessity of offering positions to provincial or local interests; or in the administrative principle of decentralization of the legislative power and the establishment of a counterbalance between the two chambers. There is, however, still another reason, which should be taken into consideration: the necessity of facilitating the participation of non-native citizens in government. In some countries members of the lower chamber are not required to be native citizens, as are the senators or members of the higher chamber. The lower chamber is thus closer to the people, while the higher chamber is more aristocratic and nationalistic. It has been thought that the senators might act as moderators of the new forces of population, who may easily come to be members of the lower chamber.

Special Rights of Congressmen. All of the countries of Latin America have certain principles which are meant to protect the members of the legislature in the free exercise of their office. These we shall not enumerate, because they are similar to those found in other countries of the world. Two of the most important are inviolability for opinions stated in the exercise of office, and immunity in the case of certain illegal acts committed as a result of office. The first principle requires little attention, since one cannot conceive of a legislator who does not enjoy liberty of expression in Congress, and who does not have the necessary protection to express and freely maintain his opinions.

The problem of parliamentary immunity is of another nature. The principle behind this right was the protection of the congressman if he was forced to violate a law because of his position. The privilege has been much abused, and many congressmen have en-

VICTORIA COLLEGE
LIBRARY
VICTORIA, B.C.

joyed this protection even in cases of common crimes committed for purely personal reasons. All of the constitutions in force today make an exception, stating that if the congressman has been arrested *in flagrante delicto,* he is not protected by parliamentary immunity. In other cases, the judicial authorities must obtain the permission of the chamber to which he belongs in order to take action against him. Some of the constitutions prohibit filing civil suits against congressmen while the Congress is in session. The purpose is to protect the congressman, who is not free to return to his province to appear in court, and to avoid advantages taken by unscrupulous plaintiffs in default. Nevertheless, Article 114 of the Mexican constitution establishes that there are no privileges or immunities for any public official of a civil nature.

The Permanent Committee. One of the features of the legislative branch in Guatemala, Mexico, Uruguay, and Venezuela is that the constitutions have created a permanent committee composed of representatives of the two chambers, which functions as a stable organ of the legislature. Besides taking charge of the administrative aspect while the Congress is not in session, this committee has special functions which we shall mention later, among others that of taking the initiative of laws and convoking the Congress to extraordinary sessions.

In Ecuador, a legislative committee is charged with taking the initiative in constitutional amendments and in laws. It is formed, in addition to the representatives of the Chambers, by representatives of the other two branches of government, the executive and the judiciary. In that country, there is also a Functional Senate which gives the legislature a special characteristic, to which we shall refer later.

In Mexico and Haiti, the Congress not only supervises the presidential elections, which is common in other countries, but acts as an electoral college.

Judicial Powers. Another aspect of the legislature in some of the Latin American countries is that in many cases it possesses judicial powers normally belonging to the judiciary, and not to a legislative, body. This is a contradiction of the principle of public law, in that the organ which makes the law should not interpret or exe-

VICTORIA COLLEGE
LIBRARY
VICTORIA, B.C.

cute it. In Costa Rica the constitution states that Congress may enact, amend, *interpret* and repeal laws. Naturally, a legislative act is required in order to do this, but many writers feel that the power of interpreting laws should belong exclusively to the judiciary. Furthermore, Congress in its first regular session reviews the acts of their predecessors and automatically decides as to their constitutionality. This function, in other countries, is generally left to private initiative, by means of judicial review.

In Ecuador, Congress is also given the power of interpreting the laws, and it adds that in case of recess of Congress, the function is exercised by the Supreme Tribunal of Justice. The Congresses of Guatemala and Peru, as well, have the power to interpret the constitution and the laws.

Sessions. Like the other countries of the world, the Latin American Congresses hold their ordinary and extraordinary sessions. The constitutions of all the countries include articles clearly stating the dates on which the ordinary sessions are held, and how long they are to last. Some countries, such as El Salvador, limit the length of the ordinary sessions to forty days.

Extraordinary sessions are given equal attention in the constitutions. As a general rule, the executive or a Permanent Committee may convoke them and may also extend the term of the ordinary sessions. In most of the countries, the legislature itself enjoys this privilege. In this case, the number of favorable votes required varies greatly. Bolivia, for instance, requires a majority vote, while in Venezuela extraordinary sessions may be assembled on petition of a fourth of the members of the Congress. Often these sessions are limited to the matters for which they are convoked. In other cases, any matters considered necessary may be included in the agenda.

Special Powers. Because the bicameral system is the prevailing one, each chamber has reserved certain special powers for itself. The most important power which always lies in the highest chamber is that of judging the members of the executive including the President of the Republic. The accusations are generally brought by the members of the lower chamber. The penalty is limited to dismissal or disqualification from public office. Any other sanction incurred by the member of the executive found guilty is imposed by the ordinary courts.

The power to accuse or judge the members of the executive has seldom been used in the Latin American countries. The strong executive of which we have spoken makes it difficult for Congress to take a hostile attitude with regard to the President and his subalterns. The President controls the bureaucratic positions, and especially the armed forces, and with this he enjoys a type of immunity, despite the constitutional right of the Congress to accuse and depose him. The privilege of the Congress generally is reduced to the possibility of exercising that right; the fact that it may be used is in itself a means of expressing political censure, without resorting to accusation or actual trial. Usually, when a President is deposed, Congress has merely legalized, *a posteriori*, a political event which has already taken place. A political leader, a *caudillo* or military chief, deposes the President, and uses the Congress to lend legal force to his act, after it has taken place. An example of this was the deposition of President Miguel Mariano Gómez of Cuba, by Colonel Batista, who forced the Congress to comply with his desires. Occasionally, Congress' threat to accuse the President may produce adverse results, with the executive resorting to a coup d'etat. This was the case in Colombia when the Liberal majority in the Congress defied President Ospina Pérez, and he assumed dictatorial powers (see Chapter 13).

The higher chamber generally enjoys the traditional power of approving important appointments, as in all bicameral systems. In the Cuban constitution, if the President or any high official of the executive is to be judged, the Senate sits with the members of Supreme Tribunal of Justice, *in plenum*. This is a result of the tendency prevailing today in Latin America, to give more political responsibility to the judiciary (see Chapter 6). In Ecuador, when the Senate acts as a tribunal of justice, it does so under the chairmanship of the president of the Supreme Court. In that country, the higher chamber is a functional senate and is composed of two senators for each province of the Sierra, which is the most thickly populated region, and one senator for each of the eastern provinces and the Archipelago of Colón. All these senators are elected by direct suffrage. Besides, there are twelve functional senators representing the following institutions: one for public education; one for private education; one for the press, scientific and literary academies; two for agriculture; two for commerce; two for industry; two for the workers, and one for the armed forces. The characteristic undoubtedly indicates a tendency toward the corporative state. The functional senators are elected by the official representatives of the institutions to which they belong, and it is required that they shall have been connected with these institutions for some period of time prior to their designation as functional senators.

Committees and Officers. Each chamber elects its president by majority vote. The form of election and the number of vice-presidents vary according to the countries. The system of creating committees to attend to legislative matters exists, as it does in other parts of the world. In many countries, the Vice-President is the president of the higher chamber. The parties, groups, or coalitions of politicians are divided in accordance with their ideologies or interests, and they have their speakers or leaders. Usually, there is a leader of the majority and a leader of the minority or opposition. But, since the two-party system is the exception rather than the rule, there are many leaders of minorities, of the left and of the right, with the result that the debates and the legislative function as a whole are complicated. Broadly speaking, the Latin American Congress resembles the European parliaments more than the legislature of the United States. Each party, group, or coalition tries to obtain advantageous positions within the standing committees. The committees do not hold so many hearings, nor do they throw open to the public their discussions on bills, as in the United States. There may be public hearings in some important cases, but they are infrequent. The committees function like technical groups, preparing and drafting bills, and often have insufficient funds to employ secretaries and personnel for this work. Congressmen frequently pay for these expenses themselves, or have the work done in their own private offices, and, as is to be expected, the most active and diligent among them can manage to have their own bills presented. The preparation of the legislative process in Latin America, in its technical aspect, is carried out as a rule in the offices of the executive. The President has the funds and the technical personnel for this purpose.

Initiative of Laws and Veto. The formal introduction of bills before the Congress may be made by means of a message of the executive, or very often by the congressmen themselves. In all of the countries, each of the chambers has this right. In Uruguay, one congressman alone may initiate the legislative process. In Venezuela, three representatives must present a bill, and in Chile, five senators or ten deputies are necessary.

The privilege of initiating laws has been extended to the judiciary in Cuba, the Dominican Republic, Ecuador, El Salvador, Guatemala, Nicaragua, Panama, Peru, and Venezuela. Cuba grants this right to organs of the executive, such as the Tribunal of Accounts, and Ecuador to the Council of National Economy. Cuba alone grants the initiative of laws to the people. The constitution states that the petition of 10,000 citizens having status as voters shall be required for this purpose. In practice, to the best of our knowledge, this privilege has not been used. In Colombia and in Venezuela, among other countries, the members of the cabinet and magistrates of the Supreme Court may take part, without the right to vote, in debates on laws referring to their respective administrative branches. In Mexico there is an interesting feature in this connection: State legislatures may present bills before the Federal Congress.

Congress, in almost all the countries of Latin America, may override the presidential veto, requiring the favorable vote of two-thirds of its members. The terminology and formalities vary according to the different constitutions, but in substance the legislature has this privilege. We may add that in practice, due to the power of the executive and the many other circumstances already mentioned, the right is seldom exercised. There is one exception in connection with the right to override the presidential veto which should be mentioned. The Peruvian constitution declares that the President must promulgate any law approved by the Congress, within ten days after its receipt. If he does not do so the Congress shall promulgate it, order its fulfillment and its publication in some periodical. Therefore, the Peruvian President really does not have the veto power. In practice, nevertheless, when the President returns the bill with his objections, or lets ten days go by without signing it, the Congress has followed the custom of tabling it until the following legislative session. The constitution cannot specifically authorize the Congress to override a veto to which the President has no written right. This situation has brought about serious friction between the legislature and the executive on many occasions.

One feature that contrasts with the United States Congress is that the President possesses the item veto, and can, therefore, partially kill a bill without turning down the whole measure. This prevents the highly objectionable "rider" by means of which a congressman introduces measures in important appropriation bills, which the President cannot stop because it would endanger the function of the whole administration.

The item veto has been, in the United States, a highly controversial point. In many states, the governor has the right to this type of veto in financial matters. In 1938, President Franklin D. Roosevelt asked Congress to give him the item veto on appropriation bills, but his request was turned down by the Senate. In Latin America, the practice is very general, and the President has this extra power over Congress. The existence of the item veto is another Latin American feature of the weakness of the legislature.

Decree-Laws. Another feature that decreases the power of Congress is the general practice of authorizing the executive to issue decree-laws. A decree in terms of contemporary Latin law (*decreto*) is a term applied to any resolution or decision made by the Executive Branch of the government. The traditional administrative practice has always been to authorize the executive to supplement or clarify positive laws in order to put into practice the principles of such legislation. It is well known that a decree cannot change or restrict the text of the statute. Properly speaking, the term "decree-law" seems a contradiction, but it is widely used and recognized in the majority of the Latin American countries as a decision issued by the executive with the force of law, in the cases in which he is empowered to do so under the constitution. In this case, the decision has all the characteristics and validity of a statute.

In practice, the Latin American presidents have abused the power of issuing decree-laws. In many cases, they have done so when not authorized by the constitution. In others, they have dissolved congress and ruled by decree-laws during the abnormal period in which the country has been deprived of its legislative organ. In still others, de-facto or provisional governments which have conquered power as a result of a revolution or a military coup, have

THE LEGISLATURE

Name of Country	HIGHER CHAMBER			LOWER CHAMBER			Special Features
	Name of Chamber	Number of Members	Terms	Name of Chamber	Number of Members	Terms	
Argentina	Senate	2 per Province	6 years	Chamber of Deputies	Proportional to population	6 years	....
Bolivia	Senate	3 per Department	6 years	Chamber of Deputies	105 Deputies	4 years	....
Brazil	Senate	3 per State	8 years	Chamber of Deputies	Proportional to population	4 years	....
Chile	Senate	45	8 years	Chamber of Deputies	Proportional to population	4 years	....
Colombia	Senate	By population in department	4 years	Chamber of Representatives	Proportional to population	2 years	....
Costa Rica	....	....	....	Legislative Assembly	45 Deputies	4 years	....
Cuba	Senate	9 per Province	4 years	Chamber of Representatives	Proportional to population	4 years	....
Dominican Republic	Senate	1 per Province	5 years	Chamber of Deputies	Proportional to population	5 years	....
Ecuador	Functional Senate	1 or 2 per Province and 12 Functionals	4 years	Chamber of Deputies	Proportional to population	2 years	Permanent Committee
El Salvador	....	....	....	National Assembly	Three per Department	1 year	....

THE LEGISLATURE (Continued)

Name of Country	HIGHER CHAMBER			LOWER CHAMBER			
	Name of Chamber	Number of Members	Terms	Name of Chamber	Number of Members	Terms	Special Features
Guatemala	......	......	......	National Congress	Proportional to population	4 years	Permanent Committee
Haiti	Senate	21	6 years	Chamber of Deputies	37 Deputies	4 years	....
Honduras	......	......	......	Congress of Deputies	Proportional to population	6 years	....
Mexico	Senate	2 per State	6 years	Chamber of Deputies	Proportional to population	3 years	Permanent Committee
Nicaragua	Senate	15 plus Ex-Presidents	6 years	Chamber of Deputies	Proportional to population	6 years	....
Panama	......	......	......	National Assembly	Proportional to population	4 years	....
Paraguay	......	......	......	Chamber of Representatives	Proportional to population	5 years	....
Peru	Senate	50	6 years	Chamber of Deputies	150 Deputies	5 years	Permanent Committee
Uruguay	Senate	30	4 years	Chamber of Deputies	99 Deputies	4 years	Permanent Committee
Venezuela	Senate	2 per State	5 years	Chamber of Deputies	Proportional to population	5 years	Permanent Committee

governed for long periods of time by means of decree-laws. One of the characteristics in those cases is the extraordinary number of decree-laws issued by the executive. The case of Argentina, after the military coup d'etat of 1943 and during the provisional government that followed, is typical. In some countries the provisional government has put into practice, by means of decree-laws, not only positive legislation, but even constitutional texts. All of this adds to the confusion and weakness of congress. There is no doubt that the governed peoples are accustomed to thinking of the executive assuming legislative functions.

ORGANIZATION AND FUNCTIONS

Argentina. Congress is composed of a Chamber of Deputies and a Senate.

The Chamber of Deputies is formed of representatives elected directly by the people. Deputies hold office for six years and may not be re-elected. The Chamber is renewed by half every three years.

The Senate is composed of two senators for each province and two for the capital city, directly elected by popular vote. The senators also hold office for six years. This body is renewed by half every three years, and its members may not be re-elected.

Laws may originate in either of the Chambers of Congress, by means of bills introduced by their members, or by the executive. The executive has twenty days in which to approve or veto a law, and, in the case of the latter, the two Chambers may override the veto by a two-thirds majority.

Bolivia. Congress is composed of a Chamber of Deputies and a Senate. Congressmen are elected by popular and direct suffrage, and plurality of vote.

The Chamber of Deputies has 105 members. Deputies hold office four years, and the Chamber is renewed by half every two years.

The Chamber of Senators is composed of three senators for each department, and they hold office for six years. One-third of the Senate is renewed every two years. Bills may be presented in either of the two chambers, and the President has ten days in which to approve or veto them. If the Congress, by a two-thirds vote of those present, declares that the President's objections are unfounded, the objections are over-ridden, and the President must promulgate the law.

Brazil. Legislative power is exercised by the national Congress, composed of a Chamber of Deputies and a Federal Senate.

The Chamber of Deputies is composed of representatives elected by means of proportional representation by the states, the federal district and the territories. The term of office is four years, and the number of deputies is fixed by law; but it may not be more than one for each 150,000 inhabitants, up to 20, and beyond that limit, the proportion must be of one for each 250,000 inhabitants. The minimum for each state and for the federal district is seven deputies. Each territory elects one deputy.

The senators are elected by the states and the federal district, for terms of eight years, and the body is renewed by half every four years. Each state, as well as the federal district, elects three senators and a substitute for each. The Vice-President of the Republic is the president of the Senate, and he may vote only in case of a tie. The initiative of laws is given to the President of the Republic or to any of the members of the Congress. Once a law is passed by both Chambers, the President has ten days to veto it, and the Congress may override the veto by two-thirds of its votes.

Chile. Congress is composed of a Chamber of Deputies and a Senate.

The deputies are elected by the departments by direct vote, for terms of four years, in the proportion of one for each 30,000 inhabitants and fraction not less than 15,000.

Senators are elected by direct ballot by the nine provincial groups that exist for this purpose. Five senators are elected by each group, for eight-year terms, and half of the Senate is renewed every four years.

The initiative of laws belongs to the President, who may present bills, or to any of the Chambers; but the legislative process in the latter case must be initiated by five senators or ten deputies. The President may disapprove a bill, for which he has a thirty-day period, and the Congress may override his objection by a two-thirds vote.

Colombia. Legislative power lies in a Congress composed of a Senate and a Chamber of Representatives.

The representatives are elected for two years, by direct suffrage, in the proportion of one for each 90,000 inhabitants and fraction not less than 45,000 in the different departments. Each department must have at least three representatives and their respective alternates.

The senators are elected by departments, for four years, at the rate of one for each 190,000 inhabitants and fraction not less than 95,000. In no case may a department have less than three senators. Their substitutes are simultaneously elected.

Laws may originate in either of the Chambers, at the proposal of their respective members or the Ministers of the State. The latter may participate in debates, as may the magistrates of the Supreme Tribunal, members of the Council of State, the Comptroller and the Attorney General of the Republic, but they may not vote. The President has from six to fifteen days to present his objections to a bill, according to its length, and the Congress may override his objections by a simple majority or by two-thirds of the votes cast, according to the case.

Costa Rica. Legislative power is delegated by the people to a body called the Constitutional Congress. This Congress is formed by deputies, elected by direct vote in the provinces, in proportion of one deputy for each 15,000 inhabitants and fraction over 7,500. They remain in office for four years, and their number is renewed by half every two years.

Laws have their origin in the Congress, at the proposal of any of its members, and in the executive, through the Secretaries of State. The President may present his objections to any bill, but the Congress may reconsider it by a two-thirds vote of its members.

Cuba. Legislative power lies in a Congress composed of a Chamber of Representatives and a Senate.

The Chamber is composed of one representative for each 35,000 inhabitants or fraction over 17,500 elected by the provinces for four years, and half are renewed every two years.

There are nine senators for each province, elected for four years, by direct suffrage. Initiative of laws belongs to the senators, representatives, the executive, the Supreme Tribunal, the Superior Electoral Tribunal, the Tribunal of Accounts, and to the people in general at the petition of 10,000 or more citizens. Once a law is approved, the President has ten days in which to veto it, and the Congress may override a veto with a vote in favor of the bill by two-thirds of the total of members of each Chamber.

Dominican Republic. Legislative power is exercised by a National Assembly, composed of a Senate and a Chamber of Deputies.

Deputies are elected by provinces, and by the federal district, at the rate of one for each 60,000 inhabitants and fraction over 30,000, and they hold office for five years.

The senate is composed of a member for each province and one for the federal district of Santo Domingo, all elected by popular vote, for five-year terms.

The initiative of laws belongs to the deputies, the senators, the President of the Republic, and to the Supreme Court of Justice in matters relating to its particular branch of administration. The President has the right to veto a law within a period which may be from three to eight days, according to the urgency of the case. Congress may override the veto by the favorable vote of two-thirds of the members.

Ecuador. Legislative power lies in a National Congress, composed of a Chamber of Senators and a Chamber of Deputies.

The Chamber of Deputies has the function of electing, from among their own members, the components of the Council of State. Deputies are elected in the provinces in the ratio of one for each 50,000 inhabitants or fraction over 25,000, and they serve for two-year terms.

The Senate is composed of two senators for each province of the *Sierra* and the *Litoral,* which are the most thickly populated, and one senator for each of the eastern provinces and the Archipelago of Colón, all of whom are elected by direct suffrage for four years. There are, in addition, twelve functional senators.

Congress or any of the Chambers at the petition of three of its members may initiate laws. The executive, the Supreme Court, the Legislative Committee and the National Economic Council also have the right to initiate laws. The President may present his objections to a bill within a ten-day term and return it to the Chamber of origin. The Congress may override the objection by majority of votes cast, in which case the President is obliged to sanction the law.

In Ecuador, there is a Legislative Committee which, in addition to the previously mentioned power, has the exclusive right to propose constitutional amendments and laws. This Committee is formed by representatives of the Chamber of Deputies, of the Senate, the executive, the judiciary, and the Dean of the Law School of the Central University.

El Salvador. Legislative power lies in a *National Assembly,* which is composed of deputies elected in the different departments by direct and popular vote, for one-year terms, and in the proportion of three deputies for each department.

The initiative of laws belongs to the deputies, the President of the Republic, and the Supreme Court of Justice (the latter in matters concerning the judiciary). The Executive may not veto acts of the Assembly which are connected with internal powers of the body, such as approval of elections of its members, regulations and so forth, but he may veto bills in general, within eight days. The Assembly may override his veto by a two-thirds vote.

Guatemala. Legislative power is exercised by a National Congress. This Congress enjoys ample legislative power, and the deputies are directly elected by the people, for terms of four years, in the proportion of one for every 50,000 inhabitants or fraction over 25,000.

The initiative of laws belong to the deputies, the Executive and the Supreme Court of Justice in matters within its jurisdiction. The President may object to bills, within a term of ten days after receiving them, but he must have the agreement of the Council of Ministers. The Congress may override his objections by the favorable vote of two-thirds of the total number of their members. Guatemala has a permanent legislative committee.

Haiti. Legislative power is exercised by a National Assembly composed of a Chamber of Deputies and a Senate.

Deputies, elected by popular vote, serve for four years. The constitution establishes that the law shall fix the number of deputies, based on population.

The Senate is composed of 21 members, elected in the departments by popular vote, and they serve for six years, with indefinite re-election permissible.

The initiative of laws belongs to each of the Chambers and to the Executive. When a bill has been passed, the President may return it with his observations within an eight-day term, and the Assembly may override the presidential resolution by a vote of two-thirds of its members.

Honduras. Legislative power is given to a Congress of Deputies. The deputies are elected for six-year terms in the departments, by popular vote, in the proportion of one incumbent and one substitute for every 25,000 inhabitants or fraction over 12,500. Besides the exclusive powers usually found in all legislative bodies, the Congress scrutinizes the votes for President and Vice-President, and declares the election of the winning candidates.

Initiative of laws belongs to the Deputies, the President of the Republic, and the Supreme Court (the latter exercising the right only in matters relating to the judiciary). The President has ten days in which to return a bill to the Congress with his observations, and the latter may override the veto by a two-thirds vote. However, the constitution establishes that presidental sanction is unnecessary when the Congress is acting on electoral matters or on laws regarding the national budget.

Mexico. Legislative power lies in a Congress composed of a Chamber of Deputies and a Chamber of Senators.

The Chamber is made up of deputies elected for three years, in the proportion of one incumbent and one substitute deputy for each 150,000 inhabitants or fraction over 75,000. The elections are by popular vote. The constitution establishes that no state may have less than two deputies, and no territory less than one. Deputies may not be re-elected.

The Senate is composed of two senators for each state, and two for the federal district, elected for six-year terms, with re-election prohibited for the following term.

The initiative of laws belongs to the President of the Republic, to the Deputies and Senators, and to the legislatures of the states. The President may "observe" a bill during a ten-day term, and Congress may override the "observations" by the vote of two-thirds of its members. The President, however, may not make objections to decisions of the Congress or of any of the Chambers, when they are exercising the functions of an electoral body or of a jury, and he may not oppose a summons to extraordinary sessions made by the permanent committee.

The permanent committee functions during the recess of Congress, and it is composed of fifteen deputies and fourteen senators, appointed by their respective chambers. This body is authorized to pass judgment on pending administrative matters, in order that the machinery of the legislative power may not be interrupted; to decide, for itself or on the proposal of the executive, upon the call for extraordinary sessions of Congress; to approve or disapprove the appointments of the magistrates of the Supreme Court, and to appoint an interim President in the case of resignation or incapacity of the President of the Republic. In this latter case, the permanent committee must immediately convoke an extraordinary session of the Congress in order to take the necessary steps.

Nicaragua. Legislative power is exercised by a Congress, composed of a Chamber of Deputies and a Senate.

Deputies are elected by popular vote for six years by the departments, in the proportion of one incumbent and one substitute for each 30,000 inhabitants or fraction over 15,000. Each department must have at least one deputy.

The Senate is composed of fifteen Senators and fifteen substitutes, besides the ex-presidents of the republic who have held office by popular vote. The senators are elected directly by the people for six-year terms, by an electoral district which comprises the entire nation.

The initiative of laws belongs to the executive, to the deputies, to the Supreme Tribunal in regard to judicial matters, and to the National Electoral Council. This latter body is a sort of electoral tribunal (see Chapter 6). The President may veto a bill within a ten-day term, but must have the agreement of the Council of Ministers, and Congress may override the veto by a vote of two-thirds of its members.

Panama. Legislative power belongs to a National Assembly composed of Deputies elected by popular vote, for four-year terms, at the rate of one for each 15,000 inhabitants or fraction greater than 7,500.

Laws may be initiated by members of the Assembly, the Ministers of State, and the Supreme Tribunal in judicial matters. The President may exercise the veto within a ten-day term, and if this is based on grounds of unconstitutionality, the Assembly may take no further steps until the opinion of the Supreme Tribunal is heard. In other cases, the Assembly may override the veto by a vote of two-thirds of its members.

Paraguay. Legislative power corresponds to a Chamber of Representatives.

This Chamber does not possess broad powers. The President of the Republic has the initiative of laws referring to the budget, expenditures, monetary questions, amnesties and military matters.

Representatives are elected by the people, in the proportion of one for each 25,000 inhabitants, for five-year terms. In the same election, a third of the total number of representatives is elected to act as substitutes.

The initiative of laws belongs to the representatives, with the exceptions mentioned above where the executive has this power. The latter may exercise two types of veto, within a ten-day period. If he completely rejects a bill, this may not be discussed until the following legislature. If he objects to only part of the bill the Chamber may override the veto by a two-thirds vote of its members.

Peru. Congress is composed of a Chamber of Deputies and a Senate. The constitution establishes that the number of Deputies is to be fixed by law, determining which shall be the electoral districts. As of the present time, there are 150 deputies, who are elected by the people for five-year terms.

The number of senators should also be fixed by law. At present, these are 50, elected for six-year terms. Article 89 of the constitution mentions a functional Senate, but we have heard nothing of its having been created yet.

The initiative of laws belongs to the Congress, to the executive, and to the Supreme Court of Justice in judiciary matters. Article 128 of the constitution establishes that the President must promulgate a law within ten days of its having been passed by the Congress. If he does not do so, the Constitution authorizes the president of the Congress to promulgate the law, and to order its publication in some periodical.

Uruguay. Legislative power corresponds to a General Assembly composed of a Chamber of Representatives and a Chamber of Senators.

The Chamber of Representatives is composed of 99 deputies, elected by popular vote, following a system of proportional representation in the different departments. Each department must have at least two deputies, and the term of office is four years.

The Senate is composed of 30 members, elected by popular vote, also by a system of proportional representation, and for terms of four years.

The initiative of laws belongs to either of the two chambers, at the petition of any of its members, or to the executive by means of his ministers. After a law has been approved by Congress, the executive may object to it within a ten-day term, and Congress, meeting in a General Assembly, may override the veto by three-fifths of their votes.

There is a permanent committee in Uruguay, composed of four senators and seven deputies, elected by their respective chambers, but always following the system of proportional representation. It is the duty of this committee to safeguard the constitution and the laws; to call the Congress to extraordinary session; and, if the Congress is dissolved, to function until the new Congress has been elected.

Venezuela. Legislative power lies in a Congress composed of a Chamber of Deputies and a Senate.

The Chamber is composed of one deputy for each 40,000 inhabitants or fraction greater than 20,000 elected by electoral districts. Each electoral district must have at least one representative. There are, in addition, two deputies for each territory, and all deputies serve for five years.

The Senate is composed of two senators and two substitutes, elected by the states and the federal district, by popular vote, for five-year terms.

Laws may have their origin in any of the Chambers, by three of its members, or at the request of the President of the Republic. Ministers of State and magistrates of the Supreme Court of Justice may participate in discussions about bills, but may not vote. After a law has been passed, the President may return it within a ten-day term with his objections, and if these refer to minor alterations, Congress may accept or reject them by simple majority vote. If the veto refers to an essential aspect of the law, Congress must have a two-thirds vote to override the veto.

There is a Permanent Committee in Venezuela, composed of the President and Vice-President of Congress, and 20 of its members elected by their Chambers. It is the duty of this committee to safeguard the constitution and to study pending bills; it calls extraordinary sessions of the Congress, collaborates with the President of the Republic in the preparation of the law on the national budget, and carries out other minor administrative functions.

SUGGESTED READINGS

English:

Amadeo, Santos P., *Argentine Constitutional Law,* New York, Columbia University Press, 1941.

Calcott, Wilford H., *Liberalism in Mexico,* Stanford University Press, 1931.

Christensen, A. N., "The Role and Organization of Legislative Assemblies in Latin America," in *The Evolution of Latin American Government,* A. N. Christensen, Ed., New York, Henry Holt & Co., 1951, pp. 446-454.

Crampton, Ethel M., "The Legislative Departments in the Latin American Constitutions," *Southwestern Political Science Quarterly,* II, September, 1921.

Fitzgibbon, Russell H., Ed., *The Constitutions of the Americas,* Chicago University Press, 1948.

Gibson, William M., *The Constitutions of Colombia,* Durham, N. C., Duke University Press, 1948.

James, Herman G., *The Constitutional System of Brazil,* Washington, D. C., Carnegie Institution, 1923.

Macdonald, Austin F., *Government of the Argentine Republic,* New York, Thomas Y. Crowell Co., 1942.

Macdonald, Austin F., *Latin American Politics and Government,* New York, Thomas Y. Crowell Co., 1949.

Schurz, William L., *Latin America,* New York, E. P. Dutton & Co., Inc., 1949.

Stevenson, John R., *The Chilean Popular Front,* Philadelphia, University of Pennsylvania Press, 1942.

Other Languages:

Antezana Paz, Franklin, *Le Regime Parlementaire en Bolivia,* Paris, 1933.

Aranha, Oswaldo, *Naturaleza Jurídica do Estado Federal,* São Paulo, 1937.

Barcena Echeveste, O., *Contribución a la Historia Política del Paraguay,* Asunción, 1948.

Baptista, Octavio, *Venezuela, Su Historia y sus Métodos de Gobierno,* Guadalajara (México), 1942.

Lazcano y Mazón, A. M., *Constituciones Políticas de América,* La Habana, 1942.

Llana Barrios, Mario, *El Juicio Político; Estudio Constitucional Histórico-Político,* Montevideo, 1942.

Mijares Palencia, José, *El Gobierno Mexicano: Su Organización y Funcionamiento,* México, D. F., 1936.

Paredes, Manuel R., *Política Parlamentaria de Bolivia,* La Paz, 1911.

Rodríguez Piñeres, E., *Táctica Parlamentaria,* Bogotá, 1937.

Roig de Leuchsenring, E., *Los Grandes Movimientos Políticos Cubanos en la República,* La Habana, 1943.

Sánchez, Viamonte, C., *Derecho Constitucional,* Buenos Aires, 1945.

Villa González, León, *El Principio de la División de Poderes en nuestras Constituciones,* México, D. F., 1942.

Wolff, Ernesto, *Tratado de Derecho Constitutional Venezolano,* 2 vols., Caracas, 1945.

CHAPTER 6

The Judiciary

On achieving independence, the Latin American countries found that they had to adapt their judicial institutions to the new form of government they had taken. During the first years, political disturbances and prevailing unsettled conditions prevented them from making much headway, and they were forced to continue using the institutions of the colonial judiciary. A gap opened between the political structure, represented by the new constitutions, and the legal structure for the administration of justice inherited from the old regime. We have seen that in colonial times there also existed a gap between the legal principles of the mother country and the colonial judiciary empowered to apply those principles in a very different environment. These two gaps continued for many years into the republican era, as a legal system is not easy to improvise. The combination of these factors has left a definite mark upon the Latin American judiciary.

Having this in mind, it is pertinent to give a brief description of the structure and functions of the colonial judiciary in order to understand more completely the place occupied by the administration of justice in the Latin American governments, as well as its function in politics.

Colonial Judiciary. The highest and final court was, of course, the Council of Indies. In theory, any case could be brought before it, but in practice, financial restrictions were placed upon the litigants who desired to use this right, which prevented most cases from reaching that Court. Distance also, with its natural delays, made many inhabitants of the colonies give up the idea of appealing to the Council. In the majority of the cases, heavy guarantees to ensure payment of the costs were required. When the Supreme Court of Spain was established, the situation remained more or less the same; therefore the highest court of justice had slight influence upon the life of the colonies.

118

After independence, the most important change introduced by the new republics was the creation of a Supreme Court that occupied the place of the Spanish higher tribunal. This Court today has a much wider jurisdiction than the Council of Indies ever had and is found in all the countries.

The *Audiencia* was, in practice, the highest court in colonial government. It was a court of appeals, although, as we indicated in Chapter 1, it performed other administrative and advisory functions not necessarily of a judicial nature. The Spanish colonial government never had the modern conception of separation of powers, and many officials of the judiciary performed administrative and legislative functions. The *Audiencia* had original jurisdiction in administrative matters, and criminal jurisdiction over violations that occurred within a certain distance of their seat. The justices, or *oidores,* were important members of the community, well familiarized with local problems, and, as a rule, greatly respected by the inhabitants.

The republican counterparts of the *Audiencia* are the appellate courts which in various countries have kept the Spanish name of *Audiencia.* The only important change introduced in this organ was the result of the principle of separation of power, and today they function mostly as courts of second instance within the administration of justice. The original jurisdiction of the *Audiencia* in administrative matters constituted the colonial antecedent to the Tribunals of Administrative Litigation that exist in many republics. In others, the Appellate Courts have kept this jurisdiction, as in the days of the colonial *Audiencia.*

The jurisdiction possessed by the colonial *Audiencia* was extended in republican days to the cognizance of all criminal cases in most of the countries. For this purpose, the courts have been divided into Chambers of Civil and Criminal Jurisdiction. In Latin America, as a rule, the District Judges in criminal cases only gather the evidence and indict the accused; cases are tried before a higher tribunal.

Under the *Audiencia* there were the provincial justices: *Gobernadores, Corregidores* and *Alcaldes Mayores.* They had original jurisdiction and tried civil and criminal cases, functioning as a rule as courts of first instance. They could also hear appeals from lower courts in some cases, and in others share their functions with the

local judges in the important urban centers. They had jurisdiction
in cases between Spaniards and Indians, but not between Indians
themselves, as this function was entrusted to the *Corregidores de
Pueblos de Indios.*

In republican Latin America, these functions are entrusted to
the Judges of First Instance, although the names used in the constitutions, as we shall see later, vary in different countries.

The municipal or local judiciary, in colonial days, was in the
hands of the *Alcalde Ordinario.* It is well to remember that he was
also a municipal official and presided over the meeting of the *Cabildo*
and, therefore, combined administrative functions with the dispen-
sation of justice, like the other organs of the colonial judiciary. The
jurisdiction of the *Alcalde* covered all minor cases arising in the
locality, and he acted on many occasions as a judge of first instance.
In larger centers of population, there were usually two *Alcaldes
Ordinarios,* and the cases were distributed equally between them.
The Latin American republics have naturally separated the administrative functions of the *Alcalde* from the judiciary ones, and today
the latter are administered by the municipal judges or justices of the
peace.

Colonial Legal System. The colonial judiciary was entrusted
with the interpretation and application of Spanish positive law. The
Laws of the Indies were especial legislation applied to the Spanish
American colonies, but together with them there existed the Spanish
laws and a series of new laws, orders, and regulations passed from
time to time by the colonial government. One characteristic of these
laws was the exaggeration of detail and absence of adequate codification which hampered the efficiency of the administration of justice.
Politics and influence played an important role, and the abuses of
litigation were in many cases a serious concern for the inhabitants
of the colonies. It is a well-known fact that on many occasions colonial officials protested against the large numbers of attorneys who
were allowed to come from Spain to practice in America, and they
demanded from the King that a ban be established on the immigration of attorneys. In general, there was little respect for the written
law, and a Spanish proverb says, *"hecha la ley, hecha la trampa"*
(as the law is made, so is the trick). Colonial monopoly stimulated
contraband and, therefore, the practice of evading the law.

Let us repeat that the Spanish civil and criminal legislation enforced in the peninsula was good enough for its time, but it was in need of important modifications when the independence of Latin America occurred. In the nineteenth century, most of the European countries followed the example of France and the Napoleonic Code, made important legislative reforms and codified their laws. Spain did the same, but not until after the independence of the South American republics, so the benefits of the Spanish reform did not reach the new countries. It is true that the republics modeled some of their legislation after the new Spanish laws, but they never experienced the direct influence of the changes. The only two countries that received the new Spanish laws were Cuba and Puerto Rico.

During the first years of the republican era, the legislative attention of the new governments was centered on the political aspects; new constitutions, constitutional amendments, and electoral laws. The colonial machinery patterned to serve a centralizing government survived. Many of the officials of the colonial regime were kept, as judges and magistrates can be improvised no more than laws. Dilatory practices, red tape, the written system in all types of cases, and the influence of the Spanish notarial institutions were barriers in the administration of justice.

The influence has been so strong that in many countries some of the practices prevail today. An illustration of this is the system that requires that all documents be written on special sealed paper provided by the government, which is a tax upon the exercise of the legal profession.

Republican Judiciary. The new republics maintained the fundamental organs of the colonial judiciary. The judicial hierarchy was kept in the same form, and the only difference, as we have said, was that each nation created its own Supreme Tribunal of Justice. All the present-day constitutions maintain the principle of absolute independence of the judiciary from the other two organs of government. There is a strong trend today to allow the higher court to control the appointments and promotions of the magistrates and judges of the lower courts. In many countries, the Supreme Court prepares the budget of the judiciary in order to assure its economic independence. The majority of the countries have established the judicial career as a branch of the civil service, with the system of promotions and tenure. The system of popular election of judges and justices has not been followed. In some countries, where election exists, it is made by the members of the legislature; therefore it is never direct and popular as in the United States. Which of the two systems is best has been the subject of long controversies. For Latin America, and for Spain, judges and justices are considered members of a learned profession and specialists, and not direct representatives of the people.

All the republics have an Attorney-General and a series of subalterns, who are the legal representatives of the state and who intervene in all cases in which public interest is involved. The function is important and has been specifically regulated in the constitutions. All countries, of course, also have a Secretary of Justice, but he is only the administrative head of the branch of the executive that deals with the legal problems of the government. In view of the trend toward independence of the judiciary, and the important position occupied by the Supreme Court, the role of the Secretary of Justice has been gradually losing political power, and he functions more as the President's representative in his relations with the judiciary as a power.

Special Institutions. During the republican era, and with variations in the different countries, the judiciary has been taking over certain functions within the machinery of government. Some of these institutions have been caused by the direct influence of the Spanish and French legal systems. Administrative Litigation and the Writ of Cassation are examples of this influence. Other institutions are of a political nature and have been caused by the desire to protect the democratic process, or to guarantee civil liberties and the sovereignty of the constitution. Examples of this are the Electoral Tribunals, the Writ of *Amparo* and the Tribunals of Constitutional Guarantees. We shall endeavor to describe, briefly, these institutions which are characteristic of the area.

Administrative Litigation. Spanish and French legal theory have always distinguished between the State as a political entity and the State as the administrator of public services. The political sovereignty of the State does not reach down into the relations between the administration and the individual when the government is acting as an administrator of the Commonwealth. If the State, in this capacity, affects private interests, the citizen has the right to legal remedies. This system was maintained in Latin America, and the State has always been considered, in this second aspect, as acting in a private capacity and subject to obligations, with full legal personality, as if it were a private person. As such, it may intervene in matters of private business, sign contracts, assume obligations and resort to the tribunals of ordinary justice to claim its rights. Of course, in this capacity, the State can also be sued by those with whom it has contracted obligations.

When the State, in its administrative function, impairs private interests, it must give legal account of its conduct and make good the damage caused. Thus a special jurisdiction to handle these matters has been created. This is the jurisdiction of Administrative Litigation, by means of which the courts of justice take cognizance of matters between the individual and the State, when the latter acts as administrator of the commonwealth or in a private legal capacity.

The procedure of Administrative Litigation requires that the parties must first exhaust the administrative channels. That is to say, individuals must file claims and appeals before the administrative branch of the government that has caused him damage. If he finds no satisfaction there, he resorts to the judicial branch, and the case is brought before the courts of Administrative Litigation. In the countries in which these courts do not exist, the cases are tried in the ordinary courts of justice. Of course the law contains detailed regulations and establishes the necessary safeguards to avoid the use of this right by unscrupulous litigants who might abuse the privilege and hinder public administration.

In practice, in many cases the executive branch of the government does not pay much attention to the decision of the courts. In matters that involve money, especially payment of taxes, when the adverse decision has been rendered on the administrative level, as a rule it is required that the amount of tax be deposited before resort to the judiciary is allowed. This, of course, discourages many claims, as once the money is in the Treasury, it is not so easy to get it back. There is always the possibility that the debt will be duly acknowledged by the Administration, but there are no funds in the budget with which to pay it.

Countries where Administrative Litigation has been constitutionally regulated are Colombia, where this jurisdiction belongs to the Council of State; Guatemala and Panama, whose constitutions carefully explain the functions of the Administrative Tribunal; Paraguay, where there is a Superior Tribunal of Administrative Litigation that functions at the same time as Tribunal of Accounts; and Uruguay, where this type of jurisdiction is defined as follows: "The Tribunal of Administrative Litigation shall be concerned with suits against illegal actions of the Administration committed in the exercise of its functions whether against individuals, private concerns or public employees."

Constitutional Guarantees and "Amparo." In all the countries, the Supreme Court is considered as the guardian of the constitution and has the right to declare the unconstitutionality of any law, decree or regulation enacted by the other branches of the government, as well as by any lower organ of the judiciary. In some countries, this right is specifically stated in the text of the constitution, and in others, it comes from the positive laws and legal precedents. The function is similar to that of the Supreme Courts of other parts of the world that have a modern constitutional structure. There are countries, Cuba being one, that have followed the precedent of the Spanish Republican constitution of 1931 and created a special court, called Tribunal of Constitutional Guarantees, that operates as a branch of the judiciary. In Cuba, this court constitutes a Chamber of the Supreme Court of Justice.

The protection of civil liberties has been the concern of Latin American countries. Mexico, for example, in its constitution of 1917, created the "Writ of *Amparo*." *Amparo*, which literally means protection, is an urgent judicial action aimed at the correction of a situation of fact, by means of which a fundamental law is violated. Roughly, it corresponds to a court injunction or a "cease and desist" order in the United States system. It has its precedent in the Spanish codes of civil procedure, in which the system of interdicts has been consecrated. An interdict is also a rapid way of getting protection when a right has been violated. There are interdicts to recover possession of property and even interdicts against potential damage caused by buildings erected by a neighbor. This principle has found its expression in constitutional law by means of the Writ of *Amparo*. When a basic civil right is violated, the citizen has the right to ask for quick protection from the courts of justice.

Cassation and Judicial Review. The Supreme Courts of Latin America, when they function as tribunals of last instance, have three types of jurisdiction. In the first place, they have original jurisdiction in special matters such as serious accusations against government officials, problems of international law and conflicts of jurisdiction between different branches of the administration. In the second place, they operate as appellate courts, and completely review the cases submitted to their consideration, basing their decision upon facts as well as upon the principles of law that have been involved in the litigation. Lastly, they take cognizance of writs of cassation. In these cases, the court deals exclusively with problems of law, and they are not empowered to examine or to pass judgment upon facts. They accept the facts as having been declared proved by the lower courts. This part of the case cannot be questioned. The court decides whether the lower court has committed an error when evaluating the facts that constitute evidence in the case and also whether any substantive law or procedural law has been violated. When the court acts in this capacity, it functions as a Court of Cassation. It realizes a purely technical function. If the court finds that a violation has been committed, it annuls the decision of the lower court and renders a new decision, judging the case on its merits. Cassation aims at guaranteeing the preservation of the legal structure of the nation, and the opinions of the court constitute legal doctrine or precedent, serving as a guide for the future interpretation of the laws and the constitution.

Judicial Review is also a right of the Supreme Court. As has been indicated, some countries specifically state this principle in their constitutions. Of course, in countries suffering from the strong executive (Chapter 4), the political power of the Supreme Court is not as efficiently exercised as in the United States. As Professor Christensen has stated, "Power struggles between the executive and the courts, or the congress and the judiciary, like those which took place in the United States in 1936-37 or 1866-68, are unknown." [1]

Nevertheless, the Supreme Court and its justices, especially the president, play an important role in politics. In many countries, after a coup d'etat, a revolution or a violent change of government, the contending parties have resorted to the practice of asking the president of the court or one of its members to take the government over provisionally, and preside over it until a new election is held. This practice has been frequent in the political life of Latin America in the twentieth century. It is another interesting trend due to the fact that, of the three powers of government, the judiciary commands the most respect.

By exercising the power of judicial review and declaring the unconstitutionality of an act, the Supreme Court also influences public opinion and gives aid and support to the political groups or parties that are contending for legality against the abuses of power of the executive. Therefore, it is fair to admit that, although judicial review in important political issues does not produce the immediate effects of stopping the unconstitutional acts of a powerful executive, it often acts as a curb to abuses of power. It is also helpful when the constitutional violation has been committed by a lower branch of the government, in which case constitutional principles are maintained with no opposition from the executive.

Electoral Jurisdiction. Another indication of the trend of giving more and more participation to the judiciary in the political life of the country is the institution of Electoral Jurisdiction. It shows the desire to put an end to electoral fraud and the recognition of the fact that the judiciary occupies an important rank in the structure of government. It is an effort to curb abuses of power of the strong executive, and it seems that the modern Latin American legislators have turned their eyes toward the judicial branch of government to secure a better balance of power. The countries that have created Electoral Tribunals follow. Those countries have given supreme authority in electoral matters to the judiciary, and have also placed in their jurisdiction administrative functions relating to the electoral process. Electoral Tribunals are empowered to issue voting certificates and even to take the electoral census.

---

[1] Christensen, A. N., "Strong Governments and Weak Courts," *The Evolution of Latin American Governments*, New York, Henry Holt & Co., 1951, p. 469.

FEDERAL JUDICIARY

Country	Supreme Court (how chosen)	Lower Courts	Other Features
Argentina	By President and the Cabinet	Courts of Appeal; District Tribunals	Juries
Brazil	By President with Senate approval	Appellate Tribunal; District Courts	Juries; military courts; electoral judiciary; labor tribunals; state courts
Mexico	By President with Senate approval	Circuit Courts; District Courts	Juries in some cases
Venezuela	By the Legislative	Courts of Appeal; District Courts	

CENTRALIZED JUDICIARY

Country	Supreme Court (how chosen)	Lower Courts	Other Features
Bolivia	By Chamber of Deputies	Courts of Appeal; District Courts	Independent, responsible only to Congress
Chile	By President and the Court itself	Courts of Appeal; Courts of First Instance	Administrative Tribunal; Electoral Tribunal
Colombia	By Congress from a panel prepared by President	Superior Tribunals; District Courts	Council of the State; Juries in Criminal Cases
Costa Rica	By the Legislative Assembly	Courts of Appeal; Courts of First Instance	Independent from the Executive
Cuba	By President from a panel prepared by Electoral College	Provincial Courts; Courts of First Instance	Electoral Tribunal; Tribunal of Constitutional Guarantees
Dom. Republic	By the Senate	Courts of Appeal; Courts of First Instance	Land Tribunals
Ecuador	By Congress	Superior Courts; Courts of First Instance	....
El Salvador	By the National Assembly	Chambers of Third and Second Instance; Judges of First Instance	Juries for some Offenses
Guatemala	By Congress	Courts of Appeal; Courts of First Instance	"Amparo" Tribunal; Administrative Courts
Haiti	By the President	Courts of Appeal; Courts of First Instance	Land Tribunal; Labor Courts
Honduras	By Congress	Courts of Appeal; Courts of First Instance	....
Nicaragua	By Congress	Courts of Appeal; District Tribunals	Electoral Courts
Panama	By President and Cabinet	Courts of Appeal; Courts of First Instance	Administrative Courts
Paraguay	By President and Council of State	Courts of Appeal; Courts of First Instance	Tribunal of Accounts
Peru	By Congress from a list prepared by the President	Superior Courts; Courts of First Instance	....
Uruguay	By the General Assembly	Courts of Appeal; Official Courts	Administrative Tribunal; Electoral Court

ORGANIZATION AND FUNCTIONS

THE FEDERAL SYSTEMS

Argentina. At the head of the administration of federal justice is the Supreme Court. Its jurisdiction covers all matters which may require the application of the constitution or of a federal law, with the exception of tax laws. It also embraces all matters of public or private international law. In some cases, the federal judiciary has original jurisdiction; in others, it functions as a court of appeals or Court of Cassation.

The Supreme Tribunal is composed of five members, appointed by the President of the Republic with the approval of the Senate, who serve for life, during good behavior. In order to be a member of the Supreme Tribunal, it is necessary to be an attorney and to have practiced for ten years.

There are, in addition, six Courts of Appeal, composed of three or five magistrates, depending on the locality, appointed in the same manner and with the same requisites as the magistrates of the Supreme Tribunal. Under these courts are the District Tribunals, having first instance jurisdiction in all matters relating to federal law. Some of these districts have more than one judge, and the cases are divided between them, separating the criminal from the civil matters. District judges must be attorneys with at least three years of practice. They are appointed in the same manner as the other components of the federal judiciary. There are juries in Argentina.

Brazil. The federal judiciary is divided into two classes: the ordinary and the special. Ordinary federal justice is administered by the Federal Supreme Tribunal, and the lower courts under it. The special judiciary comprises the Military Courts, the Electoral Courts, and the Labor Courts. The Federal Supreme Tribunal has original and appellate jurisdiction. It has original jurisdiction over criminal violation on the part of the President of the Republic, or by the high functionaries of the State; over cases of litigation between the States and the Union, or between a foreign country and the Brazilian nation, as well as other matters of public international law. It has ordinary appellate jurisdiction in matters of unconstitutionality. This tribunal is composed of magistrates appointed by the President of the Republic, with the approval of the Senate, who serve for life, during good behavior.

An Appellate Federal Tribunal, in Rio de Janeiro, is composed of nine justices, appointed in the same manner as the former. As its name implies, its principal function consists in serving as a Court of Second Instance. The constitution establishes that federal courts of appeal be created in other regions of the country.

Under the Appellate Federal Tribunal are the District Courts, functioning in the different states and in the federal district itself. These are courts of first instance having original jurisdiction. Their judges are also appointed by the President, with the approval of the Senate.

The Military Courts are regulated in the Brazilian constitution. There is no essential difference from the military justice of other nations. However, Article 108 of the constitution contains a disposition that seems a dangerous one to us since it says: "These special courts may be extended to civilians, in cases provided in the law, for the repression of crimes against the external security of the country or against its military institutions." This can permit a majority in Congress to obstruct the administration of ordinary civil justice.

The electoral judiciary has the following organs: a Superior Electoral Court; Regional Electoral Tribunals, Electoral Boards and Electoral judges. The Superior Electoral Court is located in the capital and has jurisdiction over all matters relating to the elections. It is composed of seven judges, five of whom are appointed by the Federal Tribunal of Justice, and two by the President of the Republic, but at the suggestion of the Tribunal. Decisions of the Electoral Court, which may be considered a violation of the constitution, may be appealed before the Federal Supreme Tribunal.

The organs of the administration of justice in connection with Labor are a Superior Labor Tribunal, Regional Labor Tribunals and Boards of Conciliation. These special courts have jurisdiction over labor disputes. The jury system is used in Brazil only in criminal matters.

Mexico. The federal tribunals have jurisdiction over two types of matters: (1) any controversy in which a fundamental political right has been violated, as civil liberty cases; (2) all matters which may arise from the application of a federal law, a treaty or an admiralty case, as well as those in which one of the parties is the federation or one of the states. This jurisdiction extends to certain cases of public international law and to those of writs of *Amparo*.

The supreme authority in federal matters resides in the Supreme Court, formed of 21 magistrates appointed by the President of the Republic, with the approval of the Senate. The tribunal is divided into civil, administrative, criminal and labor chambers, each with five judges. The magistrates of the Court serve for life, during good behavior, and they elect from among their number a president, who is not assigned to any particular chamber. The Supreme Court has original jurisdiction in controversies between states, between branches of the state regarding constitutionality of its acts, and in all cases in which the Federation may be a party.

The other organs of the federal judiciary are the Circuit and District Courts. These depend on the Supreme Court, who appoints their members and transfers them wherever it is considered convenient for the best administration of justice. The administration of federal justice is, therefore, considerably independent, as far as these lower courts are concerned.

For many years, Mexico employed the jury system. Today, it is maintained by the federal judiciary only in cases of freedom of speech. In some states, it is used in criminal matters.

Venezuela. The constitution declares that the judiciary is independent, and that it is integrated by the Supreme Tribunal and the other tribunals and courts established by the law. However, this independence is not clear, if one considers that the members of the Supreme Tribunal are appointed by the legislators for a term of five years. This places the members of the tribunal under the sole authority of one of the powers of the state, with no intervention from the executive, and thus makes impossible the balance between them.

The Federal Supreme Tribunal takes cognizance of accusations made against the President of the Republic, and against high functionaries of the state, and it may annul any law or government measure that violates the constitution. It has jurisdiction, as a Tribunal of Cassation, in certain important matters enumerated in the constitution, and as an appellate court in all cases of violation of criminal laws, in which the accused is subject to imprisonment. It also has jurisdiction in certain cases of administrative litigation, controversies between the states and matters of international law.

As lower organs of the federal judiciary, there are the Courts of Appeal and District Courts. The judges and magistrates of these lower courts are appointed by the Supreme Tribunal.

THE CENTRALIZED SYSTEMS

Bolivia. The Supreme Tribunal represents and administers the judiciary, and not only appoints the judges and magistrates of the lower courts, but controls the budget and orders the payment of salaries for all members of the branch. The Supreme Tribunal takes cognizance of appeals from the lower courts, matters of unconstitutionality, cases of public law and all litigation arising from the National Patronage of the Church. This tribunal is composed of ten magistrates, appointed by the Chamber of Deputies for ten-year terms, and each is chosen from a panel of three persons, proposed by the Senate. It is divided into two chambers, one for civil and the other for criminal matters. The president is elected by the magistrates from among their own number.

In the departments, there are the higher tribunals, which function as Courts of Second Instance. Their magistrates are appointed by the Supreme Tribunal for six years. There are also Courts of First Instance, whose judges are appointed in the same manner as the former, and for four years.

Chile. The Supreme Court exercises supervision and economic control of the judiciary. The members of the Court are chosen by the President from a list of five individuals, proposed by the Court itself. Two members of the Court of Appeals, oldest in service, occupy places on the list. The other three places are filled in accordance with the merits of the candidates. The jurisdiction of the Supreme Court covers appeals in matters of importance, the unconstitutionality of laws, and problems of jurisdiction and conflicts between the lower courts.

The Courts of Appeal function as organs of Second Instance in principal cities, and their magistrates are appointed by the President of the Republic, from a panel proposed by the Supreme Court. There are, in addition, Courts of First Instance, served by *"jueces letrados"* (attorneys), in the different departments. These are appointed by the President from a panel presented by the Court of Appeal.

The constitution also established Administrative Tribunals for cases of administrative litigation and of arbitrary acts committed by government officials. An Electoral Qualification Tribunal has cognizance of the election returns for the presidency, deputies and senators. This tribunal acts as a jury in the determination of the facts and gives judgment in accordance with the law. It is composed of five members, chosen from among ex-congressmen and ex-members of the judiciary.

Colombia. The judiciary is divided into two branches: ordinary justice, over which the Supreme Tribunal of Justice presides; and administrative justice, which is under the authority of the Council of State.

The Supreme Tribunal is served by twelve magistrates who are elected for five-year terms and may be re-elected indefinitely. The magistrates are appointed half by the Chamber and half by the Senate, from panels presented by the President of the Republic. The original jurisdiction of this tribunal is extended to the judgment of the high officials of the nation who may be accused before the Senate. It also takes cognizance of illegal acts committed by high administrative officers and all litigation concerning diplomatic agents, in the cases recognized by international law. As a Tribunal of Cassation and of Appeals it deals with matters of ordinary justice as well as with problems of unconstitutionality.

The national territory is divided into judicial districts, in each of which a Superior Tribunal functions as an organ of second instance,

Its magistrates are appointed by the Supreme Tribunal. Matters in
first instance correspond to the District Judges, and to the Municipal
Judges in local cases of lesser importance.

Administrative jurisdiction covers the relationship between the
government and individuals in administrative matters. It is very like
the French system, and its superior organ is the Council of the State.
The magistrates are appointed by Congress, three by each Chamber,
and the president is appointed by the national executive. There are
Administrative Tribunals in each department, whose magistrates serve
for two years and are designated by the Council of the State. In certain
criminal matters, juries are used.

Costa Rica. The Supreme Tribunal is composed of seventeen magistrates at present and is divided into various chambers. The magistrates
are appointed for four years by the Congress and may be re-elected
indefinitely. The Congress also appoints substitute magistrates to fill
any vacancies that may occur.

The Supreme Tribunal takes cognizance, as a court of cassation, of
criminal matters, civil and administrative ones, and those of unconstitutionality. It also has jurisdiction over matters of international public
law, and problems of jurisdiction among the lower courts.

There are, besides, four Courts of Appeal that function principally
as organs of second instance and, of course, the traditional Courts of
First Instance. The magistrates and judges of the latter two organs
are appointed by the executive.

Cuba. The judicial power is independent, and the Supreme Tribunal exercises supervision and control over the lower courts. Besides
the ordinary judiciary, there is a Tribunal of Constitutional Guarantee,
a Superior Electoral Tribunal and a Tribunal of Accounts. The jurisdiction of the Supreme Tribunal of Justice is broad. It takes cognizance
of writs of cassation in all civil and criminal matters, and functions as
a court of final instance in matters pertaining to administrative litigation. The magistrates are appointed by the president, with the approval of the Senate, from a panel of nine members. Of this panel, four
are designated by the Supreme Court, three by the President of the
Republic, and two by the Law School of the University of Havana.
There are also six Provincial Courts (*Audiencias*), which possess original
jurisdiction in criminal matters and take cognizance of appeals in civil
cases.

Each province is divided into judicial districts, where there are
Courts of First Instance. In important districts, the courts are divided
into civil and criminal branches. The judicial districts are subdivided

into municipal districts where the Municipal Judges function, and there are also Correctional Judges for minor offences.

The Superior Electoral Tribunal is composed of three magistrates of the Supreme Court and two from the Provincial Courts. This tribunal is entrusted with the administrative, as well as the judicial aspect, of the entire electoral procedure. The Tribunal of Constitutional Guarantees, which is meant to function as a chamber of the Supreme Court of Justice, has not been established up to the present time. The Tribunal of Accounts was already mentioned before (Chapter 4).

Dominican Republic. Judicial power is exercised by the Supreme Tribunal of Justice, the Courts of Appeal, the Courts of First Instance, and Justices of the Peace.

The Supreme Tribunal is composed of seven magistrates appointed by the Senate. It takes cognizance, in first and last instance, of actions against the President of the Republic and high functionaries of the state. It also acts as tribunal of last instance in ordinary jurisdiction, and exercises disciplinary authority over the remainder of the organs of the judiciary.

Three Courts of Appeal, whose magistrates are appointed by the Senate, function as organs of second instance in ordinary justice. The nation's territory is divided into judicial districts, with Courts of First Instance. The judges are also appointed by the Senate, for a term of five years. In the communes, the Justices of the Peace appointed by the Senate take cognizance of lesser matters.

Ecuador. The Supreme Tribunal is composed of fifteen magistrates, appointed by the Congress, for six-year terms, with re-election permissible. Its jurisdiction extends, as a Court of Cassation or of final instance, to the cognizance of matters of ordinary justice, as well as to administrative litigation, and some cases of public and private international law. The Tribunal may send a delegate to the sessions of Congress to discuss the laws, but without a vote.

Eight Superior Courts function as courts of appeal, whose magistrates are appointed by Congress for four years. The lower Courts of First Instance have original jurisdiction in ordinary matters, and its judges serve for two years. There are juries for certain criminal cases, but it is necessary to be a lawyer to serve on the jury.

El Salvador. The Supreme Tribunal is composed of seven magistrates appointed for two years by the National Assembly. Besides functioning as a higher court, with the jurisdiction common to such organs, it exercises supervision over the administration of justice, intervenes in the preparation of the budget, and appoints the judges of first instance and the subordinate employes of the judiciary.

The constitution orders the establishment of two Chambers of Third Instance in the capital, and six Chambers of Second Instance distributed throughout the national territory, whose magistrates are appointed by the National Assembly for two-year terms. These tribunals function as courts of appeal in diverse matters of ordinary justice.

The judges of the Courts of First Instance are appointed by the Supreme Tribunal for two years. There are juries in these Courts.

Guatemala. The constitution divides the judiciary into two branches, one of ordinary jurisdiction, and the other of private jurisdiction. The ordinary jurisdiction comprises the Supreme Tribunal of Justice, formed of seven magistrates appointed by the Congress for four years, which functions as an organ of final instance in civil and criminal matters, and of public law in general. The Courts of Appeal also belong to the ordinary jurisdiction, with its members appointed and removed by the Congress, and act as tribunals of second instance. There are also first instance and municipal judges, appointed by the Supreme Tribunal.

As the organs of private jurisdiction, there are the *Amparo* tribunal, which takes cognizance of violations of constitutional rights; the Tribunal of Administrative Litigation; and the Tribunal of Conflicts of Jurisdiction, which decides the cases that may arise between the different administrative branches of the government. The constitution includes the Military Courts among the organs of private jurisdiction.

Haiti. The Tribunal of Cassation takes cognizance in final instance of the matters of law only, and not of facts, but it has jurisdiction in facts as well as law in the decisions of the military courts. It also has jurisdiction over matters of unconstitutionality. The judges of this Tribunal are appointed by the President of the Republic for ten-year terms.

Three Courts of Appeal function as organs of second instance in ordinary matters, whose magistrates are appointed for ten years by the President. The President also appoints the judges of the Courts of First Instance, but their terms are for seven years. Municipal matters of lesser importance are in the hands of the Justices of the Peace.

Honduras. Original jurisdiction of the Supreme Tribunal covers common crimes committed by high authorities, cases of unconstitutionality, revision of important criminal cases, and cases of international law. This tribunal takes cognizance, on appeal, of general matters of ordinary justice. Its magistrates are appointed by Congress for six-year terms.

There are four Courts of Appeal, functioning as organs of second instance, whose magistrates are appointed by the Supreme Tribunal. First instance is in the hands of *Jueces Letrados* (attorneys), located in the different departments, and also appointed by the Supreme Tribunal. The Justices of the Peace in the municipalities are appointed by these *Jueces Letrados*.

Nicaragua. The Supreme Tribunal has economic supervision over the rest of the judiciary and prepares the budget for its approval by the Congress. It functions as a Court of Cassation, taking cognizance over writs of error, *Amparo* and revision. It has original jurisdiction in cases of unconstitutionality. Its seven magistrates are elected by the Congress for six years.

There are five Courts of Appeal in the five principal cities, functioning as organs of second instance. The magistrates are appointed by the Congress for four years. Justice, in the first instance, is entrusted to the District Courts and municipal matters, to the Local Courts. The judges of the latter are appointed by the Supreme Tribunal.

Panama. The Supreme Tribunal functions as a higher tribunal and Court of Cassation. It is composed of five magistrates, appointed by the President of the Republic, with the unanimous approval of the Cabinet and subject to the approval of the National Assembly. These magistrates serve for ten years.

There are, in addition, the Courts of Appeal, as organs of second instance, as well as Courts of First Instance. Their magistrates are appointed by the Supreme Tribunal. The constitution orders the creation of juries.

The Tribunal of Administrative Litigation is composed of three magistrates, appointed in the same manner as those of the Supreme Tribunal.

Paraguay. The Supreme Tribunal is the high chamber of justice in ordinary matters and exercises supervision over the whole judiciary. This tribunal has the power to appoint and remove, at will, the members of the judiciary. Its three magistrates serve for five years and are appointed by the Executive, with the approval of the Council of State.

The Tribunal of Accounts has the unusual feature that it is subordinate to the Supreme Tribunal, and, besides its functions of supervising the national economy, it is entrusted with administrative litigation. Its members are appointed by the President of the Republic, with the approval of the Supreme Tribunal. The magistrates and judges of the Lower Courts and tribunals are appointed in the same manner, for five-year terms. The Council of State greatly controls the judiciary, since it may judge and remove the members of the Supreme Court.

Peru. The Supreme Tribunal has original jurisdiction on all matters of public law. It also takes cognizance, in final instance, of the matters of ordinary jurisdiction and supervises the lower courts. All members of the judiciary serve for life, during good behavior. Those of the Supreme Tribunal are appointed by the Congress from a list of candidates presented by the executive.

In the departments, there are Superior Courts, whose judges are appointed by the Executive from lists proposed by the Supreme Tribunal and the judges of first instance of the respective department. These are appellate courts.

The provincial capitals have Courts of First Instance whose judges are appointed by the President from a list submitted by the superior courts. In the municipalities, there are Justices of the Peace, appointed for a year by the Superior Court.

Uruguay. Cases of ordinary jurisdiction are in the hands of the judiciary, formed of the Supreme Tribunal, Courts of Appeal, Official Courts and Justices of the Peace. There is also special jurisdiction corresponding to the Tribunal of Administrative Jurisdiction, and to an Electoral Tribunal.

The Supreme Tribunal has original jurisdiction in matters of unconstitutionality, international law and admiralty. It functions, furthermore, as the highest tribunal of justice in cases of ordinary jurisdiction, and exercises direct, consultive and economic supervision over the judiciary, whose budget it prepares.

The Tribunal is composed of five magistrates, appointed by the General Assembly, for five years. There are five Courts of Appeal, with jurisdiction in second instance. Their magistrates are appointed for life by the Supreme Tribunal, with the approval of the Senate.

Justice, in the first instance, is in the hands of Courts whose judges are appointed in the same manner as the above, with life tenure as well. Justices of the Peace are appointed by absolute majority of the total members of the Supreme Court and serve for four years. These judges carry out a very special function, consisting in the intervention in the acts of conciliation in civil matters. Article 228 of the constitution states that no civil claim may be instituted "unless it has been previously proved that conciliation has been attempted before a Justice of the Peace. . . ."

The Electoral Tribunal is composed of five members, and it functions as a special tribunal in all matters relating to the electoral process, and decides, in last instance, all electoral claims. The Tribunal of Administrative Litigation is composed of three magistrates appointed for ten years by the Congress.

SUGGESTED READINGS

English:

Amadeo, Santos P., *Argentine Constitutional Law,* New York, Columbia University Press, 1943.

Cleven, N. A. N., *The Political Organization of Bolivia,* Washington, D. C., Carnegie Institution, 1940.

Crampton, Ethel M., "The Judicial Department in the Latin American Constitutions," *Southwestern Political Science Quarterly,* December, 1921.

Christensen, A. N., "Strong Governments and Weak Courts," in *The Evolution of Latin American Governments,* A. N. Christensen, Ed., New York, Henry Holt & Co., 1951, pp. 468-476.

Cunningham, Charles H., *The Audiencia in the Spanish Colonies,* Berkeley, University of California Press, 1919.

Kahle, Louis G., "The Spanish Colonial Judiciary," *The Southwestern Social Science Quarterly,* Vol. XXXII, pp. 27-37.

Macdonald, Austin F., *Latin American Politics and Government,* New York, Thomas Y. Crowell Co., 1949.

Rowe, Leo Stanton, *The Federal System of the Argentine Republic,* Washington, D. C., Carnegie Institution, 1921.

Stuart, Graham H., *The Governmental System of Peru,* Washington, D. C., Carnegie Institution, 1925.

Weddell, Alexander W., *A Comparison of Executive and Judicial Powers under the Constitutions of Argentina and the United States,* Bulletin of William and Mary College, June, 1937.

Other Languages:

Farrera, Agustín, *El Juicio de Amparo,* México, D. F., 1942.

García, Rada, *El Poder Judicial,* Lima, 1944.

Hernández Corujo, E., *Lecciones de Derecho Constitucional Cubano,* La Habana, 1942.

Lancís Sánchez, A., *Derecho Administrativo,* La Habana, 1942.

Lazcano y Mazón, A. M., *Constituciones Políticas de América,* La Habana, 1942.

Morey Otero, S., *Constitución Anotada de la República Oriental del Uruguay,* Montevideo, 1936.

Passalacqua, Paulo A., *O Poder Judiciario na Constituçao Federal e nas Constituiçoes dos Estados,* São Paulo, 1936.

Paz, Luis, *La Corte Suprema de Justicia de Bolivia*, Sucre, 1910.

Picado G., Antonio, *Ley Orgánica del Poder Judicial*, San José (Costa Rica) 1937.

Raveau, Rafael, *Tratado Elemental de Derecho Constitucional Chileno*, Santiago de Chile, 1939.

Ruiz Guinazú, Enrique, *La Magistratura Indiana*, Buenos Aires, 1916.

Ruggeri Parra, Pablo, *Derecho Constitucional Venezolano*, Caracas, 1944.

Zavalia, Clodomiro, *Historia de la Corte Suprema de Justicia de la Republica Argentina*, Buenos Aires, 1920.

Zeledón, Marco Tulio, *Lecciones de Derecho Constitucional*, San José (Costa Rica), 1945.

CHAPTER 7

Local Government

I. PROVINCIAL ADMINISTRATION

The federal republics of Latin America are divided politically into states, which enjoy a certain degree of self-government.

The centralized republics have divided their territory into provinces or departments for the organization of their political administration. On studying these divisions, one should keep the Spanish antecedent in mind. The centralizing policy was the cause of these territorial demarcations, not based upon necessities of local economy, but arbitrarily imposed from above, by those who controlled political power in the colony.

At the time of independence, the same things occurred with the politico-administrative divisions as with the judicial system. The new republics had to keep the colonial structure, because an administrative machinery cannot be created overnight. The pattern of division was one of spatial necessity, following natural boundaries, such as mountains and rivers, with no consideration for the economic capacity or relations of homogeneity of the population. The municipalities, on the contrary, kept these last two factors in mind.

One should also consider the ideological influence exercised in the early years of the republics by the centralizing policy of the French government, when France was divided into departments. Many Latin American territories were literally divided in a straight line by politicians in the capital cities, who were totally ignorant or neglectful of the local conditions. Even French terminology prevailed, and does to this day, as most of the Latin American countries use the term "department" instead of "province." These divisions are destined to satisfy political interests rather than to serve the general needs of the region. In the federal states the local administration is organized in a constitutional document, while in the centralized governments, the local machinery is controlled by state legislation of the province or department. Political power is divided between the three traditional branches of the administration, and the executive corresponds to a governor, called *"presidente," "intendente"* or *"prefecto"* in the different countries. The terminology makes little difference, and, with the exception of Cuba and Venezuela, the governor is the real head of the local administration, although his autonomy varies greatly according to the countries, since some of them have adopted a certain degree of decentralization. The governor works with the provincial legislature whose members may either be elected by the people, or appointed by the central government. This body votes laws to govern the region and has the other characteristics of this organ.

In the federal states, the judicial machinery is more complicated and constitutes the third organ of the local government with the traditional hierarchy, from the Supreme Tribunal to the lower courts. In the centralized governments, the local judiciary exercises little influence, since it is generally controlled by the central government.

The internal organization of each of the Latin American countries will be discussed, beginning with the federal governments. Due to the structure of these, there are more motives for political friction with the central powers. Later, the internal divisions of the centralized governments will be examined, first analyzing those which have adopted a system of provincial decentralization, and concluding with the other countries.

THE FEDERAL SYSTEMS

Federalism in Latin America did not serve, as in the United States, to unite diverse and politically autonomous states, but it was made use of by *caudillos* and local leaders to disunite what had been political units during the colonial administration. These federalist ideas existed even in small countries that had no need of the flexible political organization to be found in a federation.

The nature of the federal states of Latin America is very different from that of the United States. In North America, the states existed as semi-autonomous colonies before the appearance of the national state. In Latin America, the phenomenon is directly opposite. The central power already existed, and the geographic units (states or provinces) were the result of a concession or privilege granted by the national government. Therefore the federal state was an artificial creation and not a social and historical fact that was later regulated by means of a federal constitution, as occurred in the United States.

Another characteristic of the federal states in Latin America is that the sections of poor and semi-agricultural economies, regardless of the inhabitants' enthusiasm for self-government, must of necessity be more closely connected to the national government, because the government controls the monetary resources that make possible the economic existence of the local units. This phenomenon is reproduced in the relations between the provinces and the municipalities, as we shall see later. To all of this we might add the tendency toward the strong executive and the historical antecedent of colonial administrative centralization.

The political organization of the provinces or states in Argentina, Brazil and Mexico is quite similar. In Venezuela it has more special characteristics. In the first three countries, executive power is vested in a governor or president elected by popular vote. The legislative power corresponds to an assembly or congress which in Argentina and Brazil may be unicameral or bicameral, and in Mexico and Venezuela is unicameral. In Argentina and Brazil the larger states have, as a general rule, adopted the bicameral form. The judicial branch has the normal hierarchy in its administration, ranging from the justices of the peace or municipal judges to a superior court of appeals. In some of the countries, the judges are appointed for life, while in others they are appointed for a certain period of time. As a general rule, the local courts are rather limited in jurisdiction, since the tendency is for the central government to keep for itself the important cases, especially those pertaining to economic and criminal matters.

In Venezuela, the State Legislative Assembly is in charge not only of the law-making process, but of the local administration of the state, and it has the right to remove the governor by a two-thirds vote of its members. With regard to the appointment or election of the governor, the section of the transitory provisions of the constitution left the decision of the problem for a plebiscite to be held within two years of the promulgation of the constitution. It will then be decided whether the governor is to be appointed by the President or elected by the people. Meantime, the President was authorized to appoint all state governors, until the plebiscite takes place. The peculiarity of the Venezuelan system is that administrative powers are given to the Legislative Assembly, which is elected directly by the people, and the governor is subordinated to this Assembly. The plebiscite has not been held, because the constitutional normalcy of Venezuela has been interrupted by the military coup d'etat that deposed President Rómulo Gallegos.

The most interesting problem created by the federal form of government in the four above-mentioned countries is the one of political relationship between the provinces or states and the national government. In the United States, the tendency has as a rule been to respect local autonomy and the political rights of the states. In the Latin American federal governments, the central power has always enjoyed, and does today, the right to intervene, under certain broadly stated circumstances, in local political affairs, which has made state political life trivial and, so to speak, nonexistent.

According to Argentina's constitution, intervention may be decreed by the executive in order to preserve the republican form of government. Naturally, any local election that may be considered fraudulent or that simply does not satisfy the national government, or any "suppression of civil rights," may be taken as a motive for intervention. Abuses of this right by the central government of Argentina have been quite frequent.

During the dictatorship of Getulio Vargas in Brazil, the right of intervention in the affairs of the states was so abused that the Constituent Assembly of 1946 tried to limit this power. The new constitution, in general terms, prohibits intervention in the states, and authorizes it only in certain limited cases, but of course the right to intervene to preserve the republican form of government is included. The principal limitation on this right in Brazil is that intervention must be effected by means of a law enacted by the federal Congress, in which the interests of the state in question are naturally represented. In Brazil, the central power has not intervened as often as in Argentina or Mexico.

The Mexican constitution of 1917 has an interesting provision in this connection. It deals, not with the preservation of the republican form of government, but with the disappearance of the constitutional powers of the state. That is to say, when there is a violation of the constitution or of the national laws, the federal senate has the right to declare that the offending state no longer possesses constitutional powers. Its administrative machinery ceases to exist, by will of the central government, and the federal senate appoints a provisional governor who takes over the political and administrative control of the state and convokes elections. This provisional governor is prohibited from being a candidate in the election. In Mexico, the cases in which the senate has made use of this prerogative have been frequent.

In Venezuela, because of the peculiarity mentioned above, and the fact that the form of election of state governors has not been constitutionally decided upon, the intervention by the central power has not been regulated.

Let us now glance briefly over the local political structures of the four federal nations of Latin America.

Argentina. In this country, the states are called "provinces." Each one has a governor, elected by popular vote, for a term of either three or four years. Governors may not be re-elected. In some provinces, the election is carried out through an electoral college. The Argentine provincial governor enjoys, on a local level, the executive powers generally had by the President of the Republic. He may freely appoint the functionaries of provincial administration and may veto bills passed by the legislature, which may in turn override the veto by a two-thirds vote of its members.

The legislative power corresponds to two deliberative bodies in the ten large provinces, and to a unicameral legislature in the four small ones. These latter provinces are so poor that they depend almost exclusively on subsidies from the federal government and therefore enjoy very limited political autonomy. The members of the legislature are elected by popular vote.

The provincial judiciary system is composed of a Supreme Court, various Courts of Appeal, Courts of First Instance, and Justices of the Peace. In general, members of the judiciary are appointed by the governor for a six-year term, although in some provinces they have tenure.

Apart from the provinces, there are ten territories composed of underpopulated lands which do not need a complicated administration. Each has a governor appointed by the President of the Republic.

Brazil. Executive power in the Brazilian states corresponds to a governor or President, elected by popular and direct vote, for a term which is usually four years. He may not be re-elected for the term immediately following. The governor, or president as he is sometimes designated, has similar prerogatives as in Argentina; that is, he appoints provincial employees and has the right to veto legislative bills.

The legislative power is bicameral in the more populated states, while there is only one house in the smaller ones. Members of the legislature are directly elected by the people for a three-year term. All states have their own constitution, many of them detailed and extensive.

The organization of the judiciary in the states must follow the requisites set out in the federal constitution (Article 124). The object of this limitation is to guarantee tenure, elections on the basis of a competitive examination, and promotions on merit and seniority. Salaries must equal those of members of the cabinet of the state executive. By means of this requisite, it is hoped that state funds will not be used to favor political cliques and, above all, will insure a better administration of justice, since Brazil, like many other Latin American countries, has suffered from the disadvantages of a poorly paid, and easily tempted, judiciary.

The territories, are administrative subdivisions formed, as a rule, by lands located on the borders and are under the direct control of the Federal Government.

Mexico. The state executive corresponds to a governor elected directly by popular vote, usually for a six-year term, and with no re-election allowed. The executive is politically strong, enjoying many prerogatives and usually controlling the legislature and the judiciary.

The judiciary varies in its composition and election, according to the states. In some, the judges are appointed by the governor; in others they are elected by popular vote, and in still others they are resignated by the legislature.

The powers reserved by the federal government are so broad that Mexican federalism may be said to be purely formal. The central government controls commerce, mining, public health, education, religion and the production of electric energy. The territories, which are administrative subdivisions composed of sparsely populated lands, are directly administered by the Federal Government.

Venezuela. The exercise of legislative power, as well as the administration of the states, lies in a legislative assembly, elected by popular, universal, direct and secret vote. This assembly may approve the state constitution, and its members may not hold positions in the executive branch. The legislative assembly holds political control of the state, since it may disapprove of the governor's acts and remove him from his position by means of a two-thirds vote of its members.

As mentioned previously, a transitory provision of the constitution of 1947 left to a plebiscite, not yet held, the decision of the form in which the governor is to be elected and stipulated that the federal executive would appoint the state governors for the first time.

Venezuelan federalism, like the Mexican, is not broad. The central government has reserved power with regard to electoral matters, public health, agriculture, labor, banks and monetary problems, as well as the creation of taxes.

In connection with the latter, the constitution states that one-fourth of the federal income must be distributed among the states.

As in the other countries mentioned, the territories are formed of sparsely populated lands and are governed directly by the national government.

THE DECENTRALIZED SYSTEMS

The only two countries having true decentralization, political as well as administrative, in the local institutions, are Cuba and Uruguay.

Cuba. The Cuban province functions as an administrative demarcation, composed of the union or association of the municipalities. The participation of the municipality in the provincial administration is important. Article 233 of the Constitution of 1940 states: "The Province shall be administered by a Governor and a Provincial Council. The provincial government is represented in the person of the Governor. The Provincial Council is the organ of orientation and coordination of the interests of the province."

The Provincial Council is composed of all the municipal *alcaldes* (mayors), who are elected by popular vote; therefore the municipalities have an important participation in the administration of the province.

The executive power of the Cuban province is in the hands of a governor, elected by popular, direct and secret suffrage, for a four-year term. The governor must see that the national laws are enforced and the decisions of the provincial council executed. His powers, therefore, are purely executive, although he is empowered to dictate orders, instructions and rules in order to enforce the decisions of the provincial council.

The legislative power and, in general, the provincial administration is executed by the Provincial Council which, as has been said, is composed of all the municipal *alcaldes* of the province. This council approves the budget, organizes public services, raises funds and, most important of all, appoints and removes provincial administrative em-

ployes. It may be clearly seen that political power and administrative
control is in the hands of this body and is, in fact, politically in the
hands of the inhabitants of the municipalities who elect the *alcades* that
will belong to the council. In order to protect provincial autonomy,
Article 245 of the constitution states that the governor may not suspend
or remove the members of the council.

Since Cuba is not a federal republic, there is no provincial administration of justice, and the tribunals and courts of the central government have jurisdiction over local matters.

Uruguay. In this country, the territory is not divided into provinces
but into departments, which have characteristics halfway between the
province and the municipality and enjoy local autonomy.

The executive power of the Uruguyan department is in an intendant,
directly elected by the people by a majority vote, for a four-year term,
with only one period of re-election allowed. The intendant represents
the department in its relations with other organs of the state, promul-
gates the decisions of the Departmental Board, prepares the budget,
and appoints and removes the local employes and functionaries.

Legislative power lies in a Departmental Board, composed of 31
members in Montevideo and 15 members in the other departments.
This board is elected, by popular vote, by the system of proportional
representation between the different political parties. The Departmental
Board has legislative powers and controls the local financial affairs.
The Uruguyan department enjoys the same autonomy as the Cuban
province.

THE CENTRALIZED SYSTEMS

The remainder of the Latin American countries have a highly
centralized provincial system. When some principle of decentralization exists, it is limited to administrative and sometimes legislative
matters, but executive power and political control is always in the
hands of the national government. Therefore, their provincial organization will be briefly outlined and various peculiarities stressed.

Bolivia. This country is divided into departments, provinces and
cantons, all of which are merely bureaucratic units controlled by the
national government. Each department is governed by a prefect, appointed for four years by the President of the Republic, who also has
the power to remove him at will. Each department is divided into
provinces, under a sub-prefect appointed by the President of the Republic on the recommendation of the prefect. The provinces, in turn,

are subdivided into cantons, under a *"Corregidor,"* appointed by the prefect, on the sub-prefect's recommendation. There is no local legislative power, and the executive functionaries above mentioned exercise control over their respective demarcations and govern by decrees.

Chile. The Chilean system is somewhat similar to that of Bolivia. The centralizing hierarchy rises from the national executive branch. The largest local unit is the province, whose administrative and executive powers rest in the hands of an intendant appointed directly by the President of the Republic, for a three-year term, and subject to removal by the President at will. The intendant enjoys political power over the province. Each province has a provincial assembly, whose components are elected by the municipalities. However, although this assembly is democratic in its form of election, it has only advisory powers and carries little weight in the political affairs of the community. The provinces are divided into departments under a governor, appointed by the President of the Republic, on the intendant's recommendation. As there are no provincial assemblies, the governor is the functionary in whose hands rests the administration of the locality's public interests.

The departments are subdivided into subdelegations governed by a subdelegate appointed by the governor, and the subdelegations are divided into districts, under an inspector appointed by the subdelegate. There are no advisory or legislative bodies in the subdelegations or in the districts.

The internal structure described refers to the political subdivisions of the country, since Chile has adopted a different administrative system which will be covered in the last part of this chapter.

Colombia. Although the principle that inspired the constitution now in force in Colombia was that of "political centralization and administrative decentralization" (Chapter 13), the organs of local government do not enjoy as much autonomy as in some other Latin American countries. Colombia is divided into departments, whose executive power corresponds to a governor appointed by the President of the Republic. He exercises strong control over the local administration and may freely appoint and remove the department employees.

In each department, there is an assembly whose members are elected by the people for two years. The governor has the right to veto the measures of the assembly. In theory, the governor cannot exercise the veto unless the assembly has violated the constitution or the laws, but as there is no way to contest the governor's interpretation, the political power of the assembly is very small.

Costa Rica. This country is divided into provinces, which are merely administrative divisions, with no local political autonomy. Each province is under a governor appointed by the President of the Republic and responsible directly to him, since there are no legislative or advisory organs in the province.

Dominican Republic. The Dominican Republic is also divided into provinces, which are no more than internal units of a strong administrative centralization. Each province is under a governor appointed by the President of the Republic, and there are no provincial assemblies.

Ecuador. As in Colombia, Ecuador has a centralized system with a a minimum of local autonomy. The country is divided into provinces, whose executive power is in the hands of a governor appointed directly by the President of the Republic and removed by him at will. The governor exercises all political and administrative control and appoints all provincial employes. However, in each province a legislative assembly elected by the people counterbalances to a certain extent the strong political authority of the governor.

El Salvador. The territory is divided into departments that have the same characteristics as the internal divisions of the other Central American countries, meaning to say that they are merely politico-bureaucratic units at the service and under the control of the national government. The political authority of the department is in the hands of a titular and a substitute governor, both appointed by the President of the Republic, and there are no advisory or legislative assemblies.

Guatemala. Guatemala is also divided into departments with no local political autonomy. Executive and administrative power is in the hands of a governor who is appointed by the President of the Republic and acts as his representative and delegate. There is no local legislative power.

Haiti. This country, in its internal organization, is divided into departments and *Arrondissements*. Both are headed by a prefect appointed directly by the President of the Republic.

In addition, the Council of the Prefecture, composed of the prefects, municipal magistrates, officials of public services, commissioners of the central government, justices of the peace, and school inspectors, meets twice annually and acts as the advisory board to the prefect. There is no legislative assembly elected by popular vote in the departments or in the *arrondissements,* but the municipalities (*communes*) enjoy local autonomy.

Honduras. The territory is divided into departments, under the authority of a governor appointed by the President of the Republic. There is no local political autonomy, since there are no legislative assemblies or advisory bodies in the departments.

Nicaragua. The constitution of this country offers an interesting example of administrative centralization. The national territory is divided into departments, whose administration is run by a political chief appointed by the President of the Republic. Not satisfied with this direct control, the constitution added that "in each department, there will be a Director of Police, appointed by the President of the Republic." The following article states further that "the police will be under the direct control of the President, and the budget will form part of the general budget of expenditures." Needless to say, there are no legislative assemblies or advisory bodies in the department.

Panama. The provinces are simply groups of municipalities to aid in administration, and to facilitate the relationship of the municipalities with the central government. In each province there is a governor, freely appointed by the President, who acts as his agent and representative before the municipalities forming that province. There is, therefore, administrative centralization in the provincial unit, since the governor is chosen by the national executive; but this centralization is diminished by municipal autonomy.[1]

Paraguay. Administrative centralization prevails. The territory is divided into departments, directly governed by a delegate freely appointed and removed by the President of the Republic. There are no legislative or advisory bodies in the departments.

Peru. Peru has a combined system of administration, between centralization and decentralization, and the constitution has tried to protect local autonomy. The territory is divided into departments, provinces and districts. The executive power of the department is in the hands of a prefect, appointed by the President of the Republic, subject to the approval of the Council of Ministers. Each department is divided into several provinces, governed by subprefects, also appointed by the national government. The provinces, in turn, are divided into districts, placed in charge of a governor also freely appointed by the central executive.

In the administrative sphere, and in economic matters of the de-

---

[1] Municipal autonomy is explained later in this chapter under "Municipal Administration: Panama."

partments, the people have been given participation by means of the Departmental Councils. These bodies are elected and their members serve for four-year terms. The councils are empowered to organize and administer education, health, public works, agriculture, industries, mines, social welfare, and other local interests. This is an interesting attempt to separate politics from the administration. In practice, however, we understand that the system has not given the expected results because, among other reasons, it has been difficult to break away from the political control of the national government, and because Congress has the right to approve the administrative budget of the districts.

PROVINCIAL ADMINISTRATION

I. The Federal States

Countries and Divisions	Structure of Government	Local Autonomy
Argentina (Provinces)	Governor elected by people. 2 chambers in large provinces, 1 in small ones. Judiciary.	Limited autonomy Federal "intervention."
Brazil (States)	Governor elected by people. One or two chambers according to population of states. Judiciary.	Limited autonomy. Federal "intervention."
Mexico (States)	Governor elected by people. Unicameral legislature. Judiciary.	National government controls commerce, mining, health, education and has right to "outlaw" states.
Venezuela (States)	Administration in hands of elected assembly. Governor chosen by Federal Executive. Judiciary.	National government controls basic powers. Limited autonomy.

II. The Unitary States

(a) Decentralized Systems

Cuba (Provinces)	Elected governor. Provincial Council composed of municipal mayors with ample powers.	Large degree of self-government.
Uruguay (Departments)	Intendant elected by people. Departmental Board elected by people.	Large degree of autonomy.

(b) Centralized Systems

Bolivia (Departments)	Prefect appointed by President. No elective bodies.	No self-government.
Chile (Provinces)	Intendant appointed by President. Provincial Assembly elected by municipalities.	Limited self-government.
Colombia (Departments)	Governor appointed by President. Legislative assembly elected by people.	Self-government in purely administrative matters.
Costa Rica (Provinces)	Governor appointed by President. No legislature.	No autonomy.
Dominican Republic (Provinces)	Governor appointed by President. No legislature.	No autonomy.
Ecuador (Provinces)	Governor appointed by President. Elected legislative assembly.	Limited self-government.
El Salvador (Departments)	Governor appointed by President. No assembly.	No autonomy.
Guatemala (Departments)	Governor appointed by President. No legislature.	No autonomy.
Haiti (Departments)	Prefect appointed by President. Council (Advisory Board). No elected assembly.	No autonomy.
Honduras (Departments)	Governor appointed by President. No elected body.	No autonomy.
Nicaragua (Departments)	Political Chief appointed by President. No legislature.	No autonomy.
Panama (Provinces)	Governor appointed by President. No legislature.	Centralization counter-balanced by strong municipal autonomy.
Paraguay (Departments)	Delegate appointed and controlled by President. No legislature.	No autonomy.
Peru (Departments)	Prefect appointed by President. Departmental council elected by people.	Certain degree of self-government.

II. MUNICIPAL ADMINISTRATION

The local governments in Latin America evolved directly from the colonial municipalities and were the nucleus of political resistance during the wars of independence. It should be kept in mind that the Latin American municipality does not correspond to the city of the United States; it is somewhere in between the county and the city. Local economic interests and relations of neighborhood have influenced its origin and development. But the term "municipality" does not apply, necessarily, to an urban center with the characteristics of an organized nucleus of population. In many cases it is a large rural territorial tract, and the urban section may be a group of modest houses, where the municipal government resides. In all of the countries, there are other territorial subdivisions in between the provincial and the municipal unit. Politically, these subdivisions are unimportant, because they have no government of their own—not even delegates from the central power. They are simply extensions of the national bureaucratic machinery and exist for financial or judicial reasons as, for example, the presence of an office of revenue or because, within their limits, there is a judicial demarcation with a Court of First Instance.

The city in some cases is an economic center of importance, whether it be a seaport or the central zone of an area of large production, but it is fundamentally a political center, characterized by the residence of a local or national organ of government. The municipality of the capital has always played an important political role, and most of the Latin American countries have created metropolitan districts, independent of the territorial subdivisions of the country, in order to avoid the influence of the great nucleus of population in the region to which it belongs. The political history of many nations has been written around the struggle between the capital and the provinces. There are republics, like Bolivia, where the official capital is in one city and the residence of the national government is in another.

The most important problem of the Latin American municipality, besides its form of organization, is the need of decentralization. All the systems are to be found in the constitutions, from an exaggerated centralization which deprives local inhabitants of political power to an ample autonomy guaranteed in the constitutional texts.

Argentina. Because this country is a federal state, it leaves the organization of the municipalities in the hands of the provinces. The constitution authorizes the provinces to choose their own administration of justice, municipal structure and elementary educational system. The provincial governments have been jealous of this prerogative and have been reluctant to grant much autonomy to the municipalities. In most of the provinces, the executive power of the municipalities is exercised by an intendant appointed by the governor, with the approval of the Senate. The intendant may select the employees of the municipal administration. All the municipalities have, however, a Municipal Council whose members are elected by the inhabitants of the locality. This council is the only democratic feature of the local institutions, but it has small political influence, because the intendant controls the bureaucratic machinery of the locality.

In some provinces, this system has been discarded, and the intendants are either elected by the Council or by the people themselves. In these provinces, the arrangement is more democratic, but in many of them the provincial government has reserved, by means of laws, the right to control the more important public services.

The city of Buenos Aires is a federal district, governed by an intendant, appointed by the President of the Republic, subject to the approval of the Senate.

Bolivia. The municipal, or communal, government is autonomous. The executive power is in a mayor appointed by the President of the Republic for a two-year term. The President must make the appointment from among the components of a panel of three persons, chosen by the municipal council from their own members. Two of the members of the panel must of necessity belong to the majority party of the Council, and the third to the minority. Since the Council is elected by popular vote, this lends a certain democratic appearance to the designation of the municipal executive, but the requisite of the representative of the minority party permits the President to choose a mayor who lacks the popular majority in the locality.

Legislative power in the municipality is in a Deliberative Council, elected by the people for a two-year term. This organ is invested with legislative powers in municipal matters, except that ordinances passed as to licenses and taxes should be approved by the national Senate. The Deliberative Council recommends to the mayor, by means of panels, the appointment of the municipal employees. However, the mayor has the power of the purse, since he is authorized to collect, administer, and expend municipal funds. The constitution of Bolivia guarantees the existence of rural native communities and states that the national government should promote their education.

Brazil. The municipal executive is a prefect elected by the people of the locality. This is the general rule, but in the municipalities we find exceptions, in that the prefects of state capitals, and of municipalities where there are natural water resources improved by the state or the Union, and those which have been declared by federal law to be military bases or sites of importance for the national defense, may all be appointed by the state governors. Naturally, popular election of the prefects is ruled out in all of the important municipalities of Brazil. One can, to a certain extent, agree with the exception due to reasons of defense or of investment of funds from without the municipality, but the fact that state capitals are also excluded brings out the centralizing character of the present political structure of Brazil.

Municipal councils, popularly elected, may be considered the bulwark of political autonomy. The constitution reserves certain income of a local character exclusively for the municipalities, such as that derived from urban lands and buildings, licenses, industries, professions and public recreation, all of which contributes to the local economic autonomy.

Chile. The municipality is the local administrative unit, made up of the inhabitants of the commune or a group of communes. The constitution states that the laws should gradually move toward the administrative decentralization of the country. This precept—favorable to decentralization—is more closely followed in the communes than in the other internal divisions previously examined.

The executive power of the municipality corresponds to a mayor, elected by the people, who is in charge of municipal administration. However, in cities having more than 100,000 inhabitants and in others designated by a law passed by the Congress, the mayor must be appointed by the President of the Republic. In this type of municipality, the President may also remove the mayor, but only with the approval of the provincial assembly. This is restrictive of the presidential power, because the provincial assembly is integrated by the representatives of the municipalities.

Legislative power of the municipality is in a council whose members may total not less than five, nor more than fifteen, who serve for three years, and who are elected by the citizens of the locality.

The constitution authorizes the intendant (the provincial executive) to annul municipal ordinances, as well as the resolutions of the Council he may consider to be contrary to the national constitution. The Chilean municipality is also subject to the supervision of the provincial assembly, since the latter has the power to dissolve the municipal corporation by means of a resolution taken by majority vote. This points to a strong centralizing tendency, but when we recall that the assembly is composed of representatives of the provincial municipalities, the tendency is somewhat counteracted.

Colombia. Politically, the municipality is a dependency of the department. Executive power is vested in a mayor, appointed by the governor and removable at his will. The mayor, as the governor's agent, controls the municipal administration and, of course, the bureaucratic machinery.

The Municipal Council is elected by the people and has the following powers: (a) order what is appropriate for the administration of the district; (b) vote laws, ordinances and local taxes; (c) elect municipal attorneys and treasurers, and other officials that the law may determine. The constitution establishes that municipal property and revenue belong exclusively to the municipality. It also orders that the capital city, Bogotá, should be organized as a metropolitan district, different from the general municipal system of the nation. However, no measures have been taken to put this order into effect, because the Congress has not passed the necessary laws.

Costa Rica. Each province is divided into cantons and districts. The local government of the canton is entrusted to a municipality, leaving its final organization to the law. The municipalities enjoy local autonomy, and executive power being given to a mayor elected by popular vote, who is in charge of administration. Legislative and advisory functions are performed by a Municipal Council, also elected by the people. The Council may, by means of ordinances, alter the territorial divisions of the cantons and districts in order to facilitate municipal administrations.

Cuba. The municipality, as a local political entity, possesses special jursdiction to administer its public services, carry out local improvements, and establish and administer schools, museums, public libraries and recreation centers. The municipality appoints its own employees, chooses the form of government it desires, and is authorized to elect its functionaries. In order to guarantee the autonomy of the municipalities, the constitution prohibits provincial or national authorities from suspending municipal employees, or from suspending the decisions of the municipalities. It is also established that the government of the municipality shall be democratic, and that the inhabitants may freely adopt their own municipal charter. The citizens of the municipality may select one of three systems of government—manager and commission, council and manager, or mayor and council. Up to the present time, the Cuban Congress has not passed the laws necessary to put these innovations into effect, and Cuba continues to use the traditional system of mayor-council.

The executive power in the Cuban municipality is vested in a mayor elected for four years, by popular vote, who is at the head of municipal administration. Legislature and deliberative powers are executed by a Municipal Council also elected by the people for a four-year term.

Although various of the constitutional reforms have not been carried out due to the lack of adequate legislation, the guarantees granted by the present constitution have further affirmed municipal independence. The constitution authorizes Congress to create the metropolitan district of the capital city, Havana, but this has not yet been done.

Dominican Republic. The territory of the provinces is divided into communes, whose government is in the hands of Municipal Councils. The Councils are independent but their powers are limited by law, and the citizens do not really intervene in the administration, although the constitution states that the members of the council are to be elected by popular and direct vote. The Municipal Council is invested with executive and legislative powers (within the limitations above mentioned), and its members serve for a five-year term. The old city of Santo Domingo, capital of the republic, now called Ciudad Trujillo, is not a commune but a district governed by special laws.

Ecuador. The separation between the authority of the central government and the municipal powers is clearly stated. The province, as has been said, is under a governor, and is divided into cantons and parishes. In each canton and parish a political chief and a political lieutenant, respectively, attend to the relationship of the units with the central government. However, with regard to the effects of local administration, each canton constitutes an autonomous municipality. The government of this municipality is entrusted to a municipal council elected by popular vote. The inhabitants thus have direct and democratic intervention in local affairs. In the provincial capitals, a mayor, elected by the people, is in charge of municipal administration and presides over the council.

El Salvador. The local government of the cities is directed by municipal bodies, which are independent in the exercise of their functions, but whose powers are limited to economic and administrative aspects of the community.

The government of the municipal body is composed of a mayor, who exercises executive power, and a Municipal Council formed of a syndic and two or more aldermen, in proportion to the population. These officials are elected by the people, and the constitution prohibits the interference of the central government in the appointment of municipal employees. The municipalities control the local police, which must be a civil body. The capital of the republic is under the administration of the national government.

Guatemala. The constitution guarantees municipal liberty, and states that the municipalities be governed by an autonomous municipal corporation, and that this corporation, as well as the magistrates who preside over it be elected in a direct and popular form. However, the constitution adds that the magistrates are the delegates and representatives of the departmental governor. It should be kept in mind that the governor is appointed by the national executive.

The system of government is the traditional mayor-council type, the mayor and the council being elected by the inhabitants of the locality. The mayor functions as executive and administrator, and the council as a consultative body which approves municipal ordinances.

Haiti. The municipality is autonomous, although its powers are very limited by the law, following the French influence. In each commune there is a justice of the peace, appointed by the national executive, who is the representative of the central government. As stated in the first part of this chapter, the justice of the peace forms part of the council of the prefecture, where he is supposed to represent local interests. There is, in addition, a Communal Council, whose members are elected for four years by popular vote and may be re-elected indefinitely. When a commune has insufficient funds to function as an autonomous unit, it becomes the ward of the closest commune, and subject to its authority.

Honduras. The departments are divided into municipalities. The municipal government attends solely to the economic and administrative matters of the community. It is not an entity of a political nature, but a corporation of public law. The municipality freely elects its employees and police agents. Administrative functions are performed by a mayor, and the deliberative and consultative power is in a Municipal Council elected by the people. The mayors in certain important cities are appointed by the central government, and in the smaller ones, by the citizens.

Mexico. Because it is a federal government, the relationship of the municipalities is with the states, and in many of the state constitutions and laws there are definite restrictions in connection with municipal administration. In spite of this, the federal constitution, outlining the structure of the municipalities, establishes that the states may adopt their own form of republican government and adds "and shall have the free municipality as the basis of their territorial division." Hence, municipal liberty is guaranteed in the national constitution.

The representative body of the municipality is the Municipal Council. The citizens also elect the President of the Council, who has the characteristics of a mayor and is in charge of executive and administrative matters. Legislative functions are in the hands of the aldermen forming the council. There is, besides, a municipal syndic. None of these functionaries may be re-elected for the term immediately following.

The municipality freely administers local income, but the taxes must be approved by the state legislature, which restricts economic autonomy. Another limitation is that the federal government and the state governors may control military forces in the municipalities where high officers of the federal government or the governors habitually or temporarily reside. In spite of being invested with autonomy by the federal constitution, the relationship of the municipalities with the state governments varies according to the policy followed by the latter. In some, the municipalities enjoy a true independence. In others, there is active intervention by the governors, who may suspend the decisions of the council.

The capital, Mexico City, together with a number of municipalities surrounding it, functions as a federal district. The federal congress acts as the legislative body of this district, which also has its own tribunals of justice and a Consultative Council formed by representatives of industry, commerce, professions, employees and labor.

Nicaragua. The municipal regime is an example of the rigid centralization of the country. The departments are divided into municipalities, which exist only in the cities and centers of population. The municipalities are governed by a municipal body formed by a mayor, a syndic, and an alderman. All of these officials are appointed directly by the national executive and serve for a two-year term. The people do not intervene in any manner in the election of their authorities, and the municipality has no powers other than the purely economic and administrative. The capital is a metropolitan district, governed directly by the President of the Republic.

Panama. The municipal executive corresponds to a mayor, elected by the people, who serves for a four-year term, at the head of municipal administration. He may freely employ all members of the administration. In each municipality, a municipal council, in charge of legislative and advisory functions, is always directly elected by the people. The members serve for a period of four years. The inhabitants of the municipality have the rights of initiative and referendum in local matters, and they may change their form of government, by means of a plebiscite, and select the system of municipal commission, in which case its members must also be elected by the people, and for the same four-year term. The commission would substitute for and have the same powers as the municipal council.

Paraguay. The system of centralization reaches the local administrative units. The constitution does not provide for the organization of the municipalities. Asunción, the capital city, is under the authority of the Minister of the Interior.

Peru. The constitution orders the creation of municipal councils in the provincial capitals, capitals of districts, and in the cities. These Councils represent the local interests in economic and administrative matters only, and in these they are autonomous. At certain times in the past, Peru had independent municipalities, with the traditional mayor-council system, but these were abolished under Leguía's dictatorship. In spite of the dispositions of the constitution, the municipalities have not yet been organized in a democratic manner.

Uruguay. The departments are not subdivided into municipalities, as in other countries. It should be kept in mind that the Uruguayan department is not actually a province, since its sphere of action is extended to local interests. Each community may be governed, if it so desires, by a local board of five members elected in the form and proportion in which the political parties are represented in the Departmental Board. The members of this board elect, from among their number, a president who has the executive power. Therefore, the Uruguayan municipality is a community that elects its own functionaries to attend to local interests, but always in conformity with the departmental structure.

Venezuela. Municipal autonomy is guaranteed in the constitution, which prohibits federal and state authorities from interfering in municipal affairs and from hindering the municipal officials in the exercise of their functions. The municipality freely organizes the public services of the locality, which are enumerated in the federal constitution, and receives the taxes mentioned in the constitution as belonging to the municipality. Executive and administrative power lies in the president of the Municipal Council, who is elected by the council itself from among its members.

Municipal authority, in its totality, resides in the Municipal Council, whose members are elected by the inhabitants of the community by universal, direct and secret vote for a three-year term. The number of aldermen varies in accordance with the importance of the municipality. The federal constitution authorizes the municipality to possess "communally owned lands."

The capital, Caracas, is a federal district, governed by a special law, under the authority of a governor appointed by the President of the Republic and a District Council elected by the people.

MUNICIPAL GOVERNMENT

Country	Structure of Government	Local Autonomy
Argentina	Intendant appointed by Governor. Council elected by people.	Limited by provincial government interference.
Bolivia	Mayor appointed by President from panel submitted by municipality. Council elected by people.	Large degree.
Brazil	Prefect elected by people. Popularly elected Council.	Large degree.
Chile	Mayor elected by people. Council elected by people.	Some interference by provincial authorities.
Colombia	Mayor appointed by Governor. Council elected by people.	Limited by departmental control of mayor.
Costa Rica	Mayor elected by people. Council elected by people.	Large degree.
Cuba	Mayor elected by people. Council elected by people.	Large degree of autonomy. People may adopt other systems of administration.
Dominican Republic	Communes administered by council elected by popular vote.	Not much local power in hands of councils.
Ecuador	Cantons administered by popularly elected council. Mayor elected by people in provincial capitals.	Large degree of autonomy.
El Salvador	Mayor elected by people. Council elected by people.	Power limited to economic and administrative matters.
Guatemala	Mayor elected by people. Council elected by people.	Small degree due to interference of governors.

MUNICIPAL GOVERNMENT *(Continued)*

Country	Structure of Government	Local Autonomy
Haiti	Justice of the Peace appointed by central government. Communal Council elected by people.	Very limited.
Honduras	Mayor and council elected by the people.	Limited to economic and administrative matters.
Mexico	President of Council, and Council itself elected by people.	Certain degree, but taxes must be approved by states.
Nicaragua	Mayor, Syndic and Alderman appointed by national government.	No self-government.
Panama	Mayor and Council elected by the people.	Large degree.
Paraguay	Mayor and local officer appointed by national government.	No self-government.
Peru	Municipal councils popularly elected (never put in practice).	No self-government.
Uruguay	Community governed by a popularly elected Board.	Some degree.
Venezuela	President of Council and Municipal Council elected by people.	Large degree.

SUGGESTED READINGS

English:

Cleven, N. A. N., *The Political Organization of Bolivia,* Washington, D. C., Carnegie Institution, 1940.

Co-ordinator of Inter-American Affairs, *The Government of the United States of Mexico,* Washington, D. C., 1944 (mimeograph).

Ebenstein, William, "Public Administration in Mexico," in *The Evolution of Latin American Government,* Asher N. Christensen, Ed., New York, Henry Holt & Co., 1951, pp. 477-493.

Fitzgibbon, Russell H., Ed., *The Constitutions of the Americas,* The University of Chicago Press, 1948.

Macdonald, Austin F., *Latin American Politics and Government,* New York, Thomas Y. Crowell Co., 1949.

————, *The Government of the Argentine Republic,* New York, Thomas Y. Crowell Co., 1942.

McBride, George M., *Chile; Land and Society,* New York, American Geographical Society, 1936.

Rowe, Leo S., *The Federal System of the Argentine Republic,* Washington, D. C., Carnegie Institution, 1921.

Smith, T. Lynn, *Brazil: People and Institutions,* Baton Rouge, Louisiana, State University Press, 1946.

Stuart, Graham H., *The Governmental System of Peru,* Washington, D. C., Carnegie Institution, 1925.

Taylor, Carl C., *Rural Life in Argentina,* Baton Rouge, Louisiana State University Press, 1948.

Wheless, Joseph, *Compendium of the Laws of Mexico,* St. Louis, Thomas Law Book Co., 1938.

Whetten, Nathan L., *Rural Mexico,* The University of Chicago Press, 1948.

Other Languages:

Álvarez Álvarez, M., *De las Divisiones Territoriales Administrativas,* Santiago de Chile, 1943.

Álvarez, Juan C., *Derecho Federal y Municipal,* Buenos Aires, 1943.

Álvarez Tabío, F., *Teoría General de la Constitución Cubana,* La Habana, 1946.

Angulo y Pérez, A., *Derecho Municipal Comentado y Comparado,* La Habana, 1935.

Calzada y Gonzales, O., *El Sistema Federal en México,* México, D.F., 1935 (Thesis).

Carballo G., Armando, *El Sistema Municipal en México,* México, D.F., 1936.

Carvalho, Orlando M., *Problemas Fundamentales do Município,* São Paulo, 1937.

Echeverría S., Buenaventura, *Derecho Constitucional Guatemalteco,* Guatemala, 1944.

Gonzales Irmain, Nicolás, *Por el Régimen Federal; El Derecho de las Provincias,* Buenos Aires, 1938.

Lorca Rojas, Gustavo, *La Administración Comunal,* Valparaiso, 1943.

Pareja, Carlos H., *Curso de Derecho Administrativo,* Bogotá, 1939.

Pereira Bustamante, B., *El Régimen Municipal Vigente,* Montevideo, 1936.

Portocarrero, F., *Curso de Derecho Administrativo del Perú,* Lima, 1944.

Vera Guillén, Guillermo, *Situación Jurídica-Política de los Estados Miembros,* México, D.F., 1942.

Zorraquín Becú, Ricardo, *El Federalismo Argentino,* Buenos Aires, 1939.

PART III

Conflicts of Power

Politics is struggle for power. In Latin America, as in any other part of the world, political power means control over the behavior of others. Governmental institutions are only instruments in these relationships of power. The knowledge of the institutions alone is not sufficient to have a clear picture of the complex phenomenon of political behavior. It is necessary to observe more directly the forces and institutions that in a given country intervene and participate actively in the contest for power. Later, in the last part of this study, we shall consider who are today the holders of power; how they have achieved their position, and which are the groups and forces immediately affected by the control of power.

These conflicts can be divided into four large classes. Some of them are of an economic nature and center around the control of property. Their origin is as old as civilization, but in Latin America they take special characteristics, because the ownership of property has been combined with the problem of nationalism. In many countries, those who struggle for the control of power are not members of the body politic, but represent foreign forces.

There are others of a political nature. They begin with the individual in the family circle; they condition him in his educational environment and are projected with him into party politics. Here the governments also deal with old and deep-rooted forces.

Other conflicts arise from two institutions that are typical of the area in their intervention in politics. One—the Church—controls and exercises moral and spiritual power. The other—the Army—has at its disposal the use of force or the possibility of using it.

Finally, organized labor, especially within recent years, has become more and more influential and participated in political struggles. Its role is important not only in the domestic field, but also in international life, because the majority of the unions are affiliated to organizations that function on a regional and, in many cases, a global basis.

In this part, those four types of conflict will be examined and a brief account given of the constitutional regulations of the forces in each country.

CHAPTER 8

Economic Conflicts

An examination of the texts of the present Latin American constitutions indicates that, in the majority of the countries, the State occupies a strong position in its relations with property owners. Some of the constitutional regulations aim either at the modification or control of traditional rights that have been considered as inherent to the concept of private property. There are others, of a reformist character, aimed at changing existing conditions, and still others that modify the economic position traditionally occupied by the State in relation to the business life of the country. We shall consider first the changes that regulate or modify property rights, and later the ones that give the State a different position in the economic system of the country.

Regulation of Property. The changes with regard to property rights may be classified in four large groups. In the first place, we find precepts of a reformist nature devised to put an end to the problem of the entailed estates and the abuses of *latifundia*. In the second, there are constitutional measures of a nationalistic nature, with the purpose of preventing possible abuses of power by foreign investors. In the third group, there are measures by which the State reserves for itself the title to the natural resources of the country. Lastly, there is an evident trend in most of the constitutions to redefine the concept of ownership, considering it not as an absolute privilege of the individual, but as a social function.

Rural Holdings. The strict regulation of rural holdings has its antecedent in colonial days. Recalling what was stated in Chapter 2, private individuals became owners of large extensions of land. The provisions that appear today in so many of the Latin American constitutions in connection with entails, with *latifundia,* and with agrarian reform, in general, represent an effort to correct the old problem of the land. These efforts were made in Spain at the end of the eighteenth century, and especially in the nineteenth. The Spanish government declared itself against entails, both of private individuals and of the Church. The problem in Latin American countries of the accumulation of rural property by a few was a phenomenon that had existed for centuries, and still does exist in the Iberian peninsula. Members of the rural aristocracy kept their property indivisible in the hands of the head of the family. Churches, monasteries and convents that held vast wealth in their corporate character continued to increase their property holdings. The middle classes, in Spain and America, adopted the customs of the nobility and did not divide their property among their descendants, bequeathing it to the oldest male heir with the prohibition of disposing of it. Laws were made in Spain to break these entails, called *"leyes de desamortización,"* which prohibited the accumulation of lands by means of inheritance under a sole owner. Systems of colonization were recommended to divide the lands among the peasants and the creation of new entails was prohibited.

The Spanish king, Charles IV, obtained the authorization of the Pope to break the entails of the Church, and the measures were maintained by the liberal governments of the peninsula during the nineteenth century. These reforms were started too late in Spain to be adopted fully in America, as the colonies were already engaged in their struggle for independence. Once again, the Latin American adjustment to the ideas and tendencies of the times was interrupted by historical circumstances, and the problem of the entails had to be solved by means of bitter political and economic struggles in the new nations. The owners of latifundia and the Church were naturally opposed to the changes, and the agrarian problem is still an important one in many of the countries. All of this explains the concern of the government and legislatures with latifundia and the constitutional measures that exist with the purpose of putting an end to it.

Foreign Ownership. Regulations of a nationalistic nature are introduced with the purpose of placing on an equal footing foreigners and nationals with regard to ownership of property. Other regulations discriminate against foreigners, and restrict their economic activities. Toward the end of the nineteenth century, foreign capital flowed into Latin America, with the result that in many countries non-nationals greatly influenced economic life and intervened in the political struggles. These conditions persist today in various republics. The phenomenon of economic imperialism is outside the scope of this study, but to it must be attributed the standard precepts we find in the constitutions, to the effect that non-nationals are equalized with nationals, and subject to national laws. The expression of the principle changes with the countries and their constitutions. There are some which have gone to extremes. Mexico is a typical illustration. There, the non-national must make a statement or affidavit before the Minister of Foreign Relations to the effect that he will not ask for diplomatic protection from his country. This act is required before he is allowed to acquire title to real property. It is only the constitutional acknowledgment of the old principle of public law which establishes that national laws apply territorially to all property situated within the country. Whether a citizen has the right to relinquish his diplomatic protection has been the object of long debates and discussion. The object of the precept is to avoid diplomatic claims and pressures brought by foreign governments in favor of their citizens, and it is not new in the field of international law. In numerous Latin American countries, as shall be seen later, the constitution clearly states that all foreigners shall be considered as nationals if they are engaged in business or if they own property in the country.

Eminent Domain. The constitutional measures by which the State reserves title to the subsoil and natural resources also have an antecedent in Spanish law. The principle of eminent domain of the State has obtained constitutional formulation in the Latin American republics. An example is the Mexican constitution of 1917. At the Querétaro Convention, members of the constituent assembly brought forth the Spanish historical antecedent, maintaining that the Mexican nation had acquired from Spain the rights of sovereignty and had placed itself in the same legal position as the Crown, therefore enjoying the same rights Spain had possessed in America. When this principle was debated, at the time of the expropriation of the oil companies, it was upheld by the Mexican Supreme Court, and the

United States State Department recognized that the Mexican court was correct and in keeping with the principles of the Spanish law.

The reasons for the constitutional regulation of eminent domain are the same ones that produced the nationalistic precepts in connection with foreign ownership. The Latin American governments are concerned with foreign control of natural resources and the possible intervention of their owners in the political affairs of the nation. They are also concerned with the possibility of intensive exploitation of the resources and their termination in a short period of time, with little or no benefit to the national economy.

Property as a Social Function. The most interesting change is the one that aims at the redefinition of the traditional concept of property. During colonial times and during the nineteenth century republican era, the Roman law conception of ownership as a right to use the property, to enjoy its benefits and even to abuse it, was accepted. This principle of absolute *dominium* was not changed with independence but, on the contrary, became stronger. Political liberalism, that inspired the leaders of the independence, respected private property and considered it as one of the rights of men. The principle suffered no changes and appeared in all of the early constitutions. This classic conception was limited by the right of expropriation held by the State, for reasons of public interest and always with adequate compensation. The Spanish antecedent was also strong in these early stages. The *Leyes de Partidas* defined property as the "right to enjoy and freely dispose of our things, insofar as the laws do not oppose it." [1] Despite this principle, it must be borne in mind that in many cases the titles granted by the Spanish Crown were conditioned to the extent that lands must be kept in cultivation; otherwise the title was lost. The Spanish conception of property always tended to give the State a sort of supervisory status with regard to the individuals.

Few of the modern Latin American constitutions have kept the traditional concept of property as an absolute right of the individual. Instead, most of them define property as a right of the citizen, but only when it is used in the interest of the community. In other words, property has to realize a social function in order to be respected by the State. The right to abuse your property, implied in

---

[1] Lopez, Gregorio, *Las Leyes de las Siete Partidas*, Paris, 1847.

the Roman law tradition, has disappeared. He who possesses land must cultivate it for his own good and for the good of the nation. One may not keep lands idle or property unproductive. Besides suppressing the right of abuse, the right of use is modified. Property must be exploited in a rational manner, so that it may yield better products, or so that it may serve the community.

The reason for this constitutional change could be found in the desire to put an end to the already mentioned *latifundia,* and also to prevent the possible abuses of power of large property owners. Often measures have been taken by governments confronted with the problem of large tracts of land that were not devoted to production. In many cases the landholders have been satisfied to devote their lands to the easiest crops, especially to export commodities which yield foreign exchange and allow them to live in the great urban centers or abroad as absentee owners. Governments have felt that this land should be put into cultivation of products to be consumed locally, improving the living condition of the population. Foreign investors have been restricted in their use of property for the same reason. The plantation system and large companies have devoted huge extensions of land to export materials in spite of the governments' feeling that regional needs should be considered first.

Government and Business. In many constitutions we find precepts that change the traditional position of government in its relations with the economic life of the country. Some of them are the survival of colonial economy. For example, while private monopolies are prohibited, the State is authorized to control certain types of production, as the manufacturer of matches, cigarettes or salt. The Spanish state had the monopoly on the production of certain commodities for fiscal reasons rather than for the purpose of intervening in the economic life.

There are, however, other changes of a more radical nature, and in many countries the State reserves the right to plan or direct production, intervening in economic affairs. The fact that has caused this policy comes from the desire to place the countries on the economic levels of those which have benefited from an advanced industrial development. As stated previously, Latin America has always attempted to skip over historical eras. Political and economic liberalism were late in their appearance, and industrial development is needed in the majority of the nations. Capitalism, in the sense of fostering individual initiative and an industrial economy, was also late to appear. Investors who assisted were chiefly foreign. Native capital was scarce and many native investors kept on with the tradition of devoting themselves to agriculture and a very few export industries. There has been little venture capital and local entrepreneurs. The Latin American investors have always demanded solid guarantees, preferably in real property. Therefore, the governments have tried to supplement this lack of capital, and have attempted to contribute to the development of their countries, in many cases as private investors.

Various constitutions contain specific regulations of certain types of production, especially the production upon which the country depends for its economic existence. Such cases are Venezuela with regard to oil, and Cuba with regard to the sugar industry. Practically all the countries with modern constitutions tend toward nationalization or strict regulation of industries of public services, especially the system of communications and the production of electric energy. In this, Latin America has followed more closely the European economic ideas, many of them based on socialistic thought.

In general, we will find a definite trend toward planned economy. Either the constitution or the laws of most of the countries accept the principle. Nations, or governments, with opposing political philosophies, coincide in the theory that the State must take action in economic life. An example of this was Mexico's Five Year Plan under President Cárdenas, and Argentina's Five Year Plan under President Perón. Brazil has its Mixed Companies, in which the government, together with private investors, participates in production. In the smaller countries, this has been done by means of industrial development corporations (*Compañías de Fomento*), which are government projects. This type of enterprise is found in Bolivia, Colombia, Peru and Venezuela. In many countries, the planned economy has been assisted by the United States through the Inter-American Development Commission, and work in this direction has been done in Costa Rica, the Dominican Republic, Ecuador, El Salvador, Haiti, Panama, Paraguay and Uruguay. The Rockefeller International Basic Economic Corporation is an example of private North American capital in cooperation with the Latin American governments. In their desire to establish heavy industries, the governments have also intervened directly as in the cases of the Mexican steel industry of Monterrey, the Volta Redonda enterprise in Brazil and the Paz del Río Project of Colombia.

Property and the State. It is pertinent to ask now whether, because of the strict regulation of some aspects of the national economy, the aims set by the framers of the constitutions have been achieved. The answer is not a simple one. Large holdings have disappeared in some countries but they still exist in others. Peonage conditions have improved, but large numbers of landless peasants still constitute a serious problem. Some advances have been made in the political aspect of the question. The *hacendado* of the old *cacique* type is not today the strong political factor of the past. His powers have decreased in the countries in which the constitutional restrictions on *latifundia* have been put into effect. On the other hand, in many countries the change has been only on paper, because the constitutional reforms have not been followed by adequate legislation. In some countries vested interests have regained power, especially when allied with the army, and have ignored the constitutional texts. The problem of the entailed estates has been satisfactorily corrected, and today they belong to the past.

The nationalistic measures on foreign-owned properties, and the state right of eminent domain has been more effectively maintained than some of the other measures. Friction with foreign investors and important diplomatic incidents have, of course, occurred, and the closing and withdrawal of business from some countries have on various occasions affected their economy. In general, the new system has not been really put to a test under normal economic conditions. The reforms—with the exception of Mexico—were generally introduced in the thirties, as a result of the depression of 1929, and the war period prevented a normal test. During the war, the Latin American countries, with the exception of Argentina, cooperated economically with the Allies and paid little attention to the nationalistic precepts of their constitutions. The postwar period has been still more abnormal, economically speaking, for the area. There is no doubt that private foreign capital has been conscious of the restriction and has not invested as heavily as before. But the phenomenon is not limited to Latin America, and economic nationalism exists all over the world, as evidenced by the recent Iranian oil expropriation. The constitutional changes have made foreign investors realize that, when they invest in a foreign country, they are subject to the national laws and do so at their own risk.

The redefinition of property as a social function has not seriously hindered private national initiative. The writer knows of no important case in which private individuals have been expropriated because of not using their property in the interest of the community. Regulations have been applied, of course, against absentee owners in the rural areas, but more as a part of a program of agrarian reform than as a sanction for illegal use of the property.

Participation by the government in production has given satisfactory results as stated before. Private business has not suffered from the competition because, as a rule, the government has gone into new fields and in few cases taken over an established business.

Pressure Groups. Business, farmers and propertied classes in Latin America, whether they be nationals or foreigners, function politically as pressure groups. In the majority of the countries, they do not do it as openly, nor use the propaganda media, especially the press, as in the United States. Lobbying in Congress is also not so frequent for the simple reason that political power rests with the President and his Cabinet more than with the legislature (Chapter 4). In every election, and in every important law that comes before Congress, the economic forces take their sides. Political campaigns require financing, and in countries with low standards of living ready cash is not easily found; therefore, the moneyed groups play an important part in the struggle. Buying of votes is not infrequent, and the history of Latin America is full of cases of coups d'etat and uprisings financed by business, either national or foreign. Of course, the problem is not necessarily typical of the area, and exists elsewhere.

CONSTITUTIONAL REGULATIONS

Argentina. The constitution changes the traditional concept of private property, which is now defined in Article 38 as a social function, adding that the State should supervise the utilization of rural property and endeavor to have each peasant and family become the owners of the land they cultivate. Private initiative is respected, on condition that it does not attempt to control national markets, eliminate competition or increase its profits at usury rates. Minerals, water power, deposits of petroleum, coal and gas are declared to be the property of the nation. Public services are also the property of the nation, and those remaining in the hands of private concerns shall be gradually acquired by the State. An important innovation in the new constitution is introduced in Article 4, which deals with the revenue of the federal government. This declares that the government shall provide for the expenditures of the nation with funds of the national treasury, derived from the import and export revenues, *and from its own economic activities.*[2] By this, it considers the possibility that the State may enter the field of business as if it were a private individual.

Article 39 declares that capital shall be at the service of the national economy, and have social welfare as its principal object. Article 40 establishes that the economic organization of the country and the exploitation of its wealth shall have as its sole purpose the welfare of the people in agreement with the principle of social justice. The government may intervene in the economy of the nation, and monopolize certain activities in favor of the general interest.

Bolivia. Private property is guaranteed, on condition that its use shall not be opposed to the collective interest of the nation. Foreigners, and foreign concerns, shall be considered as nationals in all matters relating to the exercises of the right to possess property, and they may not establish diplomatic claims in this respect. Aliens may not acquire land or subsoil within fifty kilometers of the frontiers. The properties of the Church and of religious institutions shall enjoy the same guarantees as those belonging to private individuals. The State has direct dominium over the subsoil in general and over all mineral deposits and article 109 reserves the right to regulate commercial and industrial activities and to assume the direction of the national economy. The State may establish monopolies upon exports, especially upon petroleum and its derivatives.

Brazil. The right of property is guaranteed, but its use is conditioned by the social interest. The law may promote the just distribution of property. An important limitation of a nationalistic nature prohibits foreigners from owning newspapers or radio concerns. This prohibition is extended to all corporations having shares payable to the bearer, since the true owner of the business cannot be ascertained.

The economic order shall be organized in conformity to the principles of social justice, and the State may intervene in the economic sphere and monopolize certain industries. Abuse of economic power is pro-

---

2 Italics by the author.

hibited, and it is ordered that rates of public services shall be set by the State, so that they shall not be greater than a just return on the capital invested.

The exploitation of the subsoil may be done only by Brazilian individuals or concerns. Coastal navigation may be made only in national ships, whose crews must be at least two-thirds Brazilian.

Chile. The right of property is considered one of the individual rights, and the constitution declares that property is inviolable, without any distinction. The exercise of the right of property is subject to limitations or regulations demanded by the maintenance of social order, and in this sense, the law may impose obligations in favor of the general interest of the State. The constitution also declares that the State should favor the division of property and the creation of the family patrimony.

Colombia. Property is considered a social function subject to obligations. In case of war, private property may be temporarily occupied by the State in order to attend to the necessities of war, or to apply its products to the defense of the nation. The income and property of the departments and municipalities belong to these administrative organs, and are as fully guaranteed as property belonging to individuals. An interesting regulation, in Article 37, disposes that there may be no real estate in Colombia that is inalienable, nor may there be irredeemable obligations.

The State reserves the right to intervene in industries, and in public or private concerns, in order to control production and see that the worker receives the remuneration to which he is entitled.

Costa Rica. This country maintains the traditional principle of private property established in the constitution as first written, in spite of the many modifications it has undergone. The constitution declares that property is inviolable, although the Congress, for reasons of public necessity, may impose limitations in the interest of society.

Cuba. The constitution has given preferential attention to the regulation of property rights. The section devoted to property opens with a statement to the effect that the State recognizes the existence and legitimacy of private property, but adds that this is understood in the fullest concept of its social functions, and with no more limitations than those that may be established by the law for reasons of public necessity or social interest. It declares that the subsoil belongs to the State, which may make concessions to individuals for its exploitation, and adds that the land, forests, concessions of mines, utilization of waters, means of transportation and public services must be exploited in a manner favorable to the social welfare. When real property is sold at public auction, the State has the right to present its bid and may acquire it at the price offered by the highest bidder. In practice, the Cuban government has made little use of this right. The constitution prohibits latifundia and disposes that the law shall stipulate the maximum extent of real property each individual or concern may own, in accordance with the manner in which the land is exploited. The family patrimony is created in rural property. The constitution prohibits perpetual liens on property. Foreigners are subject to the same conditions established by the law for nationals, and they must have in mind the socio-economic interests of the nation.

Article 256 empowers the State to establish obligatory associations of producers, as well as of professionals, in such a manner that they will be controlled by the majority of their associates.

The sugar industry, since it is Cuba's principal source of wealth, has also been constitutionally regulated. Article 275 disposes that the law shall regulate the planting and grinding of the cane done by administration, that is, the planting and grinding done by the sugar mills and not by individual owners. The purpose is to protect the independent planter or *"colono,"* and to prevent monopoly in the sugar industry. It should be kept in mind that the *"colonos"* are usually Cubans, while the sugar mills are generally controlled by foreign capital.

Dominican Republic. There are practically no constitutional limitations to the full exercise of property rights, which are declared to be inherent to the human personality. The State may, however, expropriate with justified reasons.

Ecuador. The constitution prohibits entailed estates, ordering that in Ecuador there may be no real estate which is perpetually inalienable. It also prohibits the existence of obligations that cannot be extinguished by some legal means. Property rights are guaranteed, but always with the consideration that the property fulfill a social function.

El Salvador. Private property is inviolable, but the State reserves the right, in case of war, to administer or dispose of property of enemy aliens. Article 32 contains a limitation with regard to the property of stock companies, establishing that no civil or ecclesiastical corporation whatsoever may own or administer real estate except that used directly for the aims of the corporation. That is to say, no corporation may devote its activities to speculation or administration of real estate.

Guatemala. The State recognizes the existence of private property, as a social function. Entailed estates and the existence of perpetual holdings in favor of *mortmain* are prohibited. Only citizens of Guatemala, corporations whose members are nationals, and the national banks may own real property within a zone of fifteen kilometers in width along the frontier and coast.

The State has direct dominium over its property and may grant, under conditions determined by the law, *dominium utile* over its rural real property to those that work it, preferably to families and societies, but not to stock companies or corporations. It may also grant this *dominium utile* to Guatemalan individuals, or to immigrants contracted by the State. Latifundia is prohibited, and the law is ordered to establish measures for their division. Article 99 disposes that the State will prohibit or limit the activities of concerns tending to absorb the production of one or more branches of industry, to the detriment of the national economy. All concessions granted by the State in relation to public services may not be for a term longer than fifty years, and after this length of time the business shall become the property of the State.

Haiti. Property rights are guaranteed to citizens and to aliens, but under the following limitations, the use of property must always be made in the general interest, and the owner of land must cultivate it and protect it against erosion.

Aliens as well as foreign corporations are granted the right to own property; however, they may own no more than one house in each locality. If foreigners wish to engage in business or industry, they may own the property necessary for such enterprises, but the right ceases two years after the alien has left the country.

Honduras. The constitution guarantees private property rights, but establishes that this right shall not impair the eminent domain of the State, and shall not be superior to the interests of national institutions. The State is given the right to impose upon alien ownership of lands and waters the restrictive measures necessary to the general welfare. The creation of the agrarian family patrimony is ordered.

Mexico. The constitution devotes a great deal of attention to the regulation of property rights, beginning with the declaration that the ownership of lands and waters corresponds originally to the nation, which may transfer dominium to private individuals, in this manner constituting private property.

The nation has direct dominium over all minerals, and over the subsoil in general, and the constitution carefully enumerates all classes of minerals and products of the subsoil. The waters of the ocean, to the extent fixed by international law, are also the property of the nation, as well as the lakes, rivers and other waters within the national territory.

With regard to the rights to acquire title over lands and waters, the following regulations are established. (1) Only native-born or natural-ized Mexicans may acquire dominium. The right may be granted to aliens when they agree, before the Ministry of Foreign Relations, to be considered as nationals with respect to these properties, and not to invoke the protection of their governments in case of conflict. This precept has often been misinterpreted in foreign countries, and it has been thought that a foreigner must become a Mexican citizen in order to be able to acquire lands in Mexico. It is clear that is is not the case. (2) Religious associations, regardless of creed, may not own or administer real property, or investments of capital guaranteed by real property. The real property owned by religious associations at the time of pro-mulgation of the constitution became the property of the nation. The same regulation is applied to the residence of bishops, seminaries, asylums and schools of religious associations, and to the temples which may be erected in the future, all of which are the property of the State. Therefore, all buildings of this type in Mexico belong to the State, which grants their use to a committee of citizens of the locality. This committee, in turn, authorizes the religious communities to destine them to the services of the faith. (3) Institutions of public or private welfare may acquire no more real property than needed for their aims, but they may own and administer capital guaranteed by real property. (4) Stock companies may not acquire, own or administer rural property. (5) Banks are excepted, and may own capital guaranteed by real prop-erty, but they may not own more real property than necessary for the purpose of their business.

Nicaragua. Property is inviolable, but the exercise of its right is sub-ject to limitations required by social order. Property must be regulated by the laws of the republic, whether its owner be a national or an alien. The constitution prohibits entailed estates, and endowments in favor of mortmain, with the exception of those established in order to create a family patrimony, or institutions of charity. The State may intervene in the administration of the institutions of public service, and may nationalize them, but in case of nationalization, indemnity must be paid. The wealth of the subsoil is the property of the nation, and its exploitation may be granted to individuals on the basis of participation.

Panama. Private property is guaranteed, but ownership implies obli-gations because of the social function it must fulfill. The State has the right to create enterprises and public services when these have not been established by private concerns, and may also expropriate the public services under private ownership for reasons of social interest. Owners of rural properties are obliged to see that the soil is cultivated, and the constitution establishes that the law shall prevent the existence of uncultivated land.

Article 231 prohibits foreign governments from acquiring property rights. No foreign individual or Panamanian stock company whose capital may be foreign controlled may acquire lands less than ten kilometers from the frontier. The constitution respects the rights previously acquired in this regard, but adds that foreign-owned property in this condition may be expropriated. Entailed estates and perpetual obligations are prohibited. Articles 208 states that the subsoil belongs to the State, and that the saltpits, mines and beds of all kinds may not be privately owned. The use of the subsoil and the other properties mentioned may be granted to individuals.

Concessions for the exploitation of the subsoil must always take the social interest into consideration. Although monopolies are prohibited in a general manner, the State reserves the right to establish monopolies upon imports or upon articles not produced within the national territory. This is a means of increasing State revenues, and in practice operates like a system of taxation rather than an intervention in the sphere of business. The principle of individual economic freedom is maintained, but Article 225 adds that the State shall guide the economic activities of individuals, direct, regulate or create them, according to the social necessities of the nation.

Paraguay. The constitution guarantees private property, and states in Article 21 that the law may set the maximum extension of land under the ownership of one individual or corporation, and any land over this amount may be sold at public auction or expropriated by the State for redistribution.

Peru. Property is declared to be inviolable, and subject to the national laws, regardless of the nationality of its owners. Aliens are thus considered the equals of nationals with regard to property rights, and they may in no case appeal to their own countries. The right of property must be used with consideration for the public interest. Aliens may not acquire lands, waters, mines or fuel deposits within fifty kilometers of the frontier. The mines, lands, forests, waters and other natural sources of wealth belong to the nation, which may grant its use to individuals. The State may, through adequate indemnity, nationalize public services. The State assumes the obligation of favoring the small rural holding, and for this purpose may expropriate uncultivated *latifundia*. The State has the right to receive part of the profits of mining concerns.

Uruguay. Property rights are not specifically limited in the constitution, which declares them to be an inviolable right, but subject to legal regulations for the general interest. The State may intervene in the national economy, through the "autonomous entities" and the decentralized services. However, Article 179 states that the services of post and telegraph, railways, custom houses, harbors and public health cannot be decentralized as autonomous entities, although the law may grant them a certain degree of autonomy.

The most important decentralized autonomous entities that function in Uruguay are the *Frigorífico Nacional,* a packing industry; the ANCAP (*Administración Nacional de Combustibles, Alcohol y Portland*), which has the monopoly of gasoline, alcohol and its derivatives, cement and certain chemical products; the UTE (*Administración General de las Usinas Eléctricas y los Teléfonos del Estado*) , which operates all power plants and all telephones in Uruguay, including the international communications; the Bank of the Republic, which is one of the largest and best organized of Latin America, and others of lesser importance.

Venezuela. The State guarantees the right of property, as a social function. The State has the right to establish prohibitions for the acquisition, transfer and use of certain classes of property, either because of their nature, or because of their location within the national territory. Also, it may expropriate lands to implement the agrarian reform. The right to own real property is subject to the obligation of cultivating the land in a manner which will benefit the general interests of the country.

Although private industry is protected, the State reserves the right to administer certain industries or public services, to ensure efficient functioning. A National Economic Council is created, composed of representatives of capital, labor, the liberal professions and the government. This Council is in charge, in theory, of the economic planning of the republic.

Suggested Readings

English:

Behrendt, Richard F., *Economic Nationalism in Latin America,* Albuquerque, School of Inter-American Affairs, University of New Mexico, 1941.

————, *Inter-American Economic Relations: Problems and Prospects,* New York, The Carnegie Endowment for International Peace, 1948.

Brazilian Government Trade Bureau, *Corporations, Labor and Tax System in Brazil,* New York, Brazilian Government Trade Bureau, 1945.

Commission on Cuban Affairs, *Problems of the New Cuba,* New York, Foreign Policy Association, 1935.

Ellsworth, P. T., *Chile: An Economy in Transition,* New York, The Macmillan Co., 1945.

Gordon, Wendell C., *The Expropriation of Foreign Owned Property in Mexico,* Washington, D. C., American Council of Public Affairs, 1941.

Harris, Seymour E., Ed., *Economic Problems of Latin America,* New York, McGraw-Hill Book Co., Inc., 1944.

Hughlett, Lloyd J., Ed., *Industrialization of Latin America,* New York, McGraw-Hill Book Co., Inc., 1946.

Inter-American Development Commission, *A Statement of the Laws of Bolivia, in Matters Affecting Business in its Various Aspects and Activities,* Washington, D. C., 1947 (mimeographed).

————, *A Statement of the Laws of Chile, etc.,* Washington, D. C., 1947 (mimeographed).

————, *A Statement of the Laws of Colombia, etc.,* Washington, D. C., 1947 (mimeographed).

————, *A Statement of the Laws of Cuba, etc.,* Washington, D. C., 1946 (mimeographed).

————, *A Statement of the Laws of the Dominican Republic, etc.,* Washington, D. C., 1946 (mimeographed).

————, *A Statement of the Laws of Haiti, etc.,* Washington, D. C., 1945 (mimeographed).

————, *A Statement of the Laws of Honduras, etc.,* Washington, D. C., 1947 (mimeographed).

————, *A Statement of the Laws of Peru, etc.,* Washington, D. C., 1945 (mimeographed).

————, *A Statement of the Laws of Uruguay, etc.,* Washington, D. C., 1946 (mimeographed).

Olson, Paul R., and C. Addison Hickman, *Pan American Economics,* New York, John Wiley & Sons, Inc., 1943.

Person, Harlow S., *Mexican Oil, Symbol of Recent Trends in International Relations,* New York, Harper & Brothers, 1942.

Rippy, J. Fred, *The Capitalists in Colombia,* New York, The Viking Press, 1931.

————, *Latin America and the Industrial Age,* New York, G. P. Putnam's Sons, 1944.

Woodward, Dorothy and Miguel Jorrín, *Recent Economic Developments in Latin America,* Albuquerque, School of Inter-American Affairs, University of New Mexico, 1948 (mimeographed).

Wythe, George, *An Outline of Latin American Economic Development,* New York, Barnes & Noble, Inc., 1946.

Other Languages:

Batella Asensi, Juan, *La Expropiación en el Derecho Mexicano*, México, D. F., 1941.

Bulnes, Francisco, *Los Grandes Problems de México*, México, D. F., 1926.

Bunge, Alejandro, *La Economía Argentina*, Buenos Aires, 4 vols., 1928-1930.

Cabrera, Luis, *Veinte Años Después*, 3a. Ed., México, D. F., 1938.

Canepa, Luis R., *Economía Agraria Argentina*, Buenos Aires, 1942.

Duarte, Nestor, *A Ordem Privada e a Organizaçao Politica Nacional*, São Paulo, 1939.

Fondo de Cultura Económica, Ed., *El Pensamiento Económico Latino-Americano*, México, D. F., 1945.

Friedlaender, H. E., *Historia Económica de Cuba*, La Habana, 1944.

García, Antonio, *Bases de la Economía Contemporánea*, Bogotá, 1948.

Raggi Ageo, Carlos M., *Condiciones Económicas y Sociales de Cuba*, La Habana, 1944.

Seguel C., José Miguel, *La Industria Eléctrica y la Legislación Chilena*, Santiago de Chile, 1941.

Silva Herzog, Jesús, *El Pensamiento Económico en México*, México, D. F., 1947.

CHAPTER 9

Political Conflicts

The **"Homo Politicus."** The Latin American man, in his relations with those who give orders and command obedience in the State, behaves politically. It is not maintained that in this respect the Latin Americans are different from the citizens of any other country or that there exists a special political man of a Latin American type. The use of the term "homo politicus" only attempts to indicate the political aspect of the behavior of the Latin American man, separated from other types of conduct. This behavior is conditioned naturally by his historical environment, and the conditioning process starts in the family circle. Many Latin American constitutions deal with the institution of the family and "legislate" on private matters. Of course, these regulations change from country to country, but the trend is constant, especially in the new constitutions.

The educational and intellectual environment is also of influence. In this we have the same characteristics. The constitution—a political document—carefully legislates on education. The patterns are also varied but the trend is constant. The institutions of learning play an important role in the political life of the country, not only because of their influence on individual behavior, but because of the active participation of professors, and especially students, in politics.

There is quite a common belief that Latin Americans are more politically minded and more concerned with politics than the inhabitants of other areas of the world. This generalization is frequently repeated as an explanation of the instability of government and the numerous revolutions, coups d'etat and disturbances. The point requires, in the opinion of the author, a more detailed and serious consideration. Some time ago, the Spanish philosopher José Ortega y

Gasset [1] pointed out the distinction between a revolt and a revolution. He explained that a revolt is made against the abuses of power of the rulers, while a revolution is made against the use of power. He added that there have been many revolts in the world, but only a few revolutions. When people are dissatisfied because a ruler abuses his power and they employ force to overthrow him, we have a revolt. But when the people are dissatisfied because of the way power is used, and attempt to change the institutions that permit the ruler to use power in that way, we have a revolution. A political revolution is a change in governmental institutions that necessarily creates a new state form and different social and economic structures. A revolt means only a change of direction in government or a change of those who direct the government, but does not necessarily mean an institutional change. This change is always obtained by force or violent means. In Latin America there have been many revolts but only one revolution—the Mexican Revolution of 1910.

What characterizes a revolt is the use of force as a means to introduce a change of government. But the use of force is not a political phenomenon. On the contrary, it is the negation and antithesis of politics. Politics, by its very nature, presupposes the absence of force and violence. We always speak, using the term correctly, of political solutions to conflicts. Politics also, by its very nature, presupposes dissatisfaction of a defeated group, or the group that has been unsuccessful in a struggle. There are no absolute victories in politics. A peaceful constitutional election is a purely political phenomenon. But this phenomenon can be revolutionary if the group in power changes the political, economic and social institutions of the country. When a revolt changes the group in power by the use of force it places itself outside of politics. Therefore, it is not accurate to say that in Latin America there are many revolts because of too much politics. The correct assertion might be that precisely because of the absence of politics and political changes, there are too many armed revolts. In other terms, the political groups use force because they are unable to find satisfactory solutions in their struggles for power. Of course, this does not explain why they resort to force.

When a group occupies power, by a victory in a peaceful election,

---

[1] Ortega y Gasset, José, "El Tema de Nuestro Tiempo," in *Obras de José Ortega y Gasset*, Madrid, 1932, Espasa-Calpe, S. A.

the nation has reached a political solution of possible conflicts. This is true only if those who have lost the election accept defeat and wait for their turn after a period of time. But if the defeated group does not accept defeat and uses force, we are far from having a political solution. This is what frequently happens in Latin America. It is pertinent to ask why the defeated groups do not wait. The answer in the majority of the cases is a simple one: Because economically it is not possible for them to wait. In other countries of a more advanced economy, the components of a defeated political group go back to their business and professions and wait for the next election. As a rule, it is better and more profitable to them not to occupy governmental positions as they fare better in business and professions in their capacity as private citizens. In Latin America, this is not the case. The loss of political power means, for the individual and the family, unemployment and serious economic difficulties, not counting social prestige and possibilities of doing business with the government. Politics is a serious "business" for the Latin American; he defends his right to make a living and dislikes interference with his activities as much as a United States businessman resents governmental intervention. Some Latin Americans claim that politics is the largest industry in their states.

Political Role of the Family. Spain brought to Latin America the institution of the monogamous family with its religious, juridical and economic characteristics as it existed in the peninsula. With the family there developed, as we have seen, the legal institution of the entailed estate. The Iberian family was organized by the old Roman and canon law system with great stress upon the authority of the "paterfamilias." The family was large, and kept under the authority of its head, functioning socially and politically as a unit.

In the nineteenth century, when independence came, the family was still an important social nucleus with profound influence on local and national political life. Many Latin American countries experienced long dictatorships based on family ties. The protection of family members has created the abuses of nepotism. In the administration of justice, legal infractions are tolerated when committed by relatives of influential leaders. The role of the large family is complicated by the existence of numerous relations who function as family relations, although they are not so legally. We refer to the concubinary unions. An influential man, besides his legal family, may have to take care of the relatives of his mistress, or ex-mistress, and of course, of his illegitimate children. Concubinary unions are quite frequent in the highest circles of society. This type of union and its political repercussions should not be confused with the free unions of the lower classes, since these are usually of a permanent nature and differ little from the legal or religious marriages. The abundance of the latter type of union in Latin America has been explained economically by the cost of the religious marriage that made it prohibitive for the poor classes. Another reason is that in the nineteenth century, and even today, the Church has not reached the remote rural regions. In his book on Mexico, Professor Nathan L. Whetten [2] says that the Church had no more priests in the rural areas in the days of Porfirio Díaz, when they enjoyed official support, than it has today despite the strict regimentation of the post-revolutionary period. When the institution of civil matrimony was created, the rural families still had to travel long distances to the urban centers or seats of courts to get married, so they followed their old custom of free unions.

Besides the legal and unofficial families, we must remember another type of relation of the same nature that originates with the institution of *"compadrazgo"* (godparenthood). This is the practice of giving a godfather and godmother to each child at the time of baptism. The godparents acquire the obligation of looking after the needs of the godchild, and there ensues a spiritual tie with the parents of the child, which is called *"compadrazgo."* It is not a simple relationship of friendship; but a religious and social obligation of mutual help and defense in times of need. The institution of the family is thus greatly enlarged, and of course when a member of the family occupies a political position, he feels it his duty to assist all classes of relatives. All these types of "families" exercise great influence in politics.

Having this characteristic in mind we should note the points in which matrimony and the family come in contact with the constitutions of the countries as they express the political structure and organization. To many persons it would seem strange that a document such as a constitution should contain precepts regulating the family and matrimony. But the Latin American legislatures have

2 Whetten, Nathan L., *Rural Mexico*, University of Chicago Press, 1948.

been conscious of the role of the family not only as a social and economic force, but also as a political institution. Some of the common problems between the State and the family have been education of children; legal equality of husband and wife; divorce, that did not exist under Spanish laws; the status of free unions and the protection of children resulting from them. Finally, the constitutions have also been concerned with the creation of the family patrimony and some tended to establish a family wage for workers, instead of individual ones based on personal capacity.

The Educational Environment. In the majority of the Latin American republics, we find a system of constitutional regulations and control of education. The legislators have given especial attention to the problem of illiteracy, which is predominant in many countries. Uruguay, Argentina and Costa Rica have extremely low rates of illiteracy, as compared with world figures, while others still show a large percentage. Some of the historical reasons for this phenomenon have been indicated in the first part of this book, and here we are concerned only with an explanation of the detailed constitutional regulation of education. After independence, most of the centers of learning were controlled by the Church, although there existed some lay institutions in the large cities. When independence came, the new countries could not improvise a functioning system of public education. The Church favored the political attitude of the conservative forces, whose interests were closely identified with the old colonial administration. The new liberal republics had to reckon with this interior antagonism, and one of the problems of bitter dispute was that of lay education. The nineteenth century struggles, especially in the countries where the Church was strong, resulted in constitutional precepts to protect lay education. Mexico, again, is the best example of this.

Nationalism in the educational system has been another factor. There were few native teachers in religious schools, as the Creoles were not attracted to religious life. Foreign teachers, especially Spanish ones, with no knowledge of the cultural values of the area, paid little attention to the teaching of civic duties, and some governments, to correct this situation, have required that the teaching of courses relating to national history, geography, literature and civics be in charge of natives. The Cuban constitution of 1940 illustrates this point.

All countries establish in their constitutions that primary education is compulsory. Unfortunately, the precept is not always applied in practice. There are various reasons for this situation, but the main one is of an economic nature: modest budgets in poor countries, large rural areas, lack of schools and properly prepared teachers and, above all, low salaries for teachers of primary and secondary schools. Furthermore, poor families who must depend upon the work of their children, not only in the country but in the cities, do not force the children to go to school. The social problem of child labor and mendicity is a difficult one to solve, since the authorities hesitate to apply the law knowing that the forcible school attendance of a child may often deprive a family of his small contribution, which makes the difference between subsistence and hunger.

Students in Politics. What is characteristic of Latin America is the active participation in political life of students and professors. The phenomenon is more common among university students, but it also exists in institutions of secondary education. The reasons for this behavior can be found in the nature of the institutions of learning and also in the tradition of the student body as a group different from the rest of society. Both phenomena are Spanish. Spanish literature has illustrated the character of the *estudiante* since medieval days: A person who studies, but dresses differently and enjoys a certain privileged position that allows him to behave or misbehave at will and who is tolerated by society. The Latin American university is different from the Anglo-Saxon one, and is closer to the Italian and Spanish universities. In a fairly recent article, the Peruvian author Luis Alberto Sánchez [3] makes an interesting study of student participation in university government in Latin America, and indicates that the students' political activities are the result of their conception of the role of the universities.

The Latin American university was modeled after the university of Salamanca in Spain, which in turn was influenced by the Italian universities of Bologna and Padua. Bologna was a univer-

---

[3] *Cuadernos Americanos*, No. 5, vol. XLVII, September-October, 1949, México, D. F., p. 43.

sity of students, organized in "nations," which were groups actively intervening in the administration of the institution. The system was contrasted with the university of Paris, which was a theological center of studies for teachers and members of the clergy. In Paris and in Oxford, in the middle ages, the student had no participation in the administration. The North American universities follow the French and English system, while the Latin American ones model themselves after Bologna and Salamanca. In Spain, university students for centuries had a voice in the appointments of their rectors, deans and professors. This custom came to America and in colonial days the students participated in the administration. In the university of San Marcos, in the seventeenth century, rectors were elected by university authorities, members of the faculty and a delegation of students. Toward the end of the century, student intervention in administration was abolished under the centralizing policy of the Bourbons. When independence came in the nineteenth century, the students had no intervention in administrative matters, but starting with the student protests of Córdoba (in Argentina) in 1918, the students made headway and gained more and more control over the university. Despite excesses and problems caused by student strikes and unreasonable demands, student responsibility in university affairs has produced good results. In the majority of cases, it has diminished student dissatisfaction, as suspicion and discontent has often been caused by their ignorance of the real nature of university problems. This is overcome when students are informed and asked to share responsibility and offer solutions. Student protests, revolts, riots and scandals in Latin America should not always be interpreted as manifestations of a group that is unwilling to study or submit to academic discipline. It must be borne in mind that they act and protest in the name of the university as an institution, of which they consider themselves an important part.

It is true that student movements have often been spurred on by personal ambitions of unscrupulous leaders and of politicians and demagogues in general, but in many cases the movements have been the sincere protest of a younger group of society, that is consciously aware of the political problems of their country and strive toward a solution.

Professors often contribute to intensify the political activities of the student body. As a rule, academic people are more politically minded in Latin America than in other countries, because professors are only part-time teachers and depend upon the practice of their own professions for their livelihood. They are a more active part of the social and political group than the average college professor in the United States. It is easy to understand that they share, with their students, concern over the political problems of their countries.

The Electoral Pattern. Latin America had practically no electoral experience in colonial times. Her system had to be improvised in the nineteenth century, through trial and error. Part IV of this book discusses the constitutional provisions in connection with the right of suffrage. Ages, qualifications and certain conditions change according to countries, but the right of suffrage is universally recognized. Of course there is a big difference between theory and practice, and considerable interference with the exercise of suffrage, as well as political apathy in some countries and areas. Nevertheless, the trend in recent years has been toward an increase in the number of votes cast in general elections, usually of a higher proportion than in a general election in the United States.

The ballot system and the electoral machinery in most of the countries is still obsolete. To the author's knowledge only Cuba, El Salvador, Mexico, Nicaragua and Venezuela use the Australian ballot, while the remainder of the countries allow the parties to print their own ballots, which is an inducement to fraud. The administration of the elections also offers considerable possibility for irregularity. Of course, some countries have created the Electoral Jurisdiction, placing the process under the supervision of the judiciary. This is a step forward that on the whole has produced favorable results. In countries where electoral officers are appointed by the executive, the party of the government always has an edge. Electoral corruption is frequent, and voting practices although changing from country to country, have been the cause of serious concern. Obsolete electoral registries have been one of the most serious causes of problems. In Cuba, before the creation of the Electoral Jurisdiction, there was an old joke which said that there were two All

Souls Day (*Dias de Difuntos*). One was the religious festivity, and the other the day of the national election, when all the dead people voted. Many of these defects have been corrected. Some countries require the presentation of an identification card, with fingerprints and pictures, before the voter is allowed to cast his ballot. Post-electoral fraud and ballot-box stuffing have been frequent, especially in rural and isolated areas. The best cure for all of these evils, in recent times, has been the large number of votes cast. It is easy to change an election when few have voted, but not so easy in populated regions with a large number of votes.

The Party System. Having had no colonial experience (with the exception of Cuba), the Latin Americans had to improvise their party system. During the nineteenth century, the two-party system was predominant. Countries were divided between Federalists and Centralists, representing either the interests of the rural areas or the urban centers. They were also divided between Liberals and Conservatives, but changing their names according to countries. In many cases they used as a party name the color of their emblems. The Liberals represented the urban middle class, small rural proprietors and professionals. The Conservatives were integrated, as a rule, by wealthy landowners and important businessmen and were supported by the Roman Catholic Church. This pattern has changed gradually in the twentieth century, where the trend is toward a multi-party system. The names and ideologies are varied, and often the name of the party does not really picture the ideology, as there are Radicals and Socialists who are ultra-conservative. Personalism and influence of a leader play an important role in party ideologies, and the trend to follow the man and not the organization is still persistent. A party named after Perón rules Argentina, perhaps acknowledging this reality.

One characteristic of Latin American parties is that they are not stable organizations, but as a rule remain dormant between elections and come to life for the electoral campaign. Of course, if there is a dictatorship in power, the parties remain more active in the opposition, in many cases on a conspiratorial basis. The electoral process is typical. Campaigns are bitter, and all propaganda media are used. One of the tactics used by despotic governments has been to allow freedom of speech but to control the press, radio and other means of communication. This way the elections are free but not democratic, since in most cases the parties of the opposition cannot reach the voters. This was done by Perón in the last elections. Another method is to allow freedom in the cities where there are foreign observers and a large population, and to use pressure and violence only in the rural areas.

Another characteristic of the recent parties in Latin America is the ideological influence of writers and intellectuals. Party platforms are clearly outlined and maintained, usually with a political philosophy of its own as well as a definite program of reform. These are the cases of the APRA in Peru, the Democratic Action in Venezuela, the *Colorado-Batllistas* in Uruguay and, to a lesser extent, the PIR of Mexico and the Cuban *Auténticos*.

CONSTITUTIONAL SUMMARY

Argentina. The recent constitution devotes a special section to the family, which it defines as the primary and fundamental nucleus of society. The family is declared to be under the preferential protection of the State, which recognizes its rights with regard to its composition, defense and the fulfillment of purpose. The State protects matrimony, declares the equality of man and wife, and recognizes the authority of the parents over the children. The State shall promote the economic unit of the family, under a special law to be passed to that effect; and guarantees the family patrimony, also to be under a special law. There is no divorce in Argentina. Education and instruction are the responsibility of the family, and of the private and official institutions that collaborate with it. Primary education is obligatory and shall be free in the public schools. The State declares that the professional orientation of youth is a social function promoted and protected by the State, so that the exercise of professions may benefit the family and society. The higher education offered in the universities must not only prepare youth to cultivation of the sciences, but must tend toward the growth of the nation.

Bolivia. The institution of matrimony, the family, and childhood are under the protection of the State, and the constitution specifically establishes the legal equality of the husband and wife. The Bolivian charter gives legal value to free unions or common law marriages in which the parties have lived together more than three years. Children are authorized to investigate their paternity and establish their hereditary rights. In connection with the economic aspect of the family, Article 133 of the constitution establishes the principle of unattachable and inalienable family patrimony, and states that the nation will assist families having numerous children. Education should be organized under a single school system, with attendance obligatory for all children between the ages of seven and fourteen years. It is declared the duty of the State to offer economic assistance to needy students in order that they may benefit from higher education. Private schools are subject to official regulations.

With regard to higher education, the constitution states that public universities shall be autonomous, and the only ones authorized in the republic to grant diplomas.

Brazil. Although its constitution is a recent one, we find in it the principle of the indissolubility of matrimony. Marriages may be civil or religious, and the latter have the same legal effects as the former if they have been properly registered. The family is under the protection of the nation, which especially assists parents with numerous children. All inheritance of property of foreigners residing in Brazil shall be decided by Brazilian law when this is more favorable to the widow or Brazilian children than the national law of the deceased.

Education is considered a right of all inhabitants, and may be given in the home and in schools. Primary education is obligatory and free, and shall always be offered in the national language. Industrial establishments having more than one hundred workers shall be obliged to maintain primary schools for the children of the workers. Religious instruction is an elective subject, which may or may not be received according to the beliefs of the students. The federal government shall apply at least ten per cent of the federal income of the state for the maintenance of institutions of learning. Freedom of teaching is guaranteed.

Chile. The Chilean constitution devotes but little space to the family. Article 10, Section 14, briefly mentions, in connection with the protection of labor and social welfare, that this must be given in such manner as to assure the necessities of the family. It adds that the State is favorable to the creation of family holdings. Public education is to receive the preferential attention of the State, and primary schooling is obligatory. The administrative organization includes a superintendency of public education, which exercises inspection over all the nation's education. Other educational matters are regulated by statute.

Colombia. This country does not follow the trend of regulating the institution of the family in the constitution, but merely states that this must be done by means of laws. However, the unattachable family patrimony is established. The organization of education is left to the laws, but Article 41 of the constitution declares that primary education shall be obligatory, and free in all schools maintained by the State. The same article also guaranteed freedom of instruction, and specifies that the State shall inspect public and private schools.

Costa Rica. In the Costa Rican constitution, there are only general dispositions with regard to the family. It establishes that the State shall protect the family, and shall succor mothers, children, aged persons and helpless invalids.

Primary education is obligatory and free. The constitution adds that the State shall maintain primary and secondary education, and shall create revenues for the support of the University.

Cuba. The family, maternity and matrimony are under the protection of the State. Only civil marriages are legally valid, and divorce is recognized in the constitution. Woman's legal equality is specified, and it is stipulated that she has full capacity to administer property, to engage in business, industry or profession with no necessity for marital authorization.

Common law marriages have the same effects as civil marriages, in certain circumstances. The right of the woman and children to collect alimony is given preference over any other indebtedness of the husband. Natural children are considered legally equal to legitimate children. A precept prohibits any reference with regard to the civil status of the parents, either at the time of registering the birth of a child, or at the time of his baptism, that is to say, it may not be mentioned whether the parents are married or single.

All systems of education are subject to inspection and regulation by the State. Primary education in schools maintained by the State is free and obligatory, and the secondary education offered by the State is free.

The constitution orders the creation and maintenance of schools for adults with the purpose of eradicating illiteracy, of rural schools, and of arts and crafts, commercial and technical institutions. All education, public and private, shall be inspired in the spirit of Cubanism and human solidarity. The monthly salary of the public school teachers shall in no case be lower than one millionth of the national budget. The University of Havana is autonomous, and official instruction laic. In all public or private schools, the teaching of Cuban history, literature and geography, as well as courses in civics must be entrusted to Cubans by birth, and based on texts written by native Cubans.

Dominican Republic. The constitution contains no regulations with regard to the family. Scant attention is paid to education in the constitution. Article 6 declares that freedom of instruction is one of the individual rights, and disposes that primary education is obligatory for minors and subject to State inspection. In official schools this primary education is free, as well as in schools of agriculture, of manual arts, and of home economics.

Ecuador. The constitution pays careful attention to the family beginning with the declaration that maternity is under the protection of the State, which assists mother and child "without considering antecedents." Article 163 further takes cognizance of the economic aspect, declaring that the state protects the family, as well as the family patrimony. Article 164, elaborating on these declarations of principle, especially the one protecting children without considering antecedents, does make an exception favoring legitimate children. It declares that illegitimate children have the same right to the protection of the state and of their parents as legitimate ones, but adds that when there are illegitimate and legitimate children of the same father, the illegitimate children have their right to inherit only half as much as the legitimate offspring. That is to say, the protection of the State suffers a quantitative diminution at the expense of the illegitimate children, in favor of those born of a legal marriage. Theoretically this is a contradiction, but the purpose is to stimulate marriages and to maintain the legal unity of the family.

As in Cuba, a provision forbids that any reference be made in birth certificates with regard to the civil status of the parents.

Freedom of instruction is guaranteed, as long as it is in accordance with moral principles and with republican institutions. The education of children is not only a right, but a primary duty of the parents. Primary education is obligatory, and free in schools maintained by the state. Public education must be laic. The State respects the rights of parents to give their children any religious instruction they desire. There is an interesting regulation, permitting municipalities to give economic assistance to private schools. This means that municipal funds may be used to subsidize religious schools, if the amount of the subsidy does not exceed the 20 per cent of the budget set aside for education by the municipality. The executive may also subsidize private schools, but in order to give this assistance he needs the approval of the Council of State. The problem of education of the Indians is dealt with in a clause of Article 171, which says that public and private institutions should pay special attention to the education of the native race. The constitution protects university autonomy, and disposes that the State should establish and maintain special schools for arts and crafts, commerce, agriculture and other institutions for moral and civic education.

El Salvador. There are no provisions giving equality to the natural family, with the legal one. It is merely declared that the family is the fundamental basis of the nation and is especially protected by the State, which should stimulate matrimony, as well as the protection of maternity and infancy. Article 153 orders that the law should regulate the family patrimony.

Slight attention is paid to education by the constitution. Article 33 merely guarantees the freedom of instruction, and states that primary instruction is obligatory, and shall be free in official establishments.

Guatemala. The family, maternity and matrimony are under the State's protection, and the family patrimony should be regulated by a special law. The Guatemalan constitution stipulates that there must be absolute equality of rights of husband and wife, and that, for reasons of justice, free unions may be compared to legal matrimony. Article 76 contains a provision, specifically establishing legal equality among children of all classes, and forbids any declaration as to the civil status of the parents to be made in any act or certification referring to the birth of a child.

The constitution declares that the State must guarantee a minimum of common instruction, obligatory for all citizens. Instruction in public schools is free and laic, and private schools are subject to State inspection. The only valid professional degrees are those offered by the State or the university, or by foreign institutions that shall have been duly recognized. Owners of large rural properties and industrial concerns are obliged to maintain schools for the workers. Education for indigenous groups is declared to be of national interest. The principle of freedom of education is guaranteed.

Haiti. There are no provisions in the constitution in connection with the family. Freedom of instruction is guaranteed, primary education is declared to be obligatory, and all public instruction gratuitous. In order to assist teachers and professors economically, the constitution disposes that those engaged in secondary and higher education may occupy more than one public office, remunerated by the State.

Honduras. There are only provisions of a general character related to the institution of the family. The constitution points out that the family is the basis of society, and that it is therefore under the protection of the State. It also declares that the State shall organize the family patrimony and protect maternity and childhood (Article 197).

The constitution guarantees freedom of instruction, and declares that education offered by the State shall be free and laic. Primary education is obligatory and, in general, supported by the municipalities with State assistance.

Mexico. In spite of the socialistic content of some of the provisions of Mexico's constitution, the legislators have not paid a great deal of attention to the family and, furthermore, have maintained the traditional principle that marriage is a civil contract, and not a social institution as indicated in other Latin American constitutions. Probably the Mexican legislators gave more thought to the relations of the family with the power of the Church, and stressed the civil nature of matrimony. Because of this, it is expressly stated that marriage and other acts of a civil nature are within the exclusive competence of civil functionaries. Maternity and its rights have been given consideration, but these are dealt with under the regulation of labor rights.

The constitution declares that all instruction offered by the State shall tend to develop the faculties of the human being and shall encourage love of the fatherland, international solidarity and a consciousness of independence and justice. Public education shall be independent of any religious doctrine whatsoever and, based on scientific progress, shall struggle against ignorance, servitude, fanaticisms and prejudices. Furthermore, all education shall be democratic, national, and shall encourage human cooperation, instilling the ideals of fraternity and equality of rights of all men, and avoiding privileges of race, sect, groups, sexes and individuals.

In connection with private education, the Mexican constitution has considered it necessary to regulate it carefully. Private individuals may devote themselves to teaching, but in primary, secondary and normal school institutions, they must have State authorization, and their curricula must adjust to the general dispositions above indicated. With regard to religious instruction, the constitution states that religious corporations, ministers of faith and stock companies that perform educational activities may in no manner intervene in primary, secondary or normal education, or that intended for workers and peasants. The State has the right to withdraw, at any time, official recognition of private educational institutions. Primary education is obligatory, and all education by the State is gratuitous.

Nicaragua. The constitution contains the general provision that marriage, the family and maternity are under the protection of the state. Legal investigation of paternity is authorized, and Article 72 declares that the parents have the same duties toward children born out of wedlock as those born of legal marriage. The creation of the family patrimony is ordered, and it is stipulated that the State shall protect families having numerous offspring.

Primary, secondary and professional education is subject to State inspection. Primary education is obligatory and free, and that which is given in public schools must be secular. The constitution disposes that the State alone may grant professional degrees, and orders that all agricultural and industrial concerns located outside the radius of schools, and having more than thirty children of school age, must maintain elementary schools at the expense of the owners. The constitution guarantees academic freedom, when this does not interfere with good customs and public order.

Panama. Unions in fact are considered to have the effects of a civil marriage if they have lasted for ten years or more. Article 57 states that parents will exercise jurisdiction over their children "in accordance with the social interest." There is no legal difference between natural and legitimate children, both having equal rights to inheritance. The constitution establishes the right to investigate paternity, and forbids declarations to be made with regard to the civil status of the parents in any inscription of birth or record of baptism. The family patrimony is also created.

An entire chapter of the constitution is devoted to education, which is declared to be democratic and based on ideals of aggrandizement of the country and human solidarity. Primary education is obligatory and that given by the State is free. Freedom of instruction is guaranteed, but the State is authorized to intervene in private institutions to see that the national and social principles are followed. No educational institution may refuse to admit students because of the civil status of their parents or guardians, or for social, racial or political differences. The violation of this precept may cause the loss of State recognition, and consequently loss of the right to continue in educational activities. A nationalistic regulation disposes that instruction in the history of Panama and civic education shall be entrusted to national professors, and no courses in foreign languages may be offered without the permissions of the Minister of Education. Private schools are required to include in their curricula obligatory courses in the history and geography of Panama, as well as civics.

The autonomy of the national university is guaranteed, as well as academic freedom, with no limitations except that of public order. The State must develop special technical schools, and promote a program of adult education. Although ministers of religious faiths may not hold public office, they are authorized to fill positions related to social welfare or public instruction.

Paraguay. There are only general provisions, such as that declaring that the State shall "take heed of the unity of the family." Woman is considered equal to man (Article 23), but it is added that the diversity of their respective functions in society must be considered.

Scant constitutional attention to education is given. Primary education is obligatory and free, and the government must develop secondary, professional and university instruction.

Peru. Matrimony, the family and maternity are under the protection of the State, whose duty it is to safeguard the physical, mental and moral health of childhood. Other provisions with regard to the family are left to the laws, and do not appear in the constitution.

The technical direction of education belongs to the State. Primary education is obligatory and free. Schools functioning in industrial, agricultural and mining areas must be maintained by the owners of the concerns. There must be at least one industrial school in each Department, and the State encourages the technical instruction of workers. The moral and civic education of the child is obligatory, and shall be based on national development and human solidarity. The State guarantees academic freedom, and the law must stipulate the minimum amount of funds intended for the support of education, so that this may be properly attended to.

Uruguay. The State shall protect the social development of the family, and the constitution contains an interesting provision with regard to the education of children, declaring that parents have the right to supervise their education and that this is not just a right but a duty. If the parents do not carry out their obligations, the constitution provides that the State shall protect children when abandoned by their parents or guardians, or when they are exploited or abused. The constitution also stipulates that families having numerous offspring are entitled to State assistance, and that women shall be given participation in a system set up to deal with juvenile delinquency. This indicates that the Uruguayan legislators feel that women are more qualified to attend to cases of social maladjustment of children than are men. In this country, parents have the same duties toward children born out of wedlock as toward legitimate children, and the constitution also orders, in connection with the economic aspect of the family, that its welfare shall be the purpose of special protective legislation.

Venezuela. The State protects the family, whatever its origin may be, as well as maternity, regardless of the civil status of the mother. Article 48 orders that the State should create the family patrimony, which shall be unattachable. There is an interesting article (50), found in no other Latin American constitution, declaring that the State will eliminate the social causes of prostitution and assist in the social reintegration of those affected by it.

The constitution guarantees to all inhabitants of the Republic the right to an education, and disposes that this shall be organized as an integral process to develop human personality, to prepare citizens for life, and to build the culture of the nation.

Freedom of instruction is guaranteed, and everyone may devote himself to it, with the limitations and under the conditions determined by the law. The constitution respects private instruction, and Article 56 declares that it shall be stimulated by the State, adding, however, in Article 57, that all education shall be entrusted to competent persons, this competence being verified according to law. Primary education is obligatory, and that which is offered in official institutions is free.

SUGGESTED READINGS

English:

Brazilian Government Trade Bureau, *Outline of Education in Brazil,* Brazilian Government Trade Bureau, 1946

Booth, George C., *Mexico's School-Made Society,* Stanford University Press, 1941.

Bunn, Harriet and Ellen Gut, *The Universities of Cuba, The Dominican Republic and Haiti,* Washington, D. C., Pan American Union, 1946.

Kneller, George F., *The Education of the Mexican Nation,* New York, Columbia University Press, 1951.

Logan, Rayford W., "Education in Haiti," *Journal of Negro History,* 1930.

Morgan, Katherine Lenore, *The Universities of Chile,* Washington, D. C., Pan American Union, 1944.

Nelson, Lowry, *Rural Cuba,* Minneapolis, The University of Minnesota Press, 1950.

Sánchez, George I., *Mexico: A Revolution by Education,* New York, The Viking Press, 1936.

————, *The Development of Higher Education in Mexico,* New York, Columbia University Press, 1944.

Smith, T. Lynn, (Ed.), *Brazil,* New York, The Dryden Press, 1951.

Taylor, Carl C., *Rural Life in Argentina,* Baton Rouge, Louisiana State University Press, 1948.

U. S. Office of Education, Pamphlets on *Education in El Salvador, Guatemala, Nicaragua, Peru, Colombia, Costa Rica, Dominican*

Republic, Bolivia, and Panama, Washington, D. C., U. S. Printing Office.

Whetten, Nathan L., *Rural Mexico,* University of Chicago Press, 1948.

Other Languages:

Amaral, Luis, *Aspectos Fundamentaes da Vida Rural Brasileira,* São Paulo, 1936.

Bellegarde, Dantes, *Haiti et ses Problems,* Montreal, 1941.

Bunge, A. E., *Una Nueva Argentina,* Buenos Aires, 1940.

Carneiro, Leao A., *A Sociedade Rural, Seus Problemas e sua Educaçao,* Rio de Janeiro, 1939.

Chávez Orozco, Luis, *Historia Económica y Social de México,* México, D. F., 1938.

Espinosa, Francisco, *Evolución de La Enseñanza Secundaria en El Salvador,* San Salvador, 1938.

Gamio, Manuel, *Hacia un México Nuevo,* México, D. F., 1935.

González Flores, Luis F., *La Evolución de la Instrucción Pública en Costa Rica,* San José (Costa Rica), 1934.

Labarca Hubertson, Amanda, *Historia de la Enseñanza en Chile,* Santiago, 1939.

Larrea, Julio C., *Problemas de la Educación Ecuatoriana,* Quito, 1939.

MacLean y Estenós, Roberto, *Sociología Educacional del Perú,* Lima, 1944.

México, Secretaría de Educación Pública, *La Educación Pública en México,* México, D.F., 1922.

Poblete Troncoso, Moisés, *El Standard de Vida de las Poblaciones de América,* Universidad de Chile, 1942.

Ramírez, Rafael, *La Enseñanza por la Acción dentro de la Escuela Rural,* México, D.F., 1942.

Salazar Romero, Carlos, *Problemas Educacionales del Perú,* Lima, 1943.

Salterain Herrera, Eduardo de, *Enseñanza Secundaria y temas derivados,* Montevideo, 1942.

CHAPTER 10

Institutional Conflicts

There are two institutions in Latin America that exercise great political power and cause friction and conflicts. One is the army, and the other is the Roman Catholic Church. Organized labor also intervenes, but its role shall be considered in a later chapter.

The Army in Politics. The intervention of the army in politics is the most serious problem of Latin America. Any study of the constitutions will show a number of measures introduced to curb the participation of the armed forces in political life. There are countries where no member of the army may be elected to the presidency or high offices; others where the State has the monopoly in the manufacture, import and distribution of armaments; and in most of them, the armed forces are prohibited the right to deliberate and are ordered to obey the civil authorities. To prevent nepotism, relatives of the Chief of the Army may not hold certain public offices in some countries, and in others the President is subject to military laws when he takes personal command of the troops. All of this indicates the concern of the Latin American legislators with the abuses of the army when it intervenes in politics. Unfortunately, the constitutional precepts have not been successful in changing this situation.

As this is written, militarism is extending throughout Latin America in an alarming manner. Military governments are established in Venezuela, Bolivia and Cuba; there are military dictatorships—under the cloak of legality—in the Dominican Republic and Nicaragua. Argentina is under the rule of Perón, who owes his rise to power to army force. In Panama, where there is no regular army, the Chief of Police has been "elected" president. Peru is ruled by an army man who led a successful coup d'etat and later was elected in a one-party election. Colombia has a government also elected without opposition, and kept in power with the support of the armed forces.

The army, as an armed group within the State, is one of the characteristics of the modern nations. The intervention of the regular army in politics is an old and serious problem. The role of the army is not limited to the backing of dictators and conservative forces. Every important historical revolution has been followed by a military dictatorship. In England, under Cromwell, the army's role was an important one. The French Revolution had its system of conscription and owed its success to the Army of the Republic, and later its defeat to a military leader, Napoleon I. The Russian Revolution could not have surmounted the internal and international wars had it not been for Trotsky's Red Army, and militarism today backs the dictatorship of Stalin. Certain observers believe that the bulwark of the Communist dictatorship in China has been the troops of the Eighth Route Army.

With the exception of Brazil, the Latin American republics obtained their independence through the force of arms. Since the early days of their political life, the liberating armies were among the strongest pressure groups. Marshall Sucre, himself a liberator, even then saw the problem clearly and said, "Now we have to liberate Latin America from the Liberators."

The participation of the army in the nineteenth century politics was not purely a Latin American phenomenon. The European countries with the exception of Great Britain and the northern democracies, were affected by the same troubles. France suffered from the *coup d'etat* of Napoleon III and the army's active intervention during the Third Republic. Since the time of the Revolution, French liberalism has struggled for the creation of a National Guard as an armed group of citizens to counteract the political influence of the regular army. But in Latin America, the trouble has been more acute and frequent, and we must examine its characteristics and background.

Spanish Heritage. Much of the terminology used today, and not only in Latin America, to indicate the participation of the army in politics has come to us from Spain. The Spanish term *pronunciamiento* explains the incongruous fact of the armed forces declaring themselves in favor of or against a political issue. In English, we use the French term *coup d'etat,* but the Spanish one is more graphic, because one speaks of a *cuartelazo,* or a blow from the barracks. The Spanish term *golpe de estado,* the translation of *coup d'etat,* indicates only a non-constitutional change of government in which the army has not necessarily intervened. *Cuartelazo* unfortunately describes what has most often happened in Spain and in Latin America. And, we must not forget that the famous "Fifth Column" was born in the siege of Madrid.

The political history of nineteenth century Spain is full of *pronunciamientos* and *cuartelazos,* and the memory of the Civil War and the army uprising against the Spanish Republic is so fresh that we need nothing to remind us of it. Spanish historians in many cases tell us of two Spains. Civilian Spain and *castrense* Spain, meaning the country of military encampments. The latter Spain has left a definite mark on her children overseas.

The Army and the State. In Latin America, the army is a State within a State. No one traveling through its republics will see the advertisements so frequently seen in the United States urging young men to join the armed forces. On the contrary, there are too many candidates for the positions. The possession of a uniform implies a step forward in the social ladder for the members of the masses, especially the peasants. It is not the salary alone that attracts the people to the army, but a series of small privileges attached to the wearing of the uniform. The army, too, offers the possibility of rapid promotion because of the frequent political upheavals, and it is not uncommon to see an army officer pass to an elective position in politics and then to the presidency of the republic. The army, as a class, and as a safeguard to its power and interests, has surrounded itself with an exaggerated symbolism and *esprit de corps.* In Spanish, one does not speak so often of military honor as of *pundonor,* which implies a point of honor beyond the ordinary. The politicians and governments have made use of this situation. During Urriburu's militaristic regime in Argentina, a number of army officers who led gay lives contracted sizable debts. Their creditors filed suit to collect their claims, and a scandal was in the offing. To avoid it, the President issued a decree prohibiting officers from gambling and contracting debts, and added that in order to save the honor of the army, the State would pay the debts the officers had incurred.

As a rule, the Latin American armed forces have backed conservative governments and dictators, always with their own interests in mind. A typical case was the support of the Cuban army officers of Machado's dictatorship. The army and navy officials were so detached from their troops that, after Machado was overthrown, the privates and non-commissioned officers were able to strip their superiors of command, in the military coup of September 4, 1933, without firing a single shot. This was one of the most interesting mutinies in Latin American history, and observers of other countries have found it difficult to understand such a violent break in military discipline. It can be explained only by the isolation of the officers from the troops, and by the corruption prevailing during Machado's administration.

To all of this must be added the influence of *caudillismo,* and the cult of the hero mentioned in the early chapters, so characteristic of the Latin American countries. The army intervenes in politics not as a normal political group, but by taking advantage of its organization and weapons. The people can no longer resort to the typical revolutions of the nineteenth century, with guerrilla warfare or barricades in the cities. The army's modern weapons would soon dispose of that. Furthermore, as a privileged political power, the army is used by other political groups. It is used by the lower classes as a means of advancing themselves, and by the dominating classes as a means of enjoying their privileges. While these conditions exist, the role of the army in Latin America will continue to be one of the major causes of problems and disturbances.

The armed forces function in Latin America as a mechanism of abnormal political change. In England, it is quite common to speak of a "khaki election," meaning the consultation with the electorate that takes place after a victorious war, and in which the soldiers' votes influence the results. In Latin America, it is common to ask the question, "Where will the khaki stand?", having in mind not the vote of the soldiers, but the political pressure of the armed forces. Once a cynical Cuban politician said: "You can win an election with the Army; you can win an election without the Army, but you cannot win an election against the Army." This, unfortunately, summarizes the situation in many of the Latin American republics.

Politics and the Church. The spiritual and material power of the Roman Catholic Church is still an important factor in the political life of Latin America. There are countries that, institutionally speaking, have maintained the traditional relation of colonial times, when the State exercised Royal Patronage, and the government now has National Patronage; others in which the principle of separation of State and Church exists, but in these also the power of the Church is felt. Mexico stands apart as the country in which the Roman Catholic Church has been strictly regimented.

Spanish Heritage. An historical study of the Spanish antecedent to the political role of the Church in Latin America is not intended here. An excellent book by Professor J. Lloyd Mecham covers the period well.[1] The politico-religious character of the Church in the colonial governments was discussed previously. At the time of indepence, the Pope not only refused to recognize the independence of the new republics, but took the position that since the Royal Patronage was a special, personal privilege granted to the Spanish King, and not to the Spanish State, this privilege had ceased to exist with independence, and the jurisdiction of Church matters had reverted to the Holy See. The new republics, on the other hand, held the conception that they had acquired the right of sovereignty from Spain, including the right of Patronage. It is easy to imagine the problems arising from this situation and the bitterness on both sides. In view of Rome's attitude, many governments abolished the tithe, suppressed religious orders and confiscated ecclesiastical property. This phase of the struggle was purely political. The Church participated in politics to defend its privileges. Some countries with a strong government succeeded in controlling the Church and established National Patronage. In others, where a weak government was influenced by the followers of the Church, it achieved a temporary victory; but overconfidence produced intransigence and the nationalist forces then opposed the government in bitter struggles, finally establishing the separation of Church and State.

The Church and the State. In some Latin American countries today, the government exercises Patronage over the Church. These

---

[1] *Church and State in Latin America,* Chapel Hill, University of North Carolina Press, 1934.

are Argentina, Bolivia, Costa Rica, Peru, Paraguay and Venezuela. The principle is clearly established in the constitutions, and the executive power exercises the right, in some cases with the intervention of the other branches of government. Other countries, like Colombia, deal directly with the Holy See in ecclesiastical matters by means of Concordats and following the principles of international law, as in relations between two sovereign states. All of these countries guarantee freedom of religion and of conscience in their constitutions, but the Roman Catholic Church enjoys a privileged position. In Argentina and in Paraguay, one must be a Catholic to be elected to the presidency.

A second large group of countries maintain the principle of separation of Church and State. This principle did not appear immediately after independence, except in the cases of Cuba and Panama, which obtained theirs in this century. The others had to go through long and bitter political struggles to establish separation.

Various countries have introduced restrictive measures against religious orders. Of these, Mexico is the most radical. There, the Church is placed under the strict vigilance of the State.

Points of Conflict. The most common point of conflict between the Roman Catholic Church and the State in Latin America is the control of education. However, this phenomenon is not limited to Latin America, but exists in all parts of the world where Catholicism is strong. Another point of conflict has been of an economic nature. The great economic strength of the Church has made it always a powerful enemy; therefore the nationalistic governments felt it was essential to take away some of its power by expropriation of ecclesiastical property, breaking entails and prohibition of monastic orders. The reasons for conflict have been purely administrative. In colonial days there were no civil registries, and the Church controlled the recording of all marriages, births, deaths and other matters concerning the civil status of the people. This hindered the functioning of the administrative and legal machinery of the new republics, and the governments gradually assumed these functions. That explains why today some constitutions specifically state that the civil status of a person cannot be proved by means of an ecclesiastic document.

Nominal Catholicism. Many Latin Americans are anti-clerical but not anti-Catholic. The same situation exists in Spain. There are persons who disagree with the temporal policy of the Roman Church, but in spite of that keep their religious beliefs. As a counterpart to this, many Latin Americans are nominally Catholics, but are not religious; this is true also in Spain. This fact has been well described by George Pendle [2] in his book on Uruguay:

> Uruguay is a Catholic country, but the Uruguayans are not a religious people. The general indifference to religion may perhaps be partly explained by the fact that the Banda Oriental formed part of the Spanish Empire for only a relatively short period, while immediately after the emancipation British and French influence was strong. The decline in the power of the Blancos—who traditionally received the support of the Church—assisted the secular emphasis within the State, and of course Batlle y Ordóñez was doggedly anti-clerical. Nevertheless the Uruguayan people were never intolerant in religious matters. When the Church was disestablished in 1919, it retained all its property, together with liberty of teaching and worship. The calendar was purged of Church festivals: 25 December became 'Family Day,' and Holy Week became an official seven days' holiday called 'Criollo' (*sic*) Week, and subsequently re-named 'Tourist Week;' but a large sum was raised by popular subscription to compensate the Church for its loss of State support. Before disestablishment, however, the Church had received only very limited financial aid from the State and it had never been a direct or very powerful factor in politics. In the towns the women generally are practising Catholics, and the men agnostics. There are few churches in the interior of the country, and none in the more distant villages. Religion is not taught in the schools.

Another example is Mexico, where, according to the 1940 census, 96.6 per cent of the inhabitants declared that they were Catholics. Yet that is the country where the Church is most severely regulated. Of course, it should be kept in mind that the large masses of Indians and Negroes in Latin America, who appear in the census as Catholics, often represent a combination of indigenous beliefs and Catholic principles.

---

2 *Uruguay*, Royal Institute of International Affairs, Oxford University Press, London and New York, 1952, p. 32.

Anti-clericalism and religious restrictions in Latin America have been fundamentally political phenomena. Anti-clericalism is closely allied to lay thought, and became necessary in political climates in which only one group practically monopolized all aspects of religious life. In other parts of the world, which experienced the tolerant climate that followed the Reformation and the religious wars, a better religious balance has been attained. Latin America has been deprived of the political effects of this balance.

CONSTITUTIONAL SUMMARY

Argentina. All citizens are obliged to take up arms in defense of the nation. The President of the Republic is the Chief of all the armed forces of the nation, and appoints, with the approval of the Senate, officials of higher ranks. He may appoint officials and grant promotions on the field of battle, requiring no further approval. All inhabitants have the right to practice their religious faith, but the federal government sustains the Roman Catholic Church. In order to be elected President or Vice-President of the Republic, it is necessary to belong to the Roman Catholic faith. The Argentine state, through the Executive, exercises the right of patronage and appoints the bishops, from a panel submitted by the Senate. The executive also authorizes the promulgation of Papal bulls and decrees, with the approval of the Supreme Court of Justice. When the bulls or decrees contain dispositions of a general and permanent nature, the President also needs a law passed by Congress.

Bolivia. All citizens are obliged to give military service. Members of the armed forces may not be elected to the Presidency, Vice-Presidency or the Congress. The constitution does not state that the President is the Commander-in-Chief of the army, but that the rank of Captain-General is inherent to the functions of the President of the Republic. Congress has direct intervention in the control of the armed forces, since it decides each year as to the number of the permanent army. There is a Supreme Council of National Defense, formed by the President of the Republic, the Ministers of State, the Commander in Chief and the Chief of Staff of the army.

The State recognizes and supports the Roman Catholic religion, but guarantees the public exercise of other faiths. Members of the regular clergy may not be elected to the Presidency or Vice-Presidency of the Republic. The President exercises the right of National Patronage, makes appointments of higher ecclesiastical dignitaries, and may grant or deny the exequatur to Papal bulls.

Brazil. All Brazilians are obliged to give military service. Women are excepted, but ecclesiastics are required to do so. The armed forces are under the supreme authority of the President of the Republic, and problems relating to the nation's defense are in charge of the Council of National Security, which is directed by the President and composed of the Ministers of State and the Chiefs of Staff. The national territory is divided into defense zones, and within these it is not permitted to grant land concessions, open or install means of communication, construct bridges or establish industries without the authorization of the Council of National Security. Freedom of conscience and of belief is declared inviolable, and the State guarantees free exercise of all religious faiths. Religious ceremonies and spiritual assistance in the armed forces must be in the hands of native Brazilians. The same disposition refers to penal institutions. Cemeteries must be secular, and administered by municipal authorities, and the practice of all faiths must be permitted in them.

Chile. All Chileans able to do so are obliged to give military service. Article 22 establishes that the armed forces are essentially obedient, and that no armed body may deliberate. Article 23 declares that any decision agreed to by the President of the Republic, the Congress or the tribunals of justice in the presence of the armed forces, or an officer with troops at his command, is null in law. The constitution establishes freedom of conscience and the exercise of all religions. Churches and religious institutions are subject to the common law in all matters with ownership of property. All churches, intended for the service of any sect, are exempt from taxation.

Colombia. All Colombians are obliged to take up arms when public necessity requires it, and the law determines the length of military service. The creation of a national militia and a national police force is authorized by the constitution. The State has the monopoly of importation, manufacture and possession of arms and munitions. Members of the army, the police and other armed forces may not have the right of suffrage, nor intervene in public debates. Military tribunals are created to take cognizance of illegal acts committed by members of the army in active service.

The State guarantees freedom of conscience and of religion, and orders that no one may be molested because of his religious opinions, nor compelled to profess beliefs contrary to his conscience. Article 53 disposes that the State may sign Concordats with the Holy See to establish relations between the State and the Catholic Church, and the following article declares the incompatibility of the ministerial professions with the discharge of public office. An exception is made in the case of Catholic priests, who may be employed in institutions of learning and in social work.

Costa Rica. Article 8 of the constitution states that citizens must defend the Fatherland, but does not establish obligatory military service. The armed forces are essentially obedient, may not deliberate, and are subordinated to the civil power. The President of the Republic directs the armed forces of sea and land, for the defense of the national territory, and for the maintenance of peace and order.

The Roman Catholic, Apostolic religion is that of the State, which contributes to its maintenance, without preventing the free exercise in the Republic of any other faith not opposed to morality or good customs. Clergymen or laymen may not invoke religious motives in political propaganda, or make use of the religious beliefs of the people. The Executive exercises the right of patronage, and intervenes in appointments and other acts connected with the administration of the Catholic Church.

Cuba. All Cubans are obliged to bear arms. The President of the Republic is the supreme chief of the armed forces. The profession of all religions, and the exercise of all faiths, is free, without other limitation than respect for Christian morality and public order. The Church is separated from the State, which may not grant a subvention to any religion.

Dominican Republic. The constitution disposes that the armed forces are essentially obedient, and may not deliberate. In order to belong to any armed body of the republic, it is necessary to be a Dominican, in full exercise of civil and political rights.

Freedom of conscience and of faith are considered rights of the citizen, with no limitation other than respect for good customs and public order. Article 93 declares that the relations between the State and the Roman Catholic Church shall continue to be the same, since the majority of the Dominicans profess the Catholic religion.

Ecuador. Military service is established, obligatory upon nationals and aliens domiciled in the nation. The armed forces may not deliberate, and the constitution declares that officials who give orders contrary to the constitution and the laws will bear full responsibility. The President of the Republic is the Commander in Chief of the army. All members of the armed forces in active service are subject to military jurisdiction.

Article 168 of the constitution guarantees freedom of conscience, insofar as it is not opposed to morality and public order, and the law shall make no discrimination for religious, ideological or racial motives.

El Salvador. Obligatory military service is established in case of war, and all able bodied Salvadorians between 18 and 50 years of age shall be considered soldiers. The armed forces are essentially obedient, and may not deliberate on matters of military service. In times of peace, the Congress shall fix annually the number of the armed forces, which shall be limited to the necessary number to protect the ports, military establishments and arsenals.

Freedom of all religions is guaranted with no further restrictions than required by morality and public order. No religious act shall serve to establish the civil status of persons. The purpose of this article is to guarantee the nonintervention of the Church in birth, marriage or death certificates. Churches and their dependencies shall be exempt from taxation. The State recognizes the legal personality of the Catholic Church, which represents the religion of the majority of the citizens. Other religions may obtain recognition or legal personality, in conformity with the law, but this right is not specifically granted in the constitution.

Guatemala. All Guatemalans are obliged to give military service, in accordance with the law. The President of the Republic is Commander in Chief of the armed forces.

Congress appoints the Chief of the armed forces, who holds office for six years. This official may not be related within the fourth degree to the President of the Republic, the President of Congress or the Minister of National Defense. A Superior Council of National Defense is created, to function as a consultative body and as a superior tribunal of military jurisdiction. The profession of all religions is free, as is the practice of all cults, but this must be done in the interior of the churches. Religious societies and groups, and their members as such, may not intervene in politics or in matters related to the organization of labor. Religious demonstrations outside of churches are permitted, but are governed by a special law. Article 32 specifically prohibits the establishment of conventual congregations and of monastic institutions, as well as the functioning of political organizations of an international or foreign character.

Haiti. Military service is obligatory. Members of the armed forces in active service are not eligible for public office. The Haitian army is established for the internal and external security of the republic, and to guarantee the rights of the people. Military jurisdiction is created, and its decision may be appealed before the Tribunal of Cassation.

All faith and religions are free and recognized. Everyone has the right to profess his religion, and practice his faith, as long as it does not disturb public order. It is interesting to see that this article (22) restricts the free exercise of religion for motives of public order and not principles of Christian morality.

Honduras. Military service is the duty of all male citizens from 21 to 30 years of age. Free exercise is guaranteed all religions, as long as the law is not violated. The Church is separate from the State, and the State may not grant subsidies to any denomination or for the purpose of religious instruction. No religious act may serve to establish the civil status of a person. Monastic associations are prohibited, and the entrance into the country of members of these associations shall be regulated by a special law. The constitution prohibits all foundations in favor of religious institutions, and ministers of religions may not hold public office.

Mexico. The Mexican constitution gives little space to the organization and regulation of the army, leaving this to the federal laws. Article 26 establishes that in times of peace no member of the armed forces may be lodged in a private house without the consent of the owner, nor may levies be enacted. In times of war, the armed forces may exact lodging, in accordance with martial law. Article 129 declares that, in peacetime, no military authority may engage in duties other than those directly connected with his office. All men are free to profess the religion they choose and to practice their faith in the temples or in their homes; and all public demonstrations of faith must be made precisely within the temples, which are under the vigilance of the authorities. The law recognizes no juridical personality in religious associations, and ministers of faiths are considered to be persons exercising a profession. The state laws fix the maximum numbers of ministers within their territories. To practice the ministry of any denomination, it is necessary to be Mexican by birth, and ministers may not criticize the laws of the country in any public or private assembly. Ministers shall not have the right to vote, nor form associations for political purposes. The temples are the property of the State, and each one must have someone in charge who is responsible for the compliance with laws on religious matters. Religious periodicals may not comment upon political matters. No political group may be formed whose name indicates a connection with any religious association. Ministers of denominations may not be testamentary heirs of ministers of the same denomination, or of any private individual not related within the fourth degree.

Nicaragua. Military service is obligatory, and the law determines the manner in which it is to be given. The Nicaraguan army is constituted by the National Guard, which has been controlled for many years by General Somoza. Article 273 of the constitution establishes that this National Guard is the only armed body and police force of the republic, and that any other armed body which may be created shall be under its authority and control. The Chief of the National Guard is appointed by the President of the Republic. The members of the National Guard are subject to military jurisdiction, although they may be judged by ordinary courts after they have been dismissed by that body. The Chief of the National Guard controls the manufacture, exportation and importation, as well as the use of arms and munitions of war. The State has no official religion, but guarantees freedom of conscience, as long as morals and public order are respected. Temples of faiths are exempt from taxation. No one may be compelled to declare officially his religious beliefs, except in cases ordered by the law. Public cemeteries are secular, and the ministers of all faiths may practice their religious services in them.

Panama. Although Panama does not have a regular standing army, obligatory military service is established in case of need, when required by the defense of national independence and territorial integrity. The functions of the armed forces are separate from those of the national police force. The public forces may not deliberate or exercise the right of petition, except in matters connected with the service. They may not assemble, unless by order of the authorities. Only the government may possess arms and the elements of war, and the permission of the Executive is required for their manufacture, importation and exportation.

The exercise of all religions is free, but the constitution recognizes that most of the citizens are Roman Catholics. Because of this, the Catholic religion is taught in the public schools, but students are not required to attend these classes when their parents or tutors request that they be excused.

Paraguay. Military service is obligatory for all citizens. The President of the Republic is Commander in Chief of the armed forces, and may delegate authority to an official.

Roman Catholicism is the official religion of the State, and the constitution declares that other faiths are tolerated as long as they do not oppose morality and public order.

The head of the Paraguayan Church and the bishops must be native-born citizens. The President of the Republic exercises National Patronage, with the approval of the Cabinet and Congress.

Peru. Every Peruvian is obliged to contribute toward the national defense, and submit to military obligations. The number of the armed forces, as well as of officials, is fixed by the law; and members of the forces may not exercise the right of petition. The President of the Republic is chief of the army, but Article 153 of the constitution forbids him from taking personal command without authorization from the Congress. Should he take personal command, he is subject to military jurisdiction and responsible in accordance with it. The constitution declares that, out of respect for the majority of the population, the State protects the Roman Catholic religion, although the other religions are free to exercise their respective faiths. The State exercises the National Patronage, and all relations between it and the Church are governed by Concordats negotiated by the Executive and approved by the Congress. Members of the clergy may not be deputies, senators or Ministers of State. In order to occupy the office of Archbishop or Bishop, it is necessary to be Peruvian by birth. The ecclesiastics who occupy these positions are appointed by the President of the Republic, with the Council of Ministers. The President refers these appointments to the Holy See, and approves the respective Papal Bulls.

Uruguay. The Congress exercises control over the armed forces, and annually fixes the number of its members. The constitution declares that the army may not be increased without the agreement of the majority of each of the Chambers. No citizen is obliged to render aid to the armed forces, unless by order of a civil magistrate in accordance with the law, and he shall be compensated for any losses in such cases.

All religious faiths are free, and the State supports no religion. However, the State recognizes that the Roman Catholic Churches that have been totally or partially constructed with public funds are the property of the Church, with the exception of chapels in institutions of welfare, hospitals and jails. Churches consecrated to the worship of all religions are exempt from taxation.

Venezuela. The nation alone may possess elements of war, whether they are produced within the country or imported from abroad. Members of the armed forces may not vote or belong to political parties. During elections, the army must be restricted to quarters and may leave them only when necessary to guarantee public order. The President of the Republic has supreme authority over the armed forces, and may delegate this authority to officials. The Supreme Council of National Defense is created, formed by the President of the Republic, members of the Cabinet and the delegates of the armed forces designated by law.

Liberty of conscience and of faith is guaranteed, but the practice of the faith is subject to the supreme inspection of the Executive. No one may be obliged to declare his religious faith or political ideology, except when the law requires it. No one may invoke religious beliefs in order to evade the fulfillment of the laws of the Republic. With this, conscientious objectors are eliminated. The State exercises the National Patronage, and may negotiate treaties to regulate relations between the Church and the State.

SUGGESTED READINGS

English:

Baez Camargo, G., and Kenneth G. Gruble, *Religion in the Republic of Mexico,* London, World Dominion Press, 1935.

Callcott, Wilfred Hardy, *Church and State in Mexico, 1822-1857,* New York, Durham, 1926.

————, *Liberalism in Mexico, 1857-1929,* Stanford University Press, 1931.

Holmes, Olive, "Army Challenge in Latin America," New York, Midston House, *Foreign Policy Reports, Vol. XXV,* No. 14, December, 1949.

Howard, George P., *Religious Liberty in Latin America,* Philadelphia, Westminster Press, 1944.

Josephs, Ray, *Argentine Diary,* New York, Random House, 1944.

————, *Latin America; Continent in Crisis,* New York, Random House, 1948.

Mecham, Lloyd J., *Church and State in Latin America,* Chapel Hill, University of North Carolina Press, 1934.

Portes Gil, Emilio, *The Conflict Between the Civil Power and the Clergy,* Mexico, D.F., Ministry of Foreign Affairs.

Smith, T. Lynn, *Brazil: People and Institutions,* Baton Rouge, Louisiana State University Press, 1947.

Stevenson, John Reese, *The Chilean Popular Front,* Philadelphia, University of Pennsylvania Press, 1942.

Watters, Mary, *A History of the Church in Venezuela: 1810-1930,* Chapel Hill, University of North Carolina Press, 1933.

Whetten, Nathan L., *Rural Mexico,* Chicago, University of Chicago Press, 1948.

Other Languages:

Ayarragaray, Lucas, *La Anarquía Argentina y el Caudillismo,* Buenos Aires, 1925.

————, *La Iglesia en América y la Dominación Española,* Buenos Aires, 1920.

Berthe, A., *García Moreno, President de l'Equateur,* Paris, 1887.

Caso, Antonio, *El Problema de México y la Ideología Nacional,* México, D. F., 1924.

Chaves, Julio C., *El Supremo Dictador, Biografía de José Gaspar de Francia,* Buenos Aires, 1942.

Cuevas, Mariano, *Historia de la Iglesia en México,* El Paso (Texas), 5 vols., 1921-28.

Donoso, Ricardo, *Las Ideas Políticas en Chile,* México, D.F., 1946.

García Granados, Ricardo, *La Constitución de 1857 y las Leyes de Reforma en México,* México, D. F., 1906.

Ingenieros, José, *La Evolución de las Ideas Argentinas,* Buenos Aires, 1920.

Mariátegui, José Carlos, *Siete Ensayos de Interpretación de la Realidad Peruana,* Lima, 1943.

Montalvo, Juan, *Las Catilinarias,* 2 vols., Paris, 1925.

Ortiz, Fernando, *El Servicio Militar Obligatorio en Cuba,* La Habana, 1918.

Palacio, Juan de la Cruz, *La Iglesia y el Estado,* Caracas, 1939.

Restrepo, Juan Pablo, *La Iglesia y el Estado en Colombia,* Londres, 1881.

Rodríguez Mendoza, Emilio, *El Golpe de Estado de 1924,* Santiago de Chile, 1938.

Sánchez, Gómez, Gregorio, *Sociología Política Colombiana,* Cali (Colombia), 1943.

Sender, Ramón J., *El Problema Religioso en México: Católicos y Cristianos,* Madrid, 1928.

Sierra, Justo, *Juárez, su Obra y su Tiempo,* México, D.F., 1905-1906.

Sobral Pinto, Heraclito, *As Forças Armadas en Face do Momento Político,* Rio de Janeiro, 1945.

Toro, Alfonso, *La Iglesia y el Estado en México,* México, D. F., 1927.

CHAPTER 11

Social Conflicts

Labor and the State. Labor organizations have a peculiar position in the political structure of the Latin American countries. In most of the constitutions, the rights of workers and the system of labor are enumerated in detail, or else it is specified that this shall be done by the law, taking into account the bases fixed by the constitution. In order to understand this political phenomenon, and the position occupied by organized labor in the nations south of the Rio Grande, it is necessary to devote a little time to the historical factors conditioning the development of labor organizations in Latin America.

Trade unionism came late to Latin America, and developed in unfavorable circumstances which continued well into the twentieth century. This retardation can be explained by four main factors. The first is of an economic nature. Latin America was, and is still, a continent essentially dependent upon agricultural production, while it is common knowledge that unionism is the direct result of modern industrial economy. Another factor is political, a consequence of the evolution of the Latin American governments, of the strong executive, and of the great number of dictatorships experienced. In general, dictatorial governments have violently suppressed labor movements and have delayed their normal development. The third factor, a juridical one, is that freedom of association was not recognized early enough in Latin America to facilitate the organization of the workers. The fourth factor has been the conflict of interests between agricultural and industrial workers. The persistence of *latifundia* caused the peasant to desire above all things the acquisition of land, as the sole possibility of liberation; therefore he devoted all his efforts to that end, and not toward obtaining measures for the protection of his class as a productive group. On the contrary, the urban worker has followed the general line of conduct demanding shorter hours, better wages and other improvements. To these four factors must be added an ideological one: the early influence of anarchism first, and of anarcho-syndicalism later, which were not substituted by ideas of socialism and trade unionism until after the labor movement was well on its way.

The result of all this largely explains the early social radicalism that inspired the labor movements, and the easy prey found by Marxism in the labor organizations of some countries, especially after the Russian revolution of 1917. Furthermore, working conditions in Latin America have been more severe than in the European countries, where labor movements achieved early gains. One example is sufficient to illustrate this. In Mexico until the revolution of 1910, the working day was twelve hours long, and the workers were obliged to carry with them a booklet in which the employers kept an account of their good conduct. In case of unemployment, the slightest unfavorable report from the employer made it well-nigh impossible to find a new job. Payment was made in "company stores" where the workers were obliged to make their purchases of goods, exorbitantly priced, and which were discounted from their wages. Naturally, they were always in debt and in a condition similar to peonage.

Historical Background. The best general study of the labor movement in Latin America is the work of Moisés Poblete Troncoso,[1] in which the author states that the movement has passed through three perfectly defined stages during the republican era. The first was the stage of the mutualist movements; the second, of the societies of resistance; and the third, the syndicalist and trade unionist period, still existing today. To understand the mutualist origin of organized labor in Latin America, one must recall the influence exercised by economic and political individualism, a direct consequence of the ideas of the French revolution. The French revolution did away with the guilds and corporations of the Middle Ages, and furthered the principles of freedom of work. This principle was incorporated into the penal laws of the nineteenth century, which forbade all associations with a purpose of altering the price of goods. Since work was considered a merchandise subject to the

---

[1] *El Movimiento Obrero Latinoamericano*, México, D. F., 1946.

law of supply and demand in a free market, any group of workers endeavoring to secure an improvement in wages was considered to be an association altering the price of a merchandise, and was prohibited by the penal code. The antecedent of this legislation which so retarded the labor movement was embodied in the Chapellier law, of July, 1791, stipulating that the length of the working day for each laborer was left to the free decision between individual and individual. This implicitly prohibited any collective agreement as to wages, that is to say, the workers in a group could not make any arrangement as to their pay. The principle was recognized in most of the European countries; therefore the nations that maintained the principle of freedom of association, and authorized the association of employers, did not permit associations of workers.

In order to protect their interests, the workers in many countries resorted to principles of mutualism. Mutualist associations flourished in Latin America during the republican era, due to the influence of the Spanish mutualist tradition, since Spain had had mutualist associations of merchants many years before the independence of Latin America. These groups were organized with the purpose of attending to the immediate necessities, especially in cases of sickness and death, and the workers contributed a small sum toward their maintenance. Though mutualism never functioned essentially as a labor organization, and never helped to improve working conditions because of the law mentioned above, there are still important mutualist associations in Latin America, in Argentina, Chile, and especially in Cuba. In this latter country, they are represented by the well-known regional centers organized by Spanish immigrants in the nineteenth century. In Uruguay, mutualism is also important.

While the prohibition of association continued, and although some countries like Great Britain had authorized associations of workers early in the nineteenth century, the movement in Latin America made no headway until working conditions demanded a change from the mutualistic attitude to the so-called societies of resistance. These societies functioned on the margin of the law and were temporary associations to prevent abuse or to obtain some urgent demand. Their development in Latin America is similar to that of the French societies of resistance, and served as a foundation for the syndicalism which appeared later. Another manner of influencing economic affairs used by the workers were the labor exchanges, which were also similar to the French labor exchanges. In Mexico the movement toward labor associations started actively, in the revolutionary period, with the organization of the *Casa del Obrero Mundial,* which was originally a labor exchange.

In the era of the societies of resistance and the labor exchanges, the labor movement was inspired by anarchistic philosophy. There was complete skepticism with regard to intervention in politics, and the idea was to achieve conquests by means of violent acts and direct action. The methods employed were strikes, boycott, the label and sabotage. There were direct contacts with terrorist anarchism, which produced strong repressive measures by many governments. Under this influence, the first syndicates appeared in Latin America, and the present era of labor organizations came into being.

The Domestic Front. The labor movement of today must, in turn, be subdivided into two stages, the first with a predominance of anarchistic and anarcho-syndicalistic ideology, and the second under the influence of English and North American trade unionism, democratic socialism and, later, Marxism.

The influence of anarchism and the use of its methods by Latin American labor is easily explained. Following the split between Marx and Bakunin, after the First International, Bakunin's hold was strongest in Italy and in Spain, and many anarchist leaders of these countries, especially from Spain, were the organizers of the first syndicates of Latin America. The influence of French anarchism came to Latin America through the intellectual leaders, due to the predominant position French culture has always held in the South American republics. When European anarchism changed tactics and entered into the anarcho-syndicalistic stage, there was of course a strong current from this philosophy, and the workers of Latin America placed upon it all their hopes.

British and North American socialism and trade unionism came later. In countries of German immigration, particularly in Chile and Argentina, socialistic ideas immediately made an impression and decisively influenced the first labor organizations. In still later periods, pure and simple trade unionism has also been felt, as well as Marxism.

Today's labor in Latin America is, therefore, organized under diverse ideologies, although the general trend has been toward the

decline of anarchism, at the same time that it has ceased to be important in Europe; and the growing importance of trade unionism and
socialism of all types.

Another characteristic is the form of organization. Every list of
labor unions in a Latin American country contains the following
names: syndicate, league, union, association, fraternity and brotherhood, but basically they function exactly like trade unions, with
the same variations found in labor organizations of other countries.
The craft unions persist, just as in the United States in some lines
of production. There are numerous industrial unions, which have
developed more and more during the last ten years, and there are
peasant unions, due to the agricultural nature of the countries.
These are, of course, federated in national organizations, and there
is an international labor movement, which we shall mention later.

During the last twenty years, the labor unions have multiplied,
not only because of the efforts of the workers themselves to improve
their condition, but in some cases as a result of political efforts of
local leaders, with a view to obtaining support in campaigns. Others
have been formed, although it may seem contradictory, at the request
of employers, who have found it simpler to deal with the workers in
a group. Participation in the political life of the continent by organized labor is a comparatively recent thing. As we said above, the
workers followed the practice of not intervening in politics, so as
not to cooperate with the regimes opposing them. Their intervention was mainly limited to adopting an attitude of protest against
oppression, especially dictatorships, and cooperating in the overthrow of more than one tyrant by means of strikes and armed revolts.
Later, they started to support certain parties or candidates, thinking
that their victory might contribute to the improvement of the working class; but nowadays labor organizations play an important role
in politics in Latin America.

When considering the political role of the labor movement,
another characteristic should be kept in mind: that of its leaders.
Because of the lack of education among the workers, many of the
early leaders were foreigners, who brought their European experience and knowledge. Later, the organizers of the movement were
not laborers, but rather young intellectuals coming from the professional classes. Many politicians of radical ideas have been labor
leaders, and it has only been in recent years that the working class

has advanced in education so as to produce leaders from its own files. The action of intellectuals and politicians has frequently been detrimental to the labor movement, because they have merely made use of it to further their own careers, and have not been loyal to the class once a better social position was attained.

Summing up all of these antecedents, it should be an easy matter to understand the constitutional regulations of workers' rights as found today. The conquests of the workers have been achieved with such efforts and frustrations, and have so often been at the mercy of governments, that it has been necessary to make them a constitutional right, which may not be altered without modifying the constitution. In this, the countries of Latin America followed the example of the Mexican constitution of 1917, which had a decisive influence upon all the later constitutional documents.

The International Front. The relations of Latin American workers with the rest of the world may be divided into three epochs. In the first, the international movement kept up its contacts with the anarchist internationals, an easy fact to understand because, as we have seen, that was the predominating ideology in the initial stages of organized labor. In the second, we have the relations with the Second International, characterized by the ascendancy of socialistic ideas in general, and the social-democratic philosophy in particular. The third group of international contacts were the relations with the Third International, influenced by Communism, and in which the Soviet Union played a principal part. There are, besides, scattered contacts with Catholic syndicalism, with the international organs of the League of Nations, and with other such institutions.

Just as political activities have been marked by regional movements culminating in the Organization of American States, in labor there have been purely continental fronts which may also be subdivided into three large movements. The first is represented by the Pan American Federation of Labor (COPA, *Confederación Obrera Pan Americana*), which reached the height of its power in the period between the two world wars; the second by the Confederation of Latin American Workers (CTAL, *Confederación de Trabajadores de la América Latina*), which played an important part during World War II, although it had only come into existence a short time before; and the third by the recently created Regional Organization of Latin American Workers (ORIT, *Organización Regional Inter-Americana de Trabajadores*).

The Anarchist International. At the time of the First International (International Workingmen's Association) founded by Marx and Bakunin, some of the labor publications made brief mention of the workers' organizations of Latin America, and various Latin American syndicates maintained contacts with the international institution. The contacts were few and not very influential. When the split occurred between Bakunin and Marx, and the former began to act independently and to obtain proselytes among the Italian and Spanish workers, the ties of the Latin American syndicates became closer with the labor groups of these two countries, especially with Spain. Radical and anarchist papers of the larger Spanish cities gave space to the organized labor movements of the new world, and the international connections were dominated by the anarchist ideology. In various sessions of Marx's International, reference was made to the labor movements of the south of the continent, especially those of Argentina and Brazil; while the northern republics, especially Mexico and the Caribbean, were more in contact with Bakunin and his followers. There are frequent references in anarchist periodicals to the labor movements of Mexico, and some with regard to Brazil and Uruguay. During this time, also, the Latin American anarchist syndicates were closely connected with anarchism in the United States, especially with the Industrial Workers of the World (IWW), who were popular in South America. There was no large organized movement, and no important congresses, and international labor was limited to propaganda action, celebration of the first of May, and public protests in defense of imprisoned or persecuted leaders. When the anarchist ideology declined in Europe, the same thing happened in Latin America. However, there are still important anarchist syndicates that maintain international contacts, particularly with the Anarcho-Syndicalist International.

The Social-Democratic International. When the Second International was founded in Europe, dominated by a democratic-socialist ideology, the interest of the incipient Latin American organizations

was revived, toward a more active international life. Argentine delegates were present at its inaugural congress held in Paris, and it was
immediately reported that important contacts had been made with
the workers of Bolivia, Chile, Cuba and Uruguay. During the first
years of the Second International, Argentina occupied a prominent
position in the direction of Latin American labor relations, due to
that country's active socialist party, the first to be organized in Latin
America. However, the ideological division between anarchists and
socialists kept the organized workers from presenting a united front
in the Second International.

In the initial years of the second great labor front, the contacts
with Latin America were not only with the labor organizations, but
with the political socialist parties who followed the pattern of the
times, keeping their political associations separate from the syndical
organizations, in spite of their common ideas. That was the era in
which the workers had not as yet decided to participate actively in
political life, but instead backed parties in electoral campaigns, keeping their class organizations independent. Numerically, to be sure,
this international front was much more important than the anarchist,
but due to the sluggishness of the labor movement, few countries
paid attention to the socialist internationalism. It is curious to note
that when the socialist front of the Second International experienced its schism during World War I, because of the nationalism
of the European parties which voted the war credits, Latin America
kept its faith in socialist internationalism. Contacts were kept up
with the North American socialists of the period, and there were
congresses in Latin America, with important delegations from Argentina, Chile, Uruguay, Paraguay and Peru. The Russian revolution
of 1917 had a far greater effect. The Latin American international
front, inspired by the democratic socialist ideology, made declaration in favor of the socialism triumphant in Russia. But, when the
news came of the Communist dictatorship, and its effect in Spain
in the division between socialists and Communists, the Latin American socialists themselves became divided into these two groups. The
Russian revolution of October, 1917, and the founding of the Third
International by Lenin, started the decadence of democratic socialism in the labor movement.

The Second Socialist International was active in Europe during
the years of World War I and the postwar period, but in open con-

flict with the Third Communist International. The same thing occurred in Latin America, and the socialist front maintained a languid existence, with little influence, in spite of congresses of varying significance.

Early in World War II, Latin American socialists held a conference in Chile, with representatives from political parties and delegations of workers, and resolutions were adopted condemning the Communist International. Workers from Argentina, Chile, Ecuador, Panama and Uruguay played an important part in this congress. During the war, the socialist workers of Latin America adopted resolutions against the nations of the Axis, and in defense of constitutional liberty. In general, the influence of Second International waned in Latin America for the same reasons that it was undermined in Europe, and the Latin American labor front gained little from the contact except experience in international affairs and the opportunity for some of its leaders to obtain a broader field of view on world labor problems. This no doubt facilitated the development of inter-American movements, to which we shall refer later. After World War II, and because of the cold war, socialist internationalism has again come to the foreground in Latin America, as we shall see with reference to the formation of the CIT and the ORIT.

The Communist International. When the Bolshevik party came to power in Russia, and changed its name to Communist party, Lenin founded the Third International, or Cominform. As was to be expected, the Marxist elements within Latin American organized labor directed their efforts toward the incorporation of their groups with the Russian international. Contacts were established here and there, and a number of Latin American labor leaders visited Moscow and returned to their countries highly praising the Russian system. On the other hand, as stated previously, European and Latin American socialists differed sharply in their opinions, and the revolution produced in Latin America, as in the rest of the world, the ideological division between democratic socialism and Marxist communism. At first, the Russian international paid little attention to its contacts with Latin America, due undoubtedly to its own problems at home, with civil and international war. It was not long, however, before they realized the potential importance of Latin America, as a group of semi-colonial nations, and they established closer contacts with the workers of this part of the world. Thus, in 1926, at the Third Congress of the Communist International, a Secretariat was created with the purpose of establishing relations with the workers of Spain, Portugal and Latin America, and specific instructions were given on the necessity of adjusting the tactics of international communism to the peculiarities, and political and economic conditions of Latin America.

In 1927, an important conference was held in Moscow, with delegates present from Argentina, Chile, Cuba, Uruguay, Colombia, Mexico and Ecuador. General declarations of principle were made against American imperialism, and in favor of a more effective labor organization in Latin America. Not all of the delegates were representatives of Communist unions, but there were a number of convinced Marxists, and even the non-Marxists were, for the most part, sympathetic toward the Russian political revolution.

Another conference was held in Moscow in April, 1928, and delegates attended from Argentina, Brazil, Chile, Colombia, Cuba, Ecuador, Peru and Uruguay. At this congress it was decided to create an inter-American labor international to represent all the workers of the continent before the Third International. This resulted in the establishment of the Confederation of Syndicates of Latin America (C.S.L.A.), composed of delegates from Argentina, Brazil, Colombia, Cuba, Bolivia, Ecuador, Mexico, Guatemala, El Salvador, Panama, Uruguay, Venezuela, Peru, Costa Rica and Paraguay. The organizations represented at the foundation of the CSLA were mostly Communist. This inter-American organization was quite strong until around 1933 and 1934, and held conferences in several Latin American cities. It, in turn, created the *Liga Juvenil Comunista* (Young Communists' League), and was instrumental in the formation of various governments of popular front in the continent, especially in Chile. The change in tactics of Russian communism and the internal struggles between Stalinists and Trotskyites caused the same divisions in the files of Latin American communist workers, and consequently weakened the novice international. This movement may not be considered a purely continental internationalism, because it was founded with the purpose of facilitating relations with the Third International. We shall later see how it became necessary to reorganize the inter-American labor front, due to the decadence and struggles in the heart of the CSLA.

The Pan-American Federation of Labor (Confederación Obrera Pan Americana). In the period between 1880 and 1890, the workers' organizations of Latin America were not ready, because of their ideological principles and because of their manner of organization, to approach the organization at that time most powerful in this hemisphere, the American Federation of Labor. Later, Samuel Gompers established contact with the workers of Cuba and Puerto Rico, a contact simplified due to the circumstance that Gompers had been a tobacco worker, and because a large number of Cuban and Puerto Rican workers in that field were living in Florida. When the Cubans were engaged in their struggle for independence from Spain, in 1896, the A. F. of L. convention in Cincinnati approved a motion in defense of the Cuban patriots. In 1898, the A. F. of L. condemned the attitude of the United States, which maintained its troops in Cuba without granting it independence. Later, the Puerto Rican workers asked for help of the A. F. of L. to obtain their independence, and in 1904, Gompers visited Puerto Rico and criticized working conditions on the island. These initial contacts made the Mexican workers, in particular, and the leaders of the A. F. of L. conceive hopes for the creation of an Inter-American labor front. The Mexican workers needed it in order to protect those of their number who emigrated to the United States. However, the union was made difficult, because most of the Mexican workers were drawn to anarcho-syndicalism, which was repudiated by the A. F. of L. In 1908, the Magón brothers, Mexican leaders persecuted by Porfirio Díaz, made the first important contact with the A. F. of L., and in its Denver convention requested the United States government to intercede in favor of workers imprisoned in Mexico. At the time of the Mexican revolution of 1910, the A. F. of L. demonstrated its sympathy toward Maderos' cause, and protested against his assassination by Huerta in 1913.

In 1915, when the A. F. of L. held its convention in San Francisco, Gompers proposed the celebration of a Pan-American convention in Washington, and invited labor organizations of different Latin American republics to attend, but the civil war in Mexico kept this from being carried out. When Carranza's government arrested some North American soldiers, the A. F. of L. again interceded, this time before the Mexican government, and obtained their liberty.

World War I indirectly caused the first important rapprochement between the workers of the continent. When the United States entered the war, the A. F. of L. attempted to create a continental labor front in defense of the war effort, and Samuel Gompers headed the movement, with the backing of the American government. This resulted in the celebration of the first Pan-American Congress of Labor, which took place in Laredo, Texas, in November, 1918. Delegates from the A. F. of L. attended, as well as representatives of workers' groups of Mexico and other Latin American countries, although the latter were not actually representing labor groups, but were political refugees of their countries, at the time in the United States. They were invited to the congress by the A. F. of L. to give it an international character.

The ideological conflict between the workers of Latin and North America was evident in this congress. Gompers was elected president, over the opposition of radical Mexican leaders, and there were serious accusations against the United States because of the ill treatment of Mexican laborers in this country. Nevertheless, the Pan-American Federation of Labor was constituted. Ever since its foundation, this organization met with opposition from Latin American workers of the left, and it functioned more as a regional organization of the Carabbean, including Mexico.

The second congress of the Pan-American Federation of Labor was held in New York in 1919, and various resolutions were approved. They included the eight-hour day, the creation of co-operatives, education for workers, labor participation in the League of Nations, and in Pan-American congresses. The congress was highlighted by political problems, such as the relations between Chile and Peru over the possession of the provinces of Tacna and Arica, and the participation of Latin American intellectuals as labor delegates, which did not meet with the approval of the A. F. of L. The next congress of the Pan-American Federation of Labor was held in Mexico City in 1921, with delegates attending from Mexico, Colombia, El Salvador, Guatemala, Puerto Rico and the Dominican Republic. The ideological differences between the Latin American radicals and the A. F. of L. again came to the foreground, and the Congress accomplished little except to make declarations of a general character on the principles of protection to workers. In spite of the A. F. of L.'s attempt toward appeasement, it could not avoid the accusation against the United States government because of the military occupations of Santo Domingo and Nicaragua. The Pan-American Federation of Labor held another congress in Mexico City in 1924, and still another in Washington in 1927. In the latter, declarations of a political nature were made, again with regard to the North American occupation of Nicaragua, and to the Sacco and Vanzetti case. This was the last important congress of this organization. The last congress was rather of a Mexican-North American nature than international, since there were few delegates from the other American republics, and after that date, the Pan-American Federation of Labor started to decline. To be precise, the organization never did have an international scope, because it was principally occupied with relations between the most powerful Mexican organization, the CROM (*Confederación Regional Obrera Mexicana*) and the A. F. of L. It was a movement resulting from the necessities of World War I, of Gompers' efforts, and of the semi-official position represented by the CROM in the Mexican government. It met with little interest on the part of the other countries of the continent, because the workers of Argentina, Brazil and Uruguay felt closer to the European movement in their ideology. In spite of this, it may be said that the Pan-American Federation of Labor contributed in a general manner to the development of the labor movement in the Caribbean region, and cooperated toward the formation of important trade unions in that area. It has had the disadvantage of the feeling among the Latin American labor leaders that it was too closely connected with the interests of the government of the United States.

The Confederation of Latin American Workers (CTAL). The Mexican workers were the ones who took the initiative in the formation of a new inter-American labor front, which to this day plays an important role. In 1936, a congress was held in Mexico City to unite the labor movement of the republic, and out of this congress was born the *Confederación de Trabajadores de México* (CTM). This assembly resolved to convoke a congress of all workers of Latin America for the creation of an international organization, and this was held in Mexico in September, 1938. As visitors of honor to this congress, there came labor leaders of many nations of the world, such as Leon Jouhaux, secretary of the *Confederation Generale de*

Travaille, of France; Ramón Gonzales Peña, president of the *Unión General de Trabajadores,* of Spain; leaders from Sweden and India, and John L. Lewis, founder and then president of the CIO. The most important labor groups of Latin America were present, with delegates from Argentina, Bolivia, Colombia, Chile, Cuba, Ecuador, Costa Rica, Nicaragua, Paraguay, Peru, Uruguay and Venezuela. The delegations agreed to form a Latin American international, and constituted the *Confederación de Trabajadores de la América Latina* (CTAL). Because of the active part played by Mexican labor, the president chosen was Vicente Lombardo Toledano, president of the CTM. The CTAL is formed by the trade unions of each Latin American country, each country having one representative in the international body. The seat of the confederation is Mexico City and, in order to facilitate organization, the Latin American nations are divided into regions. The regulations of the confederation state as its objectives to bring about the unification of the workers and to defend their interests; to lend assistance toward the progress of labor legislation; to struggle against imperialism, against wars of aggression and fascism. Ever since its creation, the CTAL contributed actively toward the organization of labor movements in many of the Latin American republics, since they found it necessary to form national federations in order to obtain representation in the CTAL. Thus, Cuba constituted the *Confederación de Trabajadores* in 1939, and the same was done in Colombia, Paraguay, Uruguay, Ecuador and other nations.

The CTAL held its first general congress in Mexico City in 1941, made declarations against the totalitarian regimes; stressed the necessity of fighting fascism, and backed President Roosevelt's Good Neighbor Policy. An appeal was made to all workers for continental defense, and in favor of the United Nations. In August, 1943, a Council of the CTAL met in Havana and decided to intensify relations with the labor unions of Great Britain and Russia and to invite the CIO and the A. F. of L. to a continental congress of workers, but this was never held.

The second general congress of the CTAL was held in the city of Cali, Colombia, in December, 1944, with delegates present from all Latin American countries with the exception of Brazil, Guatemala and Honduras. The CIO and the Trade Union Congress of Great Britain sent representatives as a token of brotherhood, and the workers of France and the Soviet Union sent messages of adherence. The congress made concrete recommendations for the organization of the peace and condemned the internal political system of some Latin American countries. The CTAL was represented in the World Trade Union Congress, held in London at the close of the war, and the Latin American delegates then crossed over to Paris and took advantage of their European reunion to celebrate an extraordinary congress of the CTAL. The delegates of Paraguay and El Salvador were absent, since their countries had dissolved the labor unions. The Bolivian *Confederación Sindical* was absent also, and the delegates from Peru and Venezuela reached Paris too late to attend. One important event of this extraordinary congress was the admission to the CTAL of the Brazilian workers, who had not participated previously because of the political climate of their country during Vargas' first regime.

On his return from the Paris congress, in August, 1945, Lombardo Toledano was at the height of his prestige. On that occasion he gave a lengthy lecture in Mexico City, summarizing the thirteen points of the CTAL's program to continue its continental activities. However, the political changes throughout the world in the postwar period were to have a pronounced effect upon the organization. At the beginning of the war, and during the Nazi-Soviet pact, the CTAL, through its executive committee, followed the general lines of Soviet policy, and condemned the war as imperialistic. When Russia was invaded by Germany, the CTAL changed its tactics and supported the allies.

This shift, clearly indicating that the CTAL followed the line of Russian propaganda in its international policies, somewhat affected its standing, but the Russian victories and good relations with the United States during the war and the first months of the postwar period counteracted this effect. When relations between Russia and the United States grew tense, especially after the Truman Doctrine and the beginning of the cold war, most of the Latin American governments cautiously viewed the inter-American position of the CTAL and considered its president as a potential enemy. Important countries such as Brazil and Chile outlawed the Communist party; in others, such as Cuba and Uruguay, the Communists lost ground considerably. The situation was made worse by Russia's aggressive policies and her incorporation of the countries on her eastern boundaries, particularly after the case of Czechoslovakia. Lombardo Toledano had personal difficulties within the CTM of Mexico, which resulted in his suspension and the appointment of a new president.

The political philosophy of Lombardo Toledano has been a controversial issue. Although he apparently has never belonged to the Mexican Communist party, his philosophy of labor has toed the Marxian line in the class struggle; and in international matters, he has patterned his conduct after that of Soviet Russia. The situation came to a head when the CIO invited Lombardo Toledano to participate in a congress early in 1949, and the State Department of the United States refused him a visa.

However, its President's ideology has not been the chief cause of the CTAL's present crisis. The principal reason is the ideological division within the important labor organizations of the Latin American countries, a rift widened by the anti-communist policy of many of the countries, and by the international policy of the United States which culminated in the condemnation of totalitarian regimes in the Bogotá Conference of March, 1948. Thus, the *Confederación de Trabajadores* of Cuba divided into two groups in 1947, one of which followed the political views of President Grau, and the other adopting the principles of the *Partido Socialista Popular* (Communists). In Chile, the *Confederación de Trabajadores* divided into Communists and socialists, and the socialist group separated from the CTAL. In Mexico, after the CTM broke with Lombardo Toledano, this organization ceased to belong to the CTAL. In Peru, when the Apristas, traditional enemies of the Communists, obtained control of the *Confederación de Trabajadores del Peru*, they retired it from Lombardo's organization. The suppression of the Communist party in Brazil obviously undermined the prestige of the CTAL and brought about the formation of a rival labor group. In Venezuela, when the *Confederación de Trabajadores* of that country was organized, the workers decided not to join the CTAL. In Bolivia, independent groups were formed, not belonging to the CTAL; and in Argentina, when the *Federación General del Trabajo* came under President Perón's control, its representation in the CTAL was canceled. It must be made clear that not all of the Latin American labor groups that contributed toward the organization and development of the CTAL were Communists, but many of the strongest did follow the Communist ideology, and still do. Another event that weakened the CTAL was the formation of a new rival Latin American international, inspired by the principles of the A. F. of L.

The Regional Organization of Latin American Workers (ORIT). On various occasions during the war, the A. F. of L. attempted to revive the old Pan-American Federation of Labor, and dissenting workers in the different Latin American countries made efforts to strengthen their connections with the powerful organization of the United States. As it is easy to see, the CTAL came into international existence under the auspices and with the support of the CIO, and never had good relations with the A. F. of L. It may be safely said that the feelings of antipathy between the two were mutual. Labor leaders north and south of the Rio Grande accused each other publicly, and in many meetings of the CTAL and the A. F. of L., their sentiments were freely aired. The CTAL has always held that the A. F. of L. has attempted to divide the workers of Latin America in the interests of the government of the United States, and the A. F. of L. has replied to this saying that the CTAL has been controlled by Russia.

When the CTAL reached its stage of decline, the A. F. of L. felt that the time had come to organize a rival international, and after an able campaign carried out through Latin America, by means of the regular press and of a bulletin published in Spanish, it obtained the collaboration of a number of labor leaders, and a congress was held in Lima in 1948, which resulted in the foundation of the Inter-American Federation of Labor (*Confederación Interamericana de Trabajadores,* or CIT). The congress was held under the protection of the *Apristas,* then in control in Peru, and delegates came from Argentina, Bolivia, Brazil, Chile, Colombia, Costa Rica, Cuba, the Dominican Republic, Ecuador, El Salvador, Mexico, Puerto Rico and Venezuela. Serious conflicts of ideas came to the fore in the congress, concerning the attitude of Luis Morones, for a long time a leader of the CROM of Mexico, and a bitter enemy of Lombardo Tolendano. He defended the government of Perón in Argentina, which made some of the other leaders feel that the new international would be controlled by the Argentine president. Morones' behavior was especially confusing, because the relations between the A. F. of L. and Perón are none too cordial since the visit of the A. F. of L.'s delegates to Argentina, when they were outspoken in their criticism of the lack of freedom of workers there. In that meeting, Bernardo Ibáñez of Chile was elected president of the new organization. Declarations of principle were made in favor of the support of the democratic systems of labor organizations, and against totalitarian regimes. As was to be expected, there has been strong opposition from the groups still connected with the CTAL, from the radicals in the different Latin American nations, and especially from the Communist groups and parties. Later at a meeting held in Mexico City in January 1951 the Council of the C. I. T. met in a special session and agreed to dissolve the Inter-American Federation of Workers. Their members joined a new regional organization, ORIT (*Organización Regional Inter-americana de Trabajadores*). The ORIT is the regional organization in America of the International Confederation of Free Trade Unions. Among its affiliates are the A. F. of L., the CIO, and the most important groups of the old CIT. Therefore, today there are two rival organizations in the interamerican labor front; beside other international connections with the anarchist, anarcho-syndicalist groups, and the federation of Catholic syndicates, there are also many other labor groups who have not joined international organizations.

CONSTITUTIONAL SUMMARY

Argentina. The new constitution devotes a good deal of attention to the organization of labor. It recognizes the right to work, which should be protected by society. Among the fundamental rights, the following should be mentioned: the right to a just compensation—therefore the worker should receive compensation sufficient to satisfy his material and spiritual wants; the right to capacitation, meaning that every worker should receive from society the necessary assistance to prepare him to earn his living; the right to respectable working conditions, based upon the needs of man and on the importance of work as a social function; the right to preservation of health, by virtue of which the State must maintain hygienic conditions in centers of work; the right to well-being— the worker should be assured of a home, clothing and food sufficient for himself and his family; the right to social security—in case of decrease, suspension or loss of his capacity to work, society shall offer assistance to the worker; the right to protection of the family; the right to economic betterment; and the right to defense of constitutional rights. Under the latter disposition, the worker is free to join unions and participate in other legal activities to defend his interests. The State shall protect the free exercise of this right and restrict all acts which may impede or hamper it.

Bolivia. The constitution guarantees the right to form labor unions, and recognizes collective labor contracts and the right to strike. It specifies that workers cannot be discharged, imprisoned or persecuted for their activities as members of a union. It disposes that the law shall regulate obligatory insurance for accidents, sickness, old age, maternity and death; as well as the work of women and minors, the maximum number of working hours, minimum wage, Sunday rest and workers' vacations, but these rights are not granted in the constitution. It says the law shall do so, and it has been done.

Brazil. The constitution enumerates the basic rights of workers, that is, a minimum wage sufficient to satisfy normal needs of the worker and his family; prohibition of paying different salaries for the same class of work; higher wages for night work than for day work; obligatory and direct participation of workers in the profits of concerns; maximum working day of eight hours; weekly rest on Sundays, and on civil and religious holidays; yearly vacations; sanitation and safety of labor; prohibition of work for minors under fourteen years of age; the right of an expectant mother to rest before and after childbirth; establishment of the percentage of Brazilian workers in concerns; and recognition of collective labor agreements. The constitution also guarantees the right to strike, to labor insurance, and to join unions.

Chile. The constitution deals with labor in the section devoted to civil rights. It considers as one of these the right to the protection of labor, and the works of social welfare, especially the right to sanitary dwellings and living conditions, so that each inhabitant may be assured of a minimum of well-being for himself and his family. Other dispositions regarding work are regulated by the laws. The workers enjoy all traditional rights, and the protection of labor and social security is embodied in one of the most advanced legislations of Latin America.

Colombia. The right to strike is guaranteed, but not in the public services. Freedom of work is guaranteed. Article 39 states that everyone is free to choose the profession or trade he desires. Workers' rights in Colombia are determined by law.

Costa Rica. The working period may not be more than eight hours of day work, six hours of night work, and forty-eight hours a week. Extra work must be paid at a rate 50 per cent higher than ordinary work. All workers have the right to paid yearly vacations. Employers, as well as workers, have the right to organize. Employers are guarantee the right to the lockout, and workers to the strike, except in the public services. Collective labor contracts are authorized, and the State assumes the obligation to promote the creation of cooperatives to improve the living conditions of the workers. In order to raise the economic level of the working class, it is stipulated that an equal wage shall be paid for equal work under the same conditions, without distinction of persons or sexes, and that the rural worker shall enjoy the same rights as the urban worker. Social insurance for the benefit of workers is established.

Cuba. Every worker shall have the right to a minimum wage or salary. For equal work, and in identical conditions, an equal salary shall always be paid. Employers may not make discounts on workers' wages, or employes' salaries, nor make payment in tickets, tokens or merchandise. The maximum working day shall not be more than eight hours, and forty-four hours a week, to be considered equivalent to forty-eight hours in pay. Workers are guaranteed the right to rest with pay. With regard to women, no difference with regard to work or pay may be made between married and single women, and maternity is protected, allowing a pregnant woman a rest of six weeks before and six weeks after childbirth.

The right of organization is recognized to employers and workers, as is the right to lockout of employers, and the right to strike of the workers. Collective labor contracts are recognized, and it is declared that Cubans by birth shall have a preponderant participation in labor. The fair employment system is established, and all discrimination against workers is prohibited. In general, conflicts originating from labor shall be submitted to committees of conciliation composed of equal representation of employers and workers.

Dominican Republic. The regulation of labor is left to be determined by the law. The constitution declares that work is an inherent right to the human personality, and freedom of work is recognized. The law may establish the maximum working day, rest and vacations, minimum salary, form of payment, social insurance and participation of nationals in labor.

Ecuador. The constitution declares that the law will regulate everything relative to labor, according to fundamental standards, such as collective labor contracts, minimum working hours, weekly rest, the right to organize and to strike. Typical characteristics are the establishment of a six-hour working day in the mines; the prohibition of organization to public employees, and of the strike to workers in the public services. There are special regulations with regard to the work of

Indians, and it is established that the solution of labor conflicts will be submitted to tribunals of conciliation and arbitration.

El Salvador. The constitution disposes that a labor code be promulgated, regulating all the basic rights of workers, such as minimum salary, maximum working hours, rest with pay, vacations and accident indemnification. It declares that the rights of workers are irrenounceable, and recognizes the right of the strike by workers, and that of the lockout by employers.

Guatemala. Work is an individual right and a social obligation, and vagrancy is punishable. The constitution declares and enumerates the fundamental principles of the labor system, including all the basic rights of workers as exist in Cuba, Brazil and other countries. Characteristic of Guatemala is an article disposing that Guatemalan workers be given preference, not only in the number of workers in the factories, but also in the total amount of the wages paid.

Foreigners may not intervene in matters connected with labor organizations. All rights of workers are irrenounceable, and labor conflicts are submitted to a special jurisdiction composed of labor tribunals.

Haiti. The freedom of work is recognized, but should be exercised under the control and supervision of the State. Only Haitians by birth may engage in retail trade, direct small industrial enterprises, or devote themselves to other commercial activities, such as the law may determine. The right to rest and to vacations is established, as well as the worker's right to defend his interests by means of union action.

Honduras. The maximum working day shall be eight hours, and for each six days of work there shall be one of rest. Unhealthful or dangerous work is prohibited, as well as industrial night work for women and for minors under sixteen years of age. Work is prohibited to minors under twelve years of age, and all wages must be paid in money that is legal tender in the republic.

Mexico. The Mexican constitution, in Article 123, was the first to recognize and enumerate the basic rights of the worker, and inspired most of the other Latin American constitutions. These rights are essentially the same as in Cuba and other countries, and need not be repeated, but several which are typical of Mexico should be pointed out as being of special interest. Any contract is null when its object is to diminish the liberty of the worker, whether it be because of the work, of education, or of religious vows. This means that monastic orders are not allowed, and that Mexicans should not, temporarily or permanently, renounce the liberty of performing any type of work. Labor contracts may not be made for more than one year. The strike is recognized as a general right, including workers in the public services, but in this case they are obliged to advise the committee of conciliation ten days before the strike is to take place. Strikes may not be declared illegal, unless there is an act of violence, or unless they are against a government institution. Labor conflicts are submitted to committees of conciliation and arbitration. With regard to the work of Mexicans in foreign countries, it is established that the labor contract between a Mexican and a foreign employer must be legalized by the municipal authority, and a visa obtained from the Consul of the nation to which the worker intends to go. This contract must contain a clause under which the expenses of repatriation shall be paid by the foreign employer. An interesting regulation prohibits the place of payment of employes to be in a cafe, tavern or store, with the obvious purpose of putting an end to the well-known practice of company stores.

Nicaragua. The State guarantees the freedom of work, and assures the workers the rights of maximum hours, minimum wage and payment in national legal tender, regulation of the work of women and minors, prohibition of attachment of minimum wages, and a contract of labor that may not exceed two years.

Panama. Work is a right and a duty of the individual, and articles 64 to 76 enumerate the traditional rights of workers, as indicated in other countries. All agreements made to hinder the exercise of these rights are declared void, and a labor jurisdiction is established for the solution of conflicts between capital and labor.

Paraguay. The regulation of labor in the constitution of this country is unusual. None of the basic rights of workers are recognized or enumerated, but Article 14 contains the old socialistic motto that "the exploitation of man by man is outlawed," adding that the system of contracts of labor, social security and the conditions of safety and hygiene of the workers shall be under the careful supervision of the State.

Peru. The constitution does not specifically enumerate all the rights of workers, although these are effectively regulated by the laws. Article 45 says that the State shall favor the participation of employees and workers in the benefits of concerns. Article 43 recognizes collective bargaining.

Uruguay. Labor is under the special protection of the State, and is declared to be free. The constitution states that the law shall regulate all matters relating to the rights of workers. It establishes that all concerns requiring the workers, by the nature of their work, to live on the premises shall be obliged to provide adequate food and lodging for them. The law shall promote the organization of unions; the right to strike is recognized, and it is declared that labor problems shall be submitted to tribunals of conciliation and arbitration.

Venezuela. Labor is a duty and a right, and every individual should contribute toward the progress of society by means of work. It is ordered in the constitution that the law shall recognize and effectively organize the basic rights of workers. There are two interesting dispositions, one establishing that the fulfillment of social laws is the obligation of the person in whose favor the work is done, even when the labor contract has been effected by means of an intermediary or contractor, who is also responsible; the other one, declaring that the State will favor the establishment of family wages, by means of institutions to be created for the purpose.

SUGGESTED READINGS

English:

Alexander, Robert, *Labor Movements in Latin America,* London, 1947, (Research Series of Fabian Publications, Ltd. No. 122) .

————, *Labor Parties of Latin America,* New York, League for Industrial Democracy, 1942.

Bush, Archer C., *Organized Labor in Guatemala,* Hamilton, N. Y., Colgate University Press, 1950.

Cannon, Mary M., *Social and Labor Problems of Peru and Uruguay,* Washington, D. C., U. S. Dept. of Labor, 1945.

Clark, Marjorie R., *Organized Labor in Mexico,* Chapel Hill, University of North Carolina Press, 1934.

Galarza, Ernesto, *Argentine Labor Under Peron,* Washington, D. C., Inter-American Reports, March, 1948.

————, *Labor in Latin America: A Survey,* Washington, D. C. (no date) .

International Labor Office, *Freedom of Association and Conditions of Work in Venezuela,* Washington, D. C., Int. Lab. Office, No. 21, 1950.

Lorwin, Lewis L., *Labor and Internationalism,* New York, The Macmillan Co., 1929.

Marquand, H. A., *Organized Labor in Four Continents,* London, Longmans Green & Co., 1939.

Pan American Union, *Labor Trends and Social Welfare in Latin America,* Washington, D. C., 1943.

Price, John, *The International Labour Movement,* London, Oxford University Press, 1947.

Retinger, J. H., *Morones of Mexico,* Labour Publishing Co., London, 1926.

Other Languages:

Arduz Eguía, Gaston, *Legislación Boliviana del Trabajo y de la Previsión Social,* La Paz, 1941.

Bravo, Mario, *Asociaciones Gremiales de Trabajadores,* Buenos Aires, 1936.

C.T.A.L., *Confederación Obrera Mundial,* México, 1945.

C.T.A.L., *Segundo Congreso General, Cali* (Colombia), 1944.

C.T.A.L., *Qué es la C.T.A.L?,* México (no date).

C.T.A.L., *Libro Blanco y Azul,* México, 1946.

C.T.A.L., *Congreso Extraordinario de la C.T.A.L.,* París, 1945.

Dickman, Enrique, *Marx y Bakounin, La Primera Internacional, 1864-1873,* Buenos Aires, 1922.

Granados Aguirre, Jesús, *Legislación del Trabajo en Venezuela,* Caracas, 1944.

Lagos Valenzuela, Tulio, *Bosquejo Histórico del Movimiento Obrero en Chile,* Santiago de Chile, 1944.

Lombardo Toledano, Vicente, *El Movimiento Sindical en Mexico,* México, D.F., 1926.

Oficina Internacional del Trabajo, *El Movimiento Sindical en Venezuela* (Informaciones Sociales, Junio, 1944).

Poblete Troncoso, Moisés, *El Movimiento Obrero Latinoamericano,* México, 1946.

————, *La Organización Sindical en Chile,* Santiago de Chile, 1925.

————, *Evolución del Derecho Social en América,* Santiago de Chile, 1925.

Puga Monsalves, Raúl, *Las Corporaciones Mutualistas:* Su Historia, Santiago de Chile, 1938.

Raggi, Carlos M., *Legislación Social de Cuba,* La Habana, 1942.

Revue Internationale du Travail, *Organisation des Associations Professionnelles au Brésil,* February, 1941.

————, *Mouvement Syndical à Costa Rica,* December, 1943.

————, *La Confederation des Travailleurs d'Amérique Latine,* September, 1943.

————, *Le Syndicalisme en Equateur,* June, 1943.

Salazar, Rosendo, *Historia de las Luchas Proletarias de México,* México, D.F., Editorial Avante, 1938.

Vargas Serra, Edgardo, *Sindicalismo Brasileiro,* Rio de Janeiro, 1939.

PART IV

The Control of Power

INTRODUCTORY

In this part, a brief description of each country's constitutional evolution is given. Stress is placed only on the major changes. It is not a constitutional or a political history. In many cases, but not in all, a constitutional change in Latin America reflects the political goals of the people. It is hoped that with this brief knowledge the reader will be able to find a pattern in the constitutional evolution that will help him to understand the problems of the present.

In the study of the governments in power, only the indispensable background is given. More detail is given in those cases in which the party in power derives its force from an important event like a revolution or a change in public opinion. Ideologies, policies, and party platforms are indicated, as well as the forces of opposition to the governments.

Governments change rapidly in Latin America. In spite of this, I have preferred to outline the present governments. With the information available in any college library, and by carefully following the daily press, any student can easily be aware of the important changes, using the background of the book as a starting point. Besides, it would be a good classroom project to follow the changes.

Labor is an important political factor, in many cases, underestimated. In Latin America, not only the parties of the Left have had the support of Labor, but in many cases, authoritarian rulers like Perón in Argentina and Vargas in Brazil, have had to compromise with the labor forces.

The role of organized Communism is also important. This comes not only from the international crisis, but because there is a striking similarity in the economy of Latin America and some countries in which Communism is today advancing. This similarity consists in the large number of landless peasants and the need for agrarian reform.

CHAPTER 12

Mexico and Central America

I. MEXICO

Of the countries studied in this chapter Mexico is doubtless the most important and stands out as a group in itself. Its political evolution, as well as the movement for economic and social reform, constitutes a unique experiment in Latin America.

In Mexico, the real independence, that is, the severance of political ties with Spain, was preceded by a popular uprising that failed but which clearly indicated the nature of the agrarian problems that affected the country. Independence came as a result of the desires of a class already in power that wanted to preserve its privileged position. Since independence, the democratic and popular forces were compelled to struggle against this class throughout the nineteenth century, not being able to achieve a complete victory until the revolution of 1910. The present government of Mexico is a direct result of that revolution, and as Silva Herzog [1] has so well pointed out, in Mexico the terms "government" and "revolution" are not antithetical. The constitution of 1917 created a number of political institutions that were revolutionary in nature, and outlined an ambitious program of agrarian reform, nationalization of the subsoil, labor legislation and strict regulation of all sorts of religious activities. This constitution was approved before the Russian Revolution of 1917 and represents a Mexican program of goals to be achieved. In the implementation of many of those goals, abuses have been committed by the government, and enemies have been made. There are still persons in Mexico, as there were in France after 1789, who would like to go back to *"l'ancien régime,"* but—again as in France—it is doubtful that the basic achievements of the revolution will be lost.

---

[1] Silva Herzog, Jesús, La Revolución Mexicana es ya un hecho histórico," *Cuadernos Americanos,"* No. 5, Vol. XLVII, Mexico, D. F.

Since 1920, the forces of the revolution have controlled the government. First, the PRM (*Partido Revolucionario Mexicano*) and now the PRI (*Partido Revolucionario Institucional*) have managed to remain in power. Behind the party in power are those who have advanced by the revolution, like the peasants who have received lands, the government bureaucracy that wants to preserve its positions, the large majority of organized labor who have improved their conditions, as well as the professional and intellectual classes. The party has also received the backing of the armed forces, which have remained loyal to the government.

Of course, Mexico still has a long way to go before the ambitious program and many of the goals established in the constitution of 1917 will be reached. Politically, it seems to have found the necessary structure under which to function successfully toward those goals. In this aspect, the country is far ahead of the rest of Latin American republics, with the sole exception of Uruguay.

Suffrage. All male citizens over 18 years of age, if married, and over 21, if unmarried, may vote. Married women over 18 and unmarried ones over 21 may vote, but only in municipal elections. This restriction is due to the fear that the feminine vote may influence the elections in favor of Church interests, a serious political issue in Mexico. Ministers of any religious denomination do not have the right to vote.

Constitutional Evolution. Mexico's constitutional evolution may be divided into six periods. The first starts with the wars of independence, with the *Grito de Dolores* of Father Hidalgo on the 16th of September of 1810, and lasted until the promulgation of the first constitution as a sovereign state, in October 4, 1824. This first period, however, should not properly be called constitutional, because it had only two projects of constitution or plans of government. The first of these was on October 22, 1814, under which a provisional government was organized, with an Executive Committee elected by the Congress. The second was the plan of February 24, 1821, which was the Conservative program presented in opposition to the Liberal ideas of the Spanish revolution of 1820. The 1821 program, called the *Plan de Iguala,* resulted in a political compromise between the monarchists and Conservatives, and the Liberal groups that followed the ideology of 1810. This plan consisted of the establishment of a constitutional monarchy and the maintenance of the privileges of the Church and the landowning aristocracy. General Iturbide had the army designate him Emperor, but a few months later, the opposition forced him to abdicate, and thus the first period came to an end.

The second period opened with the promulgation of the constitution of July 19, 1824, by which Mexico was organized as a federal republic, with a president elected for four years, a bicameral congress, and a Judiciary headed by a Supreme Court. This constitution was a weak effort made by the Liberals, since it still guaranteed the members of the clergy and the officers of the army the privilege of being judged by the special tribunals they had enjoyed during the colonial era. The Catholic faith was declared to be the religion of the State, and all other faiths were prohibited. This period was followed by a succession of civil wars, military dictatorships and coups d'etat, and Mexico split into the two groups that were to struggle for power continuously until the revolution of 1910. The Conservative, ecclesiastic and military elements fought for an aristocratic government, restricted suffrage and a strong central power. The Liberals strove for federalism, separation of Church and State, and a broader suffrage. The two sides formulated plans and bases for constitutions, but neither prevailed effectively until, in December, 1836, a new fundamental charter called the Seven Constitutional Laws was proclaimed; this was the beginning of the third period.

The constitution of 1836 organized the country as a centralized government, with an aristocratic and Conservative basis. There was a president elected for eight years, by a suffrage limited and qualified by the possession of property. The states were transformed into military departments and governed directly by delegates of the central power. A committee of five citizens was created, called "Conservative Power," which operated as a sort of organ of government, supervising the other powers of the State and with the purpose of maintaining a balance between them. It is not necessary to say that this constitution was most unpopular with the Liberals and Federalists. Its promulgation was followed by more civil wars and international conflicts, the most important of all being the war with the United States, in 1846, by which Mexico lost a large part of its territory. The constitutional life of the period was characterized, like the one before, by various plans, laws of bases and pro-grams of government, and even by the temporary restoration of the federal constitution of 1824.

The fourth period opened with the Liberals finally controlling power, attempting to restrict the political power of the Church, the army and the privileged classes of landowners, the three champions on whom the Conservatives depended. When the Liberals took over the government, they passed provisional statutes in May, 1856, but these did not have the nature of a constitution. A short time before this, Benito Juárez, then Minister of Justice and later the great Liberal president of Mexico, was successful in having a law passed by which the members of the clergy and the army were deprived of their special privileges. In the same year of 1856, another Liberal Minister, Lerdo de Tejada, presented a bill which became the famous Lerdo Law, with the purpose of reducing the power of the Church and supplying the Mexican peasants with land. Under it, civil and religious corporations were prohibited from holding real property not directly used for the purpose of worship, nor for the objects of the corporations. This period came to an end with the incorporation of the Liberal ideology into a new constitution, promulgated on February 5, 1857, which is a document of great importance. Without it, the present constitution of 1917 cannot be understood.

The constitution of 1857 re-established the principle of the federal government, abolished the special tribunals for ecclesiastics and members of the army, established the separation of Church and State, and embodied the principle of the Lerdo Law, by which civil and religious corporations could neither own nor administer real property. It guaranteed freedom of work, and prohibited con-tracts that might tend to diminish or sacrifice personal liberty. This clause was introduced to do away with monastic orders. The tradi-tional civil liberties were established, and capital punishment was abolished. With this constitution, Mexico reached its liberal-demo-cratic period, typical of the nineteenth century in most of the Latin American countries. If this document is especially characterized by prohibitions meant to control the economic power of the Church, we have to remember that the Church had intervened actively in politics and had controlled the government almost continually. As was to be expected, the Conservatives—and especially the Church—

were indignant. Even before the constituent convention had completed its work, the Pope instructed the faithful to disobey the constitution. This was a political error that was to weigh heavily against the Church, particularly after the revolution of 1910.

The promulgation of the 1857 constitution was followed by a civil war that lasted three years and ended with the provisional occupation of the presidency by Benito Juárez, who was elected in 1861 to continue in office. During the French intervention and the war against Emperor Maximilian, Juárez was the undisputed leader of Mexico; and after the defeat of the invaders and the execution of the Emperor, he was again elected President in 1867, holding office until his death in 1872.

After Juárez' death, the President of the Supreme Court occupied the provisional presidency, but in 1875 he attempted to extend his term; and General Porfirio Díaz, one of Juárez' most distinguished collaborators during the war with the French, rebelled against the government and finally took over the presidency in 1877. From that date until 1911 Porfirio Díaz, directly or indirectly, was the ruler of Mexico. Díaz' government was first characterized by a moderate liberalism and the absence of constitutional changes. He did not bother to have a new constitution approved, but merely ignored the one of 1857 when it suited his purposes to do so. Gradually, the conservative forces gained the ground they had lost; the Lerdo Law, far from solving the land problem, became a two-edged sword, because the indigenous communities were considered to be civil corporations and were obliged to sell their lands to individuals. The land fell into the hands of speculators to such an extent that a contemporary Mexican scholar calculates that by the end of Díaz' administration, 2 per cent of the population owned 70 per cent of the land.[2]

The federalist ideology that inspired the constitution of 1857 was nothing more than a symbol during the Díaz regime, because Díaz controlled the government of the states from the capital. Even the cultural environment contributed to the long years of dictatorship. The group of intellectuals, known as *Científicos,* animated by the positivism of Compte, Spencer and Mill, were organized in political cliques, and dominated President Díaz during the last years

---

[2] Beteta, Ramón, *Aspectos Económicos del Plan Sexenal,* México, D. F., 1935.

of his regime. The *Científicos* believed in the supremacy of the white civilization, and ignored the great masses of Indians and mestizos. Only the Creole elite had a right to political, economic and social life. In 1910, the opposition to General Díaz, headed by Madero, resolved to resist the dictator in the elections. Díaz' arbitrary measures to thwart their activities obliged the opposition to take up arms, and this fifth constitutional period came to an end with the revolutionary movement that ensued.

The final period in Mexico's constitutional evolution had its starting point when Díaz was overthrown in 1911. The first six years were marked by violence and a complete interruption of the constitutional life of the country. When, in 1916, General Venustiano Carranza succeeded in establishing himself in the de facto presidency, he convoked a constituent assembly which met in Querétaro on December 1, 1916. It drew up the present constitution, which was promulgated on February 5. 1917. The political, economic, social and educational aspects of this document have been analyzed in the second and third parts of this book. Here we merely emphasize that the Mexican constitution of 1917 is the document that has had the greatest influence in the contemporary political life of the Latin American countries, and that many of the constitutions now in force have followed in its path. It is a liberal document, with marked socialist and nationalist tendencies, and through it, attempts have been made to find normative solutions to the fundamental problems of Mexico: the problem of the *latifundia;* the problem of the political intervention of the Church; and the problem of control of mineral production by foreign capital.

The 1917 constitution has lived through thirty-five years of political life, with no essential modifications. Some amendments have been necessary, the most important one abolishing popular election of the magistrates of the Supreme Court in 1928, and establishing the system of appointments by the President of the Republic, with the approval of the Senate. Another amendment in 1933 extended the presidential term from four to six years, to provide the executive power with a better opportunity for efficient government, since no re-election is permitted. In 1946, women were given the vote in municipal elections.

Since the promulgation of the 1917 constitution, the political life of Mexico can be described as consisting of a struggle between

those who have tried to put into practice the fundamental changes
introduced in the constitution, and the once-privileged groups of
the opposition, who had lost their power as a result of the revolution
of 1910 and the reforms of the constitution, and who naturally have
tried all means to regain it. After December 1, 1920, when General
Alvaro Obregón was elected President, the presidential succession in
Mexico has been the result of the control of power by the party of
the Revolution.

In spite of some attempts at revolts and scattered acts of violence,
there have been no serious revolutionary movements. Since then,
the party of the Revolution has been victorious in the elections.
The revolutionary impetus that started in 1910 reached its apex
during the administration of General Lázaro Cárdenas (1934-1940),
afterward slowed down, and is now in an evolutionary period. This
is the opinion of most of the Mexican intellectuals of today, which
has been admirably expressed by Jesús Silva Herzog in these words:

> With the termination of the armed struggle, the Revolution
> became government; the revolutionary governments undertook
> their political and administrative tasks. Some have objected
> to the union of these two words: revolutionary and government,
> because they feel that to govern is contrary to the making of a
> revolution; they think, to all appearances reasonably, that they
> are two antithetical terms. However, the designation is correct.
> The proper term not only is, but should be so: revolutionary
> governments, because in their actions they went farther, to the
> left, than the Constitution; they were more radical than the
> fundamental law of the Republic in agrarian matters, in the
> defense of the wealth of the subsoil, and in the legislation of
> labor. Adolfo de la Huerta was more revolutionary than Car-
> ranza; Obregón more than De la Huerta; Ortiz Rubio and
> Rodríguez fell back a bit; and Cárdenas gave the strongest pos-
> sible push in favor of the interests of the people, and of the
> economic independence of Mexico. During his administration,
> in 1938, the Mexican Revolution reached its culmination. After
> that, the descent, the crisis, agony and death.[3]

Government and Opposition. The present government of Mexico took office on December 1, 1946, when the presidency was occu-

---

[3] Silva Herzog, Jesús, "La Revolución Mexicana es ya un Hecho Histórico,"
Cuadernos Americanos, No. 5, September-October, 1949, Vol. XLVII, México, D. F.
(Translation by the author.)

pied by Dr. Miguel Alemán, victorious in the general elections held
on July 7 of that year.* Of course, this government has its remote
antecedent in the revolution of 1910 and the political program set
forth in the constitution of 1917. But the immediate antecedent,
and the most important, may be found in the change in policies
initiated by Alemán's predecessor in the presidency, General Ávila
Camacho (1940-1946). During this period, the government devoted
itself to the consolidation of the conquests of the revolution, no
longer extending its sphere of action. The electoral campaign that
put Dr. Alemán in the presidency was characteristic in the change
of name of the government party, which up until that time was
called the *Partido Revolucionario Mexicano* (PRM, or Mexican
Revolutionary Party), and under that name had nominated General
Ávila Camacho. The same party nominated Dr. Alemán, but
changed its name to *Partido Revolucionario Institucional* (PRI, Institutional Revolutionary Party). This change alone is sufficient to
indicate the new political philosophy. It was no longer a question
of following the road of the revolution to new goals, but of conserving its institutions, which had been born and bred, as we have seen,
of the constitution of 1917. The opposition against Alemán nominated Dr. Ezequiel Padilla, renowned in Mexico's international
affairs, especially in the conferences held as a result of the country's
participation in World War II. The conservative groups, those who
were discontented with the revolution, the neutral classes and the
ultra-conservatives who function under the name of *Sinarquistas* (a
group formed by Catholics of the extreme right), all supported
Padilla. Another candidate, though an unimportant one, was
General Jesús Agustín Castro, nominated by a minority political
group called the *Partido Nacionalista Constitucional.* Alemán was
elected in one of the most peaceful elections in Mexico's history and
obtained a victory of three-to-one over Ezequiel Padilla.[4]

Alemán occupies the presidency today, and the opposition is
formed by the *Partido de Acción Nacional;* the *Sinarquistas'* party,
called *Partido Fuerza Popular,* which has recently been declared
illegal, and a new party headed by labor leader Vicente Lombardo
Toledano, called *Partido Popular.* Alemán's party, the *Partido Revo-*

---

* A new president was elected on July 6, 1952. See below.

4 The author was in Mexico City on the day of the elections, and made a round
of the polls.

lucionario Institucional, is still high in public favor, as evidenced in the last partial elections held on July 3, 1949, when the PRI obtained 140 seats in the House of Representatives, while the *Partido de Acción Nacional* won only four, and the *Partido Popular* one seat. For the presidential elections of July, 1952, the PRI has nominated Adolfo Ruis Cortines, a popular Veracruz man and Minister of Interior under President Alemán.†

Position of Labor. The workers' organizations in Mexico have lived through the three stages of mutualism, anarcho-syndicalism and trade unionism, to which we have referred in Chapter XI. The mutualist era reached its peak around the year 1880, when the economic conditions of the country became difficult, and when the number of urban workers increased greatly, due to the industrial development. The largest industrial growth was in textiles and in transportation. This mutualist era went on into the early twentieth century, when the first groups with a definite anarcho-syndicalistic nature appeared. In 1906, a group was organized under this ideology, by free workers of Puebla, Río Blanco, Nogales and Santa Rosa. Shortly before that, a Spanish worker, José Saldívar, and José María Pino Suárez, were publishing an anarchist periodical in Yucatán, and almost at the same time the Flores Magón brothers were organizing the workers of the capital along the same lines.

Before the revolution of 1910, there had been serious clashes between the incipient labor movement and the administration of Porfirio Díaz. The revolution naturally added momentum to the development of the labor organization. In 1911, a Typographical Conference was organized in the capital, later to function under the name of *Confederación Nacional de Artes Gráficas* (National Confederation of the Graphic Arts). The first group of a truly national character was the *Casa del Obrero Mundial,* founded in 1912, which at first operated as a labor exchange, and later took active part in revolutionary politics, organizing the famous Red Battalions that fought for Venustiano Carranza. After Carranza's victory, their contribution gave the workers of the *Casa* an important political position. In spite of this, Carranza later disagreed with the group, and had the *Casa* closed. As a result, the movement lost ground, and

---

† Cortines was elected on July 6, 1952.

another national organization, the *Confederación Regional Obrera Mexicana* (CROM), took its place.

The CROM was organized in March, 1918, and was directed for many years by Luis N. Morones.[5] During the administration of President Obregón, and later under Plutarco Elías Calles, when Morones was Minister of Industry, Commerce and Labor, the organization occupied a prominent position in Mexican politics. But Morones' political mistakes and, to a great extent, his private life, did a great deal of damage to the CROM and, when Portes Gil became president, it lost the support of the government. The workers divided into groups and sub-groups and did not come together in a national organization until February, 1936, when Vicente Lombardo Toledano was instrumental in forming the *Confederación de Trabajadores Mexicanos* (CTM). The new national federation soon attracted the most important labor groups in industrial production and attained an international position, creating the CTAL as a continental movement. The CTM enjoyed a privileged position in the political life of the country, under Lombardo Toledano's direction, especially during the administration of Lázaro Cárdenas.

Through World War II, Lombardo Toledano kept the CTM in its prominent place in politics, but the postwar split in ideologies that caused the division among the workers of the world in general, and of Latin America in particular, had the same effect on that organization.

During the present administration, the government suppressed an oil workers' strike, which weakened labor organizations. After that, because of internal differences, Lombardo Toledano lost his position as president of the CTM, as we have said before.[6]

Besides the CTM, there are other important labor groups that affect national politics. Among them, we shall mention the *Federación Nacional de Empleados al Servicio del Estado* (FNEE, National Federation of Workers in the Service of the State); the *Federación Mexicana de Trabajadores de la Enseñanza* (FMTE, Mexican Federation of Workers in Instruction), formed by public school teachers; the *Sindicato Nacional de Redactores de la Prensa* (National Syndicate of Writers of the Press); and the groups of agricultural

---

5 See Chapter 9.
6 See Chapter 9.

workers, the *Confederación Proletaria Nacional* (CPN, National Proletarian Federation) and the *Confederación de Obreros y Campesinos de México* (COCM, Confederation of Workers and Peasants of Mexico). There is also a group, called the *Confederación General de Trabajadores* (CGT, General Confederation of Workers) that follows an anarchist line and controls a number of craft unions. Although the CROM is not as important as it used to be, it is still strong among textile workers. In July, 1949, a large congress of workers was held in the capital to organize a new national federation, and so formed the *Unión General de Obreros y Campesinos de México* (UGOC, General Union of Workers and Peasants of Mexico). Agustin Guzmán, a leader of the miners, was elected Secretary-General of the new group. As we can see, organized workers in Mexico are far from presenting a homogeneous front, but in general they do come together at election times, supporting the candidates of the *Partido Revolucionario Institucional*.

Communism in Mexico occupies a peculiar position. As a political party, it has never been important. However, Marxism as a philosophy does play an important role, especially among certain writers, thinkers, artists and students.

The Communist Party was founded in 1919 and although it did manage to get a foothold in some labor unions, it was never successful in politics. Today it claims about 25,000 members, and in the presidential elections of 1946 it obtained some 40,000 votes. During the era of the popular fronts in 1935, the Communists tried to form one in Mexico and to attract the political forces of the *Partido Revolucionario Mexicano* and of the large labor unions, but the movement failed, although doubtless Marxism did exercise influence during the administration of General Lázaro Cárdenas (1934-1940). At present, there are Communist groups in many labor unions, and some of the unions are controlled by the Communist ideology.

Well-known artists, writers and intellectuals have openly professed the Marxist philosophy, but without taking an active part in politics within the Communist Party. There is, moreover, the same ideological division in Mexican Marxism as in European Marxism, and a goodly number follow the ideas of Trotsky, who lived in Mexico after he was expelled from Russia until August, 1940, when he was assassinated.

II. Central America

The Central American Republics fall into two categories. In one group may be placed Guatemala, El Salvador and Costa Rica. There we find republics which indicate that they are on the way to overcome the traditional pattern of dictatorships and *caudillos* that have burdened them in the past. The other group is composed of Nicaragua, Honduras and Panama, still in the *caudillo* stage of their political development.

Guatemala is the most advanced chronologically, because it reached its revolutionary status in 1944 with the overthrow of Ubico. This political change, not just another coup d'etat, had all the characteristics of a revolution. The new constitution has the same ambitious program of social and economic reform to be carried out from above, as the Mexicans did in 1917. As in Mexico, the party in power has the support of intellectuals, workers, peasants, and members of the armed forces. Also as in Mexico, the first administration after the revolution was troubled by extreme radicalism and social unrest. There are some indications that with the government of President Arbenz, a period of greater maturity is approaching.

The same, although in a lesser scale, can be said of El Salvador. The revolt of December, 1948, has opened another political era in the country. The election of Major Oscar Osorio was the first democratic event of this nature that the country had had in nineteen years. Major Osorio has the support of the majority of Salvadoreans.

Costa Rica has not been burdened with *caudillos* as much as her neighbors, and the revolt of March, 1948, was more of a civil war. The war directly resulted in a new constitution outlining, as in other countries, a program of reforms. The democratic tradition of the country, and the popularity of President Ulate Blanco indicate that, in all probability, it will be free from political trouble in the near future.

Panama presents a very complex picture. President Arias was overthrown in May, 1951, and Vice-President Alcibiades Arosemena took over the government. The revolt against Arias seemed to have large popular backing, but how long this will last is hard to predict.

Honduras still presents the typical nineteenth century political pattern. The *Partido Nacionalista* represents the continuation of the previous dictatorships. President Gálvez controls the army and, in spite of the fact that he has been paying lip-service to democratic principles, the armed forces in the rural areas have been active in suppressing civil liberties. His government is exactly like that of his predecessors.

Nicaragua provides the best example of the military dictatorship. Somoza is the only real political power in the country. The opposition is a "loyal" one, composed of those who have resigned themselves to live under him.

GUATEMALA

Suffrage. The constitution establishes that all male citizens over 18 years of age, and literate women over 18 have the right to vote. It is obligatory for males who know how to read and write, and they must be inscribed in the civil register. Male illiterates may exercise the suffrage six months after having registered. In order to be inscribed, illiterates must have two honorable witnesses, who can guarantee the civic capacity of the voter and his desire to exercise the right of suffrage. Illiterates may be elected only to municipal offices and no other.

Constitutional Evolution. The captaincy-general of Guatemala, during the Spanish domination, included the other Central American republics, with the exception of the territory today comprising the republic of Panama. It also included what is today the state of Chiapas, in Mexico. After independence, the Spanish province of Guatemala became a state of the Federal Republic of Central America, to which the other Central American countries belonged, as well. The Central American Federation was a political failure. Intestine divisions and rivalries of member states were an ever-present obstacle; and the political differences between the Conservatives, supported by the Church and the landowners, and the Liberals, who were struggling to give the new federation a democratic structure, made the continuation of the federation impossible. Most of the Central American countries still believe in the ideals of the federation, and several statesmen are doing their best to revive it, but they seem unable to reach a common point of agreement.

When Guatemala was a member state of the federation, it had its own constitution, dated October 11, 1825. In 1839, when the federation disintegrated, Guatemala became an independent republic, but kept the same constitution of 1825 until 1851, when a new fundamental charter was approved. This 1851 constitution has only an historical interest.

On December 11, 1879, a new constitution was promulgated, which was to remain in force—although considerably modified—until March 11, 1945, when the present constitution came into being. The 1879 constitution is interesting, because it represents the political philosophy of Latin American liberalism of the nineteenth century and, particularly, the personal philosophy of Guatemala's great statesman and president, Justo Rufino Barrios. This political document shows the liberal faith in free play of democratic forces, and the hope of prosperity and peace for the nation, if it has an honest leader who respects the laws and applies the constitution. At the time that this constitution was approved, the statesmen had not resorted to changes in the economic and social institutions, but still believed it was enough to find this honest leader. The 1879 constitution is also important when contrasted with the one promulgated in 1945, where constitutional guarantees are extended to social, economic, cultural and family problems, as we have seen in the preceding chapters. The two documents represent two diametrically opposed moments in Latin American political thought.

Like most of the Central and South American countries, Guatemala has had its times of political freedom, and its times of despotic dictatorships. The tyrannical governments of Rafael Carrera and Manuel Estrada Cabrera oppressed the country in the nineteenth century. The phenomenon was repeated in the twentieth century, with the regime of General Jorge Ubico, who assumed the presidency in 1930, and stayed there until 1944, when he was overthrown by a revolutionary general strike, in which students, workers and the people as a whole joined. After Ubico's fall, the country was first governed by a military Junta, and later by General Federico Ponce, as provisional president. In October of the same year, General Ponce was overthrown by a popular revolution, and the government taken over by a Committee of Liberation, which called for general elections. These were held in December, 1944.

Government and Opposition. The victorious candidate in the elections was Professor José Arévalo Martínez, of the *Partido Acción*

Revolucionaria. This party is a new political group that was formed after the 1944 revolution and under which professional classes, intellectuals, workers, and students were united. Arévalo Martínez is a well-known educator who was in exile for many years during the regime of Ubico, and enjoys a solid prestige among democratic elements throughout Latin America.

In November, 1950, a general election was held and the *Partido Acción Revolucionaria,* in a coalition with some small parties, won an undisputed victory with their candidate Colonel Jacobo Arbenz Guzmán. The new president is only 37 years of age and belongs to a group of young army officers who participated in the above-mentioned revolution against Ubico in 1944. He belonged to the Revolutionary Junta and later served in Arévalo's government. President-elect Arbenz was inaugurated on March 15, 1951. He announced that he will stand for the principles of the 1944 revolution, declared himself in favor of a program of social reform and opposed totalitarianism of the right and left.

The principal opposition to the government is formed by members of the old Conservative Party, that for the elections of 1950 re-grouped with members of the *Partido Unificación Democrática,* and the *Partido del Pueblo.*

Position of Labor. During Ubico's dictatorship, labor was strictly suppressed. After 1944, and especially under the guarantees of the constitution of 1945, the trade union movement developed rapidly. Communism played an important role in the organization of the workers and supported Arévalo's government, which in many cases gave the Communists positions in the administration. This situation of semi-collaboration with the Communists roused severe criticism against Arévalo, and lasted until October of 1950, when a radical change in the government policy was announced. On that date, the Minister of the Interior took drastic steps to enforce the constitutional precept prohibiting organizations of an international character. Some of the unions today, still under Communist control, are opposed both to President Arévalo and to President Arbenz. Communism is still strong in the country.

HONDURAS

Suffrage. The suffrage is established by the constitution as universal, but limited to males. Male citizens over 18 years of age may vote, if they can read and write; illiterates may vote at 20 if married, and over 21 if single. Higher officials of the armed forces may not vote, but may be elected to public office.

Constitutional Evolution. In Honduras, as in Guatemala, we find the first constitution of the country as a member nation of the Central American Federation, and later the first one as an independent state, dated January 11, 1839. This document was followed by a series of constitutions produced by shifts in the political control, from Conservatives to Liberals and back again, none of which are of importance today.

On November 1, 1880, a new constitution was approved, which marked the ideological era of liberalism, rather similar to Guatemala's constitution of Rufino Barrios. This constitution was followed by another on October 14, 1894, based on the same philosophy, which was in force, almost without interruption, until 1924. Almost without interruption is said because, between 1906 and 1908, there were violent political disturbances, and the 1894 constitution was displaced by another, but later it was restored.

On September 10, 1924, the Hondurans had another constitution, with no substantial changes. Finally, on March 28, 1936, a constituent assembly promulgated the one now in force, which did little but extend dictator Carías Andino's presidential term. Therefore, the present constitution does not contrast, as the other Latin American constitutions do, with the charters of the nineteenth century. The constitutional process has been gradual, with slight modifications, but always maintaining the basic structure of the previous one. There is no preferential attention given to economic, social, educational or labor problems, as we have seen in the others.

Government and Opposition. The country had a turbulent nineteenth century. There were struggles between Conservatives and Liberals, changes in power, and the problems caused by relations with the Federation. The antecedent of the present government goes back to 1932, when General Tiburcio Carías Andino took over political control of the country. As a dictator, and with absolute suppression of public liberties, he maintained himself in power, directly or indirectly, until January 1, 1949, when a candidate supported by him assumed the presidency. In 1948, General Carías amazed the people with the announcement that he would—finally—leave the presidency, and would call general elections, to be held on October 10 of that year. Carías' party, formerly the Conservative Party and today called *Partido Nacionalista*, nominated Juan Manuel Gálvez, who was then the Minister of War. The Liberal Party nominated Angel Zúñiga Huete, an old-time opponent of Carías, who was in exile. A short time before the elections, the Liberals retired Zúñiga Huete's candidacy, because it was obvious the government had no intention of allowing the people to express their opinion freely. The Liberals accused the government of oppressive measures during the campaign, of blocking the organization of Liberal committees in several places, and of dissolving Liberal organizations in many towns. The "elections" were held on the date planned, but many voters stayed away from the polls, and others merely deposited blank ballots. Juan Manuel Gálvez, the sole candidate, took possession of the presidency on January 1, 1949. General Carías made it clear that, although he was not interested in any public office, he meant to continue controlling the country.

However, Gálvez' first three years have been a surprise to all—including General Carías himself, no doubt—and the opposition has dared to hope that the country is headed toward a more democratic political climate. In fact, one of the first acts of President Gálvez was to offer absolute guarantees to political exiles. He announced he would work on an active plan of public works, especially on road construction; the establishment of industries, reform of the tax system, and improvement of public education and the social conditions of the country.

Position of Labor. The workers in Honduras were kept from organizing during Carías' long dictatorship, but during these first years of Gálvez' administration, they have made considerable gains. Syndicates have been formed, laws have been passed by which the payment of wages on holidays is made obligatory, and public employees have received a 25 per cent raise in their salaries. Communists have little, if any, influence in the politics of the country.

NICARAGUA

Suffrage. According to the constitution, male citizens over 18 years of age have the right to vote, if they can read and write; and those over 21 may vote even if they are illiterate. Everything connected with electoral matters is under the supervision of a National Electoral Council, located in the capital city, and under Departmental Councils in the different districts. The National Council is composed of a president and two judges, the president appointed by the Supreme Court, and the two judges by the President of the Republic, who selects their names from a list of candidates presented by the different parties.

Constitutional Evolution. The disintegration of the Central American Federation originated the first constitution of Nicaragua, as an independent state, on November 12, 1838. After a number of years of political turmoil, in which constituent assemblies approved projects of constitutions that were never promulgated, the constitution was replaced by a new fundamental charter dated August 19, 1858, which embodied the political ideas of the Conservative Party. Like Guatemala and Honduras, Nicaragua had its era of liberalism, typical of the late nineteenth century. After a revolution, the Liberal Party came to power, and approved the constitution of December 10, 1893, which introduced a series of innovations and principles of a more democratic nature. In March, 1905, a new constitution was promulgated during the regime of Zelaya, with no substantial changes, and was in force until Zelaya's fall in 1909. That was the beginning of a period marked by civil war and political confusion, with a new constitution on December 21, 1911, in the middle of it. Nicaragua then lost its sovereignty with successive interventions and military occupations by the United States, so the country was not politically independent from 1912 to 1933, when the last North American troops left the country.

Another constitution was promulgated on March 22, 1939, under the dictatorship of General Anastasio Somoza, with the sole purpose of extending his presidential term for eight years. This was replaced by the one now in force, dated January 21, 1948. How long this one will last, it is difficult to predict, since it is highly probable that another constituent assembly will be convoked before long.

Present Government and Opposition. Nicaragua's present government is based on a long and oppressive dictatorship, and there seems to be no hope for a change in the near future. In 1937, General Anastasio Somoza, who controlled the armed forces, took over political power, and since that time he has kept the country under his control, either from the presidency or appointing the presidents; and especially as Chief of the National Guard, which is the only military force of the country. In 1946, when the eight years "granted" him by the first of the transitory dispositions of the 1939 constitution were drawing to a close, Somoza proposed Dr. Leonardo Argüello as presidential candidate for the *Partido Liberal Nacionalista,* the government party. Dr. Argüello was, of course, elected and took office, but soon started to show disquieting signs of having his own ideas on how to run the country. Somoza had the Congress declare Argüello incapacitated, and obliged him to leave Nicaragua. He immediately convoked a constituent assembly that approved the present constitution and elected his uncle, Víctor Román Reyes, to the presidency. On May 6, 1950, President Román Rayes died. A few months before his death, the two major parties had reached an agreement to hold a presidential election. Under this agreement, the minority party was guaranteed 26 seats in the Congress, regardless of the number of votes received. The purpose of the pact was to assure a fixed representation of the minority in Congress giving them, therefore, a voice in the legislative process of Nicaragua.

General Somoza was nominated as candidate by his own *Partido Liberal Nacionalista,* and General Emiliano Chamorro was the choice of the Conservatives. The elections were held on May 25, and candidate Somoza won by over 100,000 votes. Voting was orderly, but far from secret. The electors were compelled to mark their ballots in public, and in the presence of a member of Somoza's party. When a vote was cast for the Liberals, the voter received a card as proof. Possession of the card was a requirement for employment with the government. This election returned to the presidency the man who has been the power behind the throne in Nicaragua since 1937. The opposition is weak within the country. In neighboring states, there are political exiles hopeful of a revolution, but a successful one is improbable, as Somoza has a firm control over the armed forces.

Position of Labor. Because of the purely agricultural economy, and the lack of freedom in Nicaragua, the labor unions are negligible. There is a small Communist group, operating under the name of *Partido Socialista de Nicaragua,* which has had some slight influence on the incipient organizations, but very little influence on the country as a whole.

EL SALVADOR

Suffrage. The constitution states that the right of suffrage is given to all Salvadorian citizens, according to the requirements and limitations set by the law. In the last elections, the electoral law granted the right to vote to all male citizens over 18 years of age, and to married males under 18 if they were high-school graduates. Women over 21, with high-school diplomas, could also vote. Other women, in order to vote, had to be over 25 and know how to read and write.

Constitutional Evolution. As a small, weak and overpopulated country, El Salvador suffered, in the nineteenth century, not only from its own domestic problems, but from the influence of the larger Central American republics, and Mexico's desires to annex it during the regime of Emperor Iturbide. As a natural measure of defense against these external pressures, El Salvador considered the possibility of annexation to the United States of America, and particularly struggled to maintain the Central American Federation as a means of protecting its independence. Like the other republics, the first constitution of El Salvador was as a member state of the Federation, dated June 12, 1824. The second, a result of the disintegration of the Federation, was dated February 22, 1841. After this there came a number of constitutions, caused by the familiar political turmoil, none of which introduced changes of importance in the fundamental institutions. The constitution of August 13, 1886, is important, because it is the typical document of nineteenth century liberalism and because it lasted until 1939.

The constitution of 1886 was replaced by another document imposed by dictator Maximiliano Hernández Martínez on January 20, 1939, which was prepared by a constituent assembly exclusively to extend his presidential term. The constitution was as unpopular with the people as the president that had inflicted it upon them, and when he was overthrown in 1944, a constituent assembly, in 1945, restored the 1886 constitution, with several amendments. The Revolutionary Junta that assumed political control in December, 1948, authorized the Congress to act as a constituent assembly, to draft a new constitution. This went into effect on September 14, 1950. The document followed the new pattern of the modern Latin American constitutions, and legislates in detail a large number of social and economic rights, as well as an ambitious program of economic reform.

Government and Opposition. The political problems of El Salvador closely parallel those in the other Central American republics, with a long dictatorship. General Maximiliano Hernández Martínez took office as provisional president in December, 1931, to complete the term of President Arturo Araujo, who had to leave the country after a military coup. Hernández Martínez kept the nation under a severe dictatorship, aided by the armed forces, for thirteen years. In February, 1944, a puppet constituent assembly extended his term for another five years, but in April the country's discontent came to a head with a revolution and a general strike propelled by students, workers, business and professional men, which forced the dictator to retire. After a provisional government under General Andrés Menéndez, Colonel Osmín Aguirre was designated provisional president, and he called for elections to be held in January, 1945. The liberal group of the country came together in the *Partido Unión Democrática,* supporting Dr. Arturo Romero as presidential candidate, but Aguirre indicated his disapproval of the selection. As a result, there was only one candidate in the elections, General Salvador Castañeda Castro, a well-known figure of the Conservative Party.

Castañeda Castro's regime introduced a few weak reforms, suppressed civil liberties, and was nothing new to the disillusioned Salvadorians. A state of seige was maintained almost without interruption, in spite of the protests of liberals and students. Finally, on December 14, 1948, another military coup disposed of Castañeda Castro and a revolutionary Junta which was called the *Consejo de Gobierno Revolucionario,* under the direction of Colonel Jesús Córdova, assumed the political control of the country. In January, 1949, the Junta accepted the resignation of Colonel Córdova, and he was replaced by Major Oscar Osorio.

Later, Major Oscar Osorio, head of the Junta, resigned from his position to run as presidential candidate for the *Partido Revolu-*

cionario de Unificación Democrática (PRUD) . This political group represents the centrist position in Salvadorean politics. The *Acción Reformista* party nominated Colonel José Asencio Menéndez, considered a democratic leader, and well respected by many of the citizenry. The elections were held toward the end of March, 1950, the first free elections in the country since 1931. Voting was large and peaceful, and Major Osorio was elected to the presidency by a comfortable margin. Osorio's party won the majority of seats in the Congress. Women participated in the elections, for the first time in the history of the country. Major Osorio was inaugurated on September 14, and he reaffirmed, in his platform, the traditional democratic principles coupled with a modern outlook on social problems. After the revolutionary process of 1944, the labor movement gradually gained momentum, and today it has a certain influence in the country. In the year of Osorio's provisional government, as we said above, a number of social measures were introduced, such as the reorganization of the Ministry of Labor. Decrees have been issued by which the payment of wages during illness is made obligatory, and others in which expectant mothers and native workers are protected. During Martinez' dictatorship, all of his political enemies were systematically accused of being Communists, when the truth was that there were very few in the country. In spite of the years of almost constant disturbances, the Communists appear to have made little headway in El Salvador.

COSTA RICA

Suffrage. Under the constitution of 1871, suffrage is granted to all male citizens over 20 years of age, and to those over 18 years of age, if married or if they have a professional degree, and on condition that they possess properties, or an honest trade sufficient to afford them a position in proportion to their social status. The constitution did not authorize the vote for women.

Constitutional Evolution. At the disintegration of the Central American Federation, Costa Rica organized as an independent state, and adopted a constitution dated April 11, 1844. This was followed by several constitutions, whose central political problem was the decision on a unicameral or bicameral legislature. The principle of a unicameral legislature emerged victorious with the constitution of 1871, the most important political document of the country, since it has lived to our own days. A unitarian system of government was adopted, with the typical threefold division of the powers of the State, and the traditional individual guarantees. Under the revolutionary government of General Tinoco, in 1917, this constitution was replaced by another, but when the government fell two years later, the 1871 constitution was restored. Various amendments of a social and economic nature were added in 1943, but the fundamental structure was maintained. During the provisional government of Colonel Figueres, in 1949, a constituent assembly approved a new constitution.

Government and Opposition. In the nineteenth century, Costa Rica had its traditional struggles between Liberals and Conservatives, with the programs and ideologies characteristic of those parties in all of Latin America. There was a period of peace and considerable progress during the early part of the twentieth century, which afforded an opportunity for development in various fields, especially education. Illiteracy was greatly diminished, to such an extent that the country today has one of the lowest percentages in Latin America. Costa Rica never had the problem of indigenous illiteracy, since there were few Indians in the region, and most of the population was of European descent. Agricultural economy was strengthened, due to the fact that rural holdings had always been small and there were few latifundia, which fitted in with the spirit of the constitution of 1871. The economic and ethnic atmosphere obviously favored the democratic liberalism of the constitution, which was not hampered by the feudalistic conditions of other countries.

The Liberals, who had been in power during the early years of the twentieth century, won the elections in 1940, under the name of *Partido Nacional Republicano,* with Dr. Rafael Calderón Guardia as their candidate. His regime was characterized by important social reforms and the constitutional amendments mentioned above. Some of the radical groups, particularly the Communists, collaborated with the government during that time. The old Conservative Party, called the *Partido Democrático,* strongly opposed Calderón Guardia and his program, but could not get enough public support to win the 1944 elections, when Teodoro Picado Michalski was elected to the presidency. Picado maintained the Liberal policy during his administration; and in the next elections of 1948, the Liberals again nominated Calderón Guardia. The Conservatives, then under the name of *Partido Unión Nacional,* nominated Otilio Ulate Blanco. The electoral campaign was turbulent and marked by violence. The Communists, who had changed their name to *Partido Vanguardia Popular,* nominated their leader, Manuel Mora Valverde. The earliest returns gave the victory to Ulate Blanco, but the other parties charged fraud and challenged the decision. The case was taken to the Superior Electoral Tribunal, which decided in favor of Ulate Blanco by a narrow margin, and recommended that the case be referred to the Congress for its final solution. The Congress declared the elections void, and ordered the formation of a provisional government to supervise new elections. The decision was followed by disturbances and armed skirmishes between the police and Ulate Blanco's followers. In March, 1948, Colonel José Figueres headed an uprising, in support of Ulate Blanco, and started a virtual civil war which lasted until the following month, on the 28th, when Figueres took the capital city. Instead of turning the government over to Ulate Blanco, as everyone expected, Figueres formed a Junta over which he presided, and announced that he would convoke a constituent assembly to decide upon the form of government to be taken.

In January, 1949, the assembly ratified Ulate Blanco's elections, complying with Figueres' request. Despite the appearance of complete accord between Figueres and Ulate, they disagreed over the draft of the constitution submitted to the Assembly. Ulate was in favor of the 1871 constitution, while Figueres wanted a new one, and Figueres' opinion prevailed. The two political groups agreed to hold elections in October, 1949, to select the first and second vice-presidents and the 45 members of the legislative assembly. The new Congress took office on November 8, when Ulate Blanco was instated as the constitutional president of the republic. For two years the central figure in national politics, Figueres apparently was satisfied to retire into the background, and his party, the *Partido Socialista Democrático,* elected only three deputies out of the 45. However, political observers believed that his apparent withdrawal obeyed an agreement with Ulate, under which Colonel Figueres will be the candidate, with Ulate's support, in the presidential elections of 1953.

Position of Labor. The higher level of education among the masses, and the better economic conditions of the country, as well as greater political freedom, have allowed the labor movements of Costa Rica to advance more than in the other countries of Central America. The strongest group of workers is the *Confederación de Trabajadores de Costa Rica* (CTCR), which in 1943 organized as a national labor union, and included important syndicates, such as the workers in streetcars, electric plants, maritime trade, the banana industry, and the metal and textile industries. Another strong labor group functions under the name of *Central de Sindicatos Costaricenses Rerum Novarum,* and is obviously Catholic in its influence.

Radicalism in labor, as in politics, has centered in the Communist Party, which was formed in 1930 by groups of intellectuals, students and workers in the capital city of San José. During Calderón Guardia's government, the party enjoyed political influence, and in the 1944 elections, they sent four deputies to the Congress. In 1943, when the Comintern was dissolved, the Communists changed their name to *Partido Vanguardia Popular,* participated in the 1948 elections and later in the revolutionary period that followed, supporting Calderón Guardia's party. The Conservative victory and Ulate's election have greatly weakened the Communists in Costa Rica.

PANAMA

Suffrage. Suffrage is universal, equal, direct and secret. All citizens over 21 years of age, regardless of education, status or sex, have the right to vote. The law prohibits the organization of political parties based on sex, race or religion, or those that might tend to destroy the democratic form of government.

Constitutional Evolution. Panama was a part of the Republic of Colombia, until it became independent, on November 3, 1903, with the aid and protection of the United States. This aid was given in order to receive the concession necessary to construct the Canal, which Colombia had at the last minute refused.

The first Panamanian constitution, dated February 13, 1904, was approved under North American influence, and organized the state as a centralized republic. The constitution stipulated that the United States would guarantee independence and that it had the right to intervene in Panama to maintain peace and constitutional order. Politically, thus, it may be affirmed that Panama was not a sovereign state under that first constitution, and that it did not obtain its complete independence until the administration of Franklin D. Roosevelt, when the treaty restricting Panamanian sovereignty was abrogated. A new constitution was approved under the regime of Arnulfo Árias, dated December 15, 1940, which did not include the clause giving the right of intervention to the United States. On March 1, 1946, Panama promulgated the present constitution, which regulates in detail the problems connected with the family, economy, labor, culture and social welfare.

Government and Opposition. Panamanian politics, during the first three decades following separation from Colombia, were generally involved with the Canal concession, relations with the United States resulting from the clause in the constitution, above referred to, and with the payment by the United States of the annual quota for the concession. Domestic political controversies were acute, because government positions are one of the few sources of income in the country, and Washington sometimes made its influence felt, even landing marines to supervise the elections.

The present political situation arises from events which took place some twelve years ago. As a result of the elections of June 2, 1940, Dr. Arnulfo Árias Madrid occupied the presidency. Árias' political program was based on a strong nationalism and opposition to the United States. His presidency and his political program became a problem for the defense of the United States, because at that time World War II was imminent, and Washington's attention was focused on the Canal Zone. In October, 1941, Árias made a short visit to Havana, announcing that he was going to consult a physician. His political enemies took advantage of the opportunity to have the National Assembly declare the presidency vacant, because the President had, they stated, left the country without authorization. Árias accused the United States of having brought pressure to bear, and the United States denied this; but in semi-official circles in Washington, he was accused of having totalitarian ideas.

After having deposed the President, the National Assembly designated Ricardo Adolfo de la Guardia as Provisional President, and this appointment was favorably received by Washington. De la

Guardia governed the country during the war years, and on May 5, 1945, members of a constituent assembly were elected, and they appointed Enrique A. Jiménez, of the Liberal Party, as Provisional President. The Assembly approved the present constitution, and voted upon their own transformation from a constituent to a legislative body, extending their powers until October, 1948.

During the years of provisional governments, Árias, then in Argentina, kept his contacts with his party members, who attempted several unsuccessful revolutionary coups. When the provisional government decided to hold elections, setting the date of May 9, 1948, Árias' party, called the *Partido Nacional Revolucionario Auténtico,* nominated their leader as presidential candidate. The old Liberals, under the name of *Partido Unión Nacional,* nominated Domingo Díaz Arosemena. The elections were held on the appointed date, and when the votes were counted, it was announced that Árias had obtained the majority. Arosemena's followers claimed there had been fraud in certain districts, and took the case before the National Electoral Jury. Árias' adherents protested violently; Provisional President Jiménez declared martial law, and again Árias was obliged to leave for a foreign country. Finally, in October of that year, the Electoral Jury decided the case in favor of Arosemena, who took office.

President Arosemena enjoyed the much disputed presidency only a short time, as he died in August, 1949, and his place was taken by first Vice-President Daniel Chanis. In November, President Chanis asked Chief of Police Colonel José Antonio Remón for his resignation, and accused him of fraud. With Panama's armed forces at his command, Remón surrounded the presidential palace, obliged President Chanis to resign, and turned the presidency over to the second vice-president, Roberto F. Chiari.

Chanis protested that his resignation was not valid, since it had been wrung from him under pressure, and appealed to the Supreme Court, which decided in his favor. To add to the confusion, Chief of Police Remón again intervened, and brushed the two vice-presidents from the picture, proclaiming Arnulfo Árias Madrid as President of the Republic. To justify his actions, he stated that the presidency actually belonged to Árias, because he had been the victorious candidate in the 1948 elections. The National Electoral Jury declared it had discovered the greatest fraud in the history of the country, and that Árias was definitely the constitutional president. Árias took office on November 25, 1949. On May 10, 1951, a bloody revolt culminated in the defeat of President Árias and Vice-President Alcibíades Arosemena assumed the presidency. The cause of the upheaval was the general dissatisfaction produced by President Árias' having adopted the 1941 constitution, thus increasing his term of office to six years. Later, Árias was tried by the National Assembly and legally removed from office on the charges that he was guilty of abusing his presidential powers and trying to establish a fascist-type dictatorship.

On May 11, a general election was held and Colonel José Antonio Remón, candidate of the Patriotic Coalition, was elected to the Presidency, to begin a four-year term on October 1. Remón, who resigned as National Chief of Police to run for the presidency, had little opposition. His principal opponent was Roberto Chiari, candidate of the Civil Alliance. Remón's chief opponent, ex-President Arnulfo Árias, did not participate in the elections. With this "election," another strong man supported by the armed forces has taken over political power in the Latin American area.

Position of Labor. The labor organizations, which enjoy an impressive number of guarantees in the constitution, have had little influence on political life. The principal problem of Panamanian workers has always been the difference between the salaries paid in the Canal Zone and the ones paid in the national territory, as well as the discrimination in wages paid by Zone concerns between white and colored workers. One of the labor groups is organized as the *Confederación de Trabajadores de Panamá,* and has tried to protect native workers, often under the direction of labor leaders from Cuba and Mexico. Some of the syndicates in this group follow a Communist ideology. There is a non-Communist group, the National Association of Labor Unions. The intervention of Communists in political affairs has been unimportant, and the party, called the *Partido del Pueblo,* has a small membership. The constitutional precept mentioned above, to the effect that no political parties may be formed that might tend to destroy the democratic form of government, has hampered Communist activities. The strongest political force in Panama is nationalism, a natural consequence of its years of dependence upon the United States.

SUGGESTED READINGS

English:

Bosques, Gilberto, *The National Revolutionary Party in Mexico and the Six-Year Plan,* Mexico, D.F., 1937.

Brenner, Anita, *The Wind that Swept Mexico,* New York, Harper & Brothers, 1943.

Calcott, W. H., *Liberalism in Mexico,* Stanford University Press, 1931.

Clark, Marjorie Ruth, *Organized Labor in Mexico,* Chapel Hill, University of North Carolina Press, 1934.

Cramer, Floyd, *Our Neighbor, Nicaragua,* New York, Stokes, 1929.

Fergusson, Erna, *Guatemala,* New York, Alfred Knopf, Inc., 1937.

Gruening, Ernest H., *Mexico and Its Heritage,* New York, Century, 1928.

Herring, Hubert, *Mexico: The Making of a Nation,* New York, Foreign Policy Association, 1942.

Jones, Chester Lloyd, *Costa Rica and Civilization in the Caribbean,* Madison, University of Wisconsin Press, 1935.

————, *Guatemala Past and Present,* Minneapolis, University of Minnesota Press, 1940.

Kepner, Charles David, *Social Aspects of the Banana Industry,* New York, Columbia University Press, 1936.

Kirk, Betty, *Covering the Mexican Front,* Norman, University of Oklahoma Press, 1942.

Macdonald, Austin F., *Latin American Politics and Government,* New York, Thomas Y. Crowell Co., 1949.

Martin, P. F., *Salvador of the Twentieth Century,* New York, Longmans, Green & Co., 1911.

Miner, Dwight Carrol, *The Fight for the Panama Route,* New York, Columbia University Press, 1940.

Munro, Dana G., *The Five Republics of Central America,* New York, Oxford University Press, 1918.

Parkes, Henry Bamford, *A History of Mexico,* Boston, Houghton Mifflin Co., 1950.

Simpson, Eyler N., *The Ejido, Mexico's Way Out,* Chapel Hill, University of North Carolina Press, 1937.

Stokes, Williams, *Honduras, An Area Study in Government,* Madison, University of Wisconsin Press, 1950.

Tannenbaum, Frank, *Peace by Revolution,* New York, Columbia University Press, 1933.

————, *Mexican Agrarian Revolution,* New York, The Macmillan Co., 1929.

————, *Mexico,* New York, Alfred A. Knopf, Inc., 1950.

Whetten, Nathan L., *Rural Mexico,* University of Chicago Press, 1948.
Wilson, Charles Morrow, *Middle America,* New York, W. W. Norton &
Co., Inc., 1944.

Spanish:

Cabrera, Luis, *Veinte Años Después,* México, D. F., 1937.
Caso, Antonio, *El Problema de México y la Ideología National,* México.
D. F., 1924.
Castellaños Tena, Fernando, *Nuestras Constituciones,* México, D.F.,
1944.
Chávez Orozco, Luis, *Historia Económica y Social de México,* México,
D. F., 1938.
Cordero Reyes, Manuel, *Nicaragua bajo el Régimen de Somoza,* San
Salvador, 1944.
Correa, Eduardo, *El Balance del Ávila Camachismo,* México, D.F., 1946.
Echeverría S., Buenaventura, *Derecho Constitucional Guatemalteco,*
Guatemala, 1944.
Mijares Palencia, José, *El Gobierno Mexicano: Su Organización y
Funcionamiento,* México, D. F., 1936.
Sierra, Justo, *Evolución Política del Pueblo Mexicano,* México, 1940.
————, *México, Su Evolución Social,* 3 vols., México, D.F., 1900-1902.
Silva, Herzog, Jesús, *La Revolución Mexicana en Crisis,* México, D.F.,
1944.
Teja Zabre, Alfonso, *Panorama Histórico de La Revolución Mexicana,*
México, D. F., 1939.
Zea, Leopoldo, *El Positivismo en México,* México, D. F., 1944.
Zeledón, Marco Tulio, *Lecciones de Ciencia Constitucional,* San José
(Costa Rica) , 1945.

CHAPTER 13

The Caribbean Area

CUBA

The most important forces contending for power in the present Cuban political arena originated in the revolutionary period against dictator Machado (1928-1933). It is true that the *Partido Liberal* is still a factor, but the leadership of the old politicians has ceased, and it is in the hands of a new generation. Institutionally speaking, the constitution of 1901 had all the characteristics of the traditional Latin American liberalism, and the constitution of 1940 represented the new nationalistic spirit, combined with the progress of social and economic reform.

To appraise Cuba's political condition today, it is necessary to remember that the country has a history different from that of most of Latin America. By remaining a Spanish colony until 1898, the island—in spite of the abuses and despotism of the colonial government—received the benefits of the institutional changes introduced in Spain during the nineteenth century constitutional monarchy. Cuban society is more integrated, because of the absence of an Indian population. The Negroes and mulattoes do not have a linguistic division or an important cultural barrier separating them from the rest of the population. Economically, the country is semi-industrialized, as the first transformation of the main agricultural crop, sugar cane, is made within the island. Because of this, organized labor plays a prominent role in politics.

Due to these circumstances, when Cuba returned to constitutional life in 1940, the country was expected to continue a more normal political evolution. Unfortunately, this did not happen. On March 10, 1952, by a military coup d'etat, ex-President Fulgencio Batista deposed the constitutional government of Prío Socarrás and assumed dictatorial powers. To be able to understand this phenomenon, it is important to have in mind that the most powerful political force that came out of the revolutionary period against Machado was the *Partido Revolucionario Cubano (Auténtico)*. But this party, especially after it achieved power in 1944, experienced important internal schisms, and only a section of it was backing President Prío Socarrás. This division, and the corruption of political leaders who had struggled gallantly in the thirties against Machado, may partly explain the coup d'etat.

Suffrage. Suffrage is universal, equal and secret, and is considered not only a right but an obligation of the citizens. Omission to vote is punishable by law. The people may also express their opinions through referenda. Cubans of both sexes, over 21, may vote, with the exception of inmates of asylums, those who are mentally incapacitated, or disqualified for criminal offenses, and the members of the armed forces and police in active service. The organization of associations and of any kind of political parties is guaranteed in the constitution, but no political groupings based on race, sex or class are permitted.

Constitutional Evolution. The constitutional evolution of Cuba may be divided into four periods. The first begins with the proclamation of the Republic in May, 1902, and ends in 1928, when President Machado, through a constituent assembly under his control, had the first constitution amended to extend his term.

Cuba's independence came late, not because the Cubans did not desire it during the nineteenth century (the first conspiracy toward emancipation took place in 1812), but because international circumstances stood in the way. After various revolutionary attempts, one of which was a long war from 1868 to 1878, the last struggle for independence started in 1895 and came to an end in 1898 with the defeat of Spain, in the war in which the United States participated. This was followed by American military occupation, until independence in 1902.

The first Cuban constitution, dated February 21, 1901, went into effect on May 20, 1902, when Tomás Estrada Palma took office as first President of the Republic. The constitution is the typical liberal document of nineteenth-century Latin America, and organized the State as a centralized republic, with a president elected for four years, a Congress composed of a Chamber of Representatives and a Senate, and an independent Judiciary headed by a Supreme Tribunal of Justice. Incorporated into the constitution was the permanent treaty signed between Cuba and the United States, containing the Platt Amendment, which had been sanctioned by President McKinley and imposed upon the Cubans as a condition for obtaining independence. The amendment was unique in constitutional theory, since it restricted the sovereignty of Cuba in many aspects and authorized intervention by the United States in the internal affairs of the republic.

When President Estrada Palma was nominated for a second term by the *Partido Moderado,* the members of the Liberal Party felt that the President would not offer the necessary guarantees to opposing parties for the elections, and withdrew. The President was re-elected by one party; the Liberals started a revolt in August, 1906, and the members of the *Partido Moderado* solicited the intervention of the United States, under the Platt Amendment. This brought about the second American military occupation that lasted until 1909, when the Liberal Party won the elections with General José Miguel Gómez as their candidate. Gómez was succeeded by General Mario García Menocal, of the Conservative Party, who held office for two consecutive terms, until 1921. When Menocal was re-elected for his second term in 1916, the elections were fraudulent, and the Liberal Party took up arms for the second time. The war lasted several months, but the Liberals were defeated, partly due to pressure from Washington, that favored General Menocal's Conservative presidency. Dr. Alfredo Zayas, elected by a coalition of the *Partido Popular* and the Conservatives, took office in 1921. During his administration, the Platt Amendment was used repeatedly as a means of exercising pressure upon the government, if not for open intervention. In spite of these disturbances, the Cuban constitution of 1901 was maintained without modifications until the presidency of the republic was occupied (1925) by General Gerardo Machado. In 1928, he convoked a constituent assembly which amended the constitution in order to extend his term. Therefore, 1928 was the last year of the legal existence of the first Cuban constitution, and the first year of the second period.

The forces of the opposition took legal steps to protest the constitutional amendment, and the case was taken before the Supreme Court. After 1930, the opposition was strengthened by the support of the students and some groups of workers. There was an unsuccessful revolt, and the dictatorship that followed was one of the cruelest that Latin America has ever seen. Machado followed the example of Latin America's traditional tyrants, ruthlessly oppressed his opponents, frequently by means of torture and murder. The opposition, and especially the students, fought terror with terror, and the life of the republic was paralyzed. The American government supported Machado until Franklin D. Roosevelt became President and sent Benjamin Sumner Welles as a special delegate to mediate in the conflict. The opposition, that had been forced underground, was given a breathing spell by this intercession, and organized a general strike which met with such sympathy among the people that not only the students and workers, but business men and professionals, joined the movement. This was early in August, 1933. The army had remained loyal to Machado, but when they realized the proportions of the movement against him, they knew his day was up. They joined the opposition, and on August 12, Machado at last was forced to leave the country. This was the close of the second period in the constitutional evolution of Cuba.

After Machado's fall, the parties of the opposition, at the recommendation of Ambassador Sumner Welles, formed a provisional government under the presidency of Dr. Carlos Manuel de Céspedes, who annulled the constitutional amendment of 1928 and restored the constitution of 1901. Some of the opposition groups, especially the students who had so persistently fought against the dictator, refused to participate in the provisional government, which they felt was a puppet of the United States, and on the 4th of September they joined in a revolt, when the enlisted men and sergeants deposed the army officers. Sergeant Fulgencio Batista immediately assumed control of the army.[1] The coup removed President Céspedes from office and appointed a provisional government, first composed of a committee of five, and later substituted by the provisional presidency of Dr. Ramón Grau San Martín. The provisional government passed a Constitutional Statute, briefly organizing the government under a Presidency, a Council of State, and the Supreme Court. The leadership of the army was formally given to Batista, promoted to the rank of Colonel. Politicians who had opposed Machado, and who

---

[1] See Chapter 10.

were thrust aside by this new government, organized a strong opposition against Grau, and the United States refused to recognize his government. Sumner Welles left Cuba and Jefferson Caffery came in his place, as a special delegate. A few months later Batista, in agreement with the old politicians of the opposition—and of course with Caffery—secured Grau's resignation. From this date until his own accession to the Presidency in 1940, Batista put in and removed the presidents at his convenience. Grau's resignation was made in favor of Carlos Hevia, but as the choice was not considered a satisfactory one, he was replaced in a matter of hours by Colonel Carlos Mendieta.

With these presidential changes, Cuba entered into a period of *de facto* governments. In 1934 the Platt Amendment was abrogated by the United States. Mendieta promulgated a provisional constitution very much like the one of 1902; this was amended several times and replaced by another on March 8, 1935. Shortly thereafter, Mendieta resigned and was replaced in the Presidency by Secretary of State José A. Barnet. General elections were held in 1936, and Dr. Miguel Mariano Gómez, son of the second President of the Republic, was elected. Dr. Gómez' term as president was short, because Batista found him less submissive than he had expected and had the Congress depose him. Vice-President Dr. Frederico Laredo Bru took Dr. Gómez' place and remained in office until 1940.

During his administration, a Constituent Assembly was convoked and a new constitution was approved that was promulgated on October 10, 1940. This constitution opened the fourth constitutional period which lasted until March 10, 1952, when Batista usurped power by a military coup.

In the elections held in 1940, Colonel Fulgencio Batista was nominated by a coalition of parties and elected to the presidency. His opposing candidate was ex-president Dr. Ramón Grau San Martín. Batista held office until October, 1944, when Grau San Martín won the elections.

Government and Opposition. During the first constitutional period (1902-1928), the Liberal party was the strongest one. However, Machado's unpopularity weighed heavily against the party and, in 1933, during the few months of the first provisional government of Grau San Martín, the Liberals' place in popular favor was taken by a new party formed by Grau with revolutionary groups, professionals and students, which they called *Partido Revolucionario Cubano (Auténtico)*. The new party was not strong enough to defeat Batista and the coalition in 1940, but it did obtain an overwhelming majority in 1944, when Dr. Grau took over the presidency. He governed until 1948, but in the last years of his administration many of his followers became disappointed with his weakness and "shilly-shallying" ways, and formed the *Partido del Pueblo Cubano*, under the leadership of Senator Eduardo Chibás.

In the elections of June 1, 1948, the PRC nominated Dr. Carlos Prío Socarrás; the old Liberal Party, again on the upward swing and the second party in membership, united with some smaller parties and nominated Dr. Ricardo Núñez Portuondo. The new *Partido del Pueblo Cubano* nominated Eduardo Chibás, and the *Partido Socialista Popular* (the Communist Party), nominated their leader, Dr. Juan Marinello. Prío Socarrás was elected by a large majority, but electoral experts were surprised by the large number of votes obtained by Chibás' party—some 320,000. The Communists, with 140,000 votes, had the smallest number of all the parties.

President Prío Socarrás continued governing the country and formed a coalition with the *Partido Liberal*. In August, 1951, Senator Eduardo Chibás committed a spectacular suicide and his death caused a crisis in the ranks of the opposition. Early in 1952, the electoral campaign for the June presidential elections was in full swing. The *Partido del Pueblo Cubano* nominated Dr. Roberto Agramonte, who had been the vice-presidential candidate with Chibás in the previous election. Prío's government, with his group of *Auténticos* and a coalition of parties, backed the candidacy of Carlos Hevia. Ex-President Batista was also a candidate, for his own party. The Communists were acting more or less underground, although they had not been outlawed, and showed little interest in the campaign. Early in March, most of the political observers believed that Dr. Agramonte had the best chance to win the elections, while Batista was running a poor third. On March 10, Batista, with a group of second-rank army officers and retired officers who had served under him during his previous administration, re-enacted the coup d'etat of 1933, marched to Camp Columbia, took command of the armed forces and sent a motorized division to the Presidential Palace, which surrendered after a slight skirmish. President Prío

Socarrás took refuge in the Mexican Embassy and later left the country.

Batista suspended the constitution of 1940 and assumed *de facto* political power, calling himself "Head of the State" (*Jefe del Estado*). Later he promulgated a constitutional statute organizing a provisional government with a Cabinet, a consultative assembly, and abolishing Congress. He announced that presidential elections would be held in 1953. These events marked the first time that a constitutionally elected president was deposed by a military coup d'etat in the history of the republic.

Batista has comparatively little popular support. The opposition is composed of the majority of the political parties that are already acting in a united front, and the leadership has been assumed, as in the days of Machado's dictatorship, by University professors, students and intellectuals. So far, there has been no violence, but it is hard to predict how long this relatively quiet situation will last.

Position of Labor. During the first two decades of the republic, the labor organizations exercised little political influence although, of course, they played their part in the social struggle, and there were strikes and labor conflicts of varying importance. The strongest unions at that time were among the workers of the railroads and transport in general, the stevedores and the workers in the tobacco industry. The movement gained strength during the last years of Machado's dictatorship, when the resistance against him was organized; and especially during the revolutionary period that followed his fall.

Today Cuba has a strong labor organization, more highly developed and coordinated than in other Latin American countries. This is mainly due to the economic conditions of the country, which is not exclusively agricultural or dependent upon mining. Most of the island's production is centered around the sugar industry, which has facilitated the formation of strong industrial unions in the sugar mills. The most important federation is the *Confederación de Trabajadores de Cuba,* and the principal unions are among the sugar, tobacco, transport and maritime workers. There are strong craft unions, as well. In 1947 there was a schism within the CTC between the Communist workers, who followed the line of the *Partido Socialista Popular,* and the non-Communists, most of whom belonged to

President Grau's PRC. The split continued during President Prío Socarrás' administration. When Batista took over, the non-Communist group of the CTC, led by Senator Eusebio Mujal, declared a general strike, but later Mujal came to an agreement with Batista and gave his support to the regime.

The Communist Party was organized in the last years of the administration of President Zayas, under the direction of young intellectuals, workers and student leaders. It played an active part during the struggle against Machado, and participated in his downfall through the general strike of August, 1933. After his overthrow, the Communists grew stronger and their membership increased. During Batista's administration (1940-1944) and later during Grau's, the Communist Party occupied various government positions and elected representatives to the Congress. Toward the end of Grau's regime, there was a break between him and the Communists, and they nominated their own candidate in the 1948 elections. At that time, the electoral census showed a Communist Party membership of approximately 164,350.

HAITI

The political life of Haiti has always been limited to a struggle between factions of the educated mulatto elite that control the economic life of the country. The large masses of illiterate Negroes in the rural areas have had little participation in politics. Because of the different nineteenth century history, the different ethnic composition and the French cultural influence, no valid comparison can be made between Haiti and Hispanic America. The educated and sincere leaders of the country have been forced to act in a sort of political vacuum, unable to influence the illiterate masses. Radicalism exists, but it has been superficial rather than real, and the army is still the true political power. Magloire's government, for the present, seems to have popular support, and a new constitution is being prepared.

Suffrage. All male citizens over 21 years of age have the right to vote. Naturalized aliens may not vote until ten years after the date of naturalization. Citizens have the right to join political parties, and this right may not be subject to any preventive measure. No one may be obliged to join an association or political party.

Members of the army in active service may not be elected to public office. The vote, and scrutiny thereof, are secret.

Constitutional Evolution. The territory that later became the republic of Haiti started its constitutional life as a province of France. On July 8, 1801, the constitution of Saint Domingue was approved, formally uniting the territory of Haiti to France, as a province, but with sufficient local autonomy and under a Governor-General. The experiment was not satisfactory, and on January 1, 1804, Haiti proclaimed its independence. Later, on May 20, 1805, an imperial constitution was adopted, to be followed by the document of December 27, 1806, by which the State was organized as a republic.

This document was followed by years of confusion and domestic struggles. The country was divided into two sections, the north and the south, functioning under political leaders as independent states among themselves. The chaotic and anarchical situation, politically speaking, lasted until 1843, when the two parts came together under a new constitution, the most liberal document Haiti had during the entire nineteenth century. More disturbances followed this constitution, and the country fell under the dictatorship of General Souloque, who proclaimed himself Emperor in 1847 and issued a constitution of an imperial nature, promulgated in September, 1849. Soulouque ruled under the name of Faustain I until 1858, when he was forced to resign. The constitution was modified in various aspects but was not discarded until June, 1867, when political changes caused the approval of a republican, and highly conservative, charter. This one suffered several amendments and was totally substituted in December, 1879, by another document, under which the State was organized with a unicameral legislature. This again was modified various times and discarded on October 9, 1889, for the constitution that was to govern the country until the occupation of Haiti by the United States.

The American intervention in Haiti had an origin similar to that of the Dominican Republic, which will be mentioned later. Domestic political problems, the condition of bankruptcy of the country, and especially debts to European nations, obliged the United States to take this step in September, 1915, to avoid intervention by other powers. As in the Dominican Republic, American troops started by taking over the custom house and applying the duties toward the liquidation of the foreign debt, but this was followed by a military occupation which lasted eighteen years. The new Haitian constitution was imposed by the government of occupation. It was made in the United States and, as a formality, submitted to a plebiscite on June 12, 1918. This document was modified twice. Under the administration of President Franklin D. Roosevelt, the American troops were finally withdrawn from Haitian soil in 1934.

With its return to independence, Haiti adopted a new constitution approved on May 16, 1935, which was amended in 1939 and 1944, and repealed in 1946. In the latter year, as a result of a military coup and the establishment of a provisional government, a constituent assembly prepared a constitution, promulgated on December 23, 1946.

Government and Opposition. The antecedent to the present government may be found in the military coup of January, 1946, when President Lescot was forced to resign, and a Junta took over the provisional government. General elections were held some months later to form a constituent assembly, which elected Dumarsais Estimé as President of the Republic on August 16, on which very day he took office. President Estimé was elected by a coalition of political groups within the constituent assembly. Under the constitutional structure of Haiti, presidential elections are based on the personalities of the candidates rather than on ideological conflicts between parties. The new government immediately placed the armed forces under the command of the President, with the purpose of curbing the participation of the army in politics.

In May, 1950, President Estimé proposed a law to alter the constitution in order to permit his own re-election. The proposed amendment was rejected by the Senate. Protest demonstrations were held all over the country, and finally a military Junta was formed which took over the government and forced the President to exile. The Junta was composed of General Frank Lavaud, Major Antoine Levelt and Colonel Paul Magloire.

A general election was held in October. Colonel Magloire resigned from the Junta to be a candidate for the presidency, which he won by a large majority. His opponent, Fenelón Alphonse, withdrew from the race, claiming that the elections had been a farce.

A commission of seventeen delegates was also elected to draft a new constitution for the country. For the first time in the history of Haiti, the President was elected by the direct vote of the people. Whether this system of election will prevail after the constitution is drafted is a matter of speculation. The election of Colonel Magloire was well received, and the people appeared to have confidence in their new leader.

Position of Labor. Haiti's constitution guarantees the right to form labor unions, but the labor movement has had little political importance. Its many dictatorships and the United States occupation were factors that impeded the development of the movement. On the other hand, the position of Communism is interesting. It started as a curious combination of French radical socialism and Russian Marxism. While political liberties were curbed, Socialists and Communists were forced to operate underground, and they joined forces. The Communist Party appeared legally after the revolutionary movement of 1946. Its political activity was characterized by the violence of its language against the government and by its independence from international communism. Another Communist group appeared in the same year which took the name of Popular Socialist Party and was ostensibly under the direction of Cuban leaders. This party did follow the line of international communism, and, since the Communist Party dissolved a few months later, the Popular Socialists controlled the field then and carries some weight in the political life of Haiti today.

DOMINICAN REPUBLIC

The Dominican Republic is still politically in the nineteenth century, under the tyranny of a typical *caudillo* and with scattered forces of the opposition living in exile.

Suffrage. According to Article 9 of the constitution, all citizens of either sex, over 18 years of age, or of any age if married, have the right to vote. Suffrage is obligatory and public, since the ballot must be marked in the presence of an electoral official. The system is a consequence of the authoritarian regime, to which we shall refer below.

Constitutional Evolution. The country obtained its independence from Spain in 1821 and promulgated a constitution dated December 1 of the same year. This first constitution lived only a few weeks, because the newborn republic was invaded by its neighbor, Haiti, and remained under its political control until 1844. The Dominicans then succeeded in shaking off the Haitian yoke and approved a new constitution on November 6. This document really marks the beginning of Dominican independence—such as it was. During the remainder of the nineteenth century, it was threatened by invasion from Haiti, and many of the country's leaders searched for protection from foreign powers.

One constitutional change followed another, but each new document that was approved had no significant political or institutional innovations. The central problem was then not of political liberty, but the constant threat of invasion by Haiti. President Pedro Santana asked the protection of France and Spain, and finally Queen Isabel II of Spain agreed to reincorporate the old colony to her Crown. This was in March, 1861, when the French had decided to invade Mexico, and when the United States had its hands full with the Civil War. In spite of protests from Haiti, from various countries of Spanish America and from the United States, Spain occupied the territory of the Dominican Republic and administered it until 1865, when she was again shaken off by Dominicans in a revolt called the War of the Restoration. During this war, the constitution of 1844 was again made effective until a new one was promulgated on September 6, 1866.

This was followed by a series of documents which were nothing more than constitutional amendments in nature. As Fitzgibbon says,[2] the Dominican custom of promulgating a new constitution every time a new amendment is introduced gives the impression of far more constitutional changes than there have actually been.

No sooner had the republic rid itself of the nightmare of Haitian domination than it fell under the danger of occupation and intervention by European powers, that threatened to use force to obtain payment of their loans. When Italian and French creditors warned that they would intervene, the United States came in and took charge of the custom house, applying part of the income to the

---

[2] Fitzgibbon, Russell H., *op. cit.*, p. 298.

payment of the foreign debt. Pressure from countries outside the continent was thus avoided but, in November, 1916, the United States established total occupation of the country by the marines, who dissolved the government and set up a military administration. The occupation lasted until 1924, and was characterized by a severe military regime, some suppression of civil liberties, and imprisonment of Dominican patriots. In 1924, elections were held under American supervision, and a new constitution was approved. The new President, Horacio Vázquez, was popular at first, since he at least represented Dominican independence, but in 1927 he had the constitution modified so that his term could be extended from four to six years. The people protested, and a movement arose against the principle of re-election. Its leader was General Rafael Leonidas Trujillo, who in 1930 established himself in power by means of a revolutionary coup. Subsequently he repudiated his anti-re-electionist past, having re-elected himself four times. Trujillo followed the old system of amending the constitution, promulgating new documents that are slight modifications of their predecessors. The present constitution, the general structure of which has already been mentioned, is dated January 10, 1947.

Government and Opposition. One of Trujillo's first acts was to dissolve political parties and transform the country into a one-party State. This is the *Partido Dominicano,* which the General controls. Since he took over in 1930, Trujillo has either had himself elected or has put one of his friends in the presidency, retaining for himself the position of Chief of the Army, from which he has controlled the presidency and, of course, the republic. Occasionally, he has ordered the formation of opposition parties to give elections an appearance of legality, but these parties have obviously been part of the stage setting. In May, 1947, Trujillo was "re-elected" for the fourth time, and the only opposition within the country was carried out by the members of the *Partido Socialista Popular,* the Communist Party. Later, as we shall see below, Trujillo permitted the legality of the Communists, but only for a few months.

The real opposition to Trujillo is organized from outside the country, principally from Guatemala, Cuba and Costa Rica, by political exiles of all ideologies who form the so-called Caribbean Legion. In September, 1947, the Cuban government captured an expedition of over 1,500 men getting ready to leave for the Dominican Republic from one of the keys off the eastern coast of Cuba. The expedition was under the command of General Juan Rodríguez García and the well-known Dominican writer, Juan Bosch. Again, in June, 1949, a group of revolutionaries landed on the northern coast of the Dominican Republic, but they were repulsed by Trujillo's troops. The Dictator immediately accused the governments of Cuba, Costa Rica and Guatemala of having helped the revolutionaries, and he obtained the authorization of the Congress to declare war on Cuba where, he said, an expedition was then being prepared with the assistance of the Cuban Red Cross. The President of Cuba firmly denied the accusations, and early in 1950 the Organization of American States appointed a commission to investigate the activities of the Caribbean Legion.*

Position of Labor. National labor unions have had small influence on the political life of the country. There are local unions organized along the lines of craft unions, but they have suffered, along with the country in general, from Trujillo's dictatorship. A Communist group, that functions clandestinely, carries weight with some of the unions. In 1946, Trujillo authorized the Communists to organize legally, so that his government would have the outward appearance of freedom. Before that date, they had operated under the name of Democratic Front (*Frente Democrático*), but when they organized legally, they took the name of *Partido Socialista Popular* and besides formed a youth movement called the *Juventud Democrática*. In October, 1946, the party conducted a public demonstration, but Trujillo ordered the police to break it up, and serious disturbances resulted. After this, the party lost its legal recognition and went back to underground operations.

Trujillo's government, of course, says that the Caribbean Legion is made up of Communists, which is not the fact, although there are Communists among them. Furthermore, the Dictator has followed the unfortunate policy of our days of accusing all enemies of being Communists, including in this accusation the governments of Cuba, Guatemala and Costa Rica.

---

* When Batista took power in Cuba, March 1952, relations between the two governments improved. On May 16, 1952, the dictator's brother, General Héctor Trujillo, was "elected" president by the country's one party.

COLOMBIA

Colombia was one of the first Latin American countries that presented an important trend toward political maturity. This came with the constitution of 1886, and with the well-organized division of political forces into two parties having clearly defined platforms and ideologies. The introduction of economic and social reforms by a succession of constitutional amendments to the basic charter has also been helpful to the country. Unfortunately, the events of April, 1948, interrupted the process. After that, the Conservatives have remained in power, through force and coercion. The Liberal Party still has the majority in the country, and this makes the political future uncertain.

Suffrage. The suffrage is exercised by all male citizens over 21 years of age. The exercise of the vote is secret, and is considered a constitutional function. The person who votes does not confer any mandate upon the official elected. This, which appears to be a deviation from the traditional doctrine that those who are elected are mandataries of the people, has been done with the purpose of assuring the independence of public functionaries with regard to political pressure from the parties.

Constitutional Evolution. The first constitution of Colombia was the Act of Federation of the United Provinces of New Granada, dated November 27, 1811, and was the result of the patriotic effort of the Colombians who were struggling for independence from Spain. As its name indicates, this document established a federal government, with only one organ, the Congress. The Congress was composed of delegates from the different provinces; but, as it had no jurisdiction over judicial matters, it was authorized to create the tribunals for the administration of justice by means of laws. There was no executive power, which was exercised by the provincial governors.

Colombia obtained her independence from Spain in August, 1819, and, in a constituent assembly that met in Angostura, approved what should be called the first constitution as a sovereign state on December 17, 1819. Another constitution was promulgated on October 6, 1821. Under this document, a President and Vice-

President were elected by an electoral college composed of provincial delegates. A bicameral congress was created, with a Senate composed of four senators from each province, and a Chamber of Representatives elected in the provinces, on the basis of population. The judicial power was independent and headed by a Supreme Tribunal of Justice.

These two constitutions governed a federation called *Gran Colombia* (Great Colombia), that comprised the territory which is today Colombia, besides the present republics of Ecuador and Venezuela. When Liberator Bolívar resigned from the Presidency, in 1830, and Great Colombia disintegrated, a constituent assembly met in Bogotá and promulgated a new constitution on May 5 of that year. This document introduced no important modifications in the organization of the three powers of the state, and created a Council of State that had consultative powers, formed by the Vice-President, the members of the Cabinet, the Attorney-General and twelve councilors appointed by the President. The true purpose of this document was to make the state organization flexible, hoping that Ecuador and Venezuela would accept it and thus keep Great Colombia together; but when these two states refused to ratify it and became independent republics, a new constitution had to be promulgated on February 29, 1832, maintaining administrative centralization and introducing some small changes. In it can be found all the characteristics of the fundamental points of future Conservative policies, that is, the strong executive and centralization.

This constitution lived until 1843, when certain political problems made it necessary to strengthen the executive power. In April of that year, a new constitution authorized the President to appoint provincial governors and to remove them at will. To make the executive even stronger, it was ordered that once the President of the Republic had been elected by the Electoral College, the election could be ratified by a simple majority of the Congress, when a two-thirds vote had previously been necessary.

A little past the middle of the century, Colombia adopted her liberal-type constitution, such as we have seen in the other Latin American republics. This was approved in 1853, and introduced a radical change in the constitutional history of the country. The document is important, not because of the structure of government, but because of the declaration of rights it contains. For the first time, we see the establishment of juries, the liberty of the press, religious freedom and the separation of Church and State. The economic qualification and the requisite of literacy in the suffrage were abolished.

In 1857, a split in the Liberal Party, similar to the one that occurred subsequently in 1945, resulted in the election of Dr. Mariano Ospina Rodríguez, of the Conservative Party, to the Presidency. A new constitution was approved in 1858, but it lasted only until 1860, when Ospina was overthrown in a revolt. After this, a provisional government under General Mosquera, who took the capital in 1861, invited plenipotentiary delegates from the different provinces to come to the city to draw up a new constitution. The Congress of Plenipotentiaries met in September, 1861, and that same month approved the constitution. It is particularly interesting, because it has more of the characteristics of a peace treaty between sovereign states than of a fundamental charter. It was not called a constitution, but *Pacto de Unión de los Estados Unidos de Colombia*. The delegates were called Plenipotentiaries and represented independent and sovereign states. The Union was directed by a President, chosen by electors designated by the states, and each state was free to choose the form of election of its representatives. The Congress was composed of two chambers—a chamber of representatives and a Senate of Plenipotentiaries—elected by the states in any manner they chose. The magistrates of the Supreme Tribunal were designated by the Senate. This document lasted no more than the previous one, because the struggles between Conservatives and Liberals (that is, between centralists and federalists) made it necessary to call another constituent assembly, and a new constitution was approved on May 8, 1863. The federal principle was maintained, and an interesting precept, indicating the nature of the future political struggle in Colombia, prohibited the religious communities and associations from owning land.

The autonomy given by this constitution to the states diminished the authority of the central power. The Conservatives continued to insist on the strong executive, and the Roman Catholic Church naturally protested against the attack on its properties. For years the struggles persisted, but the 1863 constitution remained in force until a revolution in 1885, when General Núñez invited the state governors to designate two delegates from each state for a constituent assembly. This body promulgated a new constitution on August 4, 1886, which is the most important document in Colombia's constitutional history, and whose fundamental structure has been maintained to the present day. It re-established the centralist principle of government, but reached a compromise with the federalists. This formula, called "political centralization and administrative decentralization" by Colombian statesmen, has given good results.

The government is centralized, but sovereignty resides in the nation, not in the people or the states. The states were transformed into departments. Relations between the Church and the State were re-established by means of Concordats with the Holy See. Restrictions on Church ownership of land were abolished, and Catholicism was declared to be the official religion of the State. The legislative power was composed of a Senate and a Chamber of Representatives; the former constituted by three senators for each department, and the latter by representatives elected by the departments on the basis of population. The President of the Republic was elected by an Electoral College for six years, and the Council of State and Judiciary were maintained as they had been in the previous constitutions. The constitution was a victory of the Conservatives, who remained in power constitutionally until 1930. In that year, the Liberals won the elections, with Enrique Olaya Herrera as their presidential candidate. Olaya Herrera was succeeded by another Liberal president, Dr. Alfonso López. Since the constitution of 1886 had undergone several nonessential amendments, an official text was published in 1936 with all the amendments to date. This document was called the *Codificación Constitucional de 1936*. The changes in it were with regard to the composition of the Senate, which was elected on the basis of population by the departments; the presidential term, which was reduced to four years; modifications introduced in the Judiciary, reducing the term of magistrates of the Supreme Court to five years, and giving this organ more powers in connection with unconstitutionality. The most important of the changes in this Codification referred to social rights, including the traditional rights of workers which we studied in Chapter 11. Another one was on the organization of the national economy, by which the government could supervise the production, distribution, and consumption of merchandise. Property was defined as a social function implying obligations.

In 1945, another Constitutional Codification was published, covering all amendments introduced after 1936. One addition consisted in an organ, within the Congress, to approve economic planning and develop a complete system of public works. A general comptrollership of the republic was created, and another amendment established the necessity of a two-thirds majority vote to override the Presidential veto. This Codification is still in force today.

Government and Opposition. The antecedent of the present government and of the grave political problems facing Colombia may be found in the presidential elections held on May 5, 1946. During the electoral campaign, the Liberal Party divided, and a group of Liberals of the Left nominated Dr. José Eliécer Gaitán, while another group, more to the Right, appointed Dr. Gabriel Turbay as their candidate. The Conservatives nominated Dr. Manuel Ospina Pérez. The elections were peaceful. The Conservatives won, although Ospina Pérez obtained only 42 per cent of the votes. The Liberals, naturally, had a majority in the Congress. The following year Turbay died, and the Liberals came together in support of Gaitán, who was considered to be the undisputed presidential candidate for the next elections. The Conservatives in power had a difficult time, with a minority in the Congress.

While the Pan-American Conference was being held in Bogotá in April, 1948, Dr. Gaitán was assassinated in the streets of the city. The indignant Liberals seethed in the famous riot of April 9. The populace joined in and buildings were burned and sacked. The focal point of hatred was Dr. Laureano Gómez, Conservative leader and Minister of State, who was presiding over the Pan-American Conference. The rioters attempted an attack on him, but he escaped to Spain. Impartial observers agree that the riot was a spontaneous movement. The assassination itself could be described as a spark that set off a major conflagration. The assailant was, apparently, an obscure, nonpolitical individual, and his motives were said to be purely personal; but his action was immediately given political meaning, and soon the rioters were beyond control. A large part of the police force either remained neutral or joined the mutineers, which explains why the riot reached such proportions. Comment on Communist participation in the movement will be given in a later paragraph.

After the revolt, Ospina Pérez formed a coalition cabinet, including distinguished Liberal leaders who were able, on the surface, to restore order. But in May, 1949, they resigned in protest against the abuse of force by the Conservatives in the remote rural areas, and their places were taken by three Conservatives and three members of the army. Other Liberal functionaries in the provinces followed their example and also resigned. In June, there were partial elections for the Chamber of Deputies. The Liberals maintained their majority there and in the Senate. The tension caused by Gaitán's death was still felt, and occasional clashes occurred between Liberals and Conservatives.

A government with a Conservative President and a Congress with a Liberal majority was—obviously—a problem, so the Liberals proposed and approved a law by which presidential elections would be held on November 27, 1949, instead of in June, 1950. No sooner had this law been passed than the most hated Conservative of Colombia, Laureano Gómez, returned from his voluntary exile in Spain and was immediately nominated for the Presidency by the Conservative Party. The Liberal candidate was Dr. Darío Echandía, who had been Colombia's Ambassador before the Holy See and was a member of the coalition government. Early in the campaign it was evident that the Conservatives intended to use force to impose their candidate upon the people. In the rural regions, army troops obliged the peasants to hand over their registration certificates and "spontaneously" register in the Conservative Party. A number of Liberals went into exile, and when the Congress notified President Ospina that impeachment procedures would be initiated, he used the army to dissolve the Congress, established censorship of the Press and declared martial law. Under the circumstances, the Liberals withdrew their candidate and instructed their members to boycott the elections. Two days before the elections, Vicente Echandía, a brother of the Liberal candidate, was assassinated by the police in the streets of the capital.

On the 27th of November, Dr. Laureano Gómez received some 950,000 votes, with no one but Conservatives going to the polls. The only newspaper that published the election returns was *El Siglo*, which belongs to Gómez. The other papers refused to contribute to the farce. Gómez took office on August 7, 1950.* The present situation of Colombia is explosive. One of the distinguished historians of Colombia, Germán Arciniegas, now a Professor in Columbia University, New York, in February, 1950, published an interesting analysis of his country's situation, ending with these words:

"It cost us dear in lives and suffering to gain independence,
Only God knows what it will cost us now to gain liberty." [3]

Position of Labor. The most important national labor union is the *Confederación de Trabajadores de Colombia* (CTC, Confederation of Workers of Colombia), founded in 1936 and claiming a membership of over 900 locals and 100,000 workers. For a while, Communists occupied important positions in the direction of the CTC, but they are not as strong as they had been. As in other Latin American countries, organized workers are divided among Communists and non-Communists. Within the CTC, the most important unions are among the workers in maritime and fluvial transportation, the railroads, chauffeurs, and workers in commercial establishments. There are some independent syndicates, many of them Roman Catholic, and the union of workers of the petroleum industry has grown in proportion to the development of the industry. As a general rule, organized workers have supported the Liberal Party, and Gaitán was extremely popular among them. At the time of the April, 1948, riot, the CTC declared a general strike which was instrumental in prolonging the disturbances in the whole country.

Communism has not been especially important in the political life of the country, but a number of statesmen are of the opinion that if the Ospina Pérez-Laureano Gómez dictatorship goes on, Communism is likely to grow a good deal stronger. The Communists are divided into three principal groups. One of them, the *Partido Obrero Comunista* (Communist Labor Party), follows a line of democratic socialism, favors cooperation with the Liberal Party, and a political—and not revolutionary—line of action. Another

---

* On October 31, 1951, Roberto Urdaneta was elected first designate to act as President during the temporary absence of President Gómez, who is seriously ill.

[3] Arciniegas, Germán, *Cuadernos Americanos*, Enero-Febrero, México, D. F., 1950, p. 33.

group is made up mainly of petroleum workers and follows a Marxist revolutionary line. The third is the Communist Party, which is the one appearing to maintain the closest ideological contact with Russian policies. In the presidential elections of 1946, the three groups obtained some 27,000 votes, but in the municipal elections of October, 1947, they got only 15,400. Observers believe that at the time of the Bogotá revolt, the Communists had no more than 8,000 members in all the country. Immediately after the riot, the government of Ospina Pérez, the world press in general, and United States Secretary of State Marshall attributed the uprising to a Communist plot, and Colombia severed diplomatic relations with Russia. Communist leaders were imprisoned, but they were soon released because of lack of evidence that they had instigated the uprising, although Communist groups doubtless participated in the riot after it started.

VENEZUELA

In Venezuela it seemed that the advent to power of the forces behind the *Partido Acción Democrática* and the promulgation of the constitution of 1947 marked the country's arrival at a stage of political reformism. The overthrow of President Gallegos and the role of the military junta interrupted the process. It is significant to note that Delgado Chalbaud, although an army man, did not behave like the typical ruthless *caudillo* and tried to preserve some of the institutional changes introduced by the constitution of 1947. The junta realized that the country would not tolerate the return of the *caudillo* era. The assassination of Delgado Chalbaud has not changed the picture. The appointment of a civilian to succeed him points to the possibility of a compromise that might incorporate wealthy Venezuela into the democracies of the continent.

Suffrage. All citizens of both sexes over 18 years of age may vote, if in full possession of their civil rights. Suffrage is a right and a function. It may be granted to aliens, but only in municipal elections, and when they have resided for ten years without interruption in the national territory. To be eligible for public office, one must be over 21 years of age and know how to read and write. Members of the army in active service do not have the right to vote.

Constitutional Evolution. Venezuela started its political life, after separation from Spain, as a province of Great Colombia, and had its first constitution as a federal state on December 21, 1811. When Great Colombia broke up, Venezuela adopted a constitution as an independent state, on September 27, 1830. This document, of a moderately liberal nature, was replaced by another dated April, 1857, under which the country was organized as a centralized republic. The traditional struggle between federalists and centralists, that we have seen in other Latin American republics, also occupied the central position in Venezuela's political life. Like these other nations, too, Venezuela suffered from long dictatorships, *caudillismo* and revolutions. The constitution of 1857 was discarded for another, also of a centralist type, in December of the following year; but the federalist principles got the upper hand when, in April 1864, the country adopted a constitution of that nature, which may be considered its typical nineteenth-century document of Latin American liberalism. A new constitution in May, 1875, introduced no essential changes and maintained the federalist principles. Four years before this constitution had been promulgated, Venezuela had fallen into one of the long periods of dictatorship that characterize its history. Political power was controlled until 1888 by General Guzmán Blanco, who ruled the country with an iron hand. During his regime, he had still another constitution promulgated in April, 1881.

When the dictator was overthrown, there followed a period of revolutions, coups, and unstable governments which lasted until 1909. Five different constitutions were approved, but their interest is purely historical. In 1909, Venezuela fell again under another long dictatorship, when Juan Vicente Gómez remained in power until he died—a natural death—in 1935. During Gómez' long tyranny, seven new constitutions were approved, representing changes in the formal aspect of government, and several of them promulgated only to extend his political control. When he died, Minister of War General López Contreras occupied the provisional presidency, but in April, 1936, López Contreras was appointed President by the Congress, which was the organ of government charged with the election of the President under the last constitution approved by Gómez' regime.

In July, 1936, a constituent assembly appproved a new constitution which maintained, fundamentally, the federal structure of the preceding constitutions, and with the executive continuing to be elected by the Congress. In the presidential elections of 1940, the

Congress elected General Isaías Medina Angarita, who governed until October, 1945, when he was deposed by a popular revolutionary movement, with the participation of a group of young members of the army. The government was taken over by a Junta, presided by opposition leader Rómulo Betancourt. The provisional government convoked a constituent assembly, which approved the constitution of July 5, 1947. This document was in force at the time of the coup d'etat against President Rómulo Gallegos, which will be referred to presently.

Government and Opposition. The present government of Venezuela is the result of the military coup of November 24, 1948, which overthrew the government of President Rómulo Gallegos. Its antecedent, and the unleashed political forces behind the military coup, can be traced back to the political and economic climate in Venezuela after the death of dictator Juan Vicente Gómez.

During Gómez' long years of dictatorship, political forces could hardly be organized within the country, since he tolerated none of the liberties necessary to the free development of parties. Hence, the political parties now existing in Venezuela were formed in the years after his death, and the strongest of these was the *Partido Acción Democrática*, composed of liberals, socialists, young army officers, labor leaders and intellectuals, integrating the group called in Venezuela "the generation of 1928." Their unquestioned leader is the famous novelist and educator, Rómulo Gallegos. This party was formed in 1940. Although it did not win the elections, it was active in opposition to Isaías Medina Angarita and in 1945 participated in the revolutionary coup that deposed him. The other political forces that appeared at the same time were the *Concentración de Organizaciones Políticas Electorales Independientes* (COPEI), integrated by the wealthier upper classes, groups of businessmen, conservatives in general, and supported—though not officially—by the Roman Catholic Church. The *Unión Republicana Democrática*, which controls no more than 5 per cent of the votes, and the Communists were fairly active before the military coup. The *Partido Acción Democrática* had a large majority in the Constituent Convention that drew up the constitution of July 5, 1947, and supported the provisional government of President Rómulo Betancourt.

Under Betancourt's administration, on December 15, 1947, general elections were held. This time the people, directly, voted for their President, in accordance with the new constitution, and Rómulo Gallegos, the candidate of the *Partido Acción Democrática,* won by an overwhelming majority. The COPEI nominated Rafael Caldera, and the Communists, Gustavo Machado. President Gallegos took office on February 15, 1948, with a considerable majority in the Congress, and announced that he would follow a liberal policy, although he would maintain good relations with the Roman Catholic Church, friendship toward foreign capital, and protection for capital and labor. His regime started auspiciously. Two months later, the *New York Times* made a study of political conditions in Latin America and declared that Venezuela, Argentina and Uruguay were the only countries with stable governments. The Communists offered no serious opposition, particularly after their leaders had lost control over the Federation of Petroleum Workers, which had been one of their strongholds.

In spite of all this, and for no obvious reason, Gallegos was overthrown by a military coup, whose leaders formed a provisional Junta under Lieutenant Colonel Carlos Delgado Chalbaud. President Gallegos was arrested, but later was allowed to leave for Cuba. Not only the people of Venezuela, but those of other countries where Gallegos was highly respected, were stunned. In Cuba, Gallegos declared that the foreign-owned petroleum companies were not innocent of complicity in the plot, and that a Military Attaché from the United States Embassy had cooperated with the revolutionaries. This statement he retracted when he came to the United States and said he had been able to re-check his facts and found that the United States government had not participated in the coup.

The new military government dissolved the Congress, the state legislatures, and the municipal councils, and dismissed the Supreme Tribunal of Justice. The *Partido Acción Democrática* was declared illegal, and many of its leaders were arrested. A strict censorship of the press was established. During all of 1949, the Junta reminded one of Gómez' days of tyranny. In February, it decreed the dissolution of the *Confederación de Trabajadores de Venezuela* (Confederation of Workers) and put an end to the strong Union of Graphic Arts, after a strike among its members. The Junta arrested insubmissive members of the opposition and, in October, twenty-three political prisoners, most of them students and workers, were sent to a concentration camp in El Dorado, supposedly reserved for common criminals. The two parties that continue to function freely, of course, are the COPEI and the *Unión Republicana Democrática,* which is trying to attract members from the *Partido Acción Democrática,* so far without success. In March, 1949, President Rómulo Gallegos, still considered as such by many Latin American countries, asked the United Nations to make an investigation in Venezuela, basing his request on the fact that Chalbaud's government is violating human rights and has imprisoned more than 2,000 people, without due process of law.

On November 13, 1950, Colonel Carlos Delgado Chalbaud was shot to death by a group of assailants. A few days later, Germán Suárez Flamerich, a civilian, was appointed to his place as head of the Junta. From his exile in Mexico, ex-President Gallegos condemned the assassination in the name of his party, *Acción Democrática.* The new head of the Junta has promised general elections as soon as the national census is completed. Suárez Flamerich is considered impartial in political matters and is expected to keep his promise.

Position of Labor. The labor movement in Venezuela started to grow in importance after World War I. Even under the dictatorship of Juan Vicente Gómez, in 1928, the *Federación Obrera de Venezuela* had approximately 25,000 members, However, they had no real influence in the political life of the country until 1936, when the constitution promulgated in that year granted the workers a series of basic rights. There were then three strong federations: the *Confederación Venezolana del Trabajo,* the *Federación Obrera de Venezuela,* and the *Unión General de Trabajadores.* The workers not only joined in the activities against management, but intervened in the political life of the country and supported the administration of General López Contreras. Later, they joined forces within a new national federation called *Confederación de Trabajadores de Venezuela,* affiliated to the CTAL and that, as we have seen, has been dissolved by the military dictatorship. There is, besides, a large group of employees affiliated to the *Unión Venezolana de Empleados,* formed in 1936, which remains within the sphere of trade-unionism and intervenes little in politics. Obviously, after the dissolution of the *Confederación de Trabajadores de Venezuela,* the political activities of the workers have had to be carried on underground.

The Communist groups functioned clandestinely during Gómez' long dictatorship, but they emerged to political life during the administration of General López Contreras. The party acquired legal status during the regime of Isaías Medina Angarita, and had considerable influence in the country, sometimes cooperating with the government, and other times demanding radical changes during the provisional administration of Rómulo Betancourt. Before the coup d'etat under Delgado Chalbaud, it was calculated that the Communist Party had about 20,000 members, and in the presidential elections of 1947, their candidate obtained about 52,000 votes. The principal strength of the party is the support of the oil workers. A contemporary observer calculates that more than 40 per cent of the 40,000 oil workers follow the Communist ideology. In the *Federación de Trabajadores del Distrito Federal* (Federation of Labor of the Federal District) and among workers engaged in construction, the Communists are fairly strong, but they have not made more headway in Venezuela for the same reason we have outlined in other places, that is—because of the division between them and the Socialists, who are very popular among the workers. Besides, the Communist Party is itself divided, and a group of dissident Communists have formed the *Partido Comunista Unificado* (Unified Communist Party)—which, indeed, sounds like a contradiction—and acts independently of the other group. During the present military government, the Communists have returned to their underground activities.

SUGGESTED READINGS

English:

Beals, Carlton, *The Crime of Cuba,* Philadelphia, J. B. Lippincott Co., 1933.

Chapman, Charles E., *A History of the Cuban Republic,* New York, The Macmillan Co., 1927.

Commission on Cuban Affairs, *Problems of the New Cuba,* New York, Foreign Policy Association, 1935.

Fergusson, Erna, *Venezuela,* New York, Alfred A. Knopf, Inc., 1939.

Fitzgibbon, Russell H., *Cuba and the U. S., 1900-1935,* Menasha, Wis., George Barta, 1935.

Gibson, William Marion, *The Constitutions of Colombia,* Durham,
    N. C., Duke University Press, 1948.
Henao, J. M., and G. Arrubla, *A History of Colombia,* Chapel Hill, Uni-
    versity of North Carolina Press, 1941.
Hicks, Albert C., *Blood in the Streets; The Life and Rule of Trujillo,*
    New York, Creative Age Press, Inc., 1946.
Hurston, Zora Neale, *Tell My Horse,* Philadelphia, J. B. Lippincott,
    Inc., 1938.
Linke, Lilo, *Andean Adventure,* London, Hutchinson & Co., 1945.
Millspaugh, Arthur C., *Haiti Under American Control, 1915-1930,*
    Boston, World Peace Foundation, 1931.
Ortiz, Fernando, *Cuban Counterpoint: Tobacco and Sugar,* New York,
    Alfred A. Knopf, Inc., 1947.
Rippy, J. Fred, *The Capitalists in Colombia,* New York, The Viking
    Press, 1931.
Walker, Stanley, *Journey Toward the Sunlight,* New York Caribbean
    Library, 1947.
Watters, Mary, *A History of the Church in Venezuela, 1810-1930,* Chapel
    Hill, University of North Carolina Press, 1933.
Welles, B. Sumner, *Naboth's Vineyard, The Dominican Republic, 1812-
    1928,* New York, Payson Clark, 1928.

Other Languages:

Alverez, Tabío, Fernando, *Teoría General de la Constitución Cubana,*
    La Habana, 1946.
Baptista, Octavio, *Venezuela, Su Historia y Sus Métodos de Gobierno,*
    Guadalajara, 1942.
Bellegarde, Dantes, *La Nation Haitienne,* Paris, 1938.
Franco Ornes, Pericles, *La Tragedia Dominicana,* Santiago de Chile,
    1946.
Friedlaender, H. E., *Historia Económica de Cuba,* La Habana, 1944.
Gil Fortoul, José, *Historia Constitucional de Venezuela,* Caracas, 1942.
Infiesta, Ramón, *Historia Constitucional de Cuba,* La Habana, 1942.
Pereda, Diego de, *El Nuevo Pensamiento Político de Cuba,* La Habana,
    1943.
Pérez, Francisco de Paula, *Derecho Constitucional Colombiano,* Bogotá,
    1942.
Portell Vilá, Herminio, *Historia de Cuba,* La Habana, 4 vols., 1936-1941.
Puentes, Milton, *Historia del Partido Liberal Colombiano,* Bogotá, 1942.
Raggi Ageo, Carlos M., *Condiciones Económicas y Sociales de la Repúb-
    lica de Cuba,* La Habana, 1944.

Roig de Leuchsenring, Emilio, *Los Grandes Movimientos Políticos Cubanos en la República,* La Habana, 1943.

Romero Aguirre, Alfonso, *El Partido Conservador ante la Historia,* Bogotá, 1944.

Sánchez Gómez, Gregorio, *Sociología Política Colombiana,* Cali, (Colombia), 1943.

Wolff, Ernesto, *Tratado de Derecho Constitucional Venezolano,* Caracas, 1945.

CHAPTER 14

The Andean Countries

CHILE

Chile had its typical twentieth century institutional reform with the constitution of 1925. Since independence, the country has been on the progressive side in its political evolution, as compared with the rest of the continent. It experimented early with parliamentarism, and incorporated important legislative changes. There have been difficulties, but long oppressive dictatorships of the *caudillo* type have never been tolerated.

President Videla broke with the coalition that put him in power in 1946, starting with the Communists, and later formed a cabinet composed only of his own Radical Party. Recently, all working classes have suffered extraordinarily from the high cost of living, and there have been strikes among all classes of workers, including teachers and university professors. The signs of unrest present a serious interrogation as to the future. President Videla has managed to weather the storm, but it is likely that the forces of the opposition will defeat his party in the elections of 1952.*

Suffrage. All male citizens over 21 years of age have the right to vote. Women over 21 may vote in municipal elections, a right also enjoyed by aliens under certain conditions. Members of the armed forces in active service, and priests or ministers of any denomination do not have the right to the suffrage.

Constitutional Evolution. During the French occupation of Spain, the *Cabildo* of Santiago de Chile formed a provisional government, and approved a constitutional statute, in 1811, for the country. Another provisional constitutional document was approved

---

* There is a new government. See below.

on October 27, 1812, in which the sovereignty of King Ferdinand VII was recognized, but under the obligation that he accept the constitution voted upon by the Chilean people. The country was governed, in the name of the Spanish king, by a Junta of three members appointed for three-year terms. Political power resided in the people, and in a Senate composed of seven members, whose vote was necessary in order to create taxes, declare war, coin money, establish obligatory military service and appoint diplomats and high government officials.

Later, when Chile declared its independence under the leadership of Bernardo O'Higgins, who controlled the country under the title of Supreme Director, a constitution was promulgated on October 23, 1818. The document sanctioned O'Higgins' dictatorship, then designating him Director, and concentrated political authority in his hands. Public liberties were relegated to a secondary position. No term of government was fixed for the Director, and he was granted powers similar to those of Napoleon I when he was First Consul of France. The people clamored for political guarantees, and to appease them, O'Higgins convoked a constituent assembly in 1822. The assembly promulgated a constitution, dated October 30, 1822, which established some civil liberties and separated the three powers of the state, but the constitution was unimportant, because while O'Higgins remained in power, the situation was unchanged. In January, 1823, O'Higgins was deposed and succeeded by General Ramón Freyre; in August a constituent assembly was convoked, and on December 29 of the same year, a new constitution was promulgated. This is an interesting document, establishing administrative decentralization and restricting executive powers. Political power resided, fundamentally, in a Senate of an aristocratic and conservative nature. A period of political confusion followed, and the constitution was abrogated in 1825, to be replaced the following year by a constitution organizing the country as a federal government. The system was impractical, so a new document was approved on August 8, 1828, creating a centralized republic under a president elected for a five-year term, with no re-election permitted. Legislative power was exercised by a National Congress composed of two chambers, and the administration of justice was in the hands of a Supreme Tribunal and the lower courts. The right of primogeniture was abolished, a step which sought to weaken the landed aristocracy.

On May 25, 1833, a conservative government promulgated a new constitution leaving unchanged the five-year presidential term, but allowing re-election. The President was assisted by a Council of State, with whose approval he could dissolve the Congress and assume dictatorial powers in case of war or public disturbances. He could also order the arrest of any citizen without the intervention of the courts. Legislative power corresponded to a bicameral Congress integrated by a Chamber of Representatives and a Senate. The Judiciary was presided by the Supreme Tribunal, whose magistrates were appointed by the President of the Republic. This constitution created such a strong executive that, in the opinion of Chilean historians, the President had all the powers of government under his direct control. The conservative nature of the document was evidenced by the fact that the right of primogeniture was re-established, thus strengthening the political power of the moneyed landowners.

The constitution of 1833 was unchanged until 1891, when it was amended to establish a parliamentary form of government, in which the Ministers were chosen by the President from among the majority party in Congress. The parliamentary system was unsatisfactory. Changes in the Cabinet followed each other with extraordinary rapidity, sometimes even daily. Later, the country began to show signs of interest in social—and not political—reforms, mainly because of the efforts of the Socialist Party. In spite of this, no changes were made. In 1920, Arturo Alessandri was elected President, and after political disturbances and coups, a constituent assembly was convoked. This body promulgated a new constitution on September 18, 1925, which was the work of Alessandri. The parliamentary system was abolished, and a number of important social rights were incorporated. This constitution of 1925 is still in force today and has been analyzed in the earlier parts of this book. It was modified on November 23, 1943, creating the Office of the Comptroller General of the Republic, to supervise the revenue and expenditures of the State, the provinces and municipalities. The President was authorized to alter the administrative divisions of the country, create new public services and introduce several minor administrative innovations.

Government and Opposition.† The government in power in Chile today is the result of the general elections held in September, 1946, by which Dr. Gabriel González Videla owed his victory to an electoral coalition formed by his own *Partido Radical* (Radical Party), the Liberals and the Communist Party. For the past few years, it has been the Radicals who have governed Chile. The significant point of the elections was that González Videla made use of Communist support, and that the party elected fifteen deputies and five senators.

Just a few months after he had taken office, González Videla realized that the victorious coalition could not keep together within the government. The Liberals broke with the Communists and withdrew. In August, 1947, the President ousted the Communists from the cabinet and governed with the support of the Radicals alone, forming a cabinet which he called "non-political" and composed mainly of military men. In October a CTCH strike (mentioned subsequently) among the miners caused more trouble. The Communists backed the strikers, and the President had the army take over the mines and imprisoned a number of Communist labor leaders. The government accused the Yugoslavian Chargé d'Affaires of aiding the strikers and expelled him from the national territory. Yugoslavia severed diplomatic relations with Chile, and Videla not only severed them with Yugoslavia, but with the Soviet Union as well. The change in policies was radical. Videla asked Congress to pass the necessary legislation to declare the Communist Party illegal. His request was bitterly opposed in the Congress, not only by the Communist members, but by the parties in the opposition, and by political leaders, such as ex-President Alessandri and Eduardo Cruz Coke, the Conservative candidate defeated in the presidential elections of 1946. In spite of the opposition, the law was passed, under the name of "law for the defense of democracy." It was not long before some Chileans called it the "law for the offense of democracy." It deprived the Communist Party of its political rights, but permitted the fifteen Communist deputies and five senators to remain in office until the 1949 elections in which, of course, the Communist Party was not allowed to participate.

These partial elections, to fill 147 seats in the Congress and 20

---

† There is a new government. See below.

in the Senate, were held in March, and they give a fairly clear idea of the line-up of the political forces in the country. A coalition of parties supporting the President obtained 76 seats, in the following manner: the Radical Party, 34; the Liberal Party, 32; the Moderate-Democratic Party, 7; and the Socialist Party, 3. Of these parties, the Radical Party follows a line of moderate socialism; the Liberals defend the traditional individualistic democracy; the Moderate-Democrats are right-of-center, and the Socialist Party has plans of nationalization in its program and, in general, an ideology similar to that of social democrats of the rest of the world.

The other 71 seats were won by the opposition. The Conservative Party, which represents the traditional right, obtained 33; the Agrarian Labor Party, which is even more conservative than the Conservatives themselves, got 14; and the others were divided among small groups of the right, with the exception of six seats obtained by the Democratic Nationalist Front. This is the political group backed by the Communists, now that they cannot function legally as a party. In short, the elections brought no great changes, except the loss of strength of the Communists. However, the number of votes obtained by the Agrarian Labor Party, which backs ex-president Ibáñez, was significant.

Around him revolves the political question of the future. There are many who feel that Ibáñez may reach the presidency, supported by a coalition of parties of the Right. This is all the more likely, because there does not appear to be a candidate among the popular parties who might bring these together, due to the split among Radicals, Liberals, and Socialists.‡

Position of Labor. Chile is one of the Latin American countries where the labor movement has had the most influence on political life. It started, of course, as a mutualist movement (see Chapter 11) and was decidedly influenced by the anarchist and anarcho-syndicalist ideology toward the end of the nineteenth century, especially in the mining region of the northern part of the country, where labor has always been strongest. Early in the 1900's, and before World War I, societies of resistance and labor unions made their appear-

---

‡ General Carlos Ibáñez was elected President on September 4, 1952, and took office on November 3 of the same year.

ance, resolving to defend their interests, and in 1909 the *Federación Obrera de Chile* (FOCH, Chilean Federation of Labor) was founded. In the early years of the FOCH, the mutualist and anarchist ideologies struggled to gain the upper hand among the workers. There was also a Socialist Labor Party at the time, which was later to have considerable influence.

Between 1909 and 1919, the FOCH was the most important labor movement in the country, organizing the workers and participating in a number of strikes with the purpose of improving working conditions. In December, 1919, the political direction of the workers was changed radically. In a congress held by the FOCH leaders, the organization turned toward Marxist ideas, with an openly revolutionary content, obviously influenced by the Russian revolution of 1917. In the 1921 congress of the FOCH, it joined the Communist International.

In the same period, there were other labor movements of minor importance. A federation affiliated with the IWW of the United States was created, with an anarcho-syndicalist ideology. The railroad workers functioned, for years, independently of the FOCH, under the name of *Federación Obrera Ferroviaria* (Railroad Labor Federation), and there were, as well, various Catholic syndicates inspired by Pope Leon XIII's encyclical, *Rerum Novarum*.

As a result of the financial crisis that started in 1930, the Chilean labor movement had a further incentive to improve the workers' conditions. A vigorous campaign was initiated to bring all workers together in one united front which took some time in developing, but finally in December, 1936, a national congress was held and in January, 1937, created the *Confederación de Trabajadores de Chile* (CTCH, Federation of Workers of Chile). The new union, controlled by the Marxist ideology, approved a lengthy program of action. Ever since its appearance, the CTCH carried out a huge plan of organization and greatly increased the number of its members. It is today the strongest union in Chile and is influential in the life of the country. Besides the CTCH, there are powerful agricultural unions, which are not to be overlooked in the political picture, and autonomous or semi-autonomous groups, such as the *Confederación Obrera Nacional de Empleados Particulares* (National Labor Federation of Private Employees), and the *Confedera-*

ción General del Trabajo (General Federation of Labor) of a syndicalist ideology.

As we have seen, the Communists have played an important role in contemporary Chilean politics. Needs for social reform, better organized workers, and the radicalism of European immigration paved the road for Communism. Besides this, the concentration of workers in urban zones and the condition of the workers in the mining regions have contributed to the increase in radicalism in all its forms. This became more pronounced after the constitution of 1925 that permitted free expression of thought.

The Communist Party came about as a division within the Socialist group and became more powerful within the labor organizations. In 1926, during the dictatorship of Carlos Ibáñez, they were severely persecuted, but they came into the political arena after the elections of 1932, when Arturo Alessandri became president. The ideological differences between Stalinists and Trotskyists weakened the party, but it was strong enough to give Pedro Aguirre Cerda the necessary support to put him in the presidency in the elections of 1938. Aguirre Cerda was the candidate of the Radical Party and was nominated by the "Leftist block," or popular front, at the time when Communists in other countries, such as Spain and France, were backing the popular fronts. During his administration, the Communist leaders accepted no cabinet positions, but influenced the government without accepting responsibilities. In the elections of 1946, as we have said, they again backed the Radical Party and gave González Videla the necessary majority to be elected. They obtained approximately 50,000 votes in the elections, which were undoubtedly considered important, because in Videla's first cabinet, Communists were given the portfolios of Communications, Agriculture, and Land and Colonization. The present position of the party, after the break with the government, has been explained.

BOLIVIA

The democratic institutions and social and economic principles that appear in the Bolivian constitution do not correspond to reality. Political problems and ideological issues in the country are not settled. The ethnic composition and dependency upon tin mining contribute still more to the difficulties. The country is ruled by a *de facto* government. Exaggerated nationalism, with social and economic reform and the use of revolutionary methods, has been the program of the MNR, which took power in the revolution of April, 1952. So far, the victorious group of the Army and the tin miners have backed the President. The political future of Bolivia is uncertain, and the country is far from stable.

Suffrage. Male citizens over 21 years of age, able to read and write and duly registered in the Civic Registry, have the right to the suffrage. Women over 21 may vote in municipal elections and may also be elected to municipal offices.

Constitutional Evolution. Bolivia declared its independence in January, 1825, and in May, 1826, Liberator Simón Bolívar convoked a constituent assembly that, in November of that year, approved the country's first constitution. Directly reflecting the political ideas of the Liberator, this document organized the new state as a centralized republic, with a President elected for life. Legislative power was exercised by a Senate elected for eight years, and a Chamber of Tribunes elected for four. There was, besides, a Chamber of Censors, appointed for life, which had the important duty of supervising all legislative measures of the other two organs. The judicial power was under the authority of a Supreme Tribunal, composed of magistrates appointed for life. Suffrage was limited to males over 21 years of age who met certain requirements with regard to profession and education. Under these qualifications, only some 10 per cent of the population could exercise the suffrage.

The first constitution was replaced by another on August 14, 1831, under which the presidency for life was abolished, and the executive power was entrusted to a functionary elected for a four-year term. This document established a bicameral legislature, doing away with the unpopular Chamber of Censors. After a revolutionary movement in 1839, a more liberal constitution was promulgated, which abolished slavery, among other measures. In 1843, a new constitution extended the presidential term to eight years and granted the president extraordinary powers which virtually made him the political owner of the nation. In 1851, still another constitution reduced the presidential term from eight to five years, and, in 1861, the fundamental political structure was again changed by a new document, whose essential characteristic was the creation of a unicameral congress. A number of constitutional changes followed, which involved no basic alteration of the structure, and which are interesting only from the historical point of view.

The presidential term was always a focal point of interest, and on October 28, 1880, a new fundamental document was approved, which re-established the four-year term, prohibited re-election, and restored the bicameral legislature, composed of a Senate and a Chamber of Representatives. This was Bolivia's most liberal document in the nineteenth century, and was in force until September 26, 1931, when a new constitution was promulgated which, to all practical effects, did nothing more than introduce slight modifications into the former one.

In 1936, as a result of a general strike, Lieutenant-Colonel Germán Busch took over the government, with a provisional Junta composed of socialist elements. The Junta announced that it was necessary to establish a socialist government, invited Colonel Toro to occupy the presidency and in May, 1936, suspended the constitution of 1931 and restored the one of 1880. Toro was soon deposed by Busch, and a new constitution was approved in 1938 which, with a few modifications, is still in force today. The present constitution of Bolivia is, therefore, dated October 30, 1938, and was amended on November 23, 1945.

Government and Opposition. The country is ruled by a *de facto* government that came to power as a result of a revolutionary movement that broke out on April 9, 1952. After several days of fighting, the forces of the military government, headed by General Hugo Ballivián, were defeated.

The antecedents to this revolt could be traced to the presidential elections held on May 6, 1951. In these elections, the middle-of-the-road government party nominated Gabriel Gonsálvez, an elderly banker and former diplomat. The *Movimiento Nacional Revolucionario* (MNR, National Revolutionary Movement), nominated their leader, Víctor Paz Estenssoro. There were other minor parties and candidates, but the elections were fought between Gonsálvez and Estenssoro. Estenssoro received nearly 45 per cent of the votes, but failed to reach the majority of 51 per cent prescribed by law to be elected. The Bolivian constitution provides, in such a case, that

Congress is to elect the new president from the three leading con-
tenders. It was announced that Congress was to convene on August 6
to select the President. On May 16, a queer solution of the deadlock
was reached. President Urriolagoitia resigned from office, turned
the control of the government over to a military Junta and left
Bolivia. The Junta immediately declared martial law, and issued
a decree nullifying the electoral results, stating that a new election
would be called at "a proper time." General Ballivián became
President of the Junta. From his exile, Paz Estenssoro denounced
the illegality of the coup and organized his forces to seize the position
he felt had been stolen from him.

On April 9, the revolutionary plans went into effect and the
members of the MNR finally succeeded, after a bloody revolution,
in controlling power. Estenssoro returned from Argentina, and is
today at the head of the government.

Position of Labor. As in the other countries, the first labor
unions of Bolivia were mutualist associations, and appeared in the
tin mining regions, where working conditions and the risks involved
made organization imperative. Before World War I, the Railroad
Federation was created, also of a mutualist nature, and after that
the labor movement increased and the unions multiplied, with
various ideologies. The *Federación Obrera del Trabajo* (FOT,
Labor Federation of Work) became important, and brought together workers of diverse political creeds, and the *Federación
Obrera Local* (Local Federation of Labor) had anarcho-syndicalist
tendencies.

The socialist government after the 1936 revolution tried to unite
the workers, and even decreed the compulsory formation of labor
unions, but since the government lasted only a short time, organization was not carried out as thoroughly as it might have been. Nevertheless, the *Confederación Sindical de Trabajadores de Bolivia* (Syndical Federation of Bolivian Workers) was formed, and later played
a rather important role in the political life of the country. The
miners formed the *Federación Minera de Bolivia* (Miners Federation
of Bolivia), one of the most important unions, that intervenes actively in politics under the leadership of Juan Lechín. Two of the
important political parties, the MNR and the PIR, try to outdo one
another in obtaining the support of the miners.

There are minor organizations, such as mutualist labor unions, cooperatives and societies of mutual assistance. According to the most recent statistics of the Ministry of Labor, there are nearly 300 labor organizations, of which 98 per cent are trade unions.

The position of the Communists is interesting. There is no party of that name, or any political front under any other name, that maintains official contact with the Communist parties of the continent. However, the *Partido Izquierda Revolucionaria* (PIR), with its Marxist ideology, apparently takes the place of Communism. It was founded by José Antonio Arce, a young intellectual of Marxist ideas, who maintains that his program only applies Marxism to political and economic realities, but establishes no contacts with international Communism. His party has approximately 30,000 members and obtained about 20,000 votes in the last presidential elections. Its members are mainly culled from the labor groups, students and intellectuals of the younger generation, who are principally interested in struggling against the MNR for the support of the organized workers of the country.

PERU

In 1945, with the election of President Bustamante it seemed that Peru had reached its political maturity. The forces behind Bustamante represented the best of the enlightened younger generation of Peruvians. Unfortunately, the seizure of power by Odría three years later interrupted the trend.

The political failure of the Bustamante government was caused not only by the mistakes and impatience of the *Apristas,* but by the very nature of the coalition that put him in power. A revolutionary party, like the APRA, cannot succeed in an alliance with moderate forces. The long underground tradition and the ideologies of their leaders made them restless and anxious to put into practice—at once—their political program. They did not take into consideration the need for a gradual evolution, but tried to force changes that would have taken at least a decade to mature. The result is well known—the split between Bustamante and the APRA. After that, it was easy for the opposition to take over. The future of Peru is uncertain. Haya de la Torre, the *Aprista* leader, is still a refugee in the Colombian Embassy. As long as Odría can control the army, there will probably be order, if not democracy, in the country.

Suffrage. All male citizens who know how to read and write, over 18 years of age, if married, and over 21 if single, have the right to the suffrage. Unmarried women over 21, and married ones or mothers regardless of age, may vote in municipal elections, if they know how to read and write. The vote is obligatory for all citizens up to the age of 60, and after that it is voluntary. Clergymen of all denominations are excluded from the right to the suffrage.

Constitutional Evolution. The constitutional evolution of Peru is very similar to that of the other countries of the Andean region, which we have studied. Thus, during the wars of independence, we find in Peru, as in Chile, Laws of Bases, Provisional Statutes and, in general, projects designed for organizing the territory when independence was achieved. After the war, a constituent assembly met in Lima in September, 1822, which approved the country's first constitution as an independent state. This was promulgated on November 12, 1823.

The Peruvians, influenced by the prestige enjoyed by Simón Bolívar, adopted a new constitution like the one he had established in Bolivia. The constitution became effective in November 1826, but, as in Bolivia, it was found to be impractical, and a third constitution following a policy of moderate liberalism, with a presidential system of government, was approved in March, 1828.

Domestic disturbances and changes in power brought about the approval of another fundamental charter in 1834, which did not alter the structure of the State. After this document was promulgated, Bolivia and Peru came together in a confederation, and a new constitution was passed in May, 1837, to sanction the change. When the confederation disintegrated in November, 1839, Peru had another constitution as an autonomous state, giving the government the same structure it had had before forming part of the federation.

In the middle of the century, the country had its liberal constitution approved in October, 1856, but it lasted no longer than the previous ones. It was displaced by a document of a more conservative nature in November, 1860, which was later amended and even suspended on various occasions, but that endured until 1920. On that date, dictator Augusto Leguía had a new constitution approved with the purpose of extending his presidential term, but it maintained the structure of the 1860 constitution.

Leguía was overthrown by a revolutionary movement in August 1930, and General Sánchez Cerro, who presided over the next government, convoked a constituent assembly which approved a new constitution on April 9, 1933. With several modifications, this is the document in force today, and the one we have studied in previous chapters.

Government and Opposition. Today Peru is governed by General Manuel Odría, following the pattern of dictatorship. General Odría went into power as a result of a military revolt in Arequipa, on October 27, 1948, which deposed President José Luis Bustamante and obliged him to leave the country. It is best to give a description of the political life of the last constitutional government of Peru, so that we may have a clear idea of the political forces today, their plans and purposes, and the problems of the present government.

On July 10, 1945, José Luis Bustamante was elected President in free and orderly elections. His candidacy was supported by a coalition of political parties that functioned during the electoral campaign under the name of Democratic Front. The coalition obtained a majority greater than three-to-one, against the candidate of the conservative opposition, General Eloy Ureta. The strongest group in the Democratic Front was the APRA (*Alianza Popular Revolucionaria Americana,* Popular American Revolutionary Alliance). The APRA, one of the most interesting parties of Latin America, was founded in 1924 by Víctor Raúl Haya de la Torre and a group of intellectuals and younger politicians. Its program may be described as one of democratic socialism. The *Apristas* are in favor of planned economy; of the integration of the indigenous masses to the economic and political life of the country; of the creation of a state economically independent of foreign capital; and, finally, of a political front of all the Latin American countries. Its members come, principally, from the young intellectual class, students, workers, and to a smaller extent from the lower middle classes. The economic emphasis of its ideology is taken from historical materialism, but the APRA has never accepted the political or philosophical theories of Marxian Communism, with which it broke, ideologically, soon after the formation of the party. For more than twenty years, the *Apristas* were a part of the opposition, sometimes underground, other times legally participating in presidential elections, but never reaching power. In 1945, the party changed its name to *Partido Popular* (Popular Party) , and was given legal recognition.

Bustamante took office on July 28, 1945, and at first started to govern with a nonpolitical cabinet, without giving participation to the members of the coalition which had placed him in the presidency. As was to be expected, his Ministers met such opposition in Congress (it must be kept in mind that Peru has a semi-parliamentary form of government) , that many of them were interpellated and had to resign. The APRA's activities were, then, limited to intervention in the government by means of the majority they had in Congress and trying to realize their economic and political program through legislative measures. The political atmosphere was fraught with friction and problems, and so early in 1946 President Bustamante invited the APRA to accept political responsibility in the executive and gave them three important Ministries.

The postwar economic situation and the nationalistic and socialistic policies of the APRA caused a strong current of opinion against them and produced the integration of the opposition composed of the conservative elements. The press, especially, and the conservative dailies *El Comercio* and *La Prensa* in particular, started a vigorous campaign against the government. Some leftist groups, as well, voiced their dissatisfaction with the APRA, accusing them of having sacrificed their revolutionary line of action and of haggling over bureaucratic positions. In 1946 the leftists organized the *Partido Social Republicano* (Social Republican Party) .

In January, 1947, a serious political crisis was caused by the assassination of Francisco Graña Garlán, one of the directors of *La Prensa,* because his death was attributed to a plot conceived by *Aprista* deputy Manuel Tello. Bustamante's cabinet resigned, and he formed a new cabinet without the three *Aprista* Ministers. This, the *Apristas* explained, left the government free to investigate the assassination without political pressure. The conservative opposition was not placated by the change of government; the *Apristas* continued to be the constant target of accusation, and the government to suffer from criticism against them.

The following year, in July, a rightist group, calling itself the *Unión Revolucionaria* (Revolutionary Union) , attempted a military rebellion in Juliaca but could not manage to attract the regular forces of the army, who remained loyal to the constitutional government. The revolt was put down, but all through the year the conservative opposition, especially a group called the *Alianza Nacional* (National Alliance) , boycotted Bustamante's government. The group got the support of 21 senators who followed tactics that might be called "political strike." They refused to attend the sessions of the Senate and kept it from passing the legislative measures approved by the lower house which were supported by the *Apristas* and by President Bustamante. The situation created an administrative impasse, because there was no legal way of compelling the senators to attend the sessions. Bustamante tried to solve the problem, governing by decree, but was immediately attacked by the opposition, who said this was unconstitutional. Finding no other solution, the president decided to rid himself of the *Apristas*, and issued a decree convoking a constituent assembly to modify the constitution, stating that the delegates to the assembly, once that mission was accomplished, would function as a congress or legislative chamber. The *Apristas* opposed this, saying—truthfully—that Article 236 of the constitution empowered the Congress to modify the constitution without the need of calling for a constituent assembly. They accused Bustamante of attempting to get a majority in the assembly and so, in the future Congress, to nullify the majority the *Apristas* had in the Congress as it then stood. The political situation grew so tense that there was a rebellion in Callao on October 3, 1948, in which a number of *Apristas* participated. This revolt, too, was unsuccessful, because once again the regular army remained loyal to President Bustamante. He had several *Apristas* imprisoned, although their principal leaders, Haya de la Torre and the Rector of San Marcos University, Luis Alberto Sánchez, managed to leave the country. Immediately after the Callao revolt, Bustamante's administration declared the APRA illegal.

The time was ripe for a military coup, and the forces of the Right, under the direction of Manuel Odría, organized an uprising in Arequipa, on October 27, 1948, as previously mentioned. Two days later, Odría's troops took the capital, finding no opposition this time in the regular army, which finally refused to obey the President. Bustamante did not resign, but was obliged to leave the country. From then until June 1950, Odría ruled the country with dictatorial powers. On that date, he resigned from the presidency of the Junta to become a candidate in the elections. General Zenón Noriega, another member of the Junta, became provisional president.

The only candidate of the opposition, General Ernesto Montagne, was backed by a coalition of the various political ideologies but was eliminated from the race by a decision of the National Electoral Board. This body, an institution created by Odría and composed of his supporters, ruled Montagne ineligible because of fraud in registration procedures. The election was a farce, and Odría was "elected" for a six-year term. A number of his own supporters admitted the one-sidedness of the elections. The newspaper, *El Comercio,* one of Odría's backers, advised the postponement of the elections, but its recommendations were ignored by the dictator. The opposition is carried on by some of Montagne's followers, and especially by the *Apristas* functioning underground, as they have been forced to do several times in the past.

Position of Labor. The workers began their movement toward association by forming craft unions, and in 1884 they created the *Confederación de Artesanos Unión Universal* (Federation of Artisans, Universal Union), for the exclusive purpose of protecting its members. The union was prohibited from taking part in politics. The CAUU attracted the most important of the craft unions, especially the carpenters, tailors, masons, cobblers, bakers, painters, barbers, plumbers, and later even the chauffeurs. Because they were nonpolitical, they received the protection of the State, which helped them on many occasions.

Mutualism was intensely developed, and the organizations of that type united in a central group called *Asamblea de Sociedades Unidas* (ASU, Assembly of United Societies). The railroad workers, as in other countries, were active in organization, and in 1925 constituted the *Confederación Obrera Ferrocarrilera* (COF, Federation of Railroad Workers), which later split in two because of differences among the members. After World War I, the first labor unions of a revolutionary ideology appeared, with trends from a moderate socialism to a radical Marxism. The ones following the latter tendency formed the *Confederación General del Trabajo del Perú* (CGTP, General Federation of Labor of Peru) , where the Marxist ideology naturally predominated. After unsuccessful efforts to unite the workers, the *Confederación de Trabajo del Perú* (CTP, Federation of Labor of Peru) was founded in May, 1944. It was affiliated with the CTAL, and that, as stated in Chapter 11, is the most important union in the country.

The presence of the APRA, as a revolutionary party of leftist tendencies, has taken a good deal of strength from Communism in Peru, which has been relatively unimportant politically. In the 20's, the young radicals and labor leaders who were struggling for economic and social reform, were attracted to the APRA program, when in other Latin American countries, young men in the same conditions were joining the Communist Party. When the APRA refused to form a part of the Communist International, several Peruvian Marxists and independent socialist groups organized the Communist Party in 1929. For years the Communists and the *Apristas* have bitterly opposed each other, as the Socialists and Communists have done in the European countries. The central point of friction has naturally been the efforts both groups have made to control the labor unions, and to organize the workers in the regions where there are no unions. The Communists have succeeded in organizing workers in various branches of production and attracting some followers from among them. For a long time they did not function as a political party or participate in presidential campaigns. However, when the last elections were held in 1945, they took part in political activities, and took the name of *Vanguardia Socialista* (Socialist Vanguard) . This they did for the same reason that the APRA took the name of Partido Popular, which is that Peruvian laws forbid the formation of political groups of an international character. In those elections, the Communists claimed about 50,000 members and obtained nearly 70,000 votes. We have already said that when General Odría took over control of the country, he outlawed the party. Today, they carry on their underground opposition, just as the *Apristas* have had to do. Although both groups are united in their desire to put an end to the dictatorship, collaboration between them—if there is any—is entirely due to circumstances, since they are separated by the old ideological conflict.

ECUADOR

The election of Enrique Galo Plaza in 1948 was a step forward in the political life of Ecuador. The forces that put him in power represented the best of the neutral elements of the country.

Suffrage. All citizens, men and women, over 18 years of age who can read and write, may vote. The vote is obligatory for men and voluntary for women. Members of the armed forces may not vote or be elected to public office, but the members of the clergy are not excluded from these rights.

Constitutional Evolution. The constitutional evolution of Ecuador is somewhat different from that of the other Andean countries. Due to historical circumstances, liberalism could not find its way into power until late in the nineteenth century. As we mentioned in the preceding chapter, Ecuador started its independent life as a part of Great Colombia, together with Venezuela and Colombia. When the political union of these three countries came to an end, Ecuador adopted a constitution as an independent state in May, 1830, with a presidential system and a unicameral legislature. In 1835, 1843 and 1845, new constitutions were promulgated, all of which comprise the country's first constitutional era, when the Ecuadorians were trying to organize themselves politically as an independent state. All these constitutions were of a conservative nature, as were three others that followed them, and are interesting only from an historical point of view.

Before constitutional liberalism was reached, the country went through the theocratic dictatorship of President García Moreno. During this period a constitution was approved in June, 1869, granting the Catholic Church more political powers than it had enjoyed under Spanish rule. It was necessary to belong to the Roman Catholic Church to have the right to vote. Two constitutions of minor importance followed the one of 1869, and it was not until the end of the nineteenth century, with a liberal victory, that the country could adopt the constitution of January 12, 1897, which bore the stamp of democracy. This was followed by another, on December 20, 1906, which was still more liberal, and which established the separation between Church and State. Liberalism gradually made its way, and another constitution dated March 26, 1929, took further steps on the road to democracy, while a new document on December 2, 1938, gave women the right to vote.

In May, 1944, a revolutionary coup overthrew President Arroyo del Río and placed Velasco Ibarra in power. A new constitution was approved in March, 1945, which had a liberal and democratic content and gave the workers full rights. Economically, the document had a tendency toward planned economy. President Velasco Ibarra had considerable difficulties during his administration, and when he thought his position was endangered, he blamed his troubles on the new constitution and suspended it, re-establishing the constitution of 1906. A constituent assembly convened in 1946 and approved the present constitution of Ecuador, which we have previously examined.

Government and Opposition. The antecedent of the government in power in Ecuador is the presidential election held on June 6, 1948, which elected Enrique Galo Plaza to the presidency. The elections were held under the provisional presidency of Carlos Julio Arosemena, a well-known businessman, who kept his promise to see that the law was obeyed and to maintain order. The entire electoral process was marked by an atmosphere of respect and freedom, sharply contrasting with the turbulent political years the country had traversed.

The forces in these elections were grouped in the following manner: The *Partido Liberal Radical* (Liberal Radical Party) formed a coalition with the Socialist Party and nominated General Alberto Enriquez Gallo. Although the Socialists have a considerable following, especially among the working classes, they decided to support the Liberal candidate, since they had no outstanding figure of their own. The Liberals had lost a good deal of prestige because of their support of President Arroyo del Río's dictatorship and division among themselves, but they came together in favor of a common candidate.

The Conservative Party, which follows the traditional policies of such parties throughout Latin America and is backed by landowners, Rightists, businessmen and the Roman Catholic Church, nominated Manuel Eliseo Flor. At first it seemed that the elections would be limited to the old struggle between the two traditional parties, but neither of the two candidates attracted the neutral masses, the younger politicians, nor the independent figures of the country. These formed a coalition called the *Movimiento Cívico Democrático* (Civic Democratic Movement), and nominated Galo Plaza, who had been Ecuador's Ambassador to Washington during the administration of Velasco Ibarra, and who was generally very well thought of. Galo Plaza obtained a majority of nearly 4,000 votes over his closest opponent, the Conservative candidate. He took office on August 31, 1948, and since then he has governed with no difficulties, attending to the economic and educational reforms Ecuador needs. During the first two years of government President Galo Plaza had no strong opposition.

A presidential election was held on June 1, 1952. The government of Galo Plaza favored the candidacy of José Chiriboga, of the Liberal Radical Party. The so-called Independent Liberals nominated the twice-deposed president José María Velasco Ibarra, and the Conservatives named Dr. Ruperto Alarcón Falconi. The elections were peaceful and, to the surprise of everyone, Velasco Ibarra won by a substantial majority. This victory proved the fairness of the elections and the democratic administration of President Galo Plaza, who asked the people to abide by the results, and used his personal prestige with the armed forces to keep them neutral. President Velasco Ibarra took office at the end of August.

Position of Labor. Before World War I, the workers of Ecuador were united in associations of a mutualist, or craft unionist, nature, but presented no national front, nor were they especially influential in the political life of the nation. In 1922, a number of unions came together in the *Confederación de Sindicatos Obreros* (CSO, Federation of Workers' Syndicates), that organized an active campaign to secure laws favorable to labor. Two other unions were formed years later—the *Unión Sindical de Trabajadores* (Syndical Union of Workers) and the *Confederación de Trabajadores de Guayas* (Federation of Workers of Guayas), the former following a Marxist tendency. Catholic workers formed the *Confederación de Trabajadores Católicos del Ecuador* (Federation of Catholic Workers of Ecuador), following the Catholic-socialist line. Finally, there appeared in Guayaquil, the city with most industrial activity, the *Confederación*

General de Trabajadores (General Federal of Workers), which united the workers of diverse ideologies.

When President Velasco Ibarra took office in 1944, he offered guarantees to the workers and held an important congress attended by nearly all the labor organizations of the country, including representatives from Indian communities. In this congress, the *Confederación Nacional de Trabajadores Ecuatorianos* (CNTE, National Federation of Ecuadorian Workers) was created, which joined the international organization of the CTAL. The CNTE is the most important labor group in the country, although there are other independent organizations, especially the *Confederación de Trabajadores Católicos* (Federation of Catholic Workers), which participates in political matters and carries considerable weight.

The Communists have not been very influential in politics. The party was organized in the 30's and lived a languid life, carrying on a clandestine opposition and attempting to attract followers from among the workers, whom they tried to organize. Their lack of political strength is due mainly to the opposition of the Socialists, who are much more popular among the workers. The Socialists have attracted the large masses of Indians and Mestizos and have supported agrarian reform and land distribution.

During Arroyo del Río's dictatorship, the Communists operated underground and cooperated with the forces opposing the president, which formed the group called the *Alianza Democrática* (Democratic Alliance). When Arroyo del Río was overthrown, the party participated legally in the political life of the country. However, Velazco Ibarra's ideological shift caused the Communists to withdraw their support, and today they continue to function in a semiclandestine manner. The Communist Party has only some 5,000 members, most of them in the port of Guayaquil, among the stevedores. They have some members among the workers in the sugar and rice industries, and in the railways.

There is a group of the extreme right in Ecuador, called *Acción Republicana Nacionalista Ecuatoriana* (Ecuadorian Republican Nationalist Action), formed by young men who in many ways resemble the *Sinarquistas* of Mexico (Chapter 12) and who have a great deal in common with European Fascism, especially with the Spanish *Falange*.

SUGGESTED READINGS

English:

Beals, Carleton, *Fire on the Andes,* Philadelphia, J. B. Lippincott Co., 1934.

Bolivian Commission of Inter-American Development, *Economic Resources of Bolivia,* Washington, D. C., Inter-American Development Commission, 1944.

Cleven, Andrew N., *The Political Organization of Bolivia,* Washington, D. C., Carnegie Institution, 1940.

Ecuadorian Commission of Inter-American Development, *Ecuador and Its Natural Resources,* Washington, D. C., Inter-American Development Commission, 1944.

Edwards, Agustin, *My Native Land,* London, Ernest Benn, 1928.

Fergusson, Erna, *Chile,* New York, Alfred A. Knopf, Inc., 1943.

Franklin, Albert B., *Ecuador; Portrait of a People,* New York, Doubleday, Doran, 1942.

Galdames, Luis, *A History of Chile,* Chapel Hill, University of North Carolina Press, 1941.

Hanson, Earl Parker, *Chile: Land of Progress,* New York, Reynal and Hitchcock, 1941.

International Labor Office, *Labour Problems in Bolivia,* Montreal, International Labor Office, 1943.

Linke, Lilo, *Andean Adventure,* London, Hutchinson & Co., 1945.

Martin, Percy Falcke, *Peru of the Twentieth Century,* London, Edward Arnold, 1911.

McBride, George M., *Chile, Land and Society,* New York, American Geographical Association, 1936.

Munro, Dana G., *Latin American Republics, A History,* New York, D. Appleton-Century, 1942.

Robertson, William Spence, *History of the Latin American Nations,* New York, D. Appleton-Century, 1943.

Stevenson, John R., *The Chilean Popular Front,* Philadelphia, University of Pennsylvania Press, 1942.

Stuart, Graham H., *The Governmental System of Peru,* Washington, D. C., Carnegie Institution, 1925.

Whitaker, Arthur P., *The U. S. and South America,* Cambridge, Harvard University Press, 1948.

Spanish:

Alzamora Silva, Lizardo, *Derecho Constitucional General y del Perú,* Lima, 1942.

Cox, Manuel Carlos, *Dinámica Económica del Aprismo,* Lima, 1948.

Donoso, Ricardo, *las Ideas Políticas en Chile*, México, D.F., 1946.

Donoso Torres, Vicente, *Reformas Constitucionales*, La Paz, 1947.

Echaiz, René L., *Evolución Histórica de los Partidos Políticos Chilenos;* Santiago de Chile, 1939.

Fernández, Juan F., *Pedro Aguirre Cerda y el Frente Popular Chileno*, Santiago de Chile, 1938.

Haya de la Torre, Victor Raúl, *¿A Dónde va Indoamérica?* Santiago de Chile, 1936.

————, *El Antiimperialismo y el Apra*, Santiago de Chile, 1936.

————, *La Defensa Continental*, Buenos Aires, 1946.

Mariátegui, José Carlos, *Siete Ensayos de Interpretación de la Realidad Peruana*, Lima, 1928.

O'Connor d'Arlach, Tomás, *Los Presidentes de Bolivia*, La Paz, 1912.

Pardo Zamora, Miguel, *El Sufragio Universal en Chile*, Santiago, 1946.

Pareja Paz, José, *Historia de las Constituciones Nacionales*, Lima, 1943.

Quevedo, Belisario, *Compendio de Historia Patria*, 3 vols., Quito, 1931.

Raveau, Rafael, *Derecho Constitucional Chileno y Comparado*, Santiago de Chile, 1940.

Sánchez, Luis Alberto, *Don Manuel*, Santiago de Chile, 1938.

————, *Haya de la Torre o El Político*, 2a. Edición, Santiago de Chile, 1943.

Sánchez Moreno, Manuel, *José Carlos Mariátegui*, México, D.F., 1937.

Valdez M., Salvador, *Cinco Años de Gobierno de Izquierda*, Puente Alto, Chile.

Zaconeta, José Victor, *La Democracia de Bolivia*, Oruro, 1925.

CHAPTER 15

"La Plata" Region

ARGENTINA

In spite of having indirectly originated in the military coup d'etat of 1943, the present government of Argentina cannot be classified as a typical Latin American dictatorship of the old *caudillo* pattern. Perón represents another type of ruler that has appeared in Latin America in the last few years. This ruler is undoubtedly a "strong man," but not the "strong man" who depends only upon the army and on ruthless suppression of civil liberties to keep himself in power. It is the "strong man" who succeeds in winning the support of the underprivileged masses by means of important economic and social concessions. There are some similarities between the program of Perón and Italian fascism, and even German national-socialism. Perón has been outspoken in his opposition to capitalistic individualism as well as to totalitarianism of the right and left, but he has used some of the methods and tactics employed by Hitler and Mussolini to try to win the support of the working classes.

He has called his positical philosophy a "third position," standing in the middle of the way between the exaggerations of individualism and totalitarianism. This position is characterized in his domestic policy with an effort to placate the masses. Perón has had the ability, ever since the days when he was Minister of Labor under the military government, to build up a powerful group of the working classes, who would follow him politically and with whom he could counteract the force of the army. The Argentine "strong man," knowing through his own experience the political fickleness of army leaders, had the intelligence to create another power to play against them. Of course, in doing this he has destroyed free trade-unionism in the country, but the political force of a large majority of the workers has been behind him. Besides that, Perón has profited from the mistakes made by other strong men in Latin America and in

Europe. He has never tried, like Vargas or Mussolini, to create his own vertical trade unions, but kept the structure of organized labor and won, by bribes, concessions, and other means, the backing of their leaders. His ability culminated in his two elections when he was undoubtedly chosen by a considerable majority.

In the international field, Perón profited from World War II, enriched his country by exports, and made possible the nationalization of the British-owned railroads. Later he made another important change in foreign policy, succeeding in a rapprochment with the United States and securing financial help.

If we are to judge from the recent elections, the *Peronistas* have kept their popularity. The party has a substantial majority in both houses and controls all key positions in the provinces.

Suffrage. The exercise of the suffrage is not regulated by the constitution but by the laws of the nation, with legislation for federal, municipal, and provincial suffrage. It is universal, secret and obligatory. All citizens over 18 years of age, of either sex, have the right to vote, providing they are in full possession of their civil rights. The suffrage is excluded to members of the clergy and the armed forces.

Constitutional Evolution. On May 25, 1810, the *Cabildo* of Buenos Aires formed a Provisional Junta of Government to consider the problem created by the French occupation of Spain and the cessation of sovereignty of King Ferdinand VII. On the 28th of the same month, the Junta approved by-laws and regulations for its internal organization. The city of Buenos Aires, of course, could not take upon itself the representation of the entire country, and so it was not until October, 1811, that the Provisional Junta of Government was augmented by the representatives of the provinces and began to function under the name of *Junta Conservadora de la Soberanía del Señor Fernando VII* (Junta for the Conservation of the sovereignty of King Ferdinand VII). The body adopted a set of regulations and organized the government on a national basis. The two documents to which we refer did not affirm the sovereignty of Argentina; therefore they lacked the character of constitutions, since all political acts are made in the name of the dethroned Spanish monarch.

In 1813, the provisional government convoked a general assembly to draw up a constitution, no longer mentioning the Spanish monarch, which evidenced the desire to establish the nation as an independent and sovereign state. The assembly designated a special committee to prepare the constitution, in which it was declared that the form of government was republican and that sovereignty resided in the people. However, this document was never approved. In 1815, the Junta passed a new Provisional Statute, one of its articles calling for another constituent assembly.

This assembly is known by the name of *Congreso de Tucumán*, which met on March 24, 1816. Delegates from ten important provinces were present, and in its session of July 9, the independence of the United Provinces of South America was unanimously declared. After this, the *Congreso* met in a number of secret sessions and decided to adopt a constitutional monarchy as the form of government. The sessions went on into 1819, when a centralist and aristocratic constitution was approved, much to the dissatisfaction of the provinces. The date marks the beginning of the struggle between the provinces of the interior and the city of Buenos Aires, which was to characterize the political life of the country for many years.

The legislature of Buenos Aires convoked the representatives of the provinces to a Congress which met in that city on December 6, 1824. Its sessions lasted for two years and ended with the adoption of the constitution of July 1826, which was also of a centralist nature, but which attempted to appease the provinces, granting them certain administrative autonomy and authorizing them to elect their own councils. This constitution clearly states that the nation adopts the representative, republican form of government (Article 7) and that the executive power corresponds to the President of the nation (Article 68). The effort to placate the provinces did not counterbalance the centralist nature of the constitution; the Federalists were still dissatisfied, and the struggles continued.

These struggles open a long gap in the constitutional history of Argentina, since the constitution of 1826 did not, in reality, govern the entire nation. The city of Buenos Aires functioned independently of the provinces, and after bitter rebellions which amounted to civil wars, the *Caudillo* Juan Manuel de Rosas took over the government of Buenos Aires, on April 13, 1835. He promptly became one of the most oppressive dictators in the political history of Latin

America. By the use of force, he extended his control over nearly all the country, until his opponents overthrew him in a civil war that culminated in the Battle of Caseros, on February 3, 1852. This date closes the most turbulent period of Argentina's constitutional history, and a new era opens, of a more peaceful political evolution.

On May 31, 1852, General Urquiza, eminent leader of the opposition against Rosas, met in the city of San Nicolás with the governors of the provinces, and they agreed to convoke a constituent assembly. This body met in the city of Santa Fe on November 20 of the same year, with thirteen of the provinces represented. Buenos Aires refused to participate. The assembly approved a constitution on a federal basis, dated May 1, 1853. This is the fundamental document of Argentine political life, because even the present constitution has kept its essential structure. The document was mainly inspired by the famous *Bases* of the great statesman, Juan Bautista Alberdi, but was not accepted by the province of Buenos Aires, which kept up its opposition.

After a few years, Buenos Aires reached an agreement with the other provinces, and signed the Pact of San José, on November 11, 1859. By this pact, Buenos Aires declared itself to be a part of the Argentine Federation, and convoked a convention of the inhabitants of the province, to examine and accept or reject the constitution of 1853. The convention proposed certain modifications, and the adoption of the term "Argentine Nation" to be used in all legislative acts of the state. These amendments constitute the Reform of 1860. Several historians maintain that the real constitution is dated 1860, because nineteen articles of the 1853 constitution were either reformed or modified and others were entirely abolished.

In 1866, another constituent convention met in Buenos Aires, and the 1860 text was amended slightly. The constitution was again amended in 1898, but only to decrease the number of representatives in proportion to the population. The problem of the capital had been settled in 1880, when the city of Buenos Aires was declared to be the federal district, and the city of La Plata became the capital of Buenos Aires province.

On March 11, 1949, a constituent convention convoked by President Juan Domingo Perón approved a new constitution. The political organization, insofar as it referred to the federal structure, the division of powers and the fundamental organs of the State, was left untouched in this new document. The only political change of importance was the introduction of an article authorizing the re-election of the President, which heretofore was forbidden. Minor political changes were made, such as the reduction in the number of deputies to one for each 100,000 inhabitants, and the abolition of the Electoral College. Apart from the presidential re-election, the principal innovations in the new constitution refer to the economic, social and family spheres. Property is defined as a social function; the division of latifundia is ordered, and industries may be converted into state monopolies. The public services are made monopolies of the State, and natural resources are considered state patrimony. The aged and infirm are protected by the State, and workers' rights enumerated, all of which we have already studied in the third part of this book.

Government and Opposition. The present government of Argentina is the result of general elections held on November 11, 1951, by which President Juan Domingo Perón was re-elected to the presidency.

On June 4, 1943, President Ramón Castillo was overthrown by a military coup, and a de facto government was established, lasting until Perón's first election, on February 24, 1946. For an understanding of the political forces supporting the present government, as well as the role of the opposition, we must review the origins and events of those three years of military government.

Presidential elections were to be held in 1943. The government was in the hands of the *Partido Unión Cívica Radical* (Civic Radical Union Party, moderate liberal), which was in the majority, and the President was Ramón Castillo. As Vice-President, he had taken office at the death of President Roberto Ortiz. The opposition was mainly composed of the Conservative Party, traditionally Rightist, and by the Socialist Party, the third group of importance, although it had lost strength due to lack of leadership.

On the morning of the fourth of June, the military forces of a nearby encampment marched to the city and forced the President to resign. The presidency was turned over to Colonel Rawson, who had led the movement. The conspiracy had really been directed by Colonel Pedro P. Ramírez, Castillo's Minister of War, but the President had become suspicious a few days before and had Ramírez imprisoned. Rawson occupied the Presidency for a few days, and then turned it over to Colonel Ramírez.

This military coup was organized principally by the conservative elements of the country, who doubted that President Castillo would permit honest elections. Within the army, there was a group of young officers who got control over the forces and so organized the revolt. This group, known as the *Grupo de Oficiales Unidos* (GOU, Group of United Officers) is still important in the political life of Argentina. One of them was Colonel Juan Domingo Perón.

On February 24, 1944, Ramírez was obliged to resign, again by the GOU, in favor of Vice-President Edelmiro Farrell. In this second coup, Perón's role was more important. In Farrell's provisional government, Perón was Vice-President and in charge of the ministries of Labor and Defense. It was as Minister of Labor that Perón's political reputation started to grow, as he made concessions to the workers and promised the peasants distribution of lands. His prestige was not gained without opposition, however, as public opinion turned against him considerably. He was removed from office and arrested, but after he regained his freedom he continued his political activities and organized a strong group of followers.

President Farrell had promised to hold general elections, and the date was set for February 4, 1946. The forces opposing the *de facto* government—and Perón—formed a coalition called *Unión Democrática,* composed of the Radical Party, the Socialists, Communists and other minor groups, with José Tamborini, an old Radical politician, as their candidate. The other candidate was Colonel Perón, who had formed the *Partido Obrero* (Labor Party). He was supported by large groups of workers in the cities, by the peasants, and had obtained the unofficial backing of the Roman Catholic Church, since his program included religious instruction in public schools. The campaign was a violent one, although there were no open outbreaks of importance. It was complicated by the international situation caused by the publication of the Blue Book by the U. S. State Department, which condemned the *de facto* government and Perón. Impartial observers believe that many neutral voters shifted to Perón at the last moment, precisely because of the Blue Book, which they felt was an intervention in the internal affairs of the country. It is true, however, that the opposition coalition made the mistake of choosing an elderly candidate, lacking Perón's dynamic qualities and energy. The elections were orderly, and Perón obtained a substantial majority. Of course, the government machinery was helpful in the campaign.

During his first two years, Perón introduced no important political changes, but he suppressed the opposition severely, closed down unfriendly or outspoken newspapers, and imprisoned many of his opponents. Partial elections were held in 1948, and his party obtained a resounding victory, which showed that his popularity had increased even more. To a great extent, this was attributable to the government's purchase of the railways, which had belonged to British companies. After the elections, Perón's party had 109 seats in Congress, while the opposition parties had only 49. In their minority position, the opposition kept up their campaign against the President, and there were serious crises. On one occasion, the 42 members of the Radical Party resigned in a body, but later returned to their positions feeling that it was the only way they could counteract the government forces.

Toward the end of 1948, the political groups supporting Perón started to prepare a constitutional reform, and the fifth of December was set as the date to elect delegates to the constituent assembly. Perón's followers were operating under the name of *Partido Peronista*, and won a large majority in the assembly, which approved an official program of constitutional reform on January 6, 1949.[1] The program states that the purpose of the reform was to carry out the three basic proposals the President wished to establish in the nation: social justice, economic liberty, and national sovereignty. It also justified the most important political change of the reform, the article permitting presidential re-election, and said that the principal object was to re-establish democratic principles, as it was undemocratic to deprive the people of the right to re-elect a President if they so desired.

The constitution was approved, but there was strong opposition from the anti-Perón members of the Convention, and even from several *Peronistas*. One of these, Domingo A. Mercante, who was the President of the convention, opposed the clause on re-election. He was one of the most important government figures, and did not

---

[1] "Partido Peronista," *Anteproyecto de Reforma de la Constitución, Nacional,* Buenos Aires, 1949.

withdraw his objection until Perón promised officially not to be the candidate in the 1951 elections.

Many conservatives objected to the reforms because of the modifications in the economic and social structure of the country. In spite of all the opposition, however, the constitution went into effect on April 2, 1949.

The presidential election was held on November 11, 1951. The *Peronista* Party nominated President Perón for re-election. The Radical Party nominated Dr. Ricardo Balbín. Dr. Balbín was the most distinguished leader of the opposition forces. The candidate for the Socialists was the elderly scholar, Alfredo Palacios. The Communist candidate was Rodolfo Ghioldi, and the Conservatives, functioning under the name of National Democrats nominated Reynaldo Pastor.

The electoral campaign was not free in the full democratic sense. The government monopolized the radio, television, newsreels and other means of communications, but the voting was orderly and the *Peronistas* received over 60 per cent of the total votes cast. This was the first time that a President was immediately re-elected in Argentina. The election placed Perón and his party strongly in power to rule the country for six more years.

Position of Labor. Labor organizations appeared earlier in Argentina than in any other Latin American country. There were societies of resistance as far back as 1874, and a short time after that we find mutualist organizations uniting workers according to their line of work.

Toward the end of the nineteenth century, German immigration was responsible for the introduction of socialist principles, before the other countries felt this influence. In 1882, an association of German socialist workers was created under the name of *Vorwarts Club*. It was followed by the *Círculo Socialista* (Socialist Circle) established in 1888, and later by the *Comité Internacional Obrero* (International Labor Committee) in 1889.

The first national organization to bring together workers of different regions of the country was the *Federación Obrera Argentina* (Argentine Labor Federation) which was established in 1890. From its early days, this association participated in political life, and demanded from the government improvements for the workers, especially in connection with problems of unemployment, and in general with working conditions.

The *Federación Obrera Regional Argentina* (FORA, Regional Labor Federation of Argentina) was founded in 1901, and became a powerful organization. It followed anarcho-syndicalistic tendencies, and was influenced mainly by Spanish and Italian immigrants, in whose countries the syndicalist principles were in full swing at the time. In 1902, the *Unión General de Trabajadores* (UGT, General Union of Workers) was organized. It was opposed, in its social ideology, to the FORA, followed the principles of reformist socialism and intervened in public life, along with the Argentine Socialist Party, which was the first of its kind in Latin America and then had leaders of exceptional ability. In 1922, the *Unión Sindical Argentina* (USA, Argentine Syndical Union) was created, and this organization replaced the FORA, attracted a large number of its members, and started to organize the workers on the basis of industries.

The year 1923 was important in the labor movement. It saw the creation of the *Confederación Obrera Argentina* (COA, Argentine Labor Federation) which drew its members mainly from the workers of the capital, and especially from the railroad workers who integrated the Railroad Union. Even today, this is one of the most important trade unions in the country. In 1930, the *Confederación Obrera Argentina* and some groups of the *Unión Sindical Argentina* merged and formed the *Confederación General de Trabajadores* (CGT, General Federation of Workers) with more than 150 unions affiliated and some 230,000 members. The principal unions of this new organization were those of the railroad and streetcar workers, workers in maritime trade, typographers and public employees. When the CTAL was created in Mexico, the CGT joined the international organization. In 1940, the CGT claimed more than 300,000 members, while the remainder of the organized workers in unions not incorporated to it did not exceed 160,000. Until 1942, the CGT dominated the labor movement.

In March, 1943, the CGT suffered the same schism between Left and Right that we have seen throughout Latin America. After the military coup of June, 1943, and when the *de facto* government took over the presidency and placed Perón in the Ministry of Labor, the CGT lost to Perón a sizable number of members, especially among the railroad workers, which—as we have said—was the strongest group within the organization. Perón's policy consisted in winning over the workers, offering them positive advantages, such as better wages, hospitalization plans, family assistance and paid vacations. It was logical that they should support him in the presidential elections of 1946.

Perón's policy has further consisted in the creation of a labor movement in Latin America of an international nature, and under his control. For this reason he has tried to dissolve relations between the CGT and the CTAL, and backed the foundation of the *Confederación Interamericana de Trabajadores* (CIT, Inter-American Federation of Workers) .

An interesting opinion in relation to the workers' situation in Argentina under Perón may be found in the report made by A. F. of L. delegates when they visited Argentina. They came to the conclusion that "the Argentine Federation of Labor is not a free instrument of the workers, but has become a political arm of the government." [2]

To be sure, there are still independent unions in Argentina, trying to keep their freedom, as well as the integrity of their organizations. Among them we should mention the *Unión Sindical Argentina,* which still functions and claims approximately 40,000 members; the old *Federación Obrera Regional Argentina,* and the *Comité Obrero Argentino* (Argentine Labor Committee) which is directed by the Socialists.

The Communists have never played an important role in politics, nor have they been especially influential in the labor movement, the usual condition to be found wherever socialist and syndicalist ideas have predominated. The Communist Party was organized in the early 20's and gained in strength during the economic crisis of 1929. In September, 1930, a military government outlawed them, and the party engaged in clandestine activities until December, 1945. Since that date, the Communists have followed the policy of collaborating in many cases with Perón, especially in his measures favoring labor. They agreed with the international policy of the *de facto* government, particularly in the campaign against the United States.

---

[2] Galarza, Ernesto, *Argentine Labor under Perón,* Washington, D. C., Inter-American Reports, March, 1948.

The Communists have some strength in several syndicates within the CGT, and publish two dailies of active propaganda. The article in the new constitution, declaring that international associations are illegal, is a powerful weapon in the hands of the government, and has made the party cautious in its policies. Perón has not paid much attention to Communist activities, although he has attacked their ideas in speeches and in his publicity campaigns. He has, instead, used his attitude toward the Communists to maintain that there is a real democracy in the country, refusing to follow Chile and Brazil in declaring the party illegal. In a recent study, it was estimated that the Communists have about 35,000 members in Argentina, plus about 100,000 sympathizers, and they obtained nearly 100,000 votes in the presidential elections of 1946.

URUGUAY

Uruguay, because of Batlle's reforms, its privileged geographic location, economic resources and great degree of literacy, is a model of modern and progressive democracy.

Suffrage. The suffrage, as well as inscription in the electoral registry, is obligatory. Elections are always held on the basis of proportional representation, and all citizens of both sexes, over 18 years of age, have the right to vote. Foreigners who have resided in the country for fifteen years, are married, of good conduct, have some capital or property, or are engaged in a science, art or industry in the country, also have the right to the suffrage, although they are not considered citizens.

Constitutional Evolution. The constitutional history of Uruguay is, in various aspects, quite different from that of the other Latin American republics. For years its territory was coveted by Argentina and Brazil, both of which frequently intervened and provoked international conflicts. Finally, in 1828, the country proclaimed its independence and approved its first constitution in September, 1829, which went into effect on July 25, 1830.

Although in this constitution, the nation adopted the republican form of government, what it really did was create a sort of elective monarchy, with elections every four years. The government was concentrated in the hands of the President of the Republic, who had almost absolute powers. The logical abuse of presidential power caused long and bitter civil wars between the members of the *Partido Blanco* (White Party, extreme conservatives) and the *Partido Colorado* (Red Party, moderate liberals). Unlike what we have seen in other republics, and despite civil wars and violent changes of government, the constitution of 1830 was not modified until 1917. Political dissension was limited to the struggle for power, with no effort made to alter the fundamental charter.

Before Uruguay introduced substantial changes in the constitution, it started to alter its institutional structure after 1912, when a great statesman, José Batlle Ordóñez, was elected to the Presidency for the second time. It may be said of him that he was the father of modern Uruguay, which is one of the most progressive and advanced countries of Latin America. Although he realized that the constitution of 1830 was antiquated and inefficient to cope with the political and social necessities of his time, he made no move during his first term (1903-1907) to reform it. However, in his second term, he began to introduce innovations in the laws and institutions of the country before proposing alterations in the constitutional structure. Thus in Uruguay we see the interesting—and unusual case for Latin America—of legal and institutional changes preceding constitutional ones. To appreciate the constitutional reforms to which reference will be made later, some of President Batlle's innovations should be mentioned. He created State monopoly of electric plants; nationalized the Bank of the Republic, and established the monopoly of insurance policies in favor of the State Insurance Bank. The Institute of Fishery was created, and projects were presented to establish State monopolies in the alcohol and tobacco industries. President Batlle also reformed public education, including that on the university level, so that advanced studies could be within the reach of the poorer classes. In short, early in the century Uruguay adopted many of the measures that old European countries are trying to put into practice today.

In 1913, President Batlle proposed the convocation of a constituent assembly to draw up a new constitution, suggesting one of the most interesting political innovations in the history of Latin America. He proposed that the unipersonal executive be substituted by a Junta of government, composed of nine members. The minority parties were to participate in the Junta, through a system of representation proportional to the votes received by the parties in the general elections. By this, President Batlle meant to do away with the abuses of the strong executive, which had been one of Uruguay's political troubles throughout its history. He made the proposal, but felt he should not support it openly while he was in power, and his term was up in 1916. His idea was taken up by a group of the *Partido Colorado,* and the elections for the constituent assembly were set for 1917. The *Blancos,* opposed to Battle, and a part of his own *Partido Colorado,* objected to the plural executive, while a group of *Colorados* called the *Batllistas* supported the reform. When the elections were held, the opposition to Batlle had the majority, but in spite of his defeat, his idea was partly accepted by the convention. According to several writers, Batlle's opponents were so busy struggling against him during the electoral campaign that they had no efficient constitutional program to offer. Other authors maintain that the opposition decided to create a modified plural executive, to make sure that Batlle should not occupy the unipersonal executive in the future. Probably both opinions have a good deal of truth in them.

The fact remains that a compromise was reached in the assembly, and the constitution was promulgated on January 3, 1918. Under this document, the executive power was organized in two bodies, one of which was the Presidency of the Republic, and the other the National Council of Administration, composed of nine members. The President was in charge of the Ministries of Foreign Relations, National Defense and of the Interior. The National Council of Administration had the Ministries of Finance, Public Works, Industry and Public Instruction. The President and the members of the Council were elected by universal and direct suffrage, the President for four years, and the members of the Council for six. This system differed from Batlle's proposal in that it created not a plural executive, but a *divided executive,* in which the President was entrusted with the executive functions of a political nature, while the Council took over the administrative functions. Because the essential principle of unity was lacking, the system failed. The President kept his political and military functions, but lacked administrative and economic power, as represented mainly in the Ministry of Finance. The consequence was friction between the two executives, with the resulting ill effect on the political life of the nation.

A new constitution became necessary and was approved on April 19, 1934, abolishing the National Council of Administration and re-establishing the unipersonal executive.

In 1951, under the presidency of Andrés Martínez Trueba (*Colorado Batllista Party*), a new constitutional change re-established the plural executive. The new system was inaugurated in March of 1952, and consists of a 9-man Council to take the place of the President. The Council is composed of six men from the majority party in Congress and three representatives from the parties of the opposition.

Government and Opposition. On November 26, 1950, a general election was held. The *Colorado* Party nominated three candidates for the presidency. This split does not weaken the party, because according to the electoral law, all votes for a party candidate are assigned to the one running first in votes among them, and the combined total counts as the official vote.

The Conservative element of the *Colorado* Party nominated Eduardo Blanco Acevedo, who was President of the Senate and an unsuccessful candidate in past elections. Another candidate was César Mayo Gutiérrez, Vice-President of the nation, who was supported by the group led by César Batlle, son of ex-president José Batlle Ordóñez. The other *Colorado* candidate was Andrés Martínez Trueba, former president of the Bank of the Republic, backed by the group led by President of the Republic.

The National Party, or *Blancos,* nominated their old leader, Dr. Luis Alberto Herrera, who has the unique record of having been defeated in six presidential elections. The Communists nominated Eugenio Gómez. There were other minor candidates of little political significance.

The elections were free and orderly, and Andrés Martínez Trueba received the largest number of votes among the *Colorado* Party. The combined vote of the three *Colorado* candidates were far superior to the ones cast for Dr. Herrera, and Martínez Trueba was therefore elected to be the next President of Uruguay. Significant was the decrease in power of the Communists, who lost their only senatorial seat and had their representation in the House cut down to three. The new President was inaugurated on March 1, 1951, and on March 1, 1952, he turned the government over to the Executive Council, as mentioned previously.

Position of Labor. The country had its era of mutualist organizations, but these were never important as institutions in the political and social life. The labor movement grew stronger early in the twentieth century, when there appeared the first unions of craft workers, inspired principally by anarcho-syndicalistic tendencies. The first organization of this class was the *Federación Obrera Regional del Uruguay* (FORU, Regional Labor Federation of Uruguay). Later there was another of a very similar name, the *Federación Obrera Regional Uruguaya* (Uruguayan Regional Federation of Labor), which followed the ideas of libertarian anarchism.

The *Sindicato de Industrias* (Syndicate of Industries) was created years later, and tried to organize workers of factories who employed more than 25 men, and—as the name implies—organization was by industries and not by craft unions. The *Comité Obrero de Relaciones Internacionales* (Labor Committee of International Relations) was also active, keeping close contact with labor organizations of other countries. After 1920, the Marxist influence began to be felt, and several unions were formed under it, especially the *Sindicato de Artes Gráficas* (Syndicate of Graphic Arts) and the *Sindicato de Obreros Sastres* (Syndicate of Tailors). The Marxists met in a club called *Casa del Pueblo* (House of the People), which played an important role in its time, like the *Casa del Pueblo* that existed in Spain.

The first national union was organized at the time of the economic crisis of 1930, under the name of *Unión General de Trabajadores* (General Union of Workers) which brought together workers of diverse tendencies, but in whose direction Marxism predominated. Another important union organized in those days was the *Federación General del Trabajo del Uruguay* (General Federation of Labor of Uruguay). A large congress was held in 1942 to attempt to unite the largest possible number of workers in a central union, which was organized under the same name of *Unión General de Trabajadores* mentioned above, and that joined the CTAL. Left-wing Socialists and Communists carry weight within the UGT, and brought in the largest number of independent unions, besides organizing new unions in the fields of labor where there were none. The UGT today claims about 100,000 members, although many observers doubt that this is the correct number. The organization has suffered from the usual trouble, the ideological division between Socialists and Communists. Many Socialists, especially the railroad workers, musicians, employees in the moving-picture industry and workers in the meat industry have formed the *Comité Pro-Confederación del Trabajo* (Committee Pro-Federation of Labor) to organize a strong nucleus opposed to the Marxists functioning within the UGT.

The advanced social legislation, and the real political liberty which Uruguay has enjoyed, with brief exceptions, during the nineteenth century, have hardly given the Communists the atmosphere necessary for their activities. The Communist Party claims about five or six thousand members, and perhaps some 15,000 sympathizers. It was strongest during the elections of 1946, when it obtained more than 32,000 votes, twice the number received in the 1942 elections. However, there have been various strikes organized by unions affiliated to the UGT, which hampered the economic life of the country, and this has caused the Communists to lose prestige, not only among their sympathizers, but among labor groups within the UGT itself. At present, the party has no senators and three representatives in the Congress, and some of its members hold elective positions in the municipalities and departments.

The Communists have been cautious in connection with their relations with the present government, which they have never openly attacked. They have merely insisted upon their demands in favor of the workers. They do follow a more aggressive political line in the international sphere, following the policy of Russia against the Marshall Plan, the Atlantic Pact and other measures of the western powers. The government has left the Communists in complete liberty, respected their constitutional rights, and refused to take steps against them. It has not participated in any international anti-Communist alliance, basing its decision upon the belief that this problem is up to each nation to decide for itself.

PARAGUAY

Paraguay, politically speaking, is still in the nineteenth century era of *caudillismo*. The country is an inland territory, illiteracy is high and, because of its geographic position, it is economically controlled by Argentina. Unfortunately, there is no indication of improvement.

Suffrage. The right to the suffrage corresponds to all male citizens over 18 years of age. Those who have been deprived by the law of their civil rights may not vote, nor may the armed forces and police. The vote is secret and obligatory, and the constitution specifies that all persons who recommend electoral abstention lose their rights as citizens.

Constitutional Evolution. The territory today forming the republic of Paraguay became independent of the Spanish government in 1811, and approved its first constitution on October 12, 1813. The document was drawn up by Dr. José Gaspar Rodríguez Francia, who was to head the long list of tyrants the country has had until our own days.

It is an interesting constitution, in which the great influence of French political ideas may be seen. The executive power was in the hands of two Consuls, designated by restricted suffrage, and who divided among themselves the administrative functions of the nation. Each one had his own troops under his command. There was, besides, a Congress elected by popular vote—though also restricted—which met once a year.

The curious system was adapted by Dr. Francia to suit his own purposes. As one of the consuls, he ousted the other one, took absolute control and in 1816 had himself proclaimed Perpetual Dictator, which he was until his death in 1840. This was followed by a period of anarchy and civil struggles, and the two-Consul system was temporarily re-established, with the same results. One of them, Carlos Antonio López, repeated Dr. Francia's process and made himself a dictator until 1862. However, in order to give the government a legal aspect, a new constitution was approved in March, 1844, with a president elected for ten years by limited suffrage. This document maintained the archaic administrative structure of the constitution of 1813. Its place was taken by another constitution on November 25, 1870, under which the political structure became more democratic, with the government organized in a centralized system, the classical division of the three powers of the State, a bicameral legislative, and a president elected for seven years. This was in force for seventy years, and was replaced by the present constitution, which we have previously studied, and which was dated July 10, 1940. The principal change in this last one was the unicameral legislature.

Paraguay, therefore, has not had a great many constitutional changes, but this fact does not reflect the political reality, because in all Latin America, there is no country that has had a more turbulent political history. We believe the facts disprove the theory that political disturbances are caused by the frequent constitutional changes.

Government and Opposition. The present government of Paraguay is the direct result of the dictatorship of Higinio Moríñigo. He was Minister of War under President José Félix Estigarribia, who had been taken to the presidency as a candidate of the Liberal Party (new name of the old *Partido Azul,* or Blue Party). When President Estigarribia died in an airplane accident in 1940, Moríñigo was appointed provisional president by the Cabinet, and he remained in power, with all of the typical characteristics of the nineteenth century dictator, until 1948. On February 15 of that year, Moríñigo decided to hold general elections to select his successor, and openly supported the candidate of the *Partido Colorado* (Red Party, moderate liberals), Natalicio González. Only this party participated in the elections, and González naturally obtained a large majority in the Congress as well. It is superfluous to say that the elections were undemocratic. Although there was only the one party, its members soon split up into several factions, struggling among themselves to secure the best government positions. Since those elections, the political picture in Paraguay has been limited to wrangles between the members of the *Colorado* Party.

The lame duck period between González' election and his accession to the presidency, set for August 15, 1948, was difficult for Moríñigo, because of the bickering between *Colorado* party members. To solve the problem, the party asked Moríñigo to resign, and he turned the presidency over to the president of the Supreme Court.

On August 15, González took office; a few months later there was a frustrated military coup, and on January 30, 1949, he was obliged to resign by the most influential members of his own Cabinet. The Congress accepted his resignation, and appointed General Raimundo Rolón as provisional president. The General had been González' Minister of War. Rolón remained in office only a short time, because the *Colorados* thought he would use the army to govern the country, and forced him to resign. As his successor, they appointed Felipe Molas López, who formed a purely civilian cabinet. From the presidency, he called for general elections to be held on April 17, 1949, ran as the sole candidate for the *Partido Colorado* (again the only party participating), and stayed in office. In spite of his efforts to give a legal aspect to his government, he lasted only six months. Again the *Colorados* intervened and made him resign on September 10. On the 11th, the president of the Congress, Federico Chaves, took office. By October, Chaves had to declare martial law to prevent an uprising.

On July 16, 1950, Paraguayans went to the polls to elect a president and forty members of the Chamber of Deputies. The election in this one-party nation, however, was merely a gesture. Federico Chaves, the provisional President, was elected to complete the remaining three years of former President Natalicio González. There was no other candidate in the elections, and the forty *Colorado* Party candidates for the legislature were also elected to office. The state of siege, which had been lifted for the election day, was re-established immediately after, and was to remain in effect "as long as necessary," according to President Chaves. He also made known his desire to convoke a constituent assembly for 1953, and said he hoped that for that date, other political parties might return to activity. The opposition is formed by the followers of ex-President Natalicio González ousted in January, 1949, and by members of the Liberal Party.

Position of Labor. The long dictatorships and the purely agrarian economy have retarded the labor movement, and only of recent years have the labor organizations participated in the political life of the country. To be sure, there were mutualist organizations and craft unions, but they were unimportant in the national picture. In 1936, there appeared the first organization to have some strength, called the *Confederación Nacional de Trabajadores del Paraguay* (CNTP, National Federation of Workers of Paraguay), which attracted the workers from the few industries of consumers' goods, commercial employees, and a few intellectuals. According to semi-official statistics, the union had more than 50,000 members in 1938, a number which we believe to be exaggerated. The CNTP was reorganized in 1939, and changed its name to *Confederación de Trabajadores del Paraguay* (CTP), omitting the term "National" by government order, since it was feared that it might be considered an official organization of the state. In its new form, the union incorporated a number of transport workers and other industrial groups, and joined the CTAL. In 1944, the CTP participated in a general strike against President Moríñigo, who took severe measures against the workers, and since that date the CTP has lost much of its strength.

The Communist Party has had a sluggish existence for many reasons, especially the purely agrarian economy, the turbulent political life, and the many dictatorships. Moríñigo has frequently made use of the well-known technique of accusing all his political enemies of being Communists, which makes it difficult for an impartial observer to judge the real strength of the party. For many years, the Communists operated in underground organizations, and it is estimated that, at the time, they had no more than 500 members. In 1946, Moríñigo allowed the party to function within the law, to give his regime an aspect of democracy as other dictators have done, and membership increased as a result. The Catholics, under the leadership of the Archbishop, immediately organized an anti-Communist crusade. The legal life of the Communist Party lasted only until January, 1947, when it was again outlawed, as it is still.

SUGGESTED READINGS

English:

Alexander, Robert J., *The Perón Era,* New York, Columbia University Press, 1951.

Amadeo, Santos P., *Argentine Constitutional Law,* New York, Columbia University Press, 1941.

Bradford, Sax, *The Battle for Buenos Aires,* New York, Harcourt, Brace & Co., 1943.

Burgin, Miron, *The Economic Aspects of Argentine Federalism, 1820-1852,* Cambridge, Harvard University Press, 1946.

Craig, C. W. Thurlow, *Paraguayan Interlude,* London, A. Barker, 1935.

De Ronde, Philip, *Paraguay, A Gallant Little Nation,* New York, G. P. Putnam's Sons, 1935.

Elliot, Arthur Elwood, *Paraguay: Its Cultural Heritage, Social Conditions, and Educational Problems,* New York, Teachers' College, Columbia University, 1931.

Galarza, Ernesto, *Argentine Labor Under Perón,* Washington, D. C., Inter-American Reports, March, 1948.

Greenup, Ruth and Leonard, *Revolution Before Breakfast, Argentina 1941-1946,* Chapel Hill, University of North Carolina Press, 1947.

Hanson, Simon G., *Utopia in Uruguay,* New York, Oxford University Press, 1938.

Hudson, W. H., *The Purple Land,* New York, E. P. Dutton & Co., Inc. (No date.)

Josephs, Ray, *Argentine Diary,* New York, Random House, 1944.

Koebel, William H., *Paraguay,* London, T. Fisher Unwin, 1917.

————, *Uruguay,* London, T. Fisher Unwin, 1919.

Levene, Ricardo, *A History of Argentina,* Chapel Hill, University of North Carolina Press, 1937.

Macdonald, Austin F., *Government of the Argentine Republic,* New York, Thomas Y. Crowell, Inc., 1942.

Pendle, George, *Uruguay, South America's First Welfare State,* London, Royal Institute of International Affairs, 1952.

Rennie, Ysabel F., *The Argentine Republic,* New York, The Macmillan Co., 1945.

Rowe, Leo S., *The Federal System of the Argentine Republic,* Washington, D. C., Carnegie Institution, 1921.

Taylor, Carl C., *Rural Life in Argentina,* Baton Rouge, Louisiana State University Press, 1948.

Weil, Felix J., *Argentine Riddle,* New York, John Day, 1944.

White, John W., *Argentina, The Life Story of a Nation,* New York, The Viking Press, 1942.

Spanish:

Azara, Félix de, *Descripción e Historia del Paraguay y del Río de la Plata,* Asunción, 1896.

Báez, Cecilio, *Resumen de la Historia del Paraguay,* Asunción, 1910.

Bunge, A. E., *Una Nueva Argentina,* Buenos Aires, 1940.

González, Juan Natalicio, *El Paraguay Contemporáneo,* París, 1929.

González, Julio V., *Filiación Histórica del Gobierno Representativo Argentino,* Buenos Aires, 1938.

Ingenieros, José, *La Evolución de las Ideas en Argentina,* Buenos Aires, 1918-1919.

————, *Sociología Argentina,* Buenos Aires, 1915.

Korn, Alejandro, *Influencias Filosóficas en la Evolución Nacional* (Obras, Vol. III) , La Plata, 1940.

Mallea, Eduardo, *Conocimiento y Expresión de la Argentina,* Buenos Aires, 1935.

Matienzo, José Nicolás, *El Gobierno Representativo Federal de la República Argentina,* Madrid, 1917.

Melo, Carlos R., *Los Partidos Políticos Argentinos,* Córdoba, 1945.

Oddone, Jacinto, *Historia del Socialismo Argentino,* Buenos Aires, 1934.

Partido Peronista, *Anteproyecto de Reforma de la Constitución Nacional,* Buenos Aires, 1949.

Pivel Devoto, Juan E., *Historia de Los Partidos Políticos en el Uruguay,* Montevideo, 1942.

Rodriguez Fabregat, E., *Batlle y Ordoñez, el Reformador,* Buenos Aires, 1942.

Romero, José Luis, *Las Ideas Políticas en Argentina,* México, D.F., 1946.

Sánchez Viamonte, Carlos, *Derecho Constitucional,* Buenos Aires, 1945.

————, *Historia Institucional de Argentina,* México, D. F., 1948.

Stefanich, Juan, *El Paraguay Nuevo,* Buenos Aires, 1943.

Varela, Luis V., *Historia Constitucional de la República Argentina,* La Plata, 1936.

William, José Claudio, *Una Comedia Política, 1937-1943,* Montevideo, 1943.

Zavala Muñiz, Justino, *Batlle, Héroe Civil,* México, D.F., 1945.

Zum Felde, Alberto, *Proceso Histórico del Uruguay,* Montevideo, 1930.

CHAPTER 16

Portuguese America

THE PORTUGUESE STATE

The political phenomenon of the translocation of government forms existing in Portugal to her American colony was far different from the Spanish episode. The Portuguese came to America many years after the Spaniards, and at first had no solid interest in their possessions in this hemisphere. Portugal's interest centered primarily on the colonization of her possessions in Asia and Africa, and her American territory was important only as an intermediate point for trade with the East Indies.

In their formal aspect, many of the political institutions of Portugal, as they existed at the time of the colonization of Brazil, were similar to the Spanish institutions that we have studied in the first part of this book. However, the Portuguese political structure has some characteristics of its own, and Portuguese colonial policy was so different from that of Spain that it left a mark on the institutions of government created in Brazil. Following the same method we have used with the Spanish state, we shall briefly analyze the general characteristics of the Portuguese central government, underlining only those points necessary for the understanding of the organization of Brazilian government during the colonial period.

The transformation of Portugal from a feudal state to a nation-state was not a result of a dynastic union, as in Spain, but an historical process conditioned by other factors. At the end of the eleventh century, Portugal was a barony forming a part of the Spanish kingdom of León. Because of its geographical position, the ties joining it to León were weak, and in the twelfth century, the barony of Portugal separated from León and became an independent kingdom. The monarch's political strength rose, therefore, not from a family alliance, but from the autonomous exercise of his own power; a power opposed to the feudal nobility, but supported by it, since the King was considered a member of the nobility. Thus, there was no political union of independent kingdoms, but a political liberation of a geographic unit, and the appearance of a new state.

Like Spain, Portugal had to struggle against the Moors, but the Reconquest ended two centuries, more or less, before the Spanish Reconquest. Because of this, Portugal was able to organize a strong central government which afforded the monarch greater security of command and the free exercise of his authority. For that reason, we do not find in the Portuguese administration of the American colony the same system of division of authority that the Spanish King had to maintain.

Furthermore, the discovery and part of the conquest of Brazil resulted from a geographical accident and not from a decided purpose to obtain more land for Portugal. The new territories were considered a part, or administrative division, of the European kingdom. The King of Portugal, sure of his own political position in the peninsula, did not set up a rigid control in the early days of the colonies. This gave them a degree of local autonomy, which was to be an invaluable experience for the Brazilians when they became an independent state.

At the time of the discovery, the exercise of political power in Portugal depended entirely upon the King, not only in administrative and executive matters, but in the legislative and judiciary. The kingdom of Portugal was bounded on the north and east by the Spanish kingdoms of Castile and León. When the Moors were defeated, in the middle of the thirteenth century, and expelled from Portugal, the new kingdom could not spread toward the north and the east, and the Portuguese looked toward the ocean with the hope of founding colonies in other lands. Interest in maritime trade was in this manner stimulated, followed by the great discoveries of the Portuguese sailors and the creation of a large colonial empire.

Some time before Spain, Portugal had the interesting combination of political nationalism and the necessity of trading excursions throughout the world. This is particularly important, because the wealth produced by maritime trade made the monarch's relations with his subjects different from those of the Spanish King. The Portuguese King, unlike the Spanish King, did not need to depend on economic contributions from the middle classes and urban bourgeoisie for government expenses. The Portuguese ruler was solvent.

Since he did not have to resort to loans and taxation of his subjects, he did not need to make political concessions, and the system of *Cortes* was not as important as in Spain. Another result of the early interest in maritime trade on Portugal's political life was that members of the nobility embarked on the expeditions and searched for wealth and glory away from their national territory, leaving their King to govern in peace. So, while the King had no necessity to make concessions to the incipient middle class, neither was he especially pressed by the nobility. This definitely affirmed his power.

Another characteristic to be borne in mind is that, before the conquest of Portugal by Spain (1580-1640), the central government of Portugal had not set up an elaborate system of institutions on the peninsula to attend to Brazilian matters. There were only an Inspector of Finance, in charge of Portuguese and colonial economic problems, and the *Casa da India* (Indian House) that supervised shipments and other details of commerce, and even enlisted soldiers and sailors for service overseas. These, however, were administrative offices rather than organs of government.

As in the Spanish Empire, the Roman Catholic Church functioned in Brazil and Portugal as a part of the structure of government. In 1532, the government of Portugal created the *Mesa da Consciencia e Ordenes,* an institution acting with delegated authority of the King. It exercised ecclesiastic and administrative supervision over problems related to the faith and administration of the Church, and made recommendations to the King on appointments of ecclesiastic functionaries. It had, as well, legal jurisdiction over military orders operating in Brazil. We must keep in mind that the military orders were semi-religious institutions. Portugal did have its system of *Cortes,* but these were somewhat different from those of Spain. Many specialists in the field maintain that the Portuguese *Cortes* proceeded directly, by political evolution, from the Visigothic *Curia Regis.* Following that tradition, the King would receive advice and request recommendations from a group of ecclesiastics and members of the nobility. In emergencies, the King convoked the *Curia,* but was not obliged to accept their decisions. The system gradually evolved, and the custom was established of convoking the *Curia* to special sessions, to which other important persons of the kingdom were invited. Finally, these sessions were held at fixed dates, and became the system of *Cortes* which consisted, as in Spain, in the association of the three "classes" of the kingdom: the nobility, the clergy and the representatives from the cities.

The *Cortes* declined in Portugal before they did in Spain, because of the rapid development of political centralization and the Crown's economic independence. Later, the monarch's political unification extended to the sphere of the laws, and when legislation was unified for the entire kingdom, it was established that the legislative power corresponded to the monarch, so the *Cortes'* traditional right of making or recommending laws gradually diminished. The slight political power remaining to the *Cortes* disappeared totally when Spain conquered and occupied Portugal for sixty years. After its liberation, the *Cortes* never again reached the position they had enjoyed during the Middle Ages.

The system of political organization first used by Portugal in Brazil consisted in the *Capitanias*. This was a system of colonization used by the Portuguese in the Madeira and Azores Islands, and in some areas of the East Indies. It was a concession of a determined territorial area, made directly by the Crown to certain individuals, and under which the concessionaire had quasi-absolute powers within his demarcation. The only powers reserved by the Portuguese government in the *Capitania* were those of coining money and exercising justice in certain cases where the death penalty might be imposed. Although enormously beneficial to the concessionaires, the government found the system unsatisfactory, so it later decided to exercise more supervision over its vast colonial empire. Toward the middle of the sixteenth century, the post of Governor General of the colony was created, with residence in the city of Bahia.

The concessionaires of *Capitanias,* called *Donatarios,* were in reality feudal lords who controlled everything within their territories. They were the government. They did not exercise delegated authority, and thus did not form part of a complicated administrative hierarchy, like the local functionaries in the Spanish dominions. When the post of Governor General was created, he theoretically received the political power over all the colony. He was a functionary of the Portuguese central administration, appointed by the King, and responsible to him. The last Governors of Brazil often received the name of Viceroy and used one or the other title at choice. As we shall indicate, the friction between the *Donatarios* and Governors was constant for many years.

The administrative organization of Brazil changed radically during the union of Spain and Portugal, under the Spanish government. The Spanish monarch extended to Portuguese America the system functioning in Spanish America. In 1591, a Council of Finance was established, depending directly upon the central government of Madrid, and in charge of the economic problems of Portugal and her dominions. This council was subdivided into four sections, one of which was devoted to Brazilian affairs. The Spanish Council of the Indies was divided into two sections, one for Brazil and Africa, and the other for the East Indies, so that during that period Brazil had an organ similar to the Spanish one. But, since this was imposed by a foreign power, and all decisions were made in Madrid subject to the pressure of court politicians, the Brazilian section of the Council of the Indies never enjoyed the prestige of the Council of the Indies in the Spanish colonies. The other organs of the Spanish government that we have mentioned in the first part of this book were also extended to Brazil during the Spanish administration, and by 1608, there was an *Audiencia* in Bahia.

When Spain's control over Portugal came to an end, the Portuguese kings conserved the political institutions created by the Spanish monarchs. The Council of Indies became the Overseas Council and, as a Portuguese organ of government, was entrusted with all problems concerning Brazil, with authority and jurisdiction over military, civil, and religious matters, as well as supervision over Tribunals of Justice. This organ, however, did not designate governors or other colonial functionaries, this power being kept, as before, by the King. For this reason, the Council never had the political authority of the Council of the Indies in the Spanish colonies.

The private nature of the rights granted to the *Donatarios* under the system of *Capitanias* provoked serious conflicts between these feudal lords and the central government of Brazil. The King often followed the policy of appointing special agents to deal with administrative and political problems in certain localities. Thus there appeared the *Corregidores* in Brazil, similar to the ones in Spanish America, except that, instead of supervising local administration, they dealt only with the private interests of the *Donatarios*. They had judicial and military powers, and even heard complaints of residents of the *Capitanias* against the *Donatarios*. The system produced mixed results, because the *Corregidores* occasionally decided against the influential—and displeased—*Donatarios*. Although the cases were exceptional, the intervention of the *Corregidores* protected the inhabitants from abuses of power by the *Donatarios*.

Despite this encroachment upon his power, the *Donatario* enjoyed great local autonomy, especially during the early days of the colony. He was generally a member of the nobility, and his title was hereditary. He functioned, as we have indicated, as a military chief; lord and master of his fief, although he was obliged, as a condition established on receiving the concession from the Crown, to distribute lands to colonists who desired to settle there. He enjoyed ample judicial powers, in civil and criminal matters, administered justice, and was empowered to grant concessions, found cities, and appoint subordinate civil and military officials. At first, he could enslave Indians and sell them into foreign markets, but this power was later restricted by the Portuguese Crown. In this, the system was different from that of Spain, whose monarchs never officially authorized the slavery of Indians.

The *Donatarios* were in charge of economic and financial matters. They could create new taxes and collect and administer existing ones. Like the Spanish monarchs, the Portuguese established the *quinto,* a tax of one-fifth of the products of the new world, and the *Donatarios* collected this to pay the Portuguese government. The Roman Catholic Church also established, as it had in the Spanish dominions, the *dizimo* (one tenth) which the *Donatarios* collected for a commission. So, from a political point of view, we may see that all power within the jurisdiction of the *Capitania* rose from the *Donatario* or his subordinates, over whom the central government of Portugal exercised only a weak supervision. This form of administration may be described as American neofeudalism, an institution maintained in Brazil after it had disappeared from Europe.

Portuguese policy in Brazil, if there was one, has been described by Lillian E. Fisher as "limited to the exercise of a type of protectorate over the *Capitaneas* (sic), in exchange for the payment of certain taxes. The intention of the central government was to maintain each territory indivisible within the same family, although royal confirmation was required to obtain the privileges of hereditary title to it." [1]

The system of great power and local autonomy in the hands of the *Donatarios* gradually changed, as the colonists and the small landowners improved their economic condition and increased their political power. The loss of the *Donatarios'* power also went hand in hand with the centralizing tendencies of the Portuguese monarchy, and by the end of the seventeenth century, they were no longer especially influential. Another reason for this change was the appearance of new organs of government in Brazil. When the system of Governors General was established, official bodies were created around them to attend to local policy. There was the Commissioner of Finance, in charge of fiscal and economic matters—which weakened the *Donatarios;* the *Ouvidor Geral,* who supervised the administration of justice, with the same effect; and other minor officials, as well as military authorities entrusted with the defense of the coasts.

Our remarks in the first part of this book with regard to the Spanish *Municipio,* especially its origin and development, may be applied to the Portuguese municipality. There Sánchez Albornoz has been cited as saying: "The municipality was born in the valley of the Duero, when the *Terra Portucalensis* formed a part of the kingdom of León, and it was *one and the same* on either side of the artificial frontier which history has created between Castile and Portugal." [2] The same process was repeated in Portugal and Spain. Municipalities and cities appeared as a result of the Reconquest, and those that arose south of the Duero River, where there were large areas of uninhabited land and where danger from the infidels was greater, enjoyed more freedom than the ones north of the river. The *Conselho* of the Portuguese municipality may be compared to the Spanish *Consejo,* which has already been discussed. In a study of the modern municipalities of Brazil, the administrative structure of the Portuguese municipality need not be described in detail, but mention should be made of its similarity to the Spanish city and the fact that the Portuguese municipalities had lost their special prerogatives years before the conquest of Brazil. It was the Portu-

---

[1] A. Curtis Wilgus, Ed., *Colonial Hispanic America,* The George Washington University Press, 1936, pp. 167-199.

[2] *Op. cit.,* p. 129. Italics and translation of the author.

guese municipality of the sixteenth century that was taken to Brazil. The centers of population that integrated the municipalities were administered by a Council whose powers varied in accordance with the charter adopted by each city when it was founded. Some of their powers were often stipulated by the *Donatario* or by the Governor. At first, the residents of each locality elected their own officials, but gradually, as in the Spanish colonies, the municipal functionaries came to be appointed by the central government of Brazil.

Colonial Brazil. In describing the general characteristics of Brazil's evolution as a Portuguese colony, mention will be made only of those that differ from the basic institutions of the Spanish colonies. The characteristics that have influenced the political life of the country as an independent state will also be stressed.

The well-known Brazilian author, Gilberto Freyre,[3] says that the history of Brazil was marked by two apparently contradictory tendencies, but that these actually complemented one another. The first he calls the vertical tendency, represented by the settlers who became permanently established along the coast and devoted themselves to the cultivation of sugar cane, employing slaves and living on their plantations like true feudal lords. They founded a permanent and static culture during the colonial period and resided in the mansions called *Casas Grandes*. The second were nomadic settlers, whom Freyre calls horizontal. Moving from one place to another in search of gold and Indians, whom they could sell into slavery, these nuclei of population were free from the feudal organization. They were independent, enjoyed not only political liberty, but greater moral and religious freedom, and possessed numerous women. The ethnic group thus mingled rapidly with the indigenous population. These nomads and their descendants, called *"bandeirantes"* or *"Paulistas"* according to the region, soon created a population that ceased to be Portuguese, to become *mestizos*.

Portuguese feudalism, as formed by the lords of the *Casas Grandes,* was somewhat different from the Spanish institution. The privileges enjoyed by the lords were so ample, the distances were so vast, their isolation so complete—and Brazilian decentralization

---

[3] Freyre, Gilberto, *Interpretación del Brasil*, México, D. F., 1945.

so much greater—that they developed a spirit of independence which they used first against the Portuguese crown, and later against the central government of the nation. Also, the Church in Brazil was never as powerful as it was in Spanish America. In the plantations and *Casas Grandes*, each feudal lord had his own church as a part of his domain, and the church depended more upon his will than upon the Bishop of the ecclesiastic hierarchy of Portugal. There was never a strong clergy in Brazil—no bishops who dominated the economic and political life of the colony. This explains why there are no grave religious problems in modern Brazil. The first Brazilian constitution, although it declared Roman Catholicism to be the official religion of the State, permitted the exercise of other faiths. In that climate of liberty, there was little of the struggle between the Roman Catholic Church and the government that there was in the Spanish American countries. The Church did, however, occupy an important place in Brazilian economic life, since the early days of the colony. The monasteries and missions, especially the Jesuit ones, engaged in agriculture and made a profit of their products. The Jesuit Missions of southern Brazil and Paraguay are famous, functioning as economic rivals of the lords of the *Casas Grandes*, with whom they had serious conflicts. The main problem was the issue of Indian slavery. Although the missionaries used Indian labor, they were in favor of the abolition of slavery, and the landowners said their reason was purely economic, to deprive them of the work of the slaves whom they needed for their industries.

The *Casa Grande* had an extremely aristocratic structure, but it was—to a certain extent—more democratic than the *Haciendas* in the Spanish colonies. The feudal lords had few moral scruples, and had extra-matrimonial relations with Indian and Negro women, creating a *mestizo* population which was to be an important ethnic factor in the integration of modern Brazil. Nomad Brazil, of the moving cities, also produced the same results of the ethnic mixture, and maintained the spirit of individualism within the political system of the Portuguese crown.

As an important consequence of the situation we have described, there was an almost absolute absence of *caudillismo* in Brazil, especially during the nineteenth century. It is true that there were a few *caudillos* in the early years of the republic, but their influence was not as negative as in Spanish America. Neither had Brazil great heroes or military leaders, since it achieved independence through political evolution—as we shall see below—and not by means of a war. Altogether, the country was better prepared for independence than the other republics of the continent.

Some years before independence, toward the end of the eighteenth century, the Portuguese crown introduced certain reforms in Brazilian administration, as Spain did with her colonies. The Marquis of Pombal, a Minister of the Crown, granted great authority to the Viceroys, which diminished the autonomy enjoyed, to a certain extent, by the provincial governors. He expelled the Jesuits and freed the Indian slaves, although the Negroes were kept in bondage.

The ideas of eighteenth century European liberalism came to Brazil, as to the Spanish colonies, and provoked protest movements, demands of reform and even an attempted revolt to achieve independence, in the region of Minas Geraes (1789) which was quelled by the armed forces.

When Napoleon I occupied Portugal in 1807, the royal family and the court escaped to Brazil. The Portuguese government-in-exile was another contributing factor to Brazil's eventual independence. King João VI was surrounded by members of his court and of the nobility, who became extremely unpopular with the colonial aristocracy. Although the King introduced reforms, such as freedom of trade, and tried to develop local industries, still the Brazilians were displeased with the regime and even resorted to open revolts, some of which had to be repressed by force. The King returned to Portugal when the French domination came to an end, leaving his son Pedro as Regent of Brazil. Pedro was later called by the peninsular government, but he decided to remain in Brazil, and the country proclaimed its independence in 1822.

Independent Brazil. Having achieved independence by evolution and not by force, Brazil freed itself from nineteenth century *Caudillismo*. Many Brazilians have correctly remarked that they were more fortunate than the rest of the Latin American countries, because they had no great liberators and heroes to satisfy when they became free from Portugal. Also, the lesser amount of centralization under Portuguese rule accustomed the people to a certain degree of self-government, from which the new republic greatly profited.

The recent peaceful election of Getulio Vargas and his acceptance of the constitution of 1946 is an indication that Brazil is well prepared to rule its own destiny. An old "strong man" of the *caudillo* and dictatorial type has been returned to power by the vote of the lower classes and of many neutral citizens who were dissatisfied with the high cost of living and unnecessary waste under the administration of President Dutra. Observers believe that Vargas will try to put into practice a program with a left-of-center ideology. Among the various groups of the country, the wealthy class will probably be heavily taxed; the middle class and white-collar workers will remain more or less in the same condition, while the lower classes and peasants will certainly receive most of the benefits under the new administration. If Vargas manages to exercise a definite influence upon the Congress, it is very probable that we shall see a large program of economic planning and social legislation.

Constitutional Evolution. After independence, Dom Pedro took the title of Defender and Protector and promised to accept the constitution which was to be drawn up by a constituent assembly. Then he adopted the title of Emperor Pedro I. However, the Emperor refused to accept the constitution prepared by the assembly and dissolved the body by force. He then appointed a commission to prepare another constitutional document. The result was the first constitution of Brazil as an independent state, to which the Emperor swore allegiance on March 25, 1824. Under this document the nation was organized as a limited and hereditary monarchy, and the State was integrated under a centralized form of government. The executive power corresponded to the Emperor, who was the head of the national administration, and the moderating power in the relations between the three branches of the state. The legislative power was composed of a Senate, whose members were appointed for life by the Emperor, taking their names from a list of candidates elected by an indirect and extremely limited suffrage. There was a Chamber of Deputies, also elected by indirect suffrage, for four years. This form of government and the Emperor's abuses of power produced countless protests from the people, who had enjoyed more autonomy in colonial times. In April, 1831, there was a serious insubordination in the capital. The army refused to obey the government, and Dom Pedro was obliged to abdicate in favor of his son, who was only six years old at the time.

Until the heir to the throne was fifteen years of age, the country was governed by a regency, composed at first of a committee of three persons appointed by the Congress. In 1834, the Congress changed the system of a plural regency for a unipersonal one, and a Regent was elected by general and indirect suffrage. The constitution of 1824 was also amended on that date, granting certain rights to the provinces, by which the system became less centralized.

Needless to say, the government of Brazil was far from being a democracy, but the reforms were a step forward to federalism, which was demanded by the inhabitants of the provinces. In 1840, in order to put an end to political conflicts caused mainly by conservatives in Rio Grande do Sul, the Congress declared the heir to the throne of age, although he was only fifteen. He was proclaimed Emperor with the name of Dom Pedro II.

The new government maintained the constitution of 1824. adapting it to the political necessities of a rapidly progressing country. A constitutional amendment in 1847 created a parliamentary form of government and the position of Prime Minister, making him and the other members of the cabinet politically responsible before the Congress.

Dom Pedro II proved to be a progressive ruler. He followed the typical liberalism of the Enlightenment, and was in favor of scientific and rationalistic teaching, which incurred the displeasure of the Roman Catholic Church. His abolitionist ideas made him unpopular with the wealthy landowners, which, of course, contributed toward his downfall, but were beneficial to the country. In 1888, Dom Pedro made a trip to Europe, leaving his daughter, the Princess Isabel, in charge of the government. Following her father's ideas, the Princess favored the total abolition of slavery, which was approved by the Congress. The landowners became more aggressive, and Dom Pedro returned to Brazil, but could not control his opponents, nor the liberal and republican group of the army, who forced him to abdicate. A federal republic was proclaimed on November 15, 1889.

The army organized a provisional government and approved several measures of a liberal nature, especially the absolute separation of Church and State (1890). A constituent assembly was convoked, which approved the first republican constitution of Brazil, dated February 24, 1891.

The new constitution organized the country as a federal republic, with the three traditional powers of the state, in a form similar to the constitution of the United States. The executive power corresponded to a president elected for four years, by direct suffrage, and there was also a vice-president. The legislative power was composed of a bicameral congress: a Senate integrated by three senators for each state, and a Chamber of Representatives elected by popular vote on the basis of population. The judicial power corresponded to a Supreme Tribunal with power of judicial review. Suffrage was granted to all male citizens over 21 years of age. This constitution did away with the parliamentary system in favor of the presidential system, leaving the secretaries in absolute liberty as regarded their responsibility before the Congress. The states enjoyed a certain degree of autonomy, but the executive had the right to appoint interventors, by which autonomy was curbed.

The constitution of 1891 remained in force until 1930. In October of that year, Getulio Vargas took over the presidency of the republic through a revolutionary coup and immediately issued a decree suspending the constitution and dissolving the federal and state legislatures. He kept for himself all the powers of government until a constituent assembly should be convoked, but this he seemed unhurried to do. The body did not meet until 1933, and the constitution it prepared was promulgated on July 16, 1934. It is an interesting one, clearly reflecting the totalitarian tendencies under which President Vargas administered the country. The federal structure was maintained, but the president was given more powers, taking them away from Congress. The number of senators was reduced to two for each state. The lower house was still composed of deputies elected by popular vote, on the basis of population, but in addition there were fifty deputies appointed by the President, and chosen from among commercial, industrial and agricultural associations, the liberal professions, and organizations of employers and workers. A semi-parliamentary system of government was created, the members of the cabinet being responsible before the Congress for their actions. Citizens could vote at 18 years of age, instead of 21, and the suffrage was extended to women who could read and write. The new charter was short lived. In November,

1937, President Vargas again dissolved the Congress and assumed dictatorial powers. It is interesting and unusual that within a very few days he produced a constitution that undoubtedly had been prepared secretly beforehand, probably by one of his Ministers, Dr. Francisco Campos, a well-known lawyer of totalitarian ideas.

Under the new constitution of 1937, the state was organized in what was called the *Estado Novo* (New State). If one reads the document in the normal order of numeration of articles, it is evident that Brazil adopted a corporate form of government, very similar to that of Fascist Italy, or the one Portugal has today under Oliveira Salazar. But, if the reader starts at the end, and reads the transitory dispositions, he may easily see that the object of the constitution was to place all the powers of the state in the hands of Vargas. One of these dispositions stated that until the new constitution should be approved by a plebiscite, the President was empowered to govern by decree.

The new document contained institutions of a purely corporative character. The Senate, for example, became a Federal Council, some of whose members were elected by the states, but others freely appointed by the President of the Republic. The National Council of Economy and Finance was created and composed of delegates from the associations of producers and labor organizations recognized by the government. It was the function of this Council to approve or disapprove all legislative measures passed by the Congress on economic and social matters.

Vargas' dictatorship was more original than that of the European totalitarian dictators. In Italy and Germany in those days, and in Russia, Spain, and Portugal today, only one party is tolerated, the official party of the government. Vargas went still further and declared that political parties were necessary only in countries where there were differences of opinion among the people, but as all of Brazil was with his government, there was no need of political parties. So Brazil was a non-party state. In his new constitution, Vargas granted a number of rights to labor, and got the support of several vertical unions. His dictatorship was maintained during the entire period of World War II, using the technique of organized propaganda, censorship and the symbols of totalitarian systems, until a military coup obliged him to resign in October 1945. The President of the Supreme Court assumed the provisional presidency and convoked a constituent assembly which, on September 18, 1946, gave Brazil the constitution in effect today.

Government and Opposition. The provisional president who took over after Vargas' downfall, Dr. José Linhares, called for general elections to be held on December 4, 1945, the first free elections to be held in Brazil since the beginning of Vargas' dictatorship in 1930. The political forces of the country came together in new parties, in preparation for the elections. The two most important were the Democratic National Union, following a tendency of moderate liberalism, and whose members came mainly from the middle classes and small landowners. The other party, called Democratic Socialists, was composed of the upper classes, and received the non-official support of the Roman Catholic Church and the armed forces. Its political philosophy is, generally, the traditional philosophy of the Latin American conservatives. The Democratic National Union nominated Eduardo Gomes for the presidency, a man who was then extremely popular, and who had directed the air corps during World War II. The other party nominated General Eurico Dutra, a politician of the old school, whom public opinion considered closely connected with ex-dictator Vargas. The Communists, under the leadership of Luis Carlos Prestes (to whom we shall refer further) organized as an independent party and nominated Yeddo Fuiza.

Dutra defeated Gomes by nearly one million votes and was inaugurated as constitutional President on January 31, 1946. The Communists obtained more votes than commonly expected, receiving over half a million. They elected 14 deputies to the lower house, and their leader, Prestes, to the Senate.

Shortly after the elections, Vargas again came into the political arena, formed his own party (Labor Party) and, together with the Communists, took the opposition to Dutra. The Democratic National Union was also in the opposition, but they adopted a more moderate attitude, and often collaborated with the government.

Partial elections were held in January, 1947, for state governorships, members of the state legislatures, municipal functionaries, and some vacancies in the federal congress. The Communists gained amazingly in power, obtaining a large vote in the Municipal Council of the capital, and about 70 seats in the legislatures of the different states. The government immediately took steps to stop the party's advancement, and the Attorney General filed a claim before the Superior Electoral Tribunal, requesting the dissolution of the Communist Party, on the grounds that they violated Article 141 of the constitution, prohibiting political parties having a program contrary to the democratic form of government. In May, the Tribunal, by a vote of three to two, ordered the dissolution of the Communist Party, as requested by the government. After that, the problem was reduced to the legal situation of the Communists who had been elected in the partial and general elections, and who occupied government positions prior to the declaration of illegality. In October, Dutra's government took a further step against Communism, severing diplomatic relations with the Soviet Union, because of an incident produced by an article offensive to President Dutra in a Russian newspaper. The situation of the Communist deputies in the Congress and in the local bodies was decided in favor of the government in January, 1948, when the Congress approved a law canceling their credentials.

General elections were scheduled for October 4, 1950. In May, the Democratic National Union again nominated Eduardo Gomes; the Social Democrats nominated Cristiano Machado, a prominent engineer from the powerful state of Minas Geraes. The Socialist Party backed their old leader João Mangabeira, and Getulio Vargas was the candidate of his own Labor Party. The whole electoral process, as well as the campaign, was calm, and Vargas won by a large majority, with Gomes as runner-up. Vargas returned to the Presidential Palace on January 31, 1951. This victory of Vargas opened an interesting political interrogation in Latin America. Observers believe that there is no danger of his returning to corporatism or Fascism, as the old Fascist minority voted for Gomes. It is well known that Vargas is a bitter enemy of the Communists, whose leader, Carlos Prestes, served a long term during his previous administration. The new President announced that he would follow a policy of laborite orientation, modeled after England and the Scandinavian countries.

Position of Labor. Toward the end of the nineteenth century, and early in the twentieth, the workers of Brazil were organized, as were those of other Latin American countries, in mutualist associations and societies of resistance. The most important mutualist groups were composed of transport workers, carriers, and workers in the coal industry, but they were not noticeably influential in political matters.

The first unions were formed in the capital, among the railroad workers and stevedores, and—to a lesser extent—among the textile workers. The labor movement gained in strength after World War I, when unions were organized in other parts of the country. One of the most important was the Confederation of Fishermen, which reached a membership of 30,000 and founded a school for fishermen. All of these groups functioned independently, with nothing to tie them together nationally.

When the economic crisis of 1929 developed, there were strikes all over the country, and the workers made their first effort to create a central union, founding the General Confederation of Workers of Brazil. The Marxist tendency predominated in this organization, which drew up a program openly favoring the class struggle, and preaching noncollaboration with the government. The most important groups within this union were the railroad workers and stevedores. The same year, certain groups of workers who refused to accept the Marxist ideology of the union organized a rival union called the National Federation of Brazilian Workers.

A short time before the organization of the two unions mentioned above, the workers of Porto Alegre founded a political party called the Labor Party, which spread throughout the country. It adopted a democratic-socialist program, but many Communist unions either supported or sympathized with it. The party program favored the representative form of government, the defense of national sovereignty, and collaboration with international organizations of workers. It demanded important social reforms for the workers, including participation in the profits of industries. Poblete Troncoso says of this political group that it was "a party of heterogeneous strength, without a definite professional or syndical basis, and lacking an ideological structure founded on economic principles, all of which destined it to a rapid disappearance."[4] The groups comprising the Labor Party mainly represented workers in trade, railways, maritime trade, transportation and the textile industries. Gradually the party lost what strength it had, especially after 1930, when

---

4 Poblete Troncoso, Moisés, *El Movimiento Obrero Latinoamericano*, México, D. F., 1946, p. 112. (Author's translation.)

Getulio Vargas appeared upon the scene with his dictatorship, and by 1935 it had practically vanished.

The General Confederation of Workers of Brazil functioned during Vargas' first years, but becoming weaker as the dictator's repressive measures grew stronger, particularly after the corporative constitution of 1937. Many of the unions changed their tactics and found they had to organize in vertical unions to obtain the government's approval and to continue protecting their members. Nevertheless, the GCW had a clandestine life at the same time, maintaining its early syndical structure, and when Vargas was overthrown, it was ready to resume its legal life with considerable strength. Today it is the most important union in Brazil. Many of the unions within it are controlled by the Communists, but there are others of a socialist tendency, and there are even syndicalist groups.

We have already said that the Communists have played an important role in Brazil's contemporary political life. The party started its activities, in a clandestine manner, in 1922, and was relatively unimportant at first. In general, the governments of Brazil have always adopted a severe policy against Communism. In 1927, after a series of strikes, the Congress passed a law called Repression of Communism, authorizing judicial authorities to close down, without further action, any association considered dangerous to the social order. In spite of the governmental policy, Communism has progressed in Brazil more rapidly and become stronger than in any other country of Latin America. To a great extent, the Communists owe their increase in strength to a leader of military and political experience, whose reputation has spread over the entire country. This man is Luis Carlos Prestes. An army man in 1924, Prestes headed an uprising against President Arturo Bernardes. For twenty-eight months the campaign went on, and Prestes was undefeated, but was finally forced to retreat into Bolivia and disarm his column. Despite the unsuccessful ending to the story, the episode gave him tremendous popularity, and when Vargas came into power in 1930, Prestes returned to Brazil and—for a while—collaborated with the government. When the inevitable disagreement with the dictator occurred, Prestes again left his country. On this occasion, he went to Europe and stayed in the Soviet Union for a period of time. In 1935, he returned to Brazil, a convinced Communist, and organized the National Liberation Front against Vargas, which the president dissolved. Prestes was put in prison, where he remained until 1945, when Vargas was forced to resign. We have explained how Prestes reorganized the Communist Party as soon as he regained his freedom, and how the party participated in the 1945 elections.

Once again the Communists are outlawed, but they maintain their clandestine agitation and many undercover centers of propaganda. Today the party has an estimated membership of 150,000, with its strongest centers in the state of São Paulo, the Federal District and the city of Pernambuco.

SUGGESTED READINGS

English:

Cunha, Euclides da, *Rebellion in the Backlands,* University of Chicago Press, 1944.

Denis, Pierre, *Brazil,* London, T. Fisher Unwin, 1911.

Freyre, Gilberto, *Brazil: An Interpretation,* New York, Alfred A. Knopf, Inc., 1945.

———, *The Masters and the Slaves (Casa Grande e Senzala),* New York, Alfred A. Knopf, Inc., 1946.

Hambloch, Ernest, *His Majesty, the President of Brazil,* New York, E. P. Dutton & Co., Inc., 1939.

James, Herman G., *The Constitutional System of Brazil,* Washington, D. C., Carnegie Institution, 1923.

James, Preston E., *Brazil,* New York, The Odyssey Press, Inc., 1946.

Loewenstein, Karl, *Brazil under Vargas,* New York, The Macmillan Co., 1942.

Nash, Roy, *The Conquest of Brazil,* New York, Harcourt, Brace & Co., 1926.

Normano, João, *Brazil: A study in Economic Types,* Chapel Hill, University of North Carolina Press, 1935.

Oliveira Lima, Manoel de, *The Evolution of Brazil Compared with that of Spanish and Anglo-Saxon America,* Stanford University Press, 1914.

Pandia Calogeres, João, *A History of Brazil,* Chapel Hill, University of North Carolina Press, 1939.

Pierson, Donald, *Negroes in Brazil,* University of Chicago Press, 1942.

Ramos, Arthur, *The Negro in Brazil,* Washington, D. C., Associated Publishers, 1939.

Smith, T. Lynn, *Brazil: People and Institutions,* Baton Rouge, Louisiana State University Press, 1946.

Smith, Marchant A. (and Editors), *Brazil: Portrait of Half a Continent*, New York, The Dryden Press, Inc., 1951.

Tavares de Sa, Hernane, *The Brazilians: People of Tomorrow*, New York, John Day, 1947.

Zweig, Stefan, *Brazil, Land of the Future*, New York, The Viking Press, 1941.

Portuguese:

Amaral, Luis, *Aspectos Fundamentaes da Vida Rural Brasileira*, São Paulo, 1936.

Calmon, Pedro, *Espírito da Sociedade Colonial*, São Paulo, 1935.

Campos, Francisco, *Antecipações, à Reforma Política*, Rio de Janeiro, 1940.

Carneiro, Leão, *A Sociedade Rural, seus Problemas e sua Educacão*, Rio de Janeiro, 1939.

Devinelli, Carlos, *Política Brasileira*, Rio de Janeiro, 1942.

Duarte, Nestor, *A Ordem Privada e a Organizacão Politica Nacional*, São Paulo, 1939.

Goulart, Jorge Luis, *A Formação do Rio Grande do Sul*, Porto Alegre, 1933.

Rocha Pombo, Jose Francisco, *História do Brasil*, Rio de Janeiro (no date).

Rodrigues Alves, Francisco M., *As Bases da Unidade Nacional*, São Paulo, 1940.

Saenz Hayes, Ricardo, *El Brasil Moderno*, Buenos Aires, 1942.

Santos, José Maria dos., *A Política Geral do Brasil*, São Paulo, 1930.

Conclusions

We have endeavored to indicate the main features of the governmental structures found in the Latin American area. We have synthesized the phenomenon of government in three main characteristics: strong executive powers, weak legislatures, and politically powerless judiciaries. Uruguay is today an exception.

In contrasting political institutions with practices, many anomalies are to be noted. Politics is a serious game in Latin America, and all social forces participate actively in the political life of the countries. Authoritarianism in the family, education, and religion make political struggles bitter. Militarism and organized labor shifting their allegiances from right to left further complicate the problems.

European ideologies have deeply influenced Latin American politics. The traditions of the Enlightenment inspired their movements for independence and guided them in the creation of their early forms of government. These traditions derived mainly from the intellectual antecedents of the British and French Revolutions. Both of these were revolts of the nascent middle classes against the absolute monarchies backed by an established church. In England and France, they succeeded in establishing the rule of the middle class. In Latin America, this was not the case. As we have seen, the new republics were governed, at the beginning, by the landed Creoles or a militaristic caste.

Furthermore, Latin American liberalism was more of the authoritarian and anti-rationalistic type, based on Rousseau's philosophy, than the tolerant type that followed Locke and Voltaire. Latin American independence never resulted in a compromise of political issues and never respected the rights of dissenting minorities. Independence was only a victory of the principle of authority of the new states against the authority exercised by the mother countries. The new republics adopted many of the features of the constitution of the United States, but not the American philosophy of liberalism. Political authoritarianism appeared in Latin America disguised in democratic forms. This situation has continued, with few exceptions, until today.

In this book we have tried to stress the above-mentioned characteristics. After describing governmental structures, we have endeavored to contrast them with the political role of some institutions and the political reality represented by actual conditions and practices in the different countries. This divorce between theory and practice, between the ideal represented by the constitutions and legal structures, and the real as shown by political conditions, is the most disquieting factor in the whole area. It is a phenomenon quite similar to the one witnessed in contemporary Spain, during the reign of Alfonso XIII, before the Republic of 1931. Some Spanish writers describe this divorce as official Spain opposed to real Spain. In Latin America, we also have the official side of the state, embodied in constitutional provisions, which also extends abroad to diplomatic missions and their representatives in the United Nations and the Organization of American States. But this official side differs from the political realities of the countries.

Governmental structures, in the Latin American area, have the character of ideal postulates and not of positive legal institutions, characterized by enforcement. Governmental institutions fail in the technical and administrative level of government. This phenomenon can be partially explained, and we are perfectly aware of the situation, by the absence of well-qualified and well-paid personnel. Rapid political changes bring about instability, and this absence of personnel widens the gap between theory and practice. Latin America needs well-trained administrators and an adequate budget for them far more than it needs theoretical plans of reform.

Today the political condition of the area is unstable. Only some half dozen countries have governments resulting from democratic processes. It is probable that further changes may occur before this book is in print. The patterns of dictatorship are different. Some are typical of the traditional *Caudillo* and militaristic style. Some have "legalized" dictatorships by pseudo-democratic processes. Some have demagogic rulers, not only supported by the armed forces but by large groups of the population, including organized labor. We hope that the situation is temporary, and that Latin America will free itself from this epidemic of dictators.

Glossary*

Adelantado Mayor: Royal functionary entrusted with judicial powers in colonial days.

Adelantado Menor: Or *"fronterizo."* Royal functionary stationed along the borders of the provinces, performing chiefly military duties.

Alcalde: Mayor, municipal official.

Alguacil: Minor employee generally in charge of the execution of administrative orders.

Audiencia: Territorial division and judicial tribunal also in charge of administrative matters in colonial days.

Autos-De-Fe: Public punishment of those sentenced by the Tribunal of the Inquisition.

Ayuntamiento: Municipal corporation.

Bandeirante: Nomadic explorer and frontierman of Brazil.

Cabildo Abierto: Open meeting of the members of the *ayuntamiento* with important members of the locality.

Cabildo Cerrado: Meeting of the members of the municipal government.

Cacique: Indian chief.

Caja de Comunidad: Community chest.

Capitán General: Primarily a military official, but also in charge of civil matters of a territory.

Capitania: Vast territory covered by the grant received by a *Donatario* in Brazil.

Capitulación: Charter or agreement signed between the Spanish Crown and a *conquistador*.

Casa de Contratación: Institution in charge of economic, political, legal and scientific matters in America, subordinated to the *Consejo de Indias*.

Casa de las Indias: Same as *Casa de Contratación*.

Casa Grande: Residence of a *Donatario* in Brazil.

---

* Includes terms not translated in the text.

Caudillo: Leader or chief.

Cimarrón: Run-away Negro slave.

Colegio: Institution of secondary education or, in general, a school.

Compañía: Commercial company.

Composiciones: Procedure to legalize the title to lands by means of an agreement with the government.

Comuneros: Members of a *commune* or municipality.

Conquistador: Conqueror; chief of an expedition that conquered a territory in America.

Consejo de Indias: Highest legislative and administrative authority of the Spanish Empire in America.

Consejo Real: Advisory board of the King, formed by members of the clergy and nobility.

Conselho: Municipal council in Brazil.

Corregidor: Executive officer in a territory or city.

Corregidor de Pueblos de Indios: Executive officer in an Indian village.

Cortes: General assembly of persons in the old kingdoms of Castilla, Aragón, Valencia, Navarra and Cataluña, in which legislative measures for the kingdom were approved.

Curas Doctrineros: Priests in charge of teaching Indians.

Curia Regis: Council or advisory board to the Portuguese King.

Depositario: Depositor.

Diezmo: Church tithe meaning one-tenth.

Dizimo: Same as *diezmo* (Brazil).

Donatario: Brazilian landholder receiving a grant (*capitania*) from the Crown.

Ejido: Land that belongs to a city or village, for common use of inhabitants.

Empadronado: Person registered in a census.

Encomendero: Person receiving Indians entrusted to him.

Encomienda: Institution for the distribution or allocation of Indians.

Flota: Fleet.

Fronterizo: See *adelantado menor.*

Fueros Municipales: Municipal prerogative or rights.

Gobernador: Governor.

Gracia: Grant or concession given by the King.

Hacendado: Landowner, generally controlling a large tract of land.

Hacienda: Large landholding.

Intendencia: Administrative division created in the eighteenth century.

Intendente: Functionary in charge of the *intendencia.*

Juicio de Residencia: Investigation to which a functionary in America was submitted.

Latifundia: Large landholdings.

Letrado: A person with legal knowledge.

Leyes de Indias: Laws of the Indies.

Leyes de Partidas: Code of laws of Spain.

Mayorazgo: Entailed estate.

Merced: Concession made by the King.

Mesa Da Consciencia E Ordenes: Portuguese institution in charge of religious matters.

Mestizo: Mixture of Indian and European.

Mita: Indian system of rotation of labor adopted later by Spaniards who enslaved Indians.

Monte Pío: Institution lending money at a moderate interest.

Municipio: Municipality.

Navíos de Aviso: Ships conveying information concerning production and market conditions between America and Spain.

Ñáñigos: Name given in Cuba to secret underworld societies.

Obraje: Workshop or factory system in colonial Spanish America.

Oidor: Magistrate or judge of the *Audiencia.*

Ouvidor Geral: Functionary in charge of the administration of justice in colonial Brazil.

Paulista: A native of São Paulo, also explorer and frontiersman of that region.

Peninsular: Spaniard in America, born in Spain.

Peonaje: System of work in rural areas, by means of which the farm hand has the status of a serf.

Presidente: President.

Presidio: Frontier institution generally formed by a military garrison.

Pulque: Alcoholic beverage of Mexico.

Quinto: One-fifth of products, to be paid to the Spanish Crown.

Real y Supremo Consejo de las Indias: Same as *Consejo de Indias.*

Recopilación de las Leyes de los Reinos de las Indias: Compilation of the Laws of the Indies.

Reducciones: Territories reserved for Indians.

Regalía: Patrimony reserved by the Spanish King in America.

Regidores: Aldermen.

Repartimiento: In some cases land grants; in others, distribution of Indians similar to *encomiendas.*

Superintendente: Post created in the eighteenth century, with delegated powers from the King.

Terra Portucalensis: Portugal.

Tienda de Raya: Company store in which payment in kind is made to workers.

Vecinos: Usually property owning residents.

Veedores: Municipal inspectors.

Virrey: Viceroy.

Virreina: Vicereine.

Visita: Inspection made by a higher officer of a lower functionary.

Visitador: Functionary making the *visita.*

Zambo: Mixture of Negro and Indian.

Index

Entries are generally limited to subjects, persons, and institutions of the Latin-American area, or its historical background. Other names and topics mentioned are not included. Topics and names appearing in the constitutional summaries are also omitted, as they can be found under the headings of each country. For a general treatment of topics, the table of contents appearing on page ix should be consulted.